TEACH OUR CHILDREN WELL

Why the January 21, 2017 Marches Matter

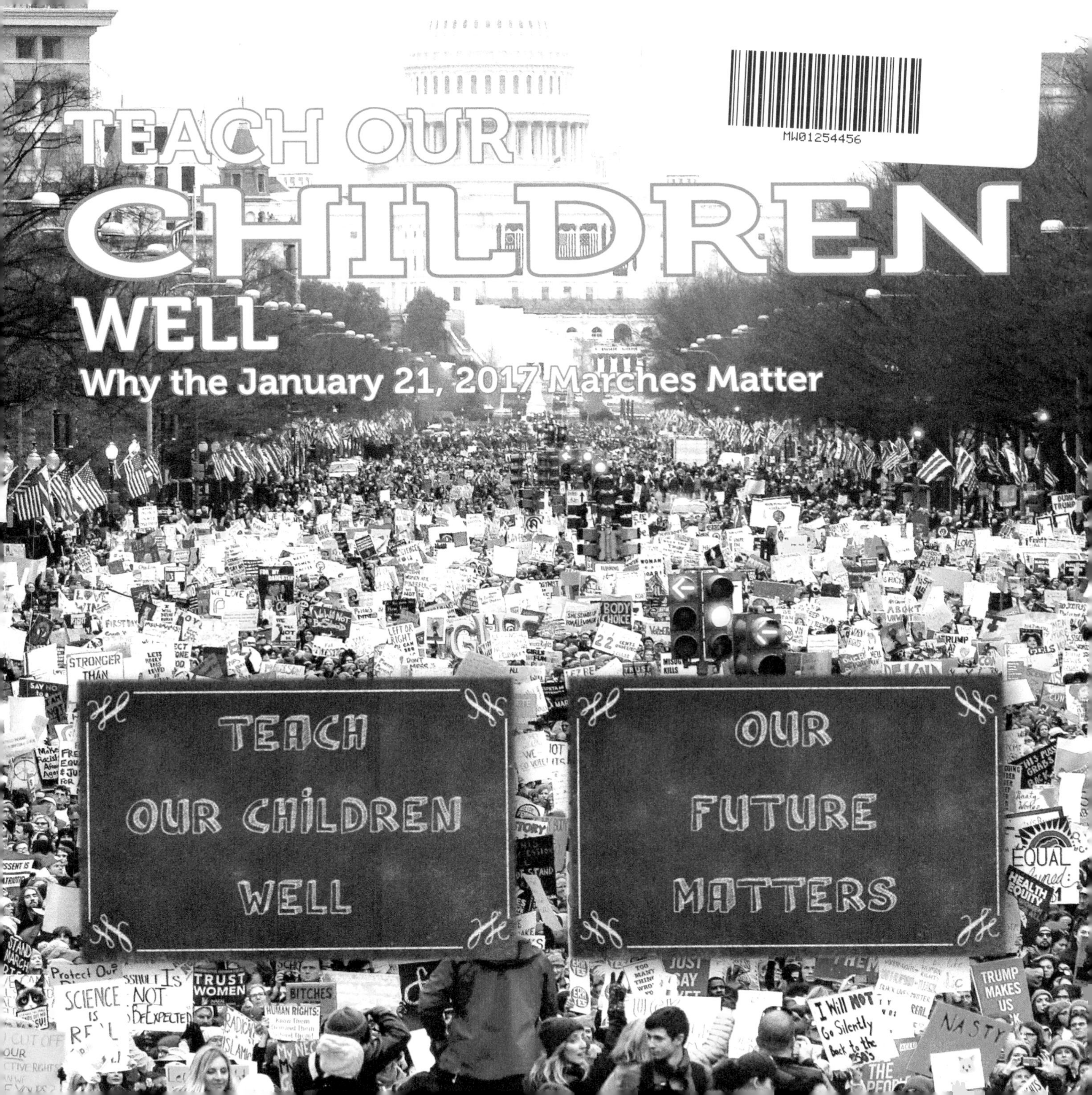

TEACH
OUR CHILDREN
WELL
OUR
FUTURE
MATTERS
STRONGER THAN
BODY CHOICE
TRUST WOMEN
SCIENCE IS REAL
TRUMP MAKES US
I Will NOT Go Silently Back to the 1950's
EQUAL
HEALTH EQUITY

TEACH OUR CHILDREN WELL

Why the January 21, 2017 Marches Matter

Copyright ©2017 by Karen Gross • Debbi Wraga

All rights reserved. No part of this book may be reproduced in any form, manner, or by any means without the prior written permission of the authors.

A portion of the net profits from the sale of this book will be donated to non-profit organizations that support our civil liberties.

ISBN: 978-1-60571-347-2
Library of Congress Control Number: 2017934286

©2017 Photographs courtesy of: Alexander Family, L. Barad, J. Benjamin, M. Colaizzi, M. Cornwell, N. Donovan, J. Fine, G. Galer, O. Galer-Noel, A. Guidone, P. Guttmacher, L. Jankowski, H. Kreisle, H. Mayes Gleason, D. Golden, K. Gross, N. Halbeck, P. Heller, D. Kohan, H. Kreisle, K. James, W. Lubin, C. Morrow, J. Murphy, E. Rodolfy Russell, M. Wagner, J. Winkelman J. Wood, and D. Wraga.

SHIRES PRESS
www.northshire.com

Printed in the United States of America

TEACH OUR CHILDREN WELL

Why the January 21, 2017 Marches Matter

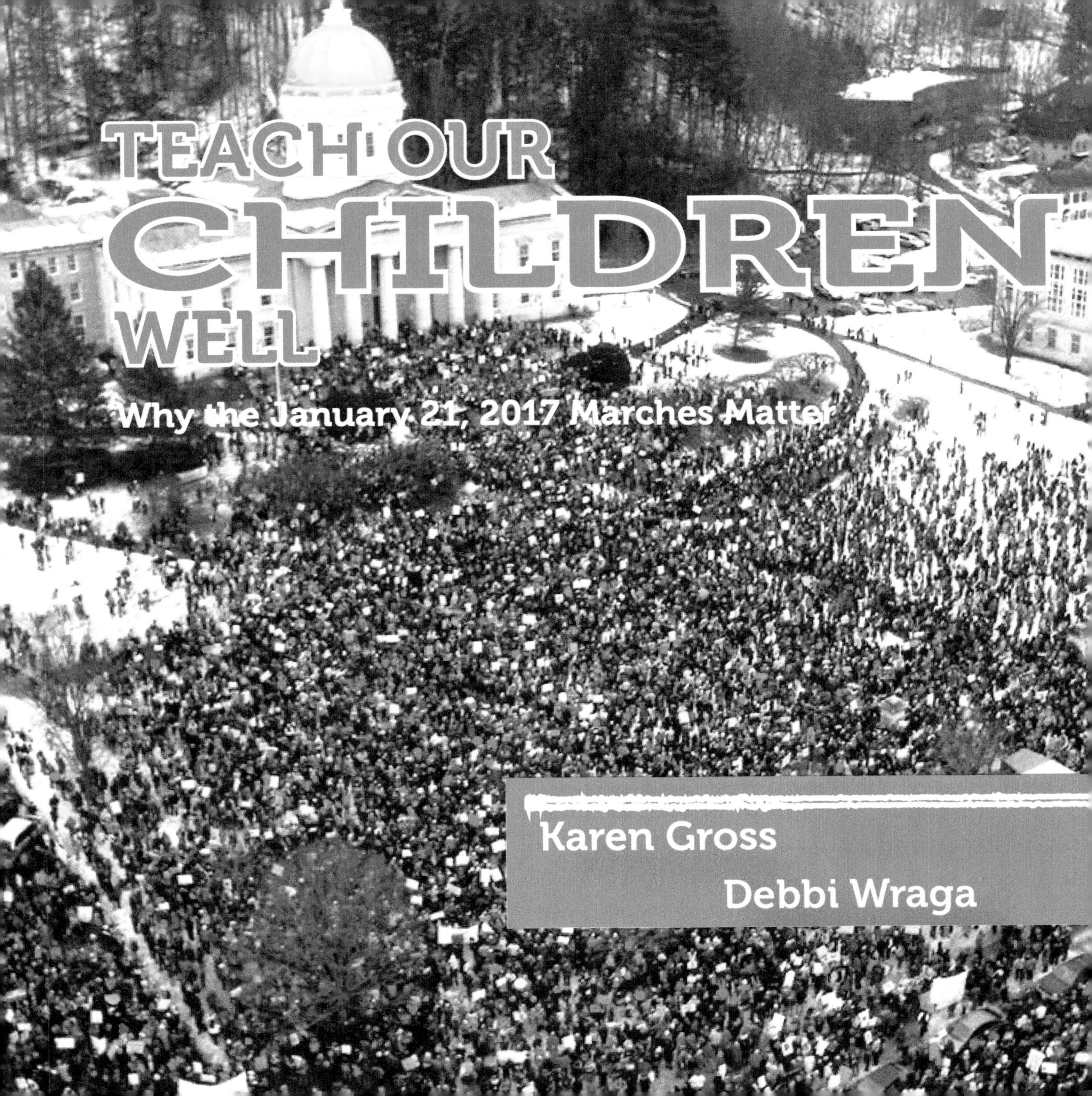

Karen Gross

Debbi Wraga

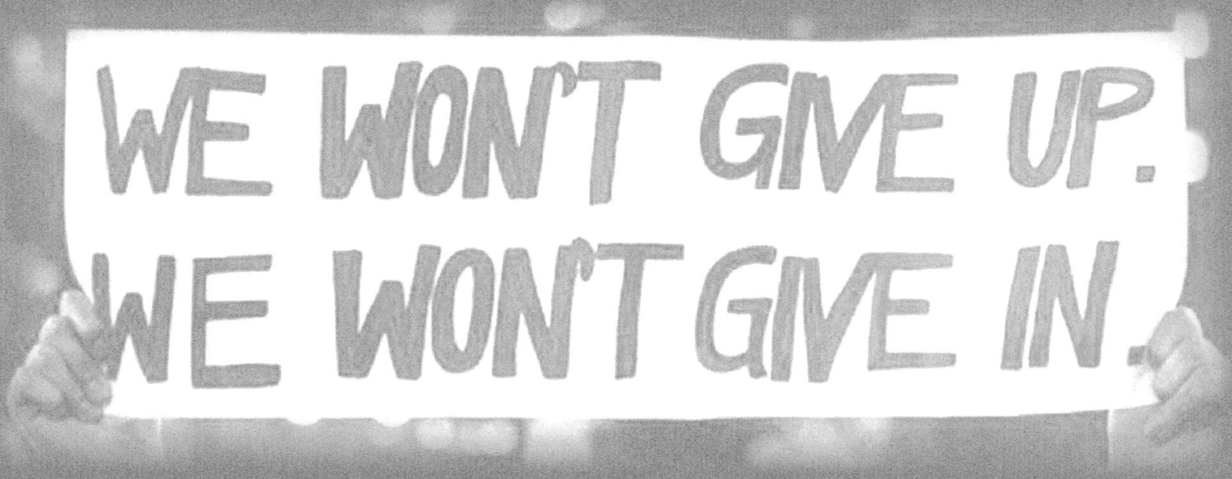
WE WON'T GIVE UP.
WE WON'T GIVE IN.

To all our children and
our children's children —
to whom we owe a better world

The Declaration of Independence (1776) An excerpt

When in the Course of human events it becomes necessary for one people to dissolve the political bands which have connected them with another and to assume among the powers of the earth, the separate and equal station to which the Laws of Nature and of Nature's God entitle them, a decent respect to the opinions of mankind requires that they should declare the causes which impel them to the separation.

We hold these truths to be self-evident, that all men are created equal, that they are endowed by their Creator with certain unalienable Rights, that among these are Life, Liberty and the pursuit of Happiness. — That to secure these rights, Governments are instituted among Men, deriving their just powers from the consent of the governed, — That whenever any Form of Government becomes destructive of these ends, it is the Right of the People to alter or to abolish it, and to institute new Government, laying its foundation on such principles and organizing its powers in such form, as to them shall seem most likely to effect their Safety and Happiness. Prudence, indeed, will dictate that Governments long established should not be changed for light and transient causes; and accordingly all experience hath shewn that mankind are more disposed to suffer, while evils are sufferable than to right themselves by abolishing the forms to which they are accustomed. But when a long train of abuses and usurpations, pursuing invariably the same Object evinces a design to reduce them under absolute Despotism, it is their right, it is their duty, to throw off such Government, and to provide new Guards for their future security. — Such has been the patient sufferance of these Colonies; and such is now the necessity which constrains them to alter their former Systems of Government. The history of the present King of Great Britain is a history of repeated injuries and usurpations, all having in direct object the establishment of an absolute Tyranny over these States. To prove this, let Facts be submitted to a candid world.

Why We March With Signs

Since (if not before) the birth of our nation, we have had revolutions, demonstrations and protests to protect values we hold dear. All one has to do is read the Declaration of Independence – over which much blood was spilt – to appreciate the depth of our commitment to a government that represents the "people" and to freedom and equality (yes, thankfully, equality's meaning has improved, grown and changed).

Interestingly and importantly, a goodly number of us who protested recently at the Women's March on January 21, 2017 were marching for the first time in decades. We had marched in the 60's and 70's related to civil rights, the war in Vietnam and/or in support of the then emerging feminist movement. Thereafter, most of us did not march. Marching seemed singularly something in the wheelhouse of youth.

When millions of us decided to march on the day following the Trump Inauguration, many people asked: Why? What's the point? What does one accomplish through marching? Are you simply marching against someone? Surely marches won't change the rude, disrespectful and misogynistic speech and behavior or attitude of the new

US President, although that was the stated purpose of some of us. And marches now are not needed to stop an illegal war where young Americans (our friends) are dying in record numbers by the minute on foreign soil. And, why not use our skills for something more likely to cause change: work for a new candidate running for state or federal office; speak at state legislatures on budget allocations; work with organizations that can lobby and push government? What are you marching for? Good points all.

During the hours of the march, many of us kept focusing on the signs – the signs held high by young and old, by parents and grandparents and children and grandchildren, by minorities, by people of wide ranging ethnicities. Some signs were literally tied to marchers' bodies. Other signs were tied to or floated above wheelchairs and walkers.

The signs ranged from the handmade to the formal, from the handwritten to the printed. Some were powerful statements; some were just a word or two; some contained angry messages; some were funny; some were clever; some were lewd; some were serious; many were powerful; some were unique in their take on the new President; some kept repeating phrases that blazed across the sea of pink pussy hats. Collectively they messaged loudly. Collectively they spoke: voices matter and people matter and we cannot proceed for the next four years by standing still and silent. And the signs represented vastly more than words. They represented the free and collective voice of women and men and children. And the signs were not just reactive – although some were; they were also pro-active, about topics and values that matter regardless of who sits in the Oval Office or on the Supreme Court.

When the march ended and we learned about the simultaneous marches all over the globe through social media and friends and Facebook and other outlets, the value of these marches and their signs started to become clearer. These were simultaneous events across the globe – as if there were a connective tissue in the air. Families around the world were doing the same thing – separately but together. And there is some power in knowing that. There is a power in shared experiences separated by water and miles and air and culture and time zones.

And it was then that I and many others realized that the power of the signs at the marches across the world needed to be memorialized and preserved and remembered. They were too powerful to be lost with the passage of time. And their messaging needed to serve as a constant reminder of the true power of the people. And we needed our children and our children's children to see that there is value in speaking up and out, that grown men and women of all shades and shapes can raise their voices through their signs and peacefully shout out about what matters to them – not just what angers them in the form of a new leader but what they care about for the wellbeing of our world.

Yes, the messages at the marches post-Inauguration were varied. They did not just focus on women's issues (reproductive rights; non-harassment; dignity of body), and the word "intersectionality" kept being raised. A goodly number of the signs focused on America's new President, although in many ways he was a stand-in for our concerns about deeply held beliefs about personhood and integrity and rights of women. The signs lauded our diversity and open borders and absence of walls. They focused on the threats to our Democracy; they addressed race relations and relationships; they pushed for an America that was fairer; they chastised us for our governmental failures past and present; they begged for us to wake up and care. They asked us – loudly – to focus on our nation and its future.

For these reasons, among many, these varied signs need to be combined in one place and then heralded and highlighted for our children and our children's children. We have an obligation to teach our children — and that can happen in many ways both formal and informal.

One way we can teach our children well: we can remind them and ourselves that they are our future and that that future depends on them. And we are there to help them build a future of which they can be proud. We can help create a world that is deserving of them and children everywhere – a world of freedom and equity and fairness and clean air and clean water and plentiful food and suitable housing, and decency and the absence of discrimination whether one is white or black or brown or tall or small or abled or disabled or thin or fat or whether one hails from Boston or Botswana or Washington or the West Indies.

The story of the signs is what this book aims to share. It is not about one man who was elected President of the United States and those whom he chose to nominate for high positions. It is a story for us all – a story that can push us forward, that can remind us of our obligation to fight for what we believe in.

At the end of the day, this book of the post-inaugural march signs is a story for our children. Children everywhere need to know and believe that adults will not only protect them from harm but will help them live in a world that honors our values. This book, written through the signs and the words and images on them, is an adult story but it is a commitment too.

My hope is that this book, to which so many contributed their amazing photographs and who are all listed in the front piece to this book, sits in your living rooms and on your coffee tables. These signs – these plentiful and powerful signs – can serve as reminders of what we can do for our children, with our children and on behalf of our world.

And one more thing: marches are not ending as best I can tell; in fact they are just beginning. We already have marches on seeking to enable immigration and eliminate unlawful detention based on ignoble efforts to transform a nation of immigrants into a nation of homogenized people. And, when each new tweet or Executive Order threatens the world as we know it, people will march. Weekly or perhaps even daily. But, remember this: it is not a person we are marching against; it is values we are marching for. That's a big difference.

This book can also serve, then, as a reminder of the story we are telling and will be telling — to preserve history and to make history and to restore history. That's one important book then that was created by the people, for the people and with the people.

Karen Gross

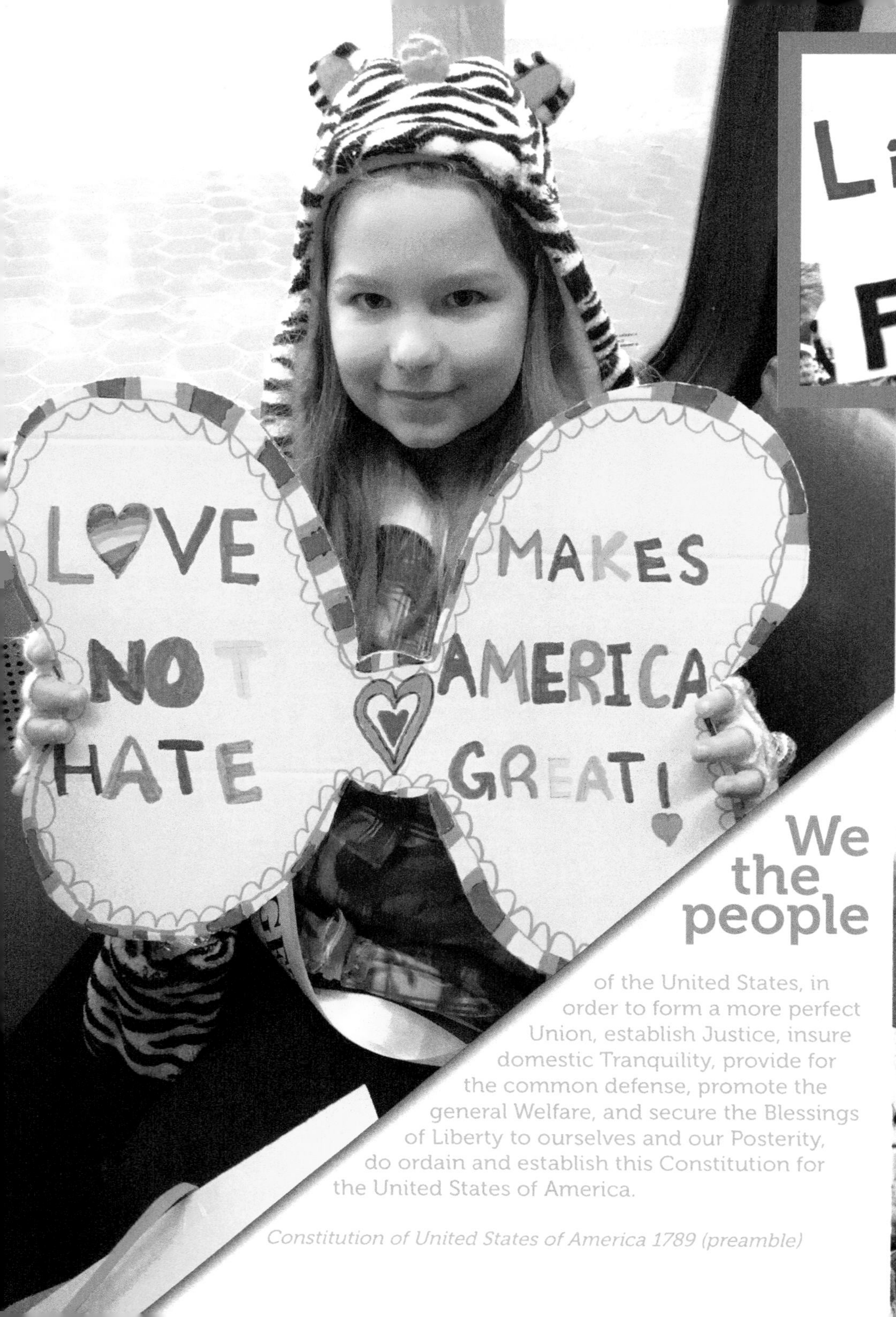
LOVE
NOT
HATE
MAKES
AMERICA
GREAT!

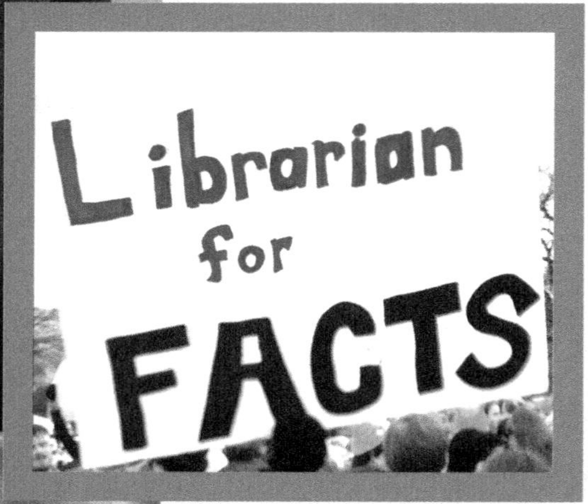
Librarian
for
FACTS

We the people

of the United States, in order to form a more perfect Union, establish Justice, insure domestic Tranquility, provide for the common defense, promote the general Welfare, and secure the Blessings of Liberty to ourselves and our Posterity, do ordain and establish this Constitution for the United States of America.

Constitution of United States of America 1789 (preamble)

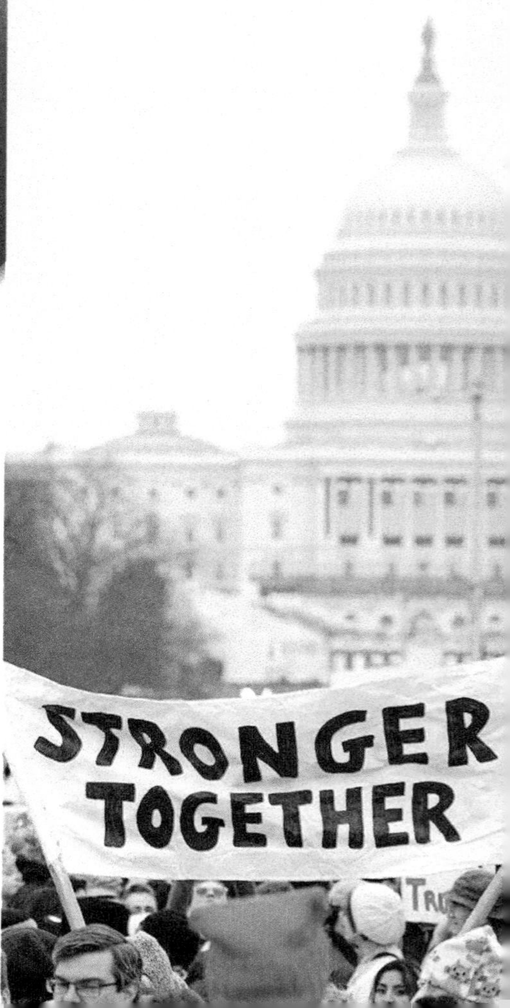
STRONGER
TOGETHER

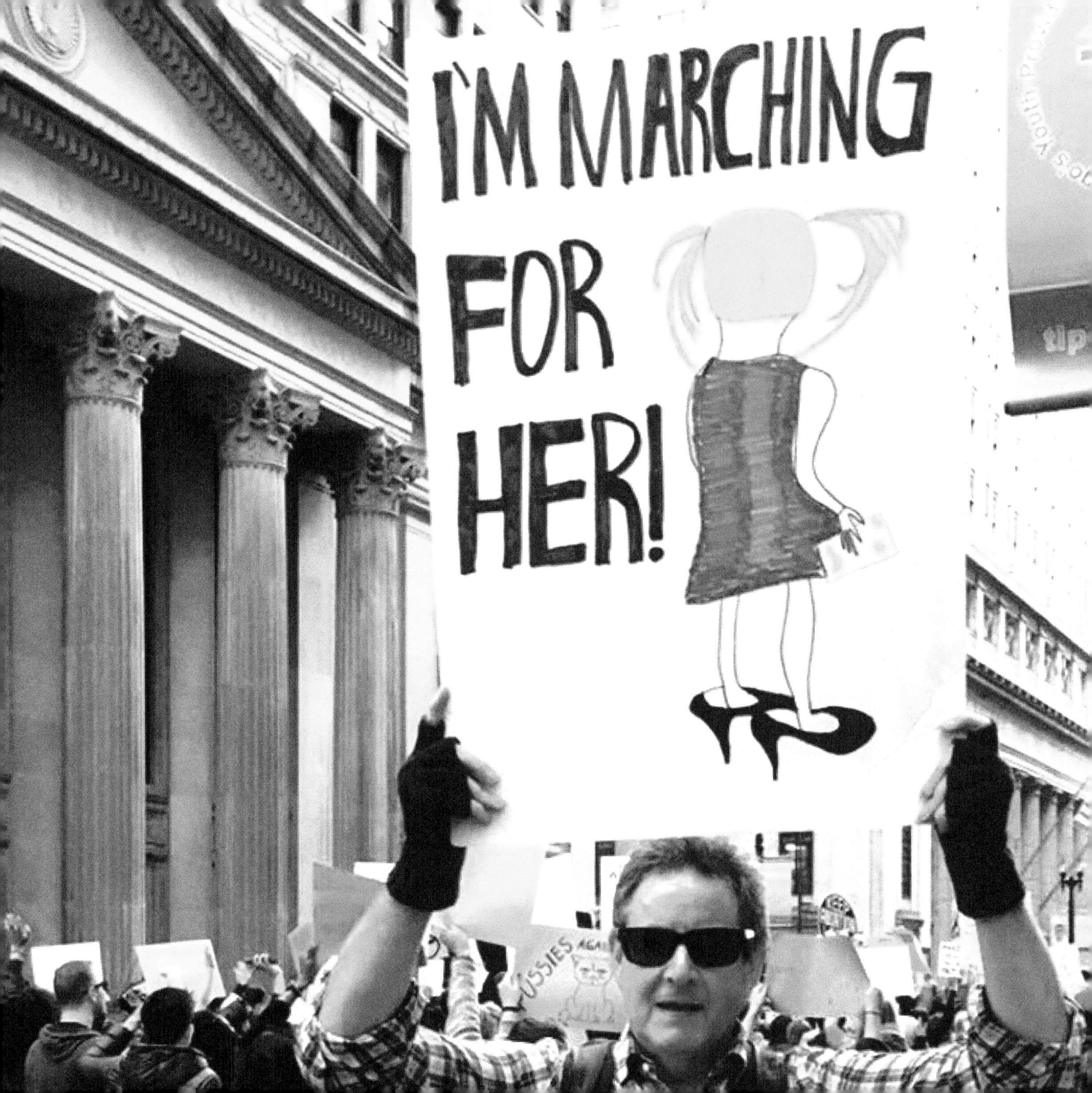
I'M MARCHING
FOR
HER!

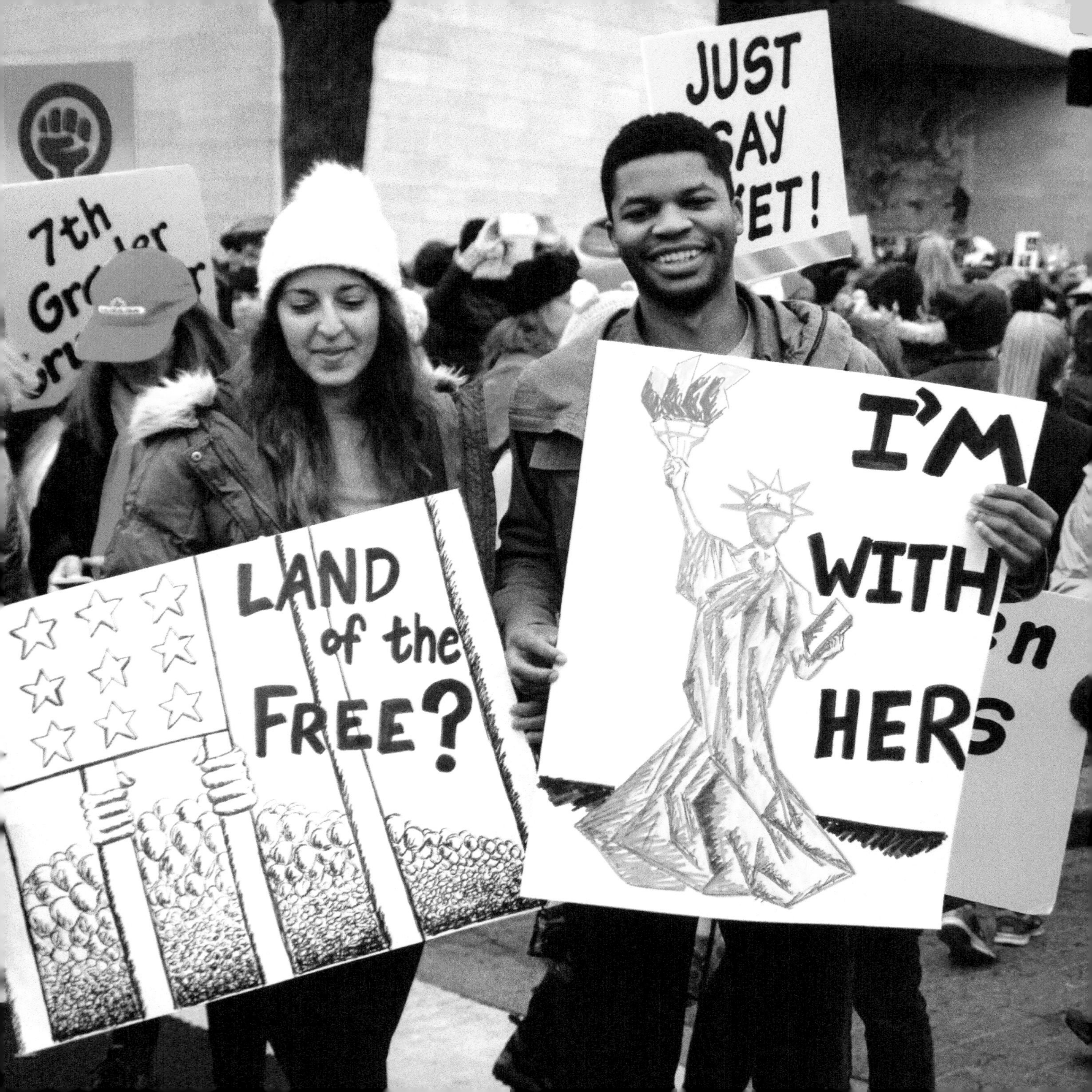
7th
JUST
LAND of the FREE?
I'M WITH HERS

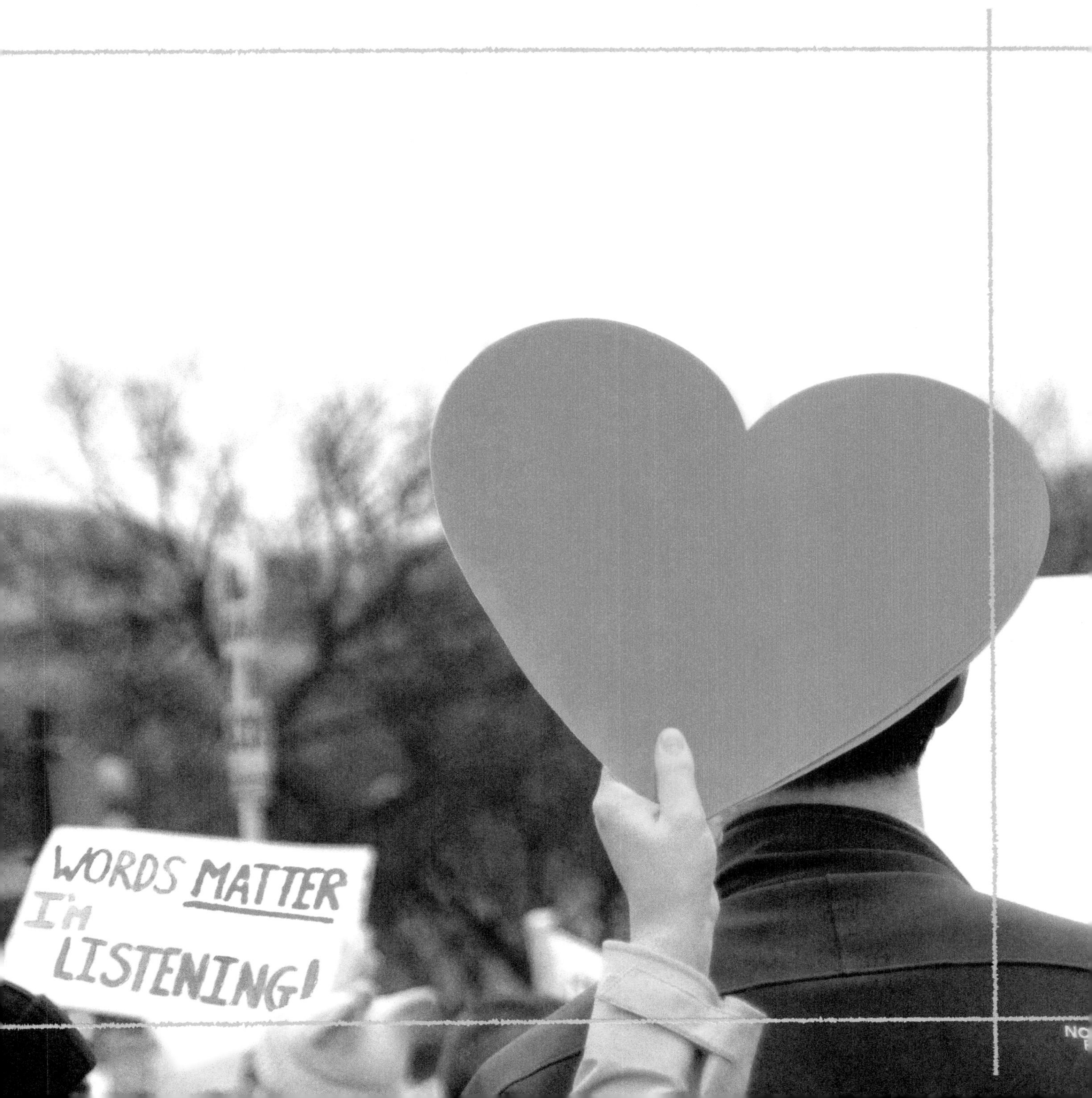
WORDS MATTER
I'M
LISTENING!

These signs – these plentiful and powerful signs – can serve as reminders who what we can do for our children, with our children and on behalf of our world.

Karen Gross

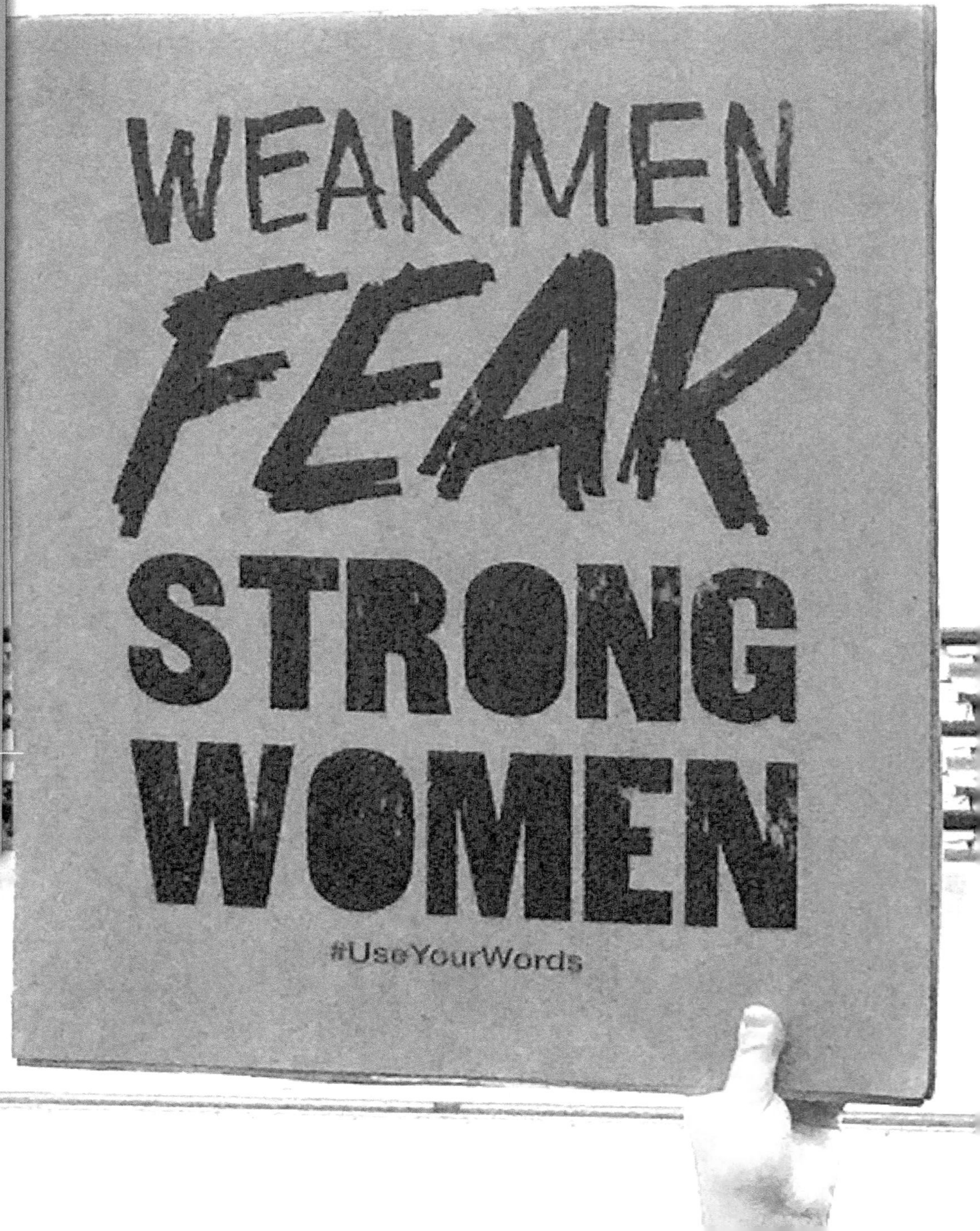
WEAK MEN
FEAR
STRONG
WOMEN
#UseYourWords

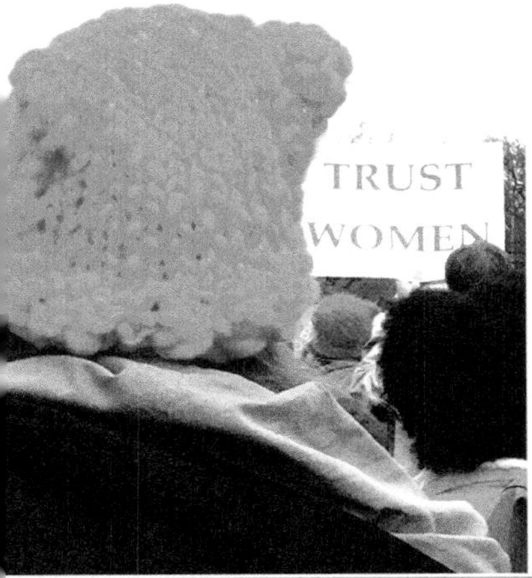
TRUST
WOMEN

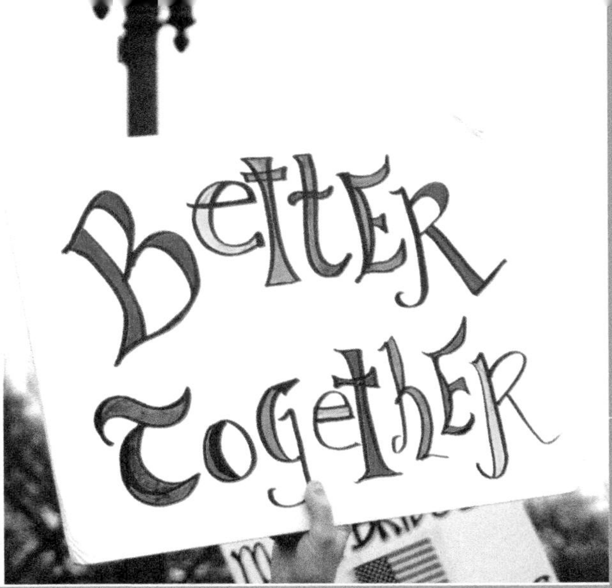
Better Together

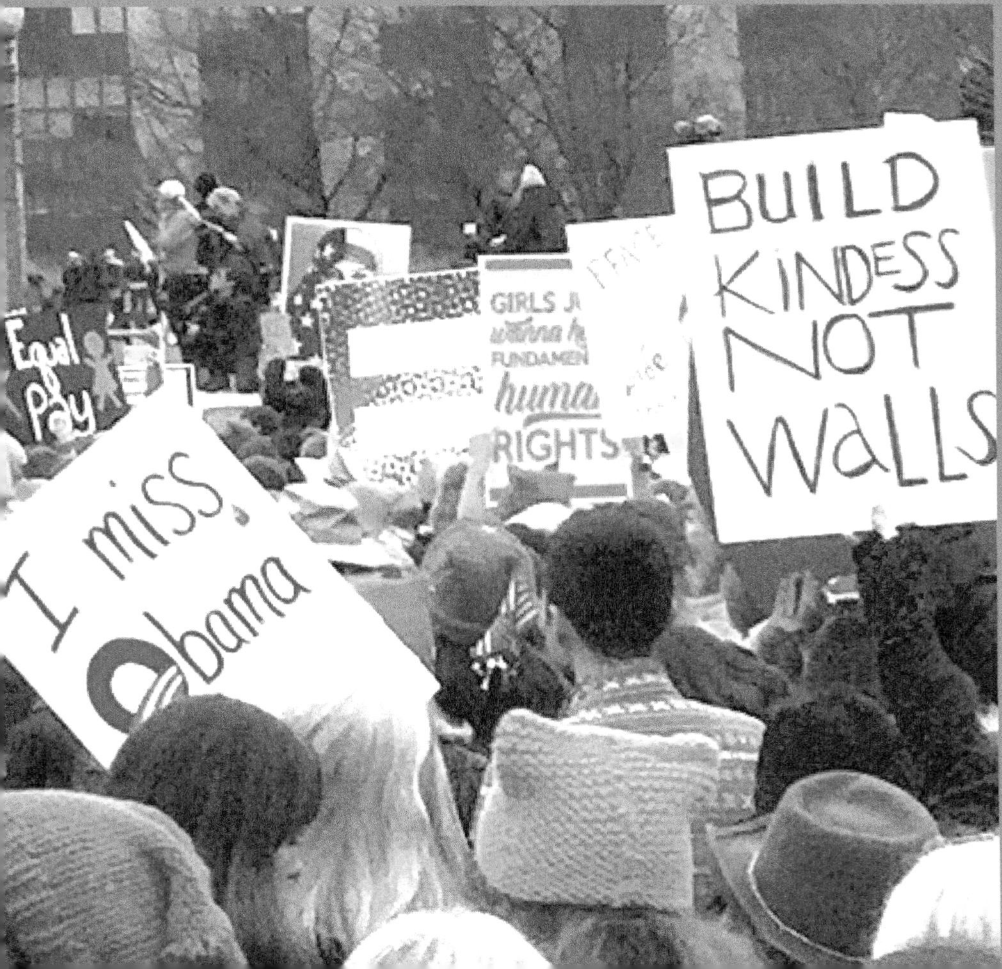
BUILD KINDESS NOT WALLS
Equal Pay
I miss Obama
RIGHTS

I
am
marching
for
her!

Anonymous

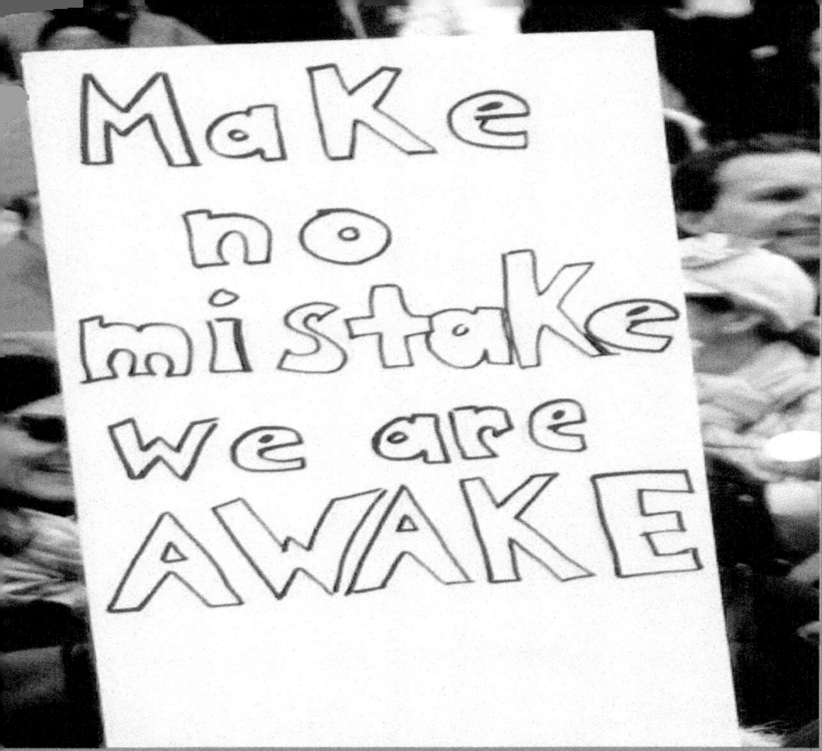
Make
no
mistake
we are
AWAKE

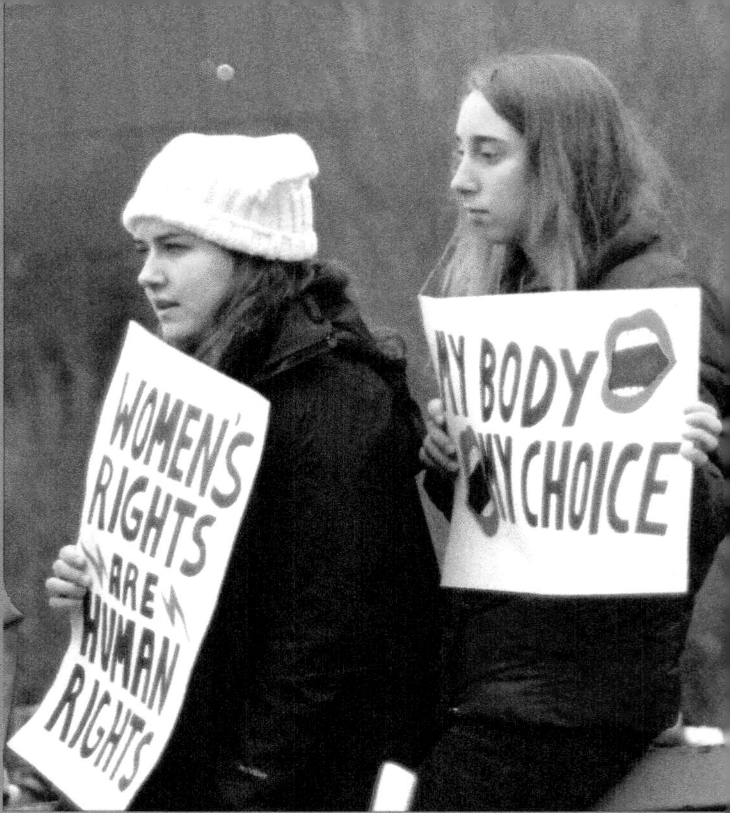
WOMEN'S
RIGHTS
ARE
HUMAN
RIGHTS
MY BODY
CHOICE

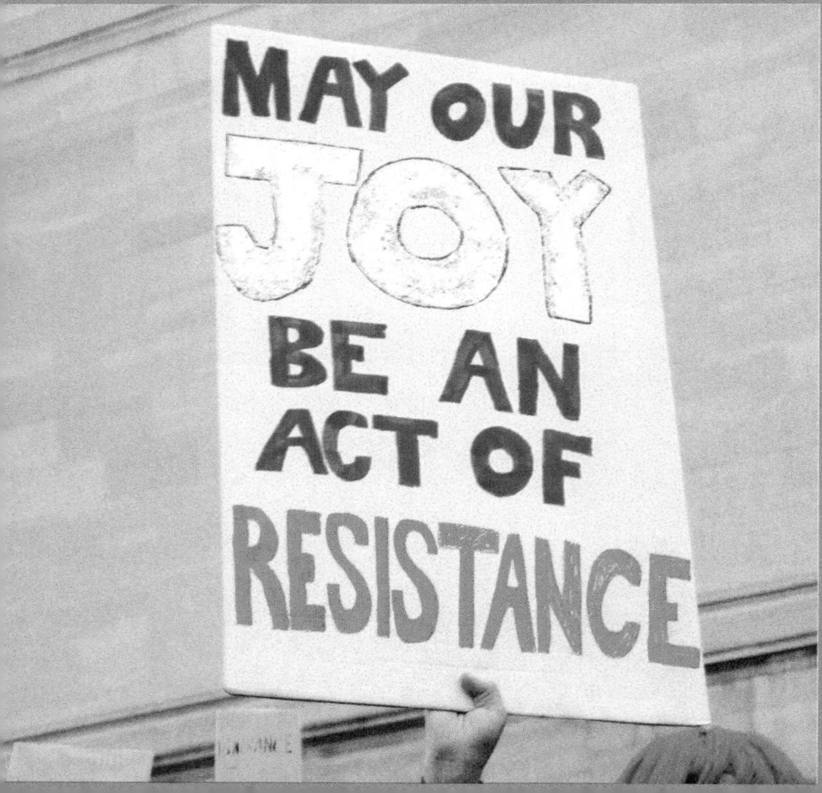
MAY OUR
JOY
BE AN
ACT OF
RESISTANCE

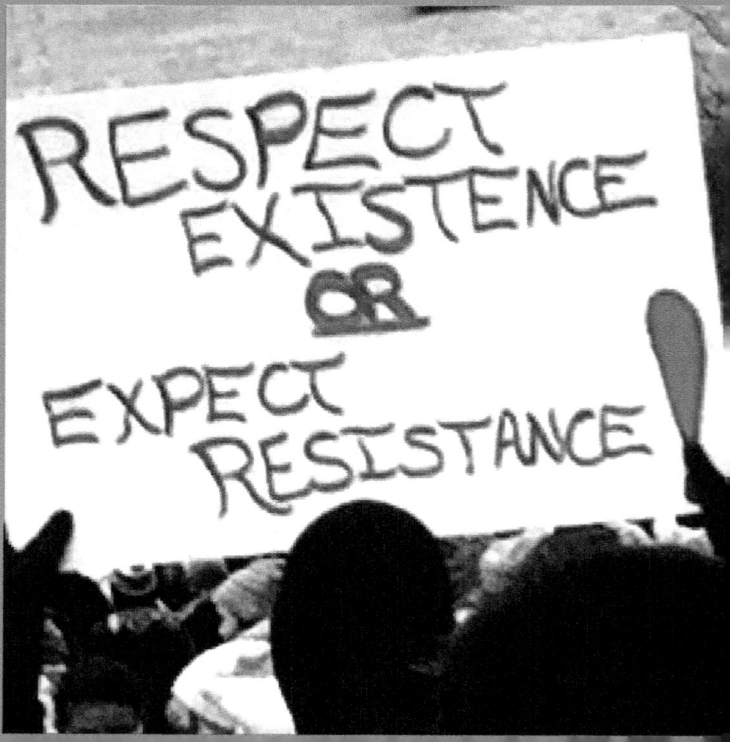
RESPECT
EXISTENCE
OR
EXPECT
RESISTANCE

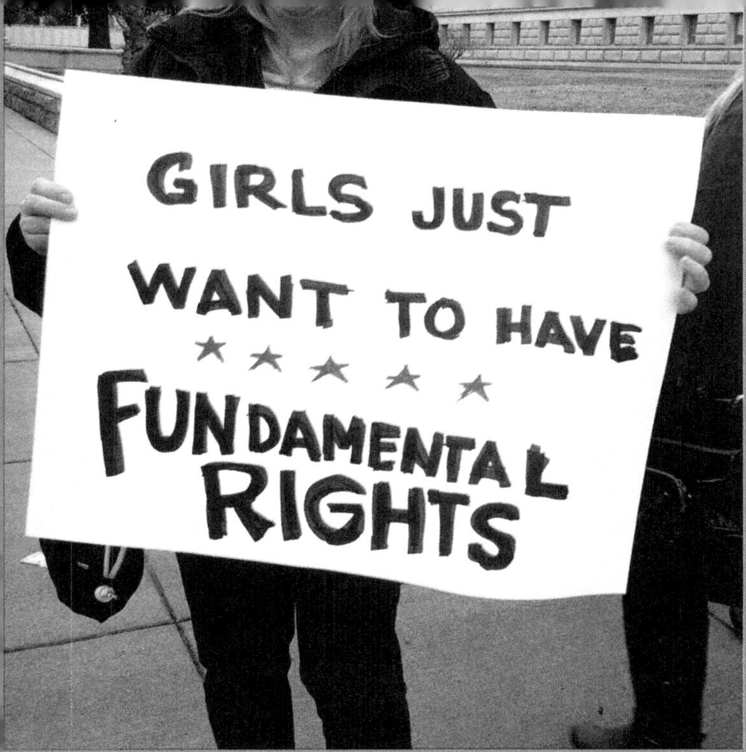
GIRLS JUST
WANT TO HAVE
FUNDAMENTAL
RIGHTS

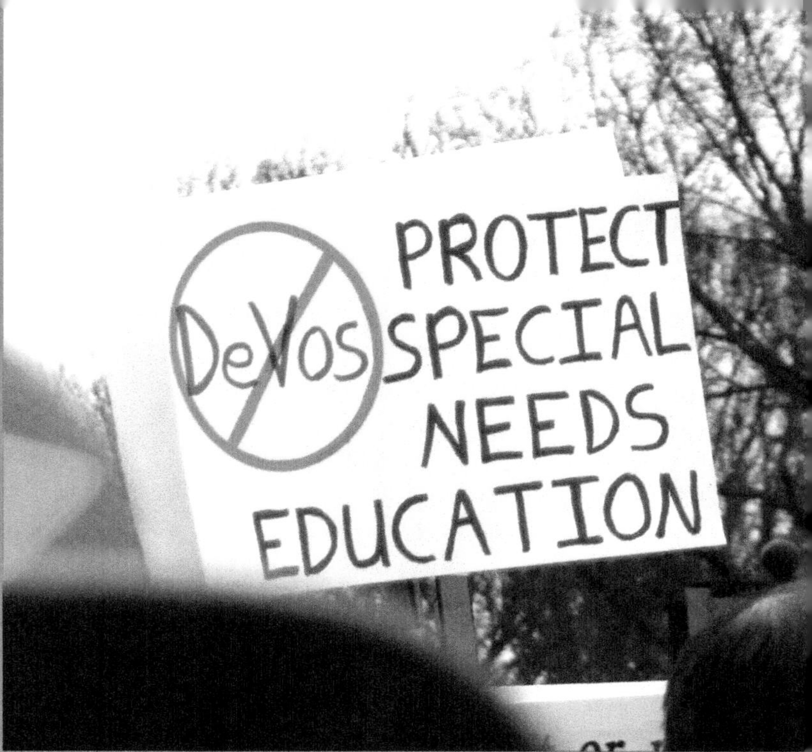
DeVos
PROTECT
SPECIAL
NEEDS
EDUCATION

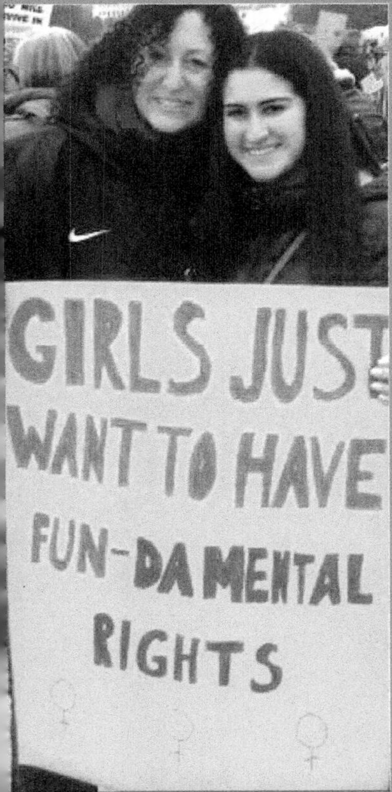
GIRLS JUST
WANT TO HAVE
FUN-DAMENTAL
RIGHTS

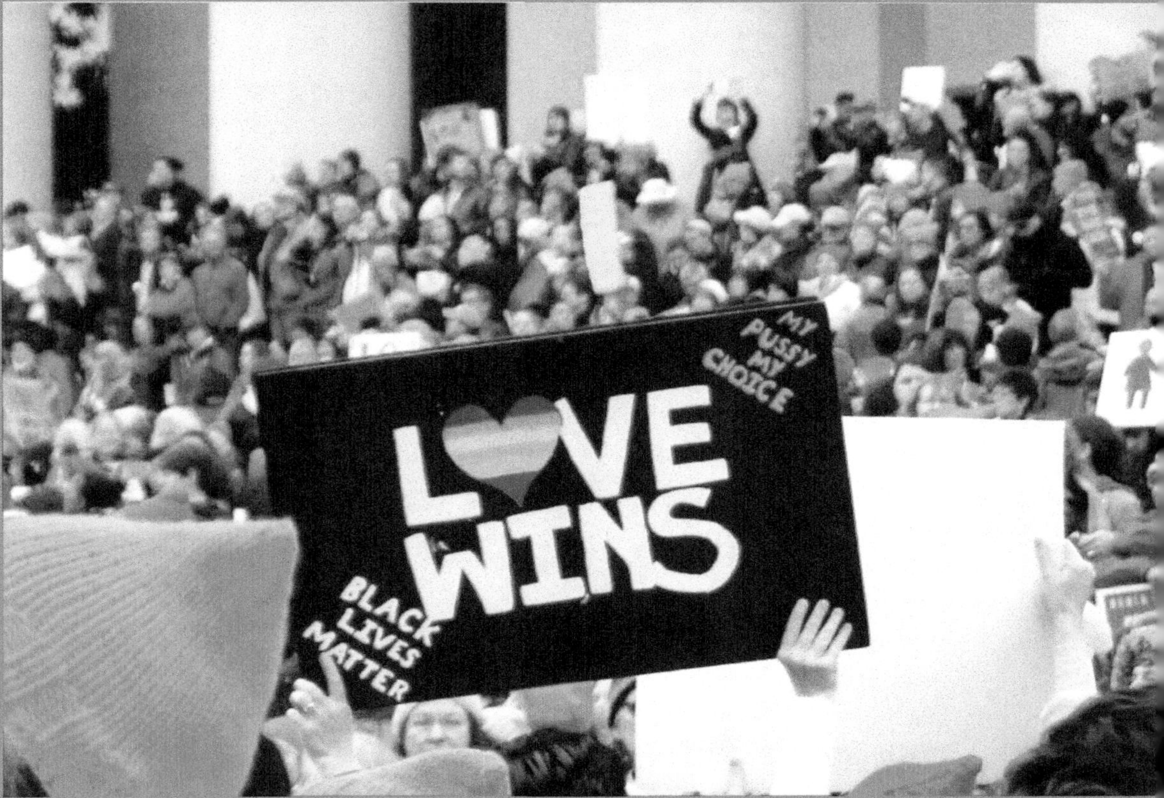
MY PUSSY MY CHOICE
LOVE
WINS
BLACK LIVES MATTER

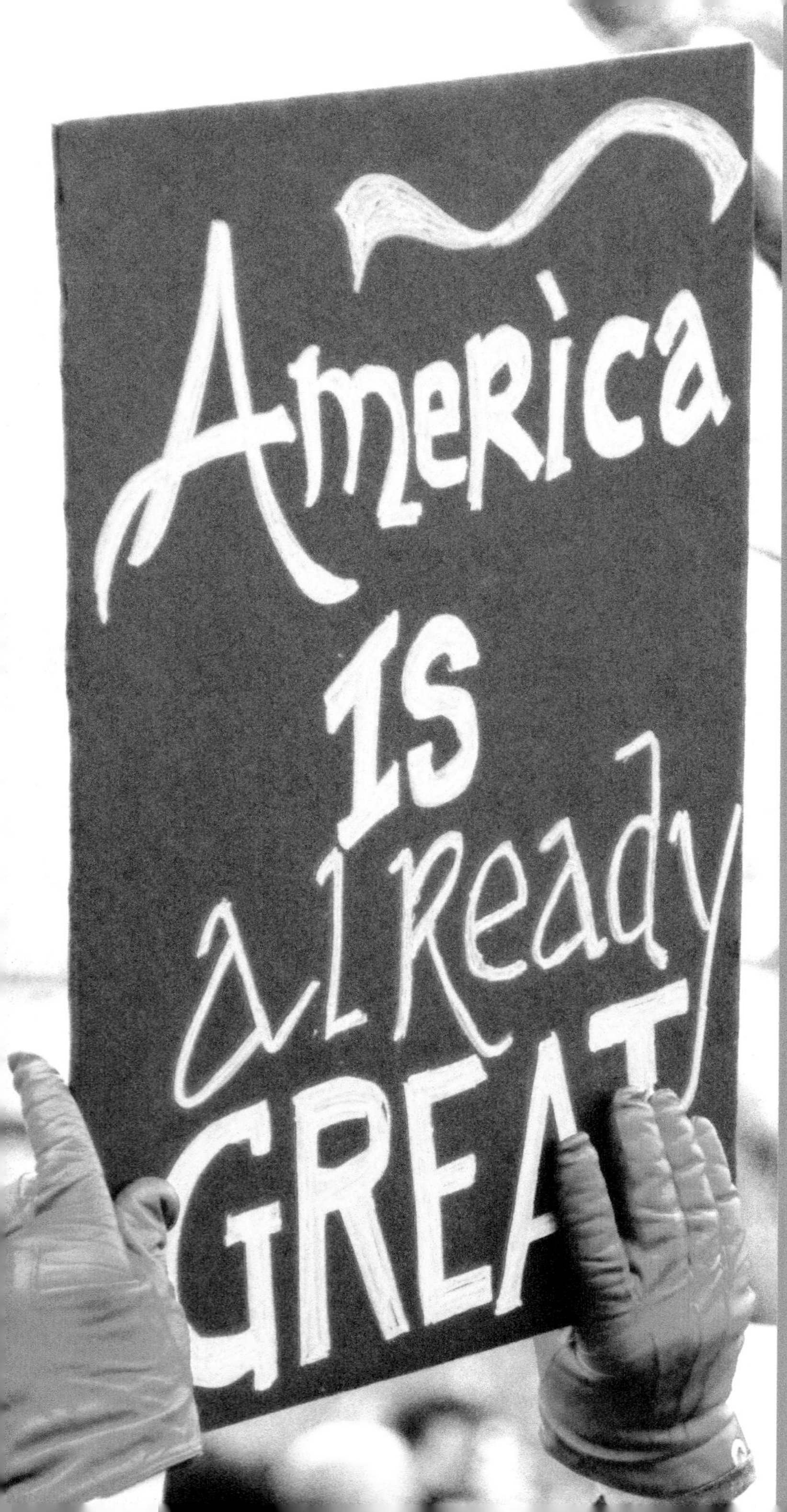
America
IS
already
GREAT
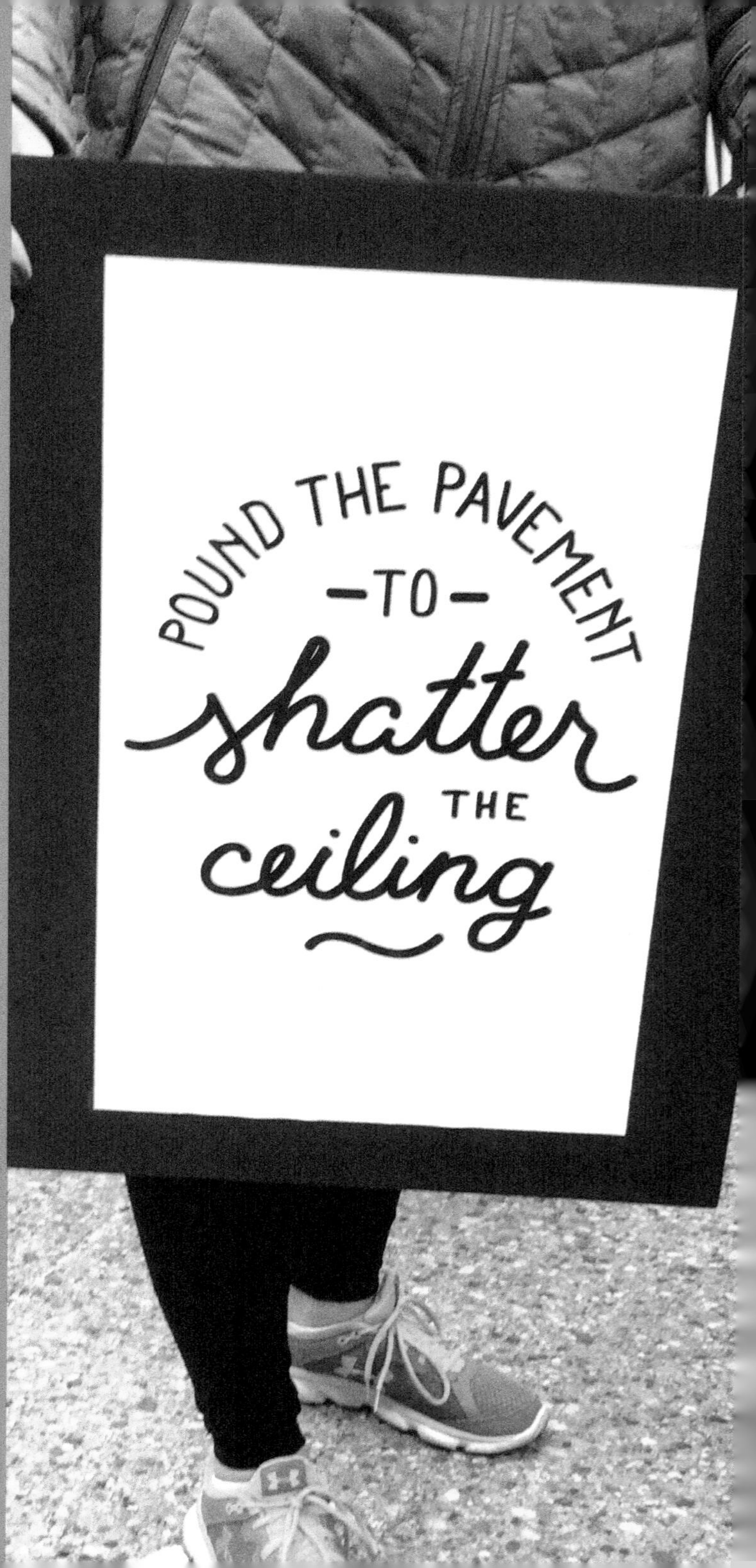
POUND THE PAVEMENT
-TO-
shatter
THE
ceiling

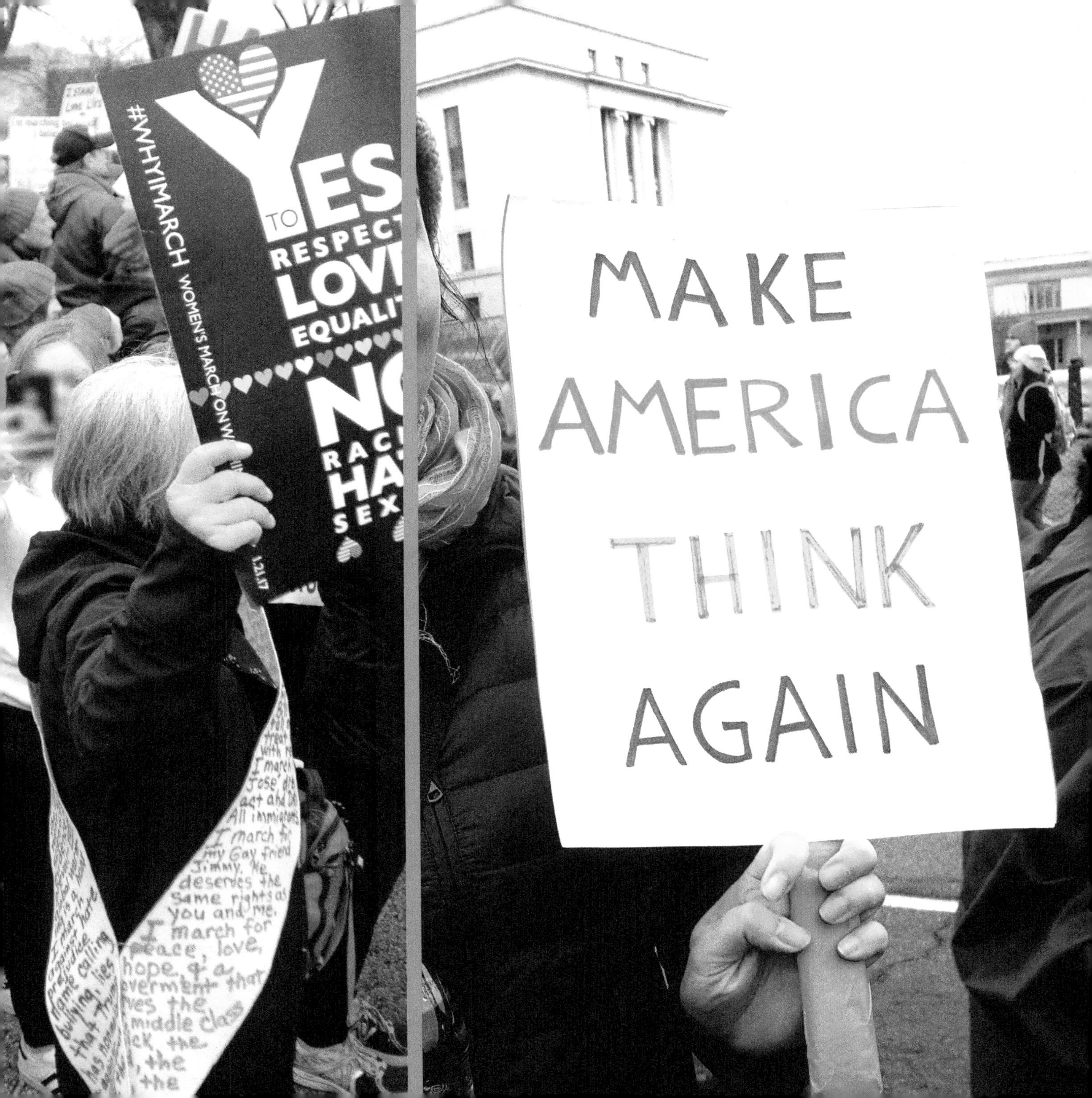
#WHYIMARCH
RESPECT
MAKE
AMERICA
THINK
AGAIN
I march for
my Gay friend
Jimmy. He
deserves the
same rights as
you and me.
I march for
peace, love,

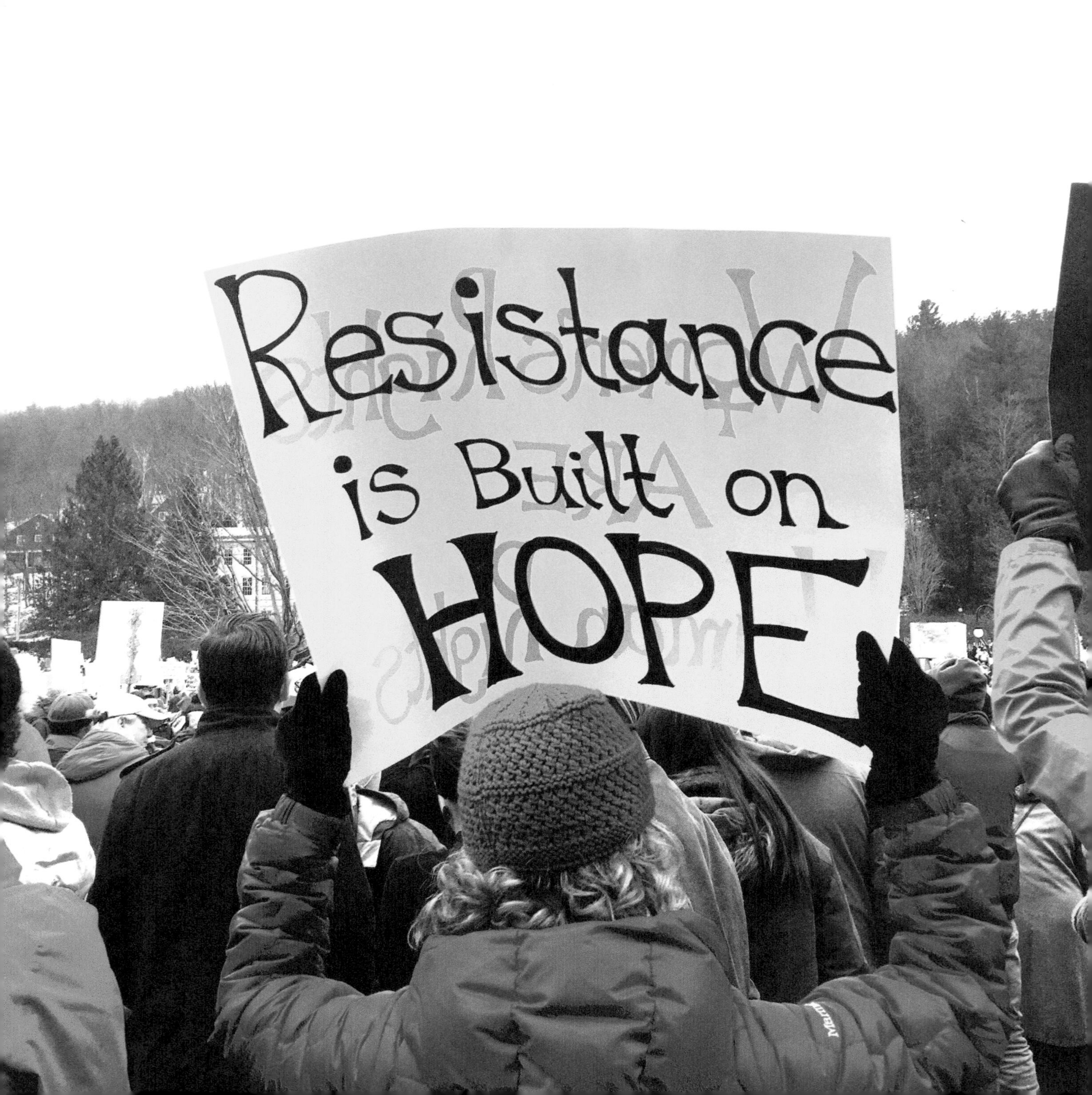
Resistance
is Built on
HOPE

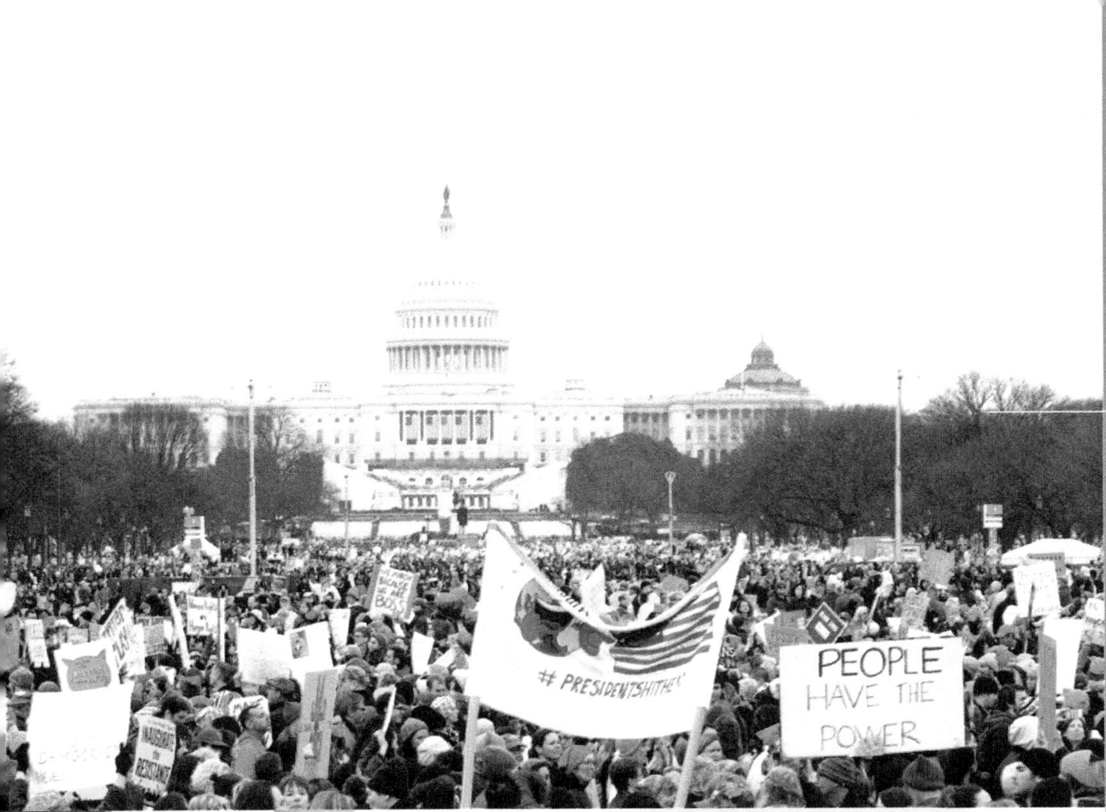
PEOPLE
HAVE THE
POWER

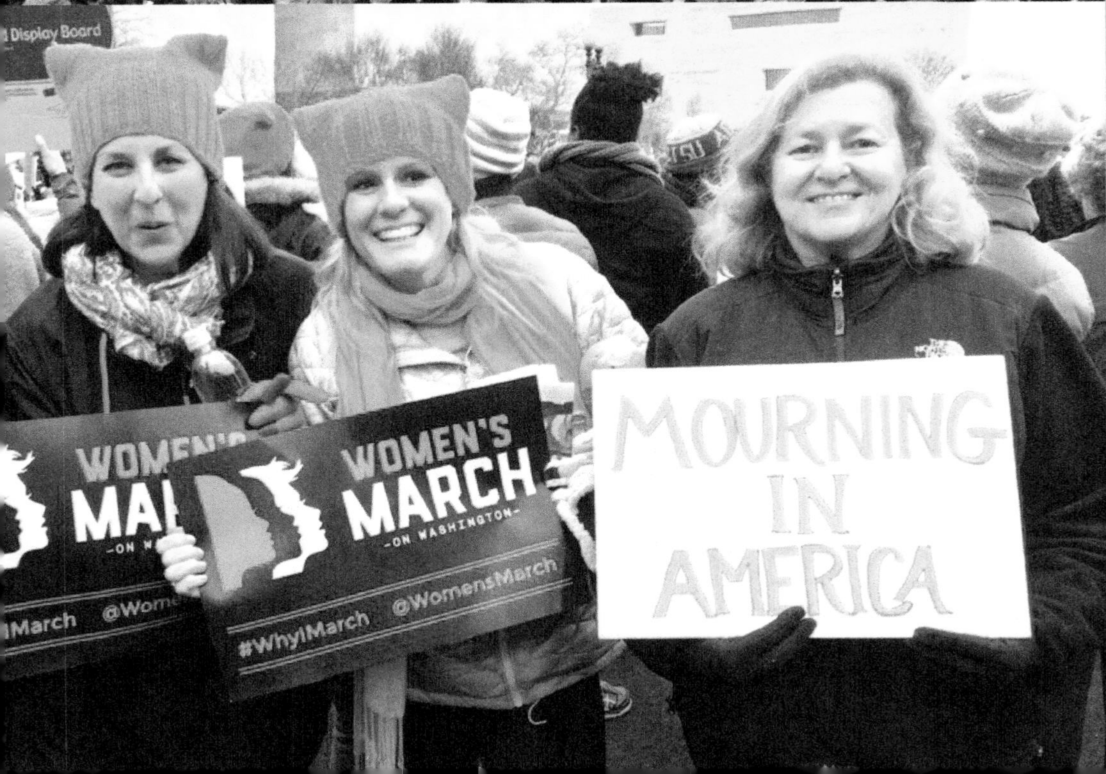
WOMEN'S
MARCH
-ON WASHINGTON-
#WhyIMarch
@WomensMarch
MOURNING
IN
AMERICA

The point isn't that there is only one pathway forward. There are many – and they are not all straight.

Karen Gross

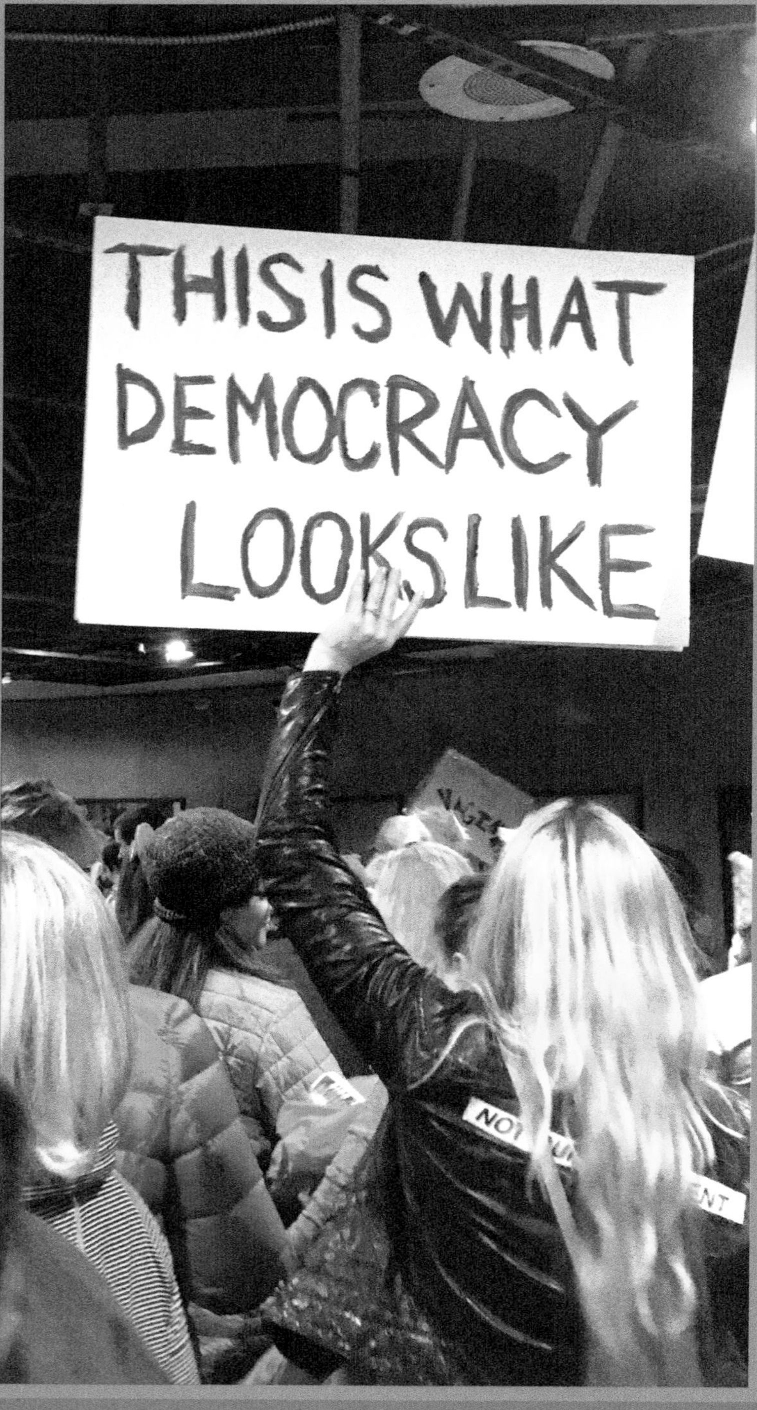
THIS IS WHAT
DEMOCRACY
LOOKS LIKE

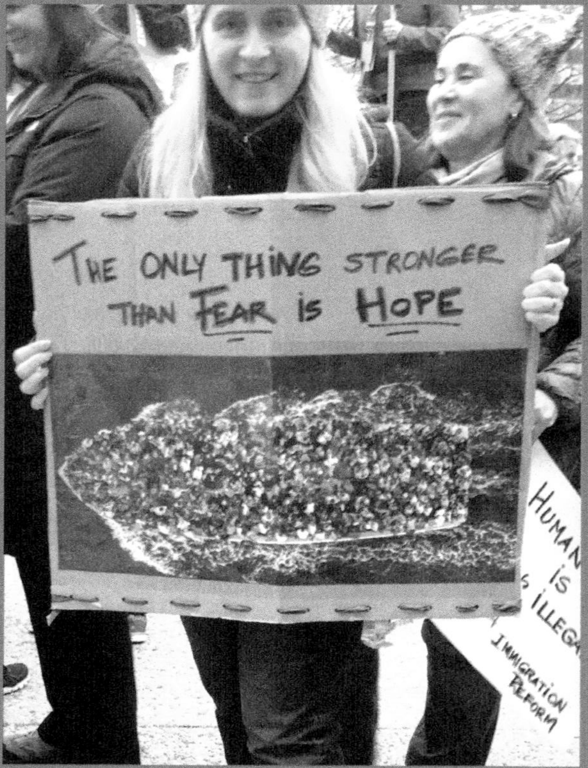
THE ONLY THING STRONGER
THAN FEAR IS HOPE
IMMIGRATION
REFORM

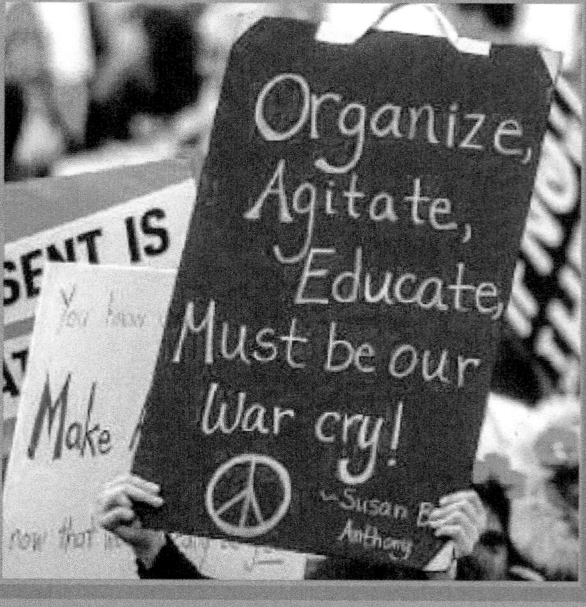
Organize,
Agitate,
Educate,
Must be our
War cry!
~Susan B
Anthony

Marches are not ending as best I can tell;
in fact they are just beginning.

Karen Gross

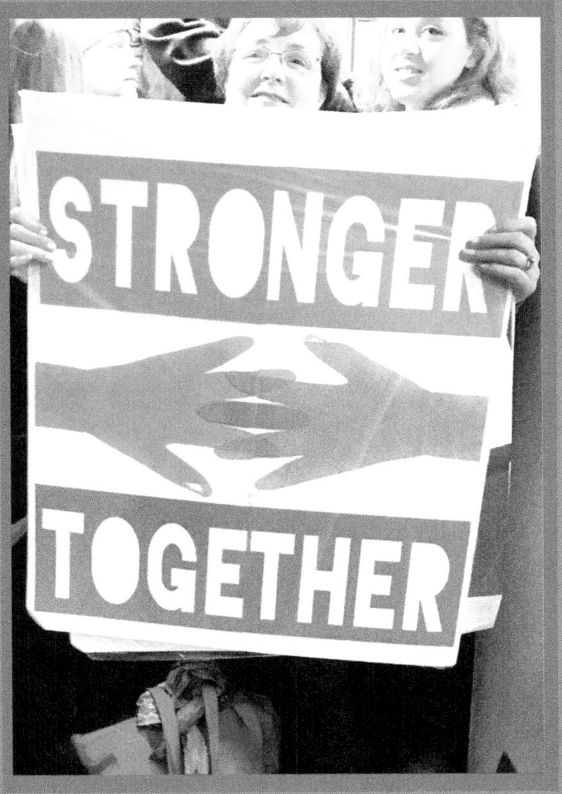
STRONGER
TOGETHER

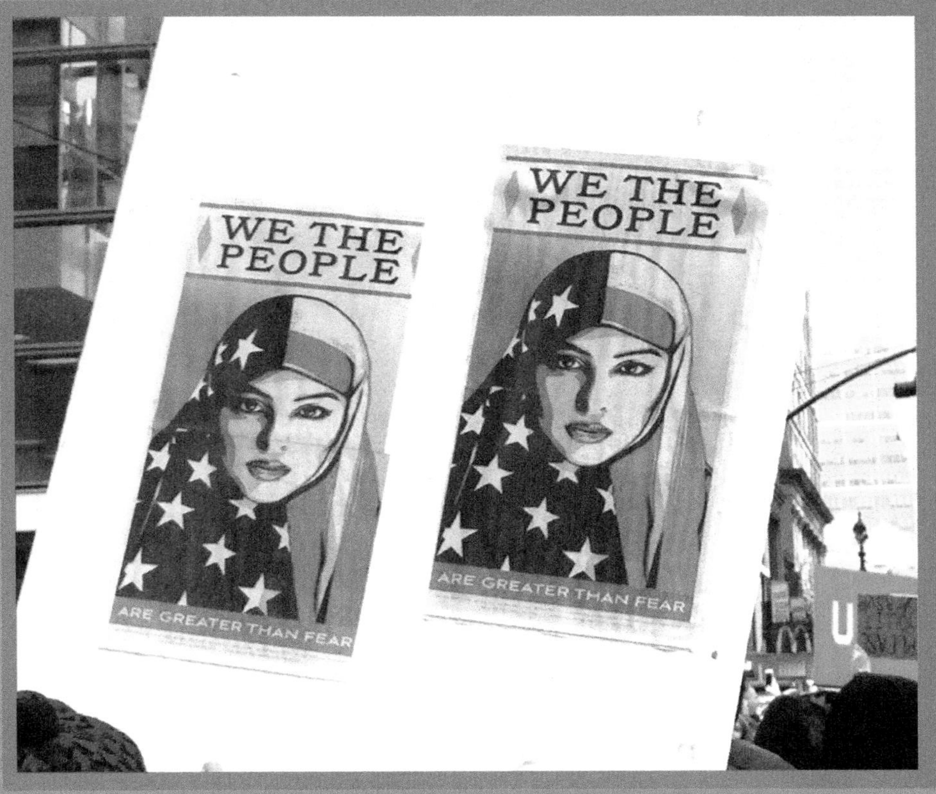
WE THE PEOPLE
ARE GREATER THAN FEAR
WE THE PEOPLE
ARE GREATER THAN FEAR

We already have marches on seeking to enable immigration and eliminate unlawful detention based on ignoble efforts to transform a nation of immigrants into a nation of homogenized people.

Karen Gross

> Some people are caregivers, within and outside the home, whether or not they earn actual dollars. Some people are focused on raising their child or children and helping raise other children.
>
> Karen Gross

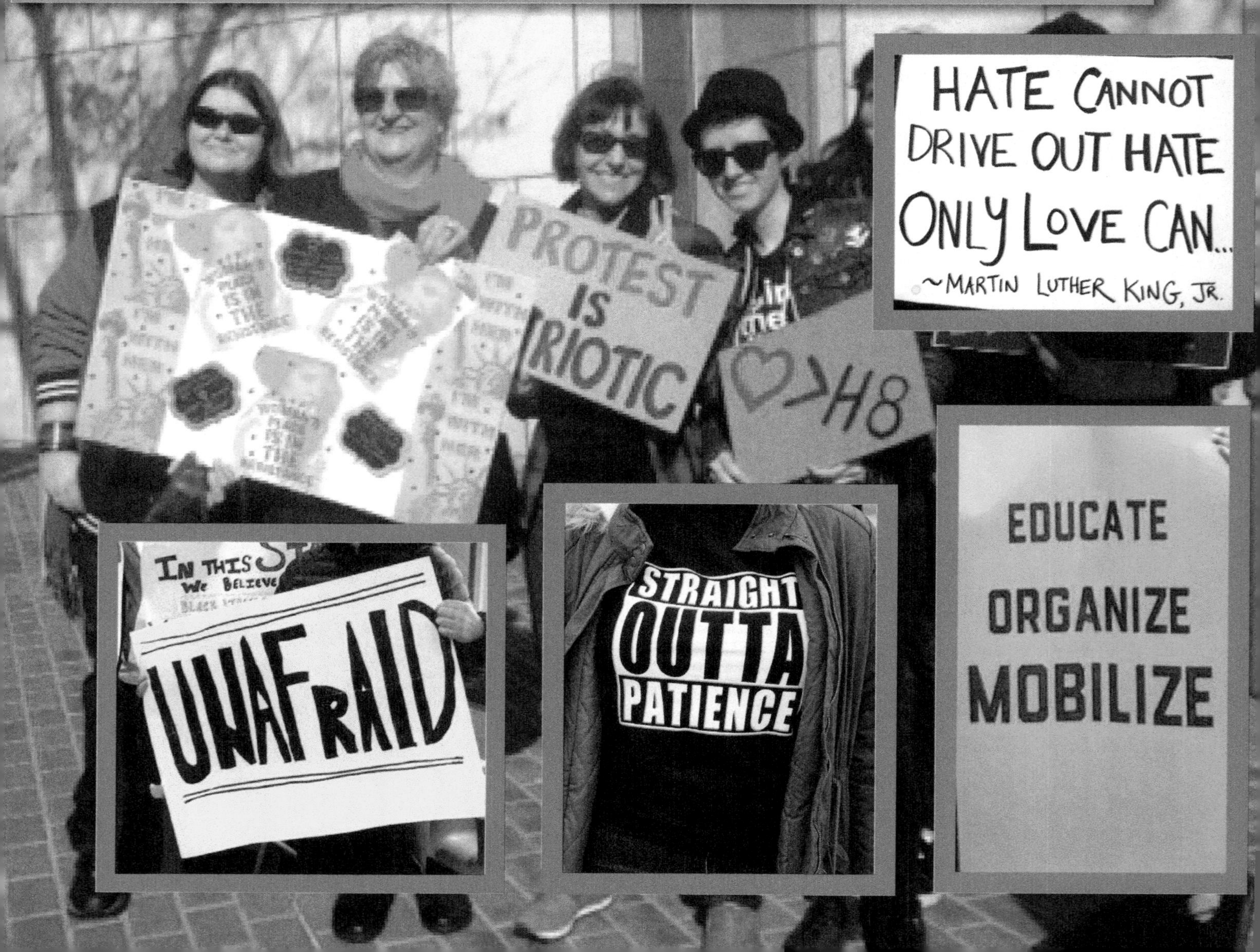
PROTEST IS RIOTIC
♥ > H8
HATE CANNOT DRIVE OUT HATE ONLY LOVE CAN...
~MARTIN LUTHER KING, JR.
IN THIS
WE BELIEVE
UNAFRAID
STRAIGHT OUTTA PATIENCE
EDUCATE
ORGANIZE
MOBILIZE

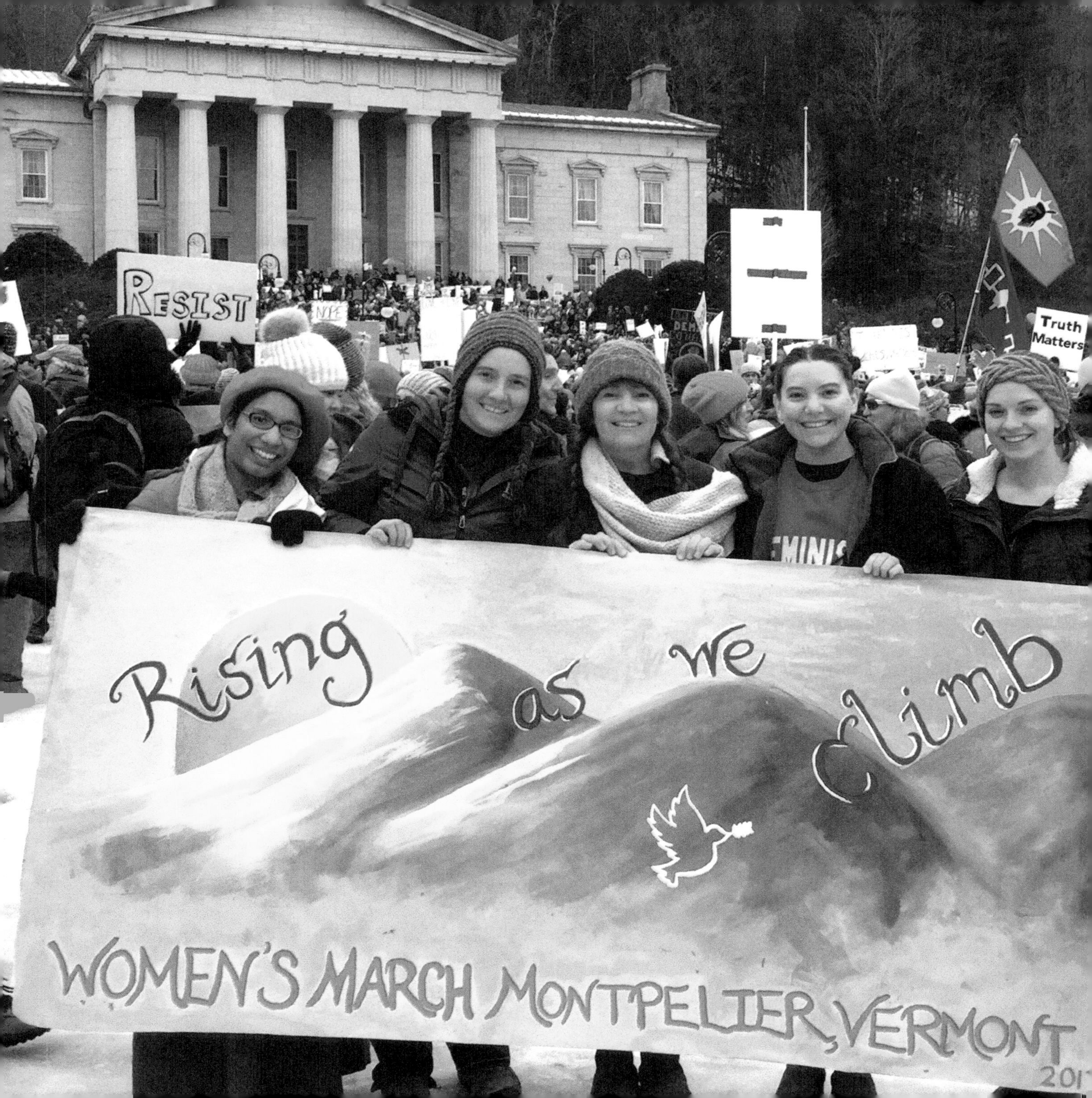
RESIST
Truth Matters
Rising as we Climb
WOMEN'S MARCH MONTPELIER, VERMONT
2017

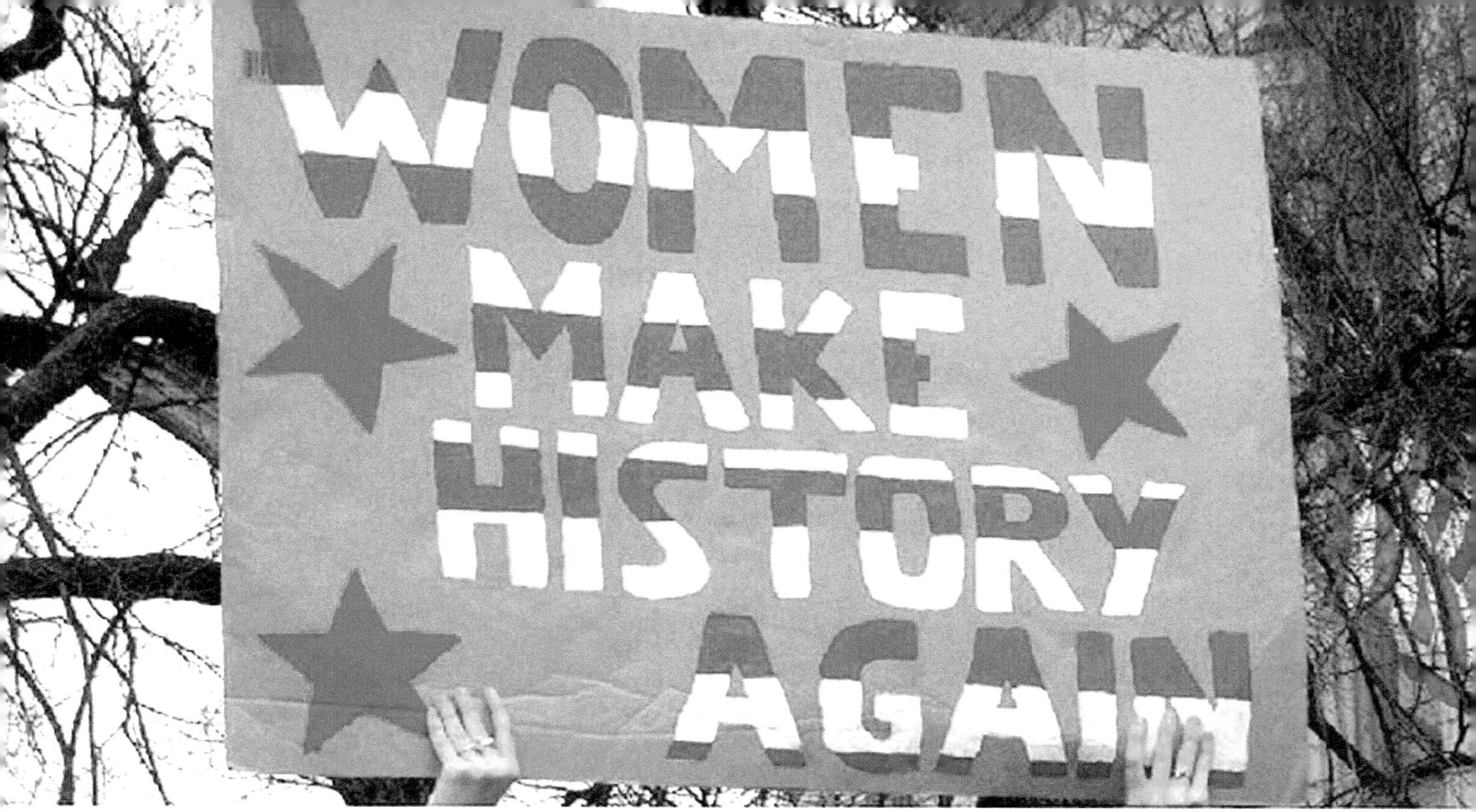
WOMEN
MAKE
HISTORY
AGAIN

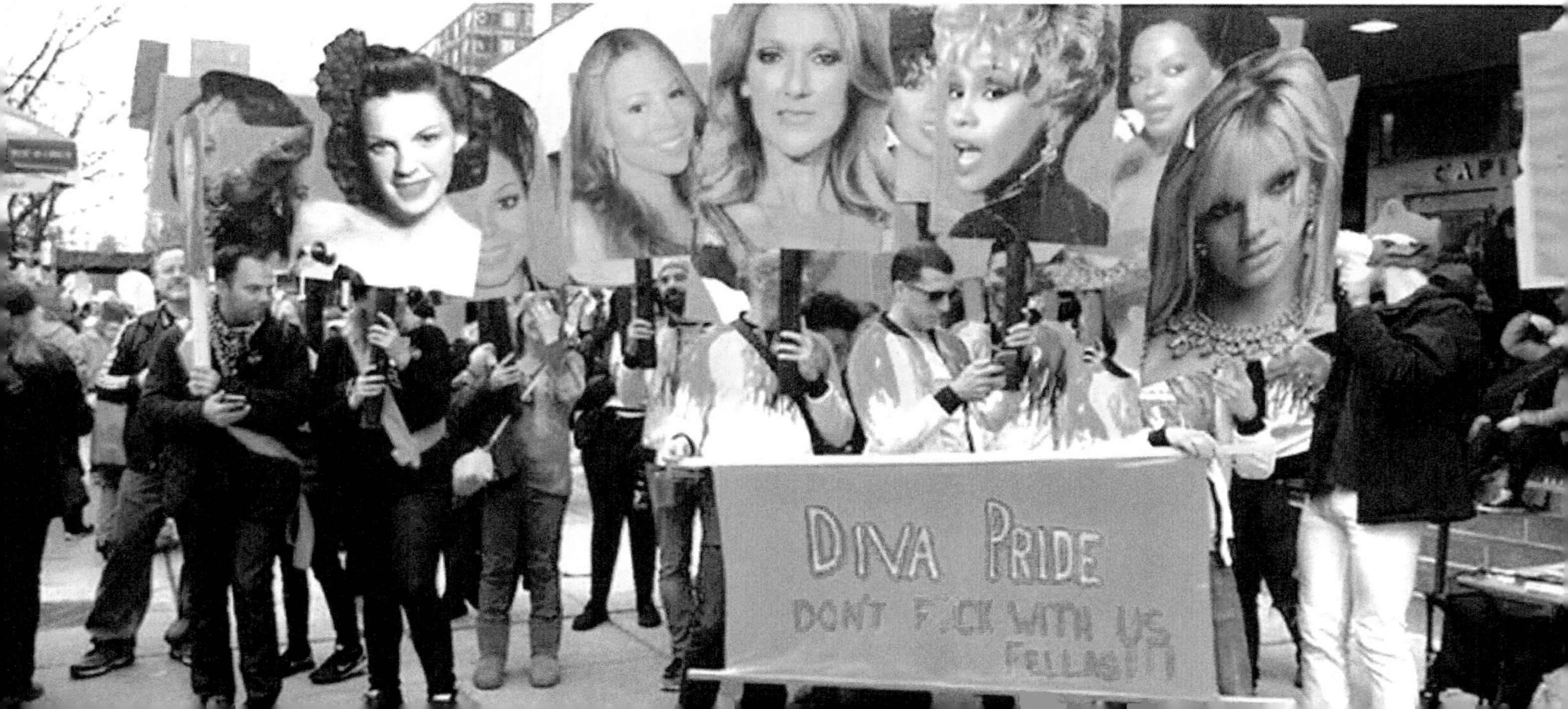
DIVA PRIDE
DON'T F.CK WITH US
FELLAS!!!

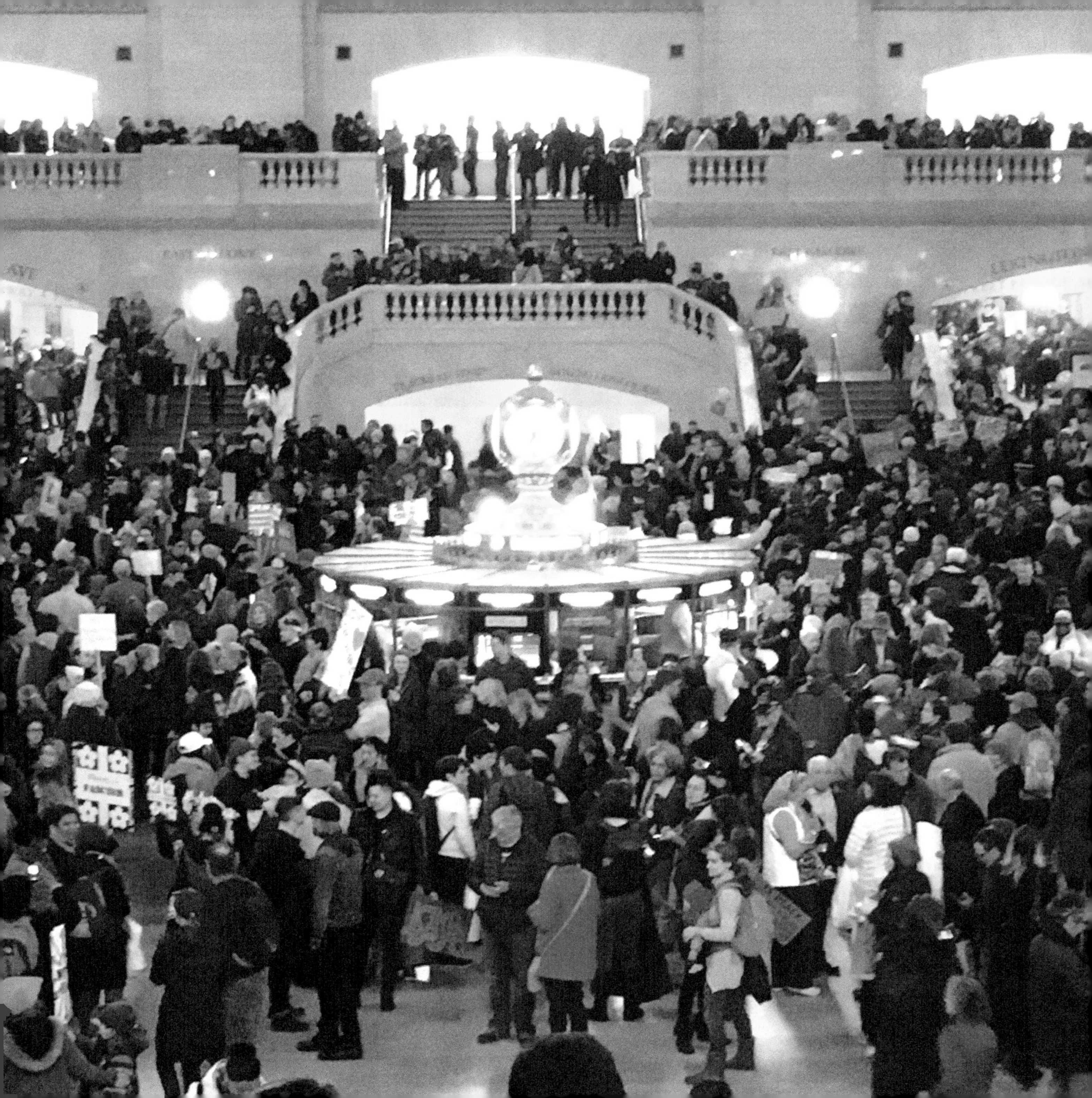

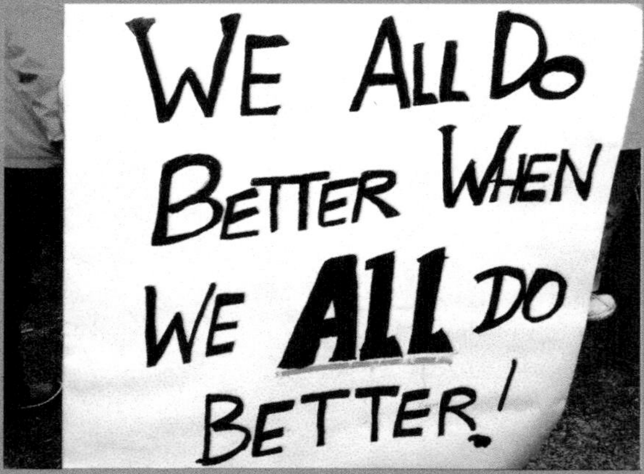
WE ALL DO
BETTER WHEN
WE ALL DO
BETTER!

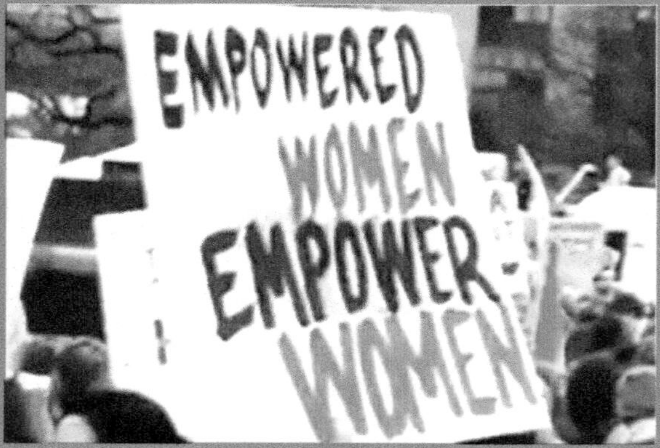
EMPOWERED
WOMEN
EMPOWER
WOMEN

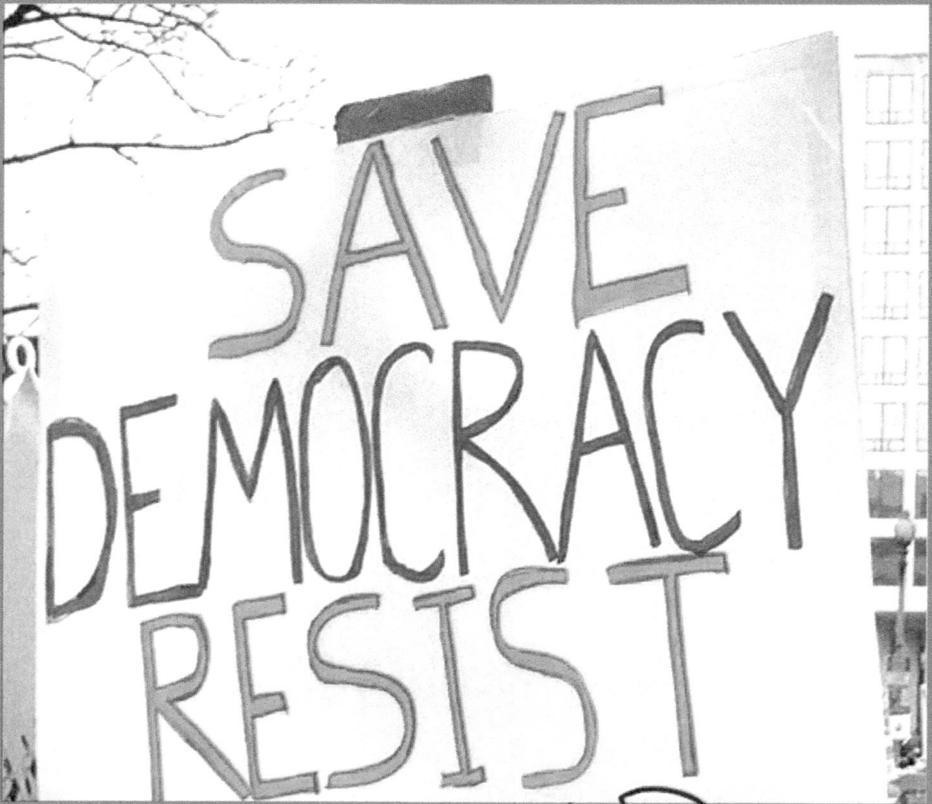
SAVE
DEMOCRACY
RESIST

Many years ago, Caroline Kennedy edited a book called *A Patriot's Handbook.* The book had and still has a powerful message: there are many ways to be a Patriot.

Karen Gross

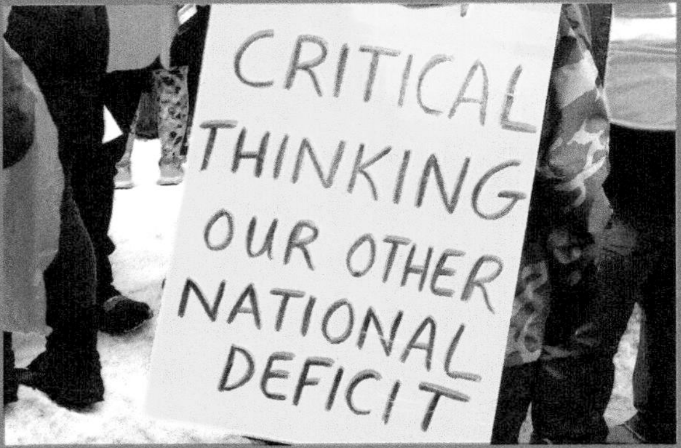
CRITICAL
THINKING
OUR OTHER
NATIONAL
DEFICIT

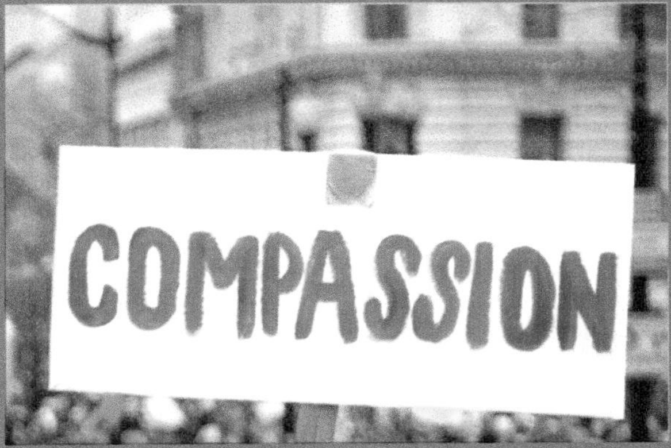
COMPASSION

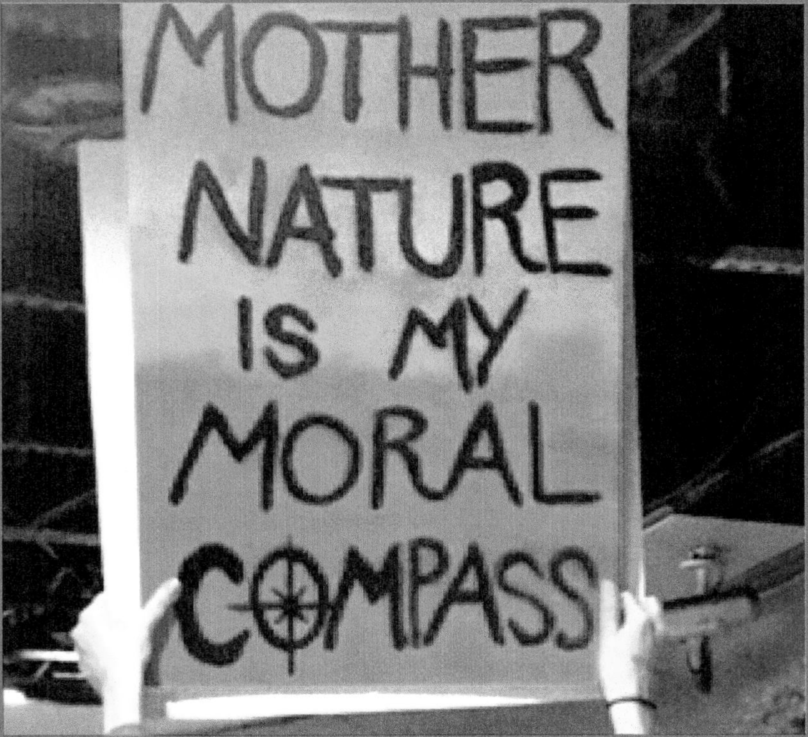
MOTHER
NATURE
IS MY
MORAL
COMPASS

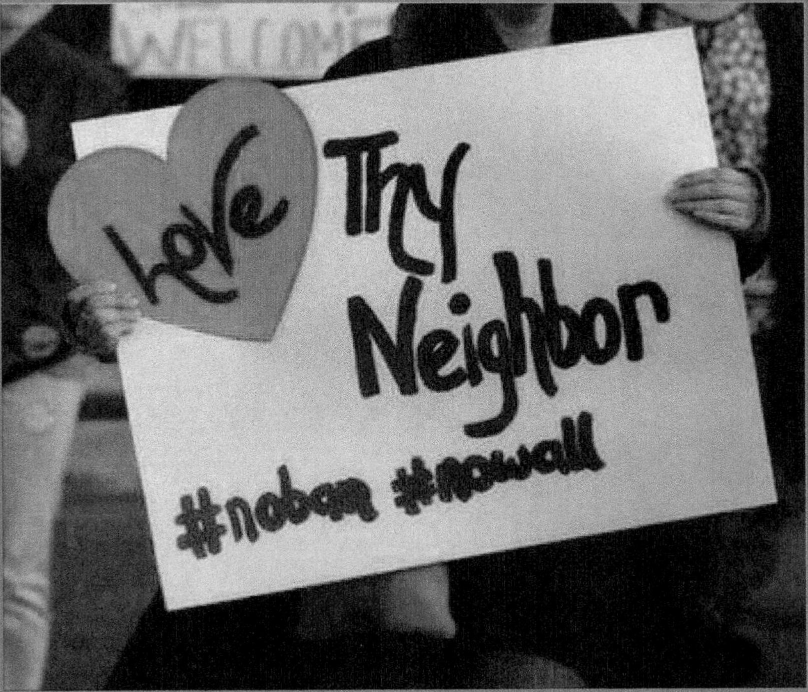
love Thy
Neighbor
#noban #nowall

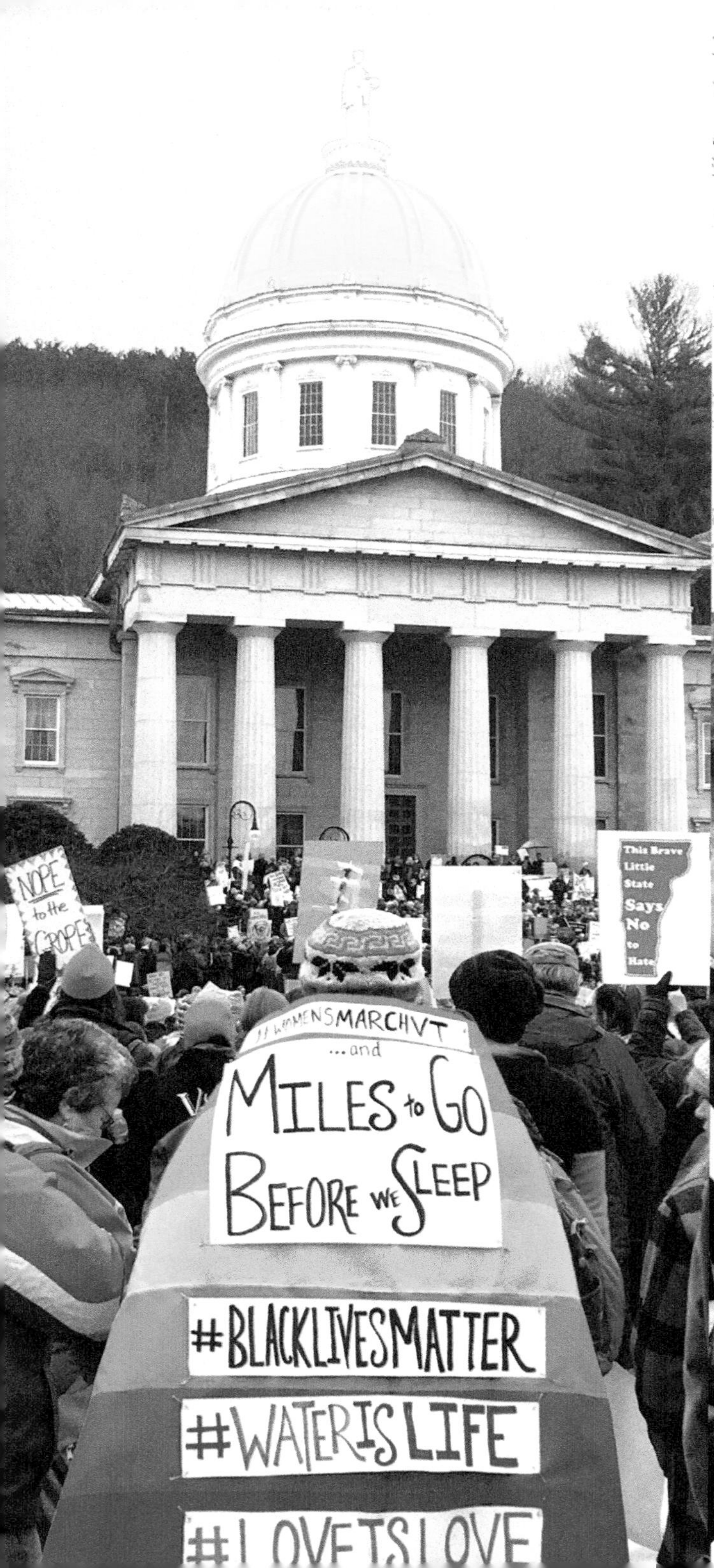
NOPE to the GROPE
This Brave Little State Says No to Hate
#WOMENSMARCHVT
...and
MILES to GO BEFORE WE SLEEP
#BLACKLIVESMATTER
#WATERISLIFE
#LOVEISLOVE

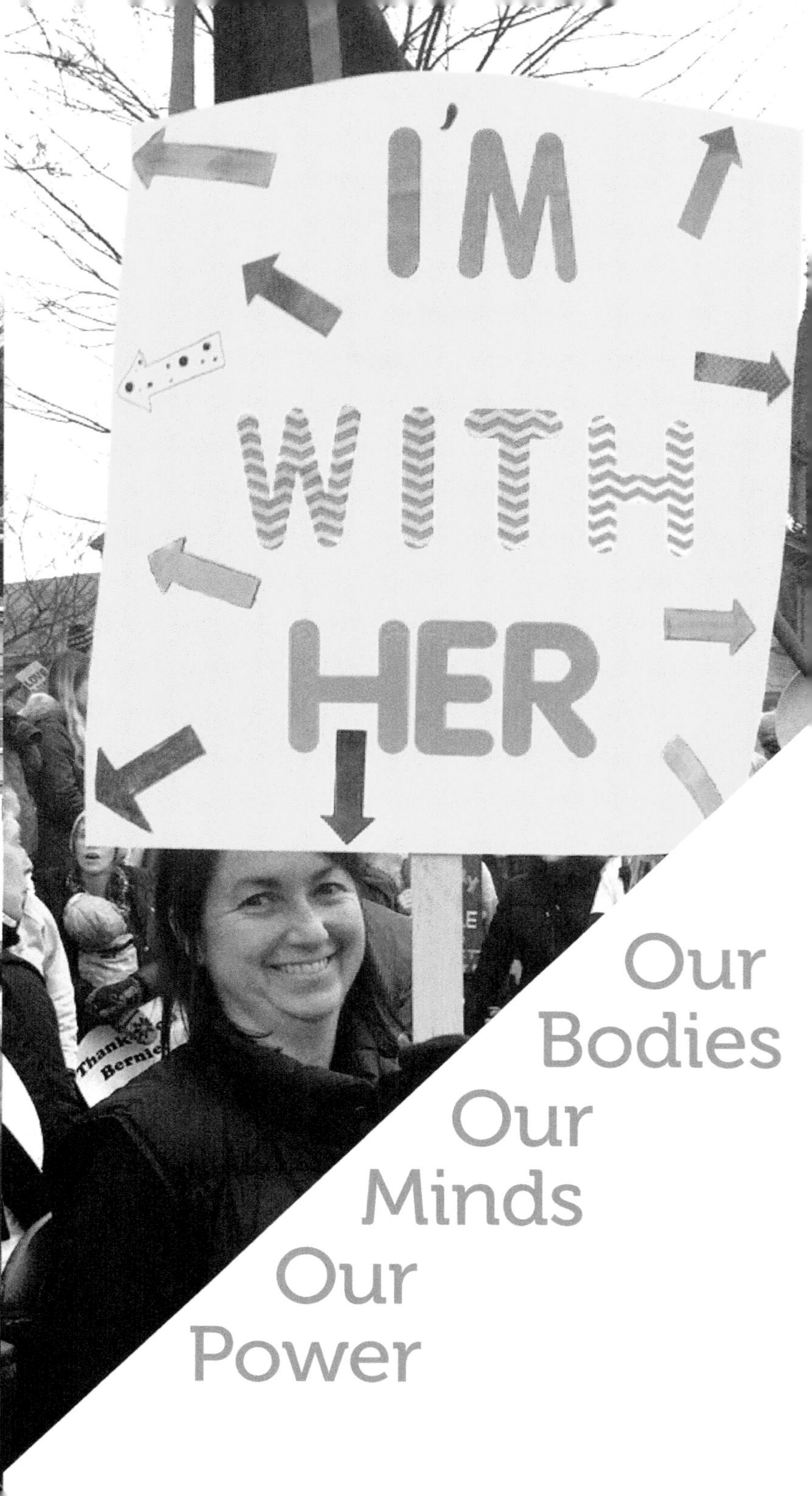
I'M WITH HER

Our Bodies
Our Minds
Our Power

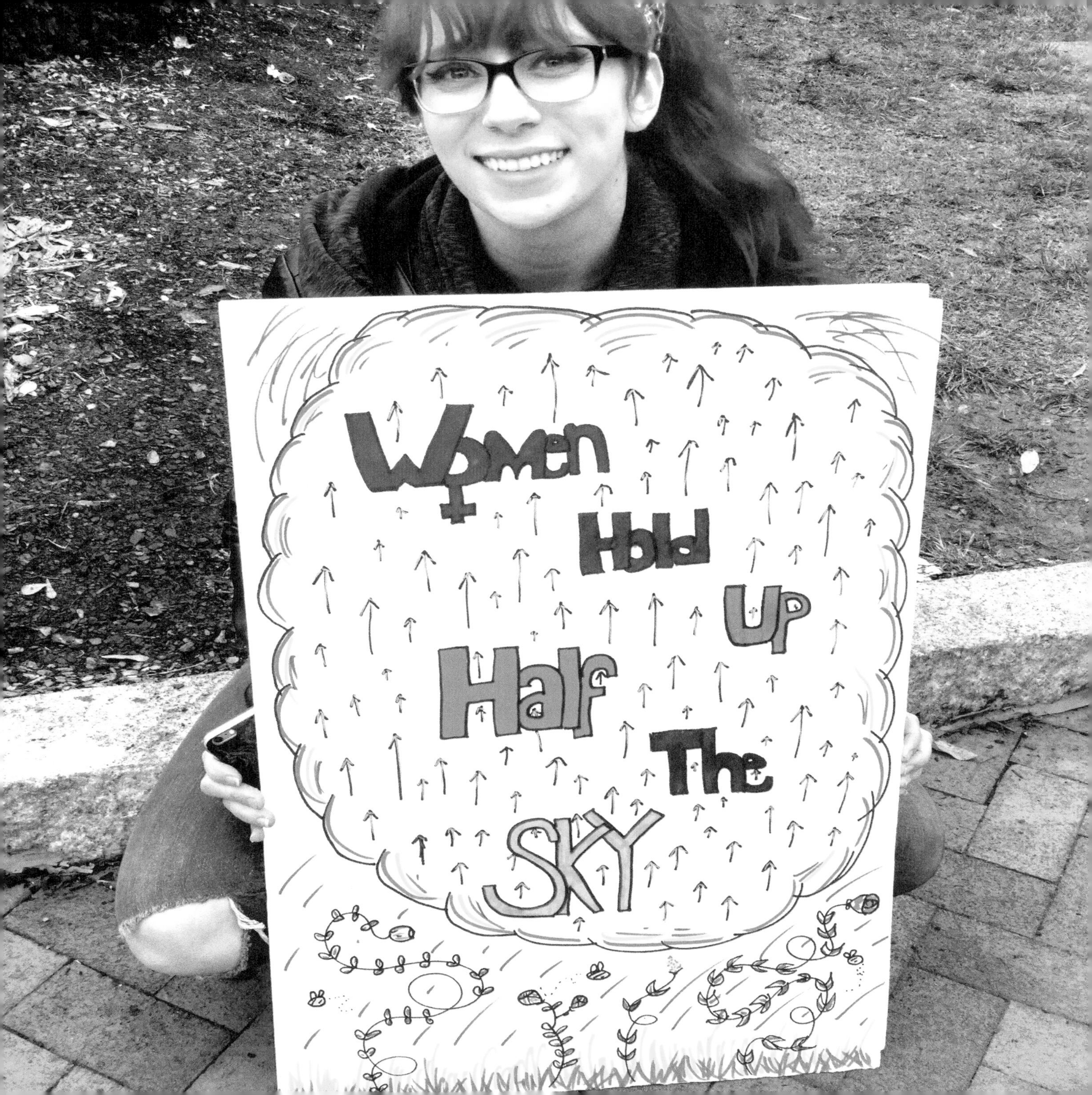
Women
Hold
Up
Half
The
SKY

We need
to see,
experience and
use our
collective
web-like power to
utilize a myriad of
strategies –
simultaneously –
to teach our
children.

Karen Gross

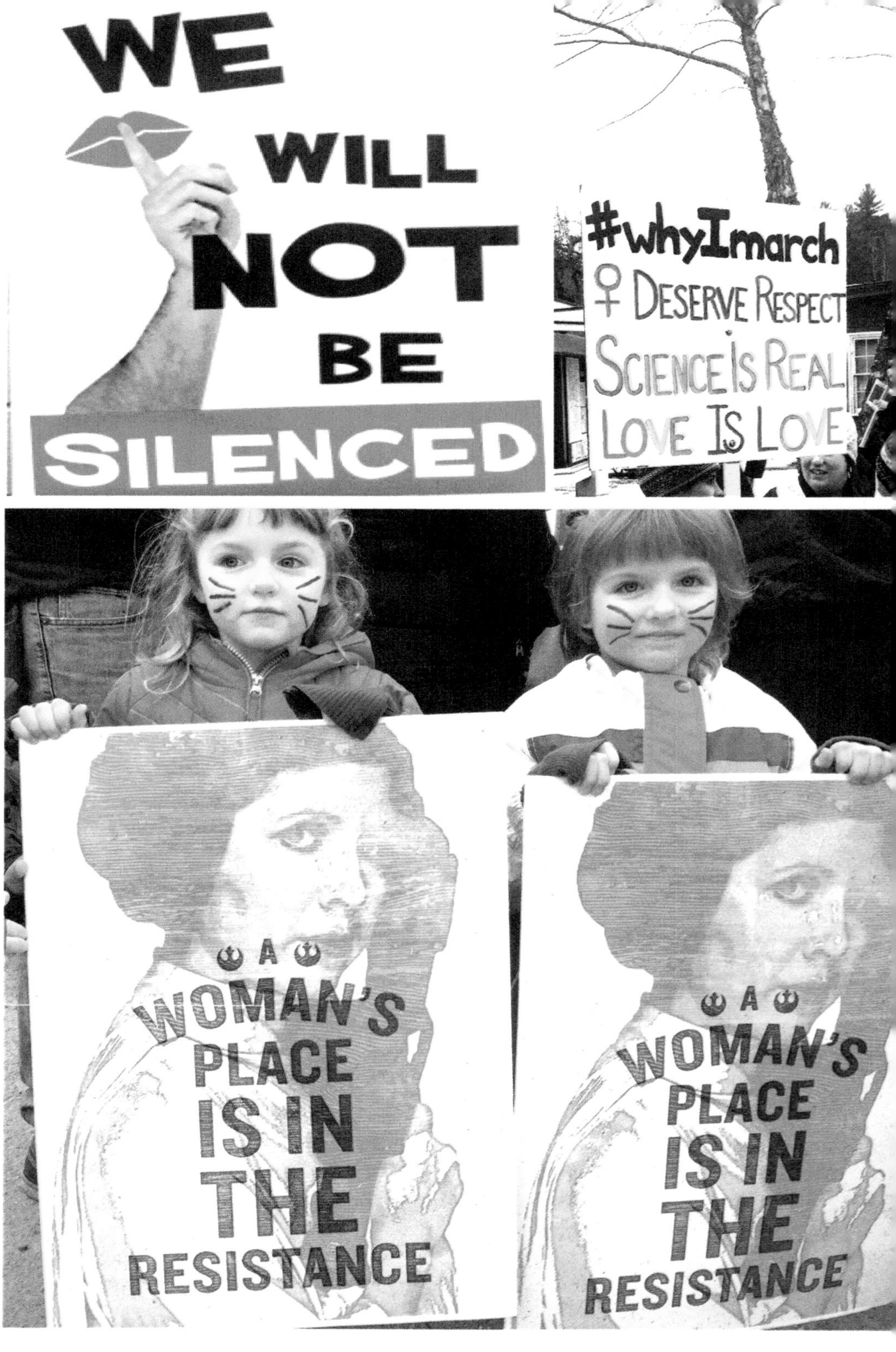
WE WILL NOT BE SILENCED
#whyImarch
♀ DESERVE RESPECT
SCIENCE IS REAL
LOVE IS LOVE
A WOMAN'S PLACE IS IN THE RESISTANCE
A WOMAN'S PLACE IS IN THE RESISTANCE

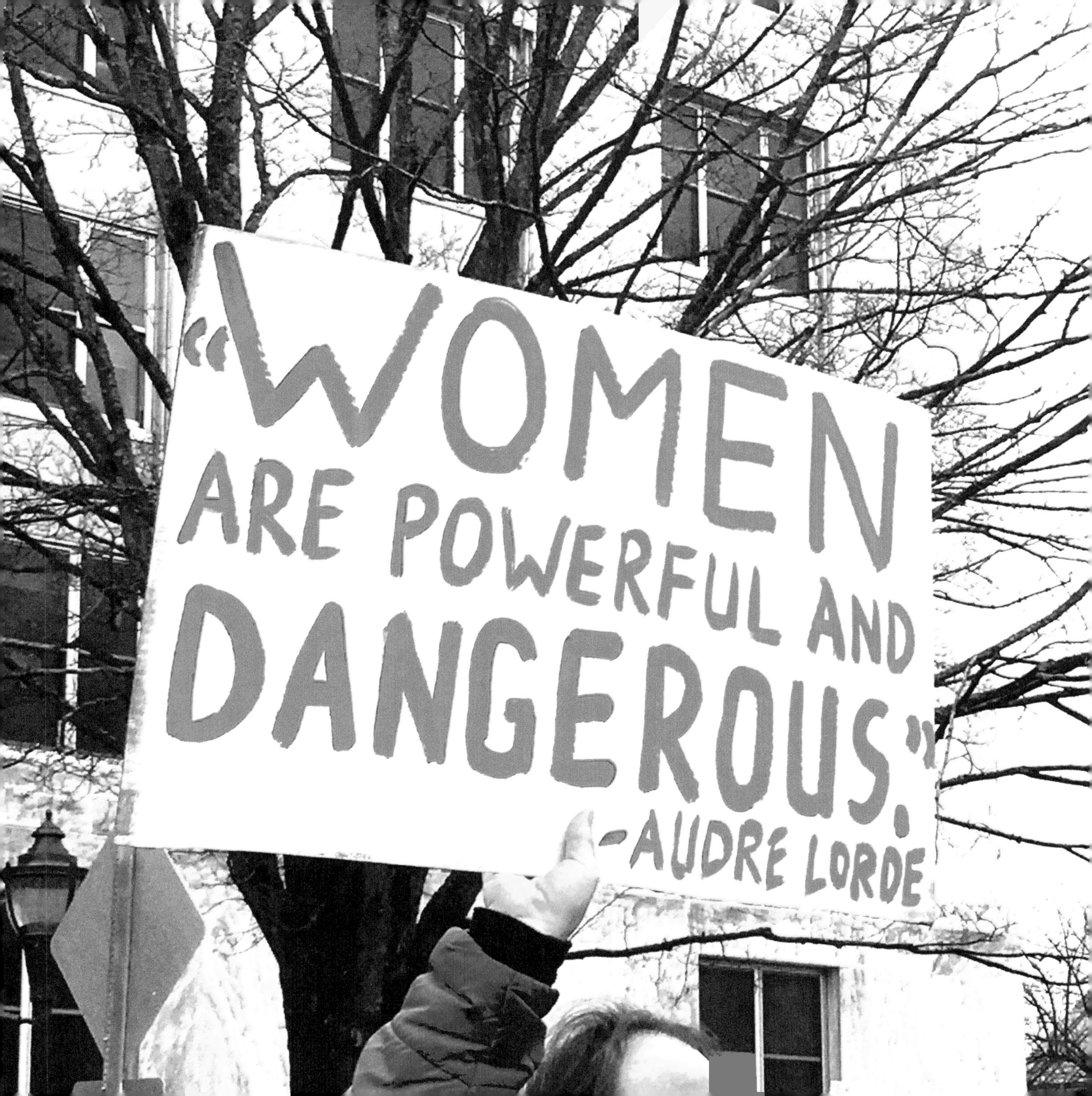
"WOMEN
ARE POWERFUL AND
DANGEROUS."
-AUDRE LORDE

Original saying: Rosa sat so Martin could march; Martin marched so Obama could run; Obama ran so our children could fly....

Khari Mosley

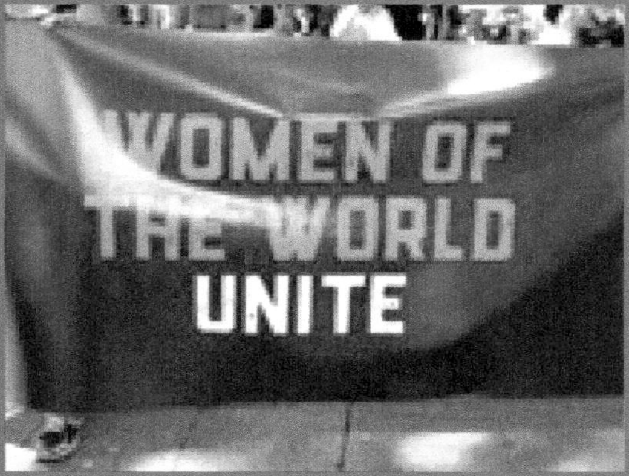
WOMEN OF
THE WORLD
UNITE

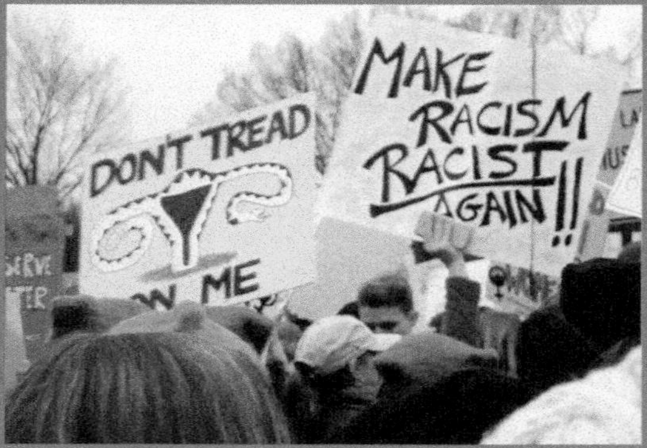
DON'T TREAD
MAKE
RACISM
RACIST
AGAIN!!

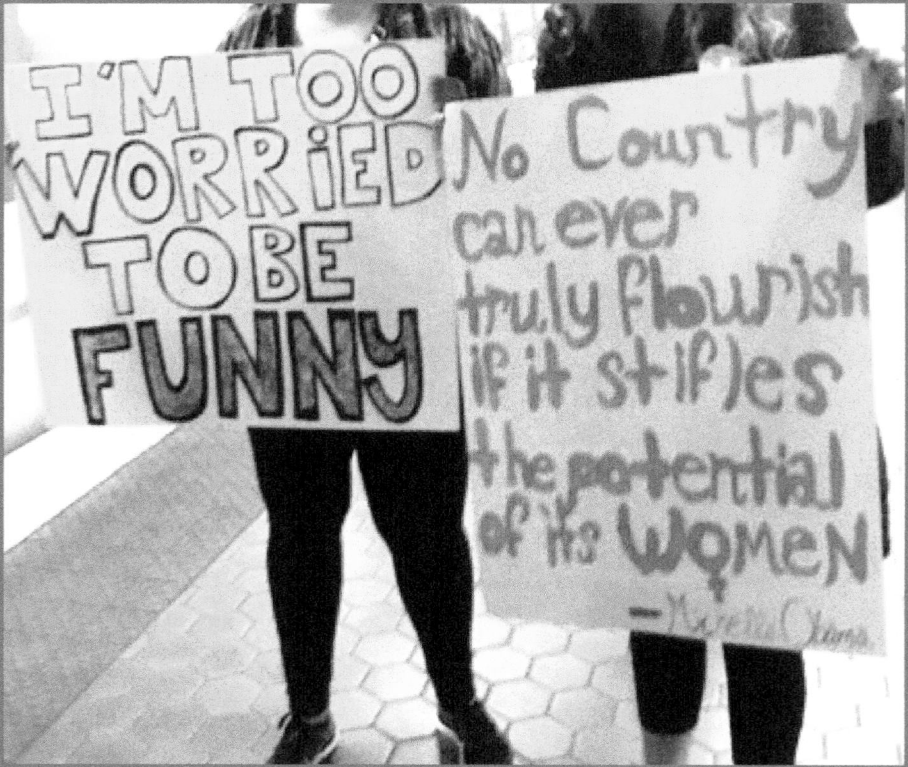
I'M TOO
WORRIED
TO BE
FUNNY
No Country
can ever
truly flourish
if it stifles
the potential
of its WOMEN

Now we need to revise this to: Rosa sat, and Martin marched, and Obama ran, and it is our time to rise.

Anonymous

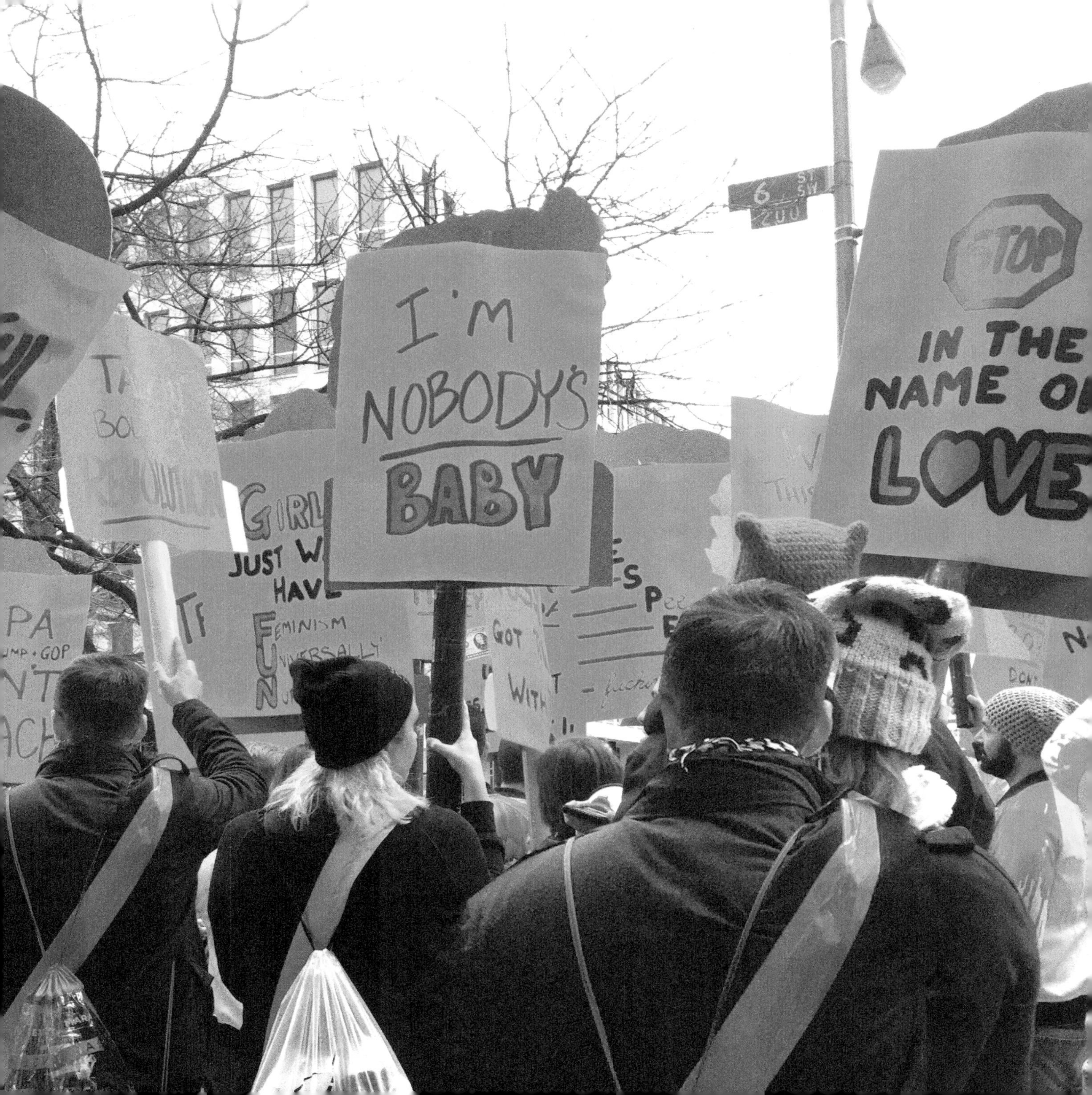
I'M NOBODY'S BABY
STOP
IN THE NAME OF LOVE
6 ST SW
200
FEMINISM
UNIVERSALLY

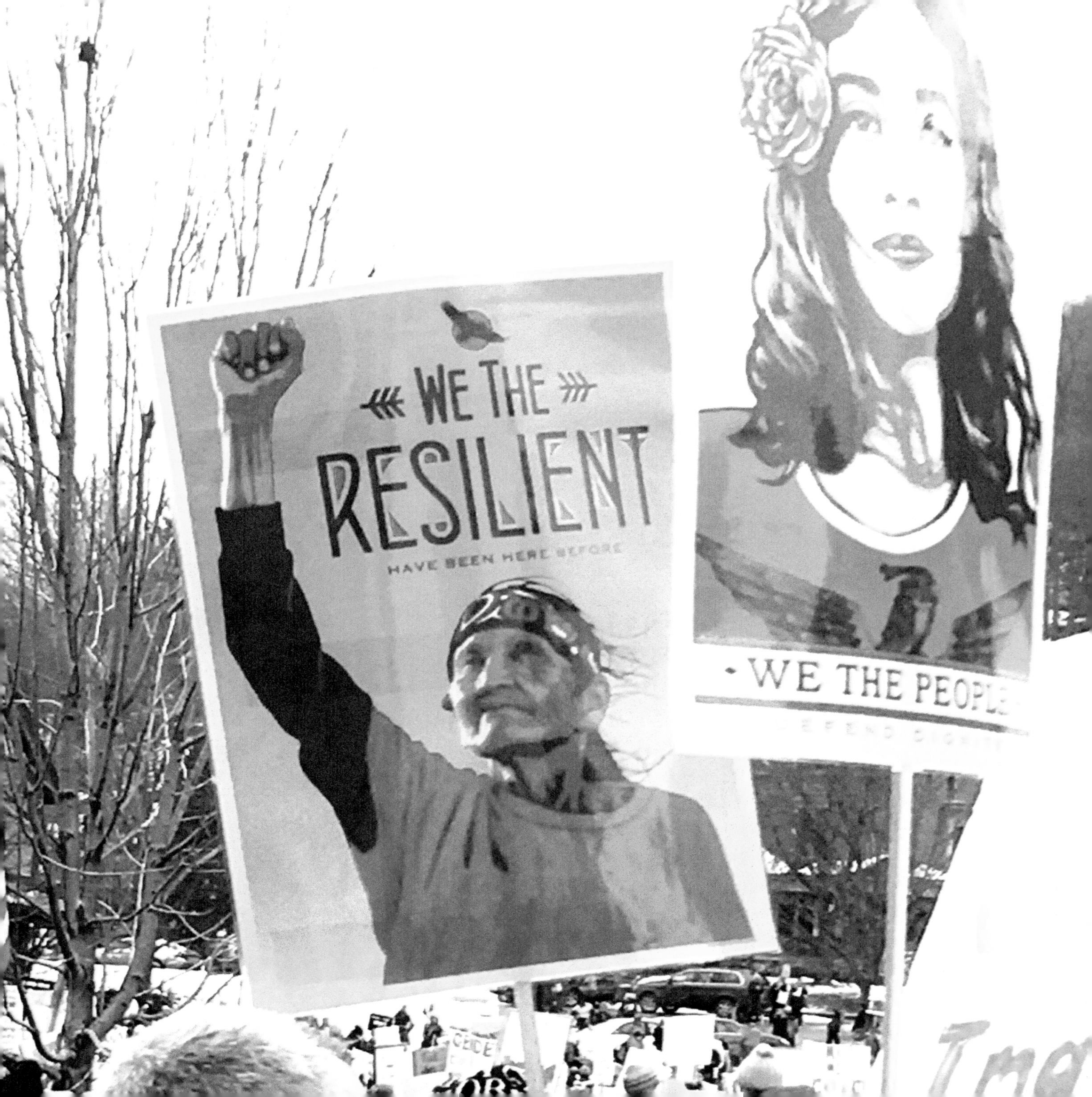
WE THE
RESILIENT
HAVE BEEN HERE BEFORE
WE THE PEOPL

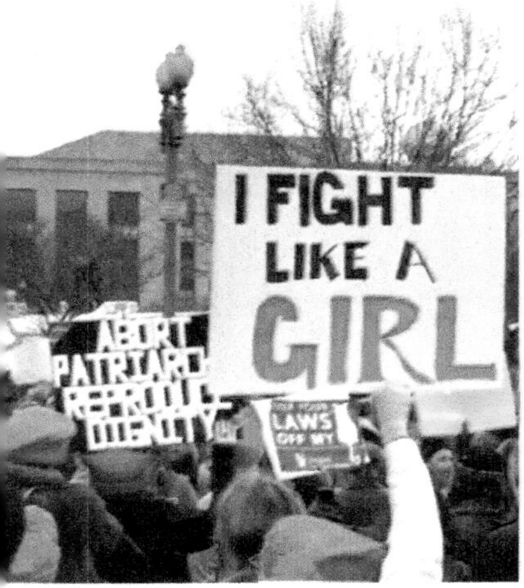
I FIGHT
LIKE A
GIRL
LAWS

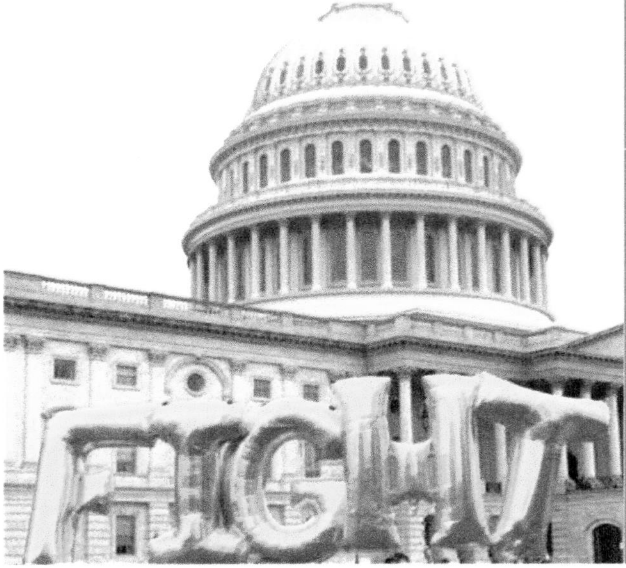

Everyone will and can contribute to improving our world in different ways.

Karen Gross

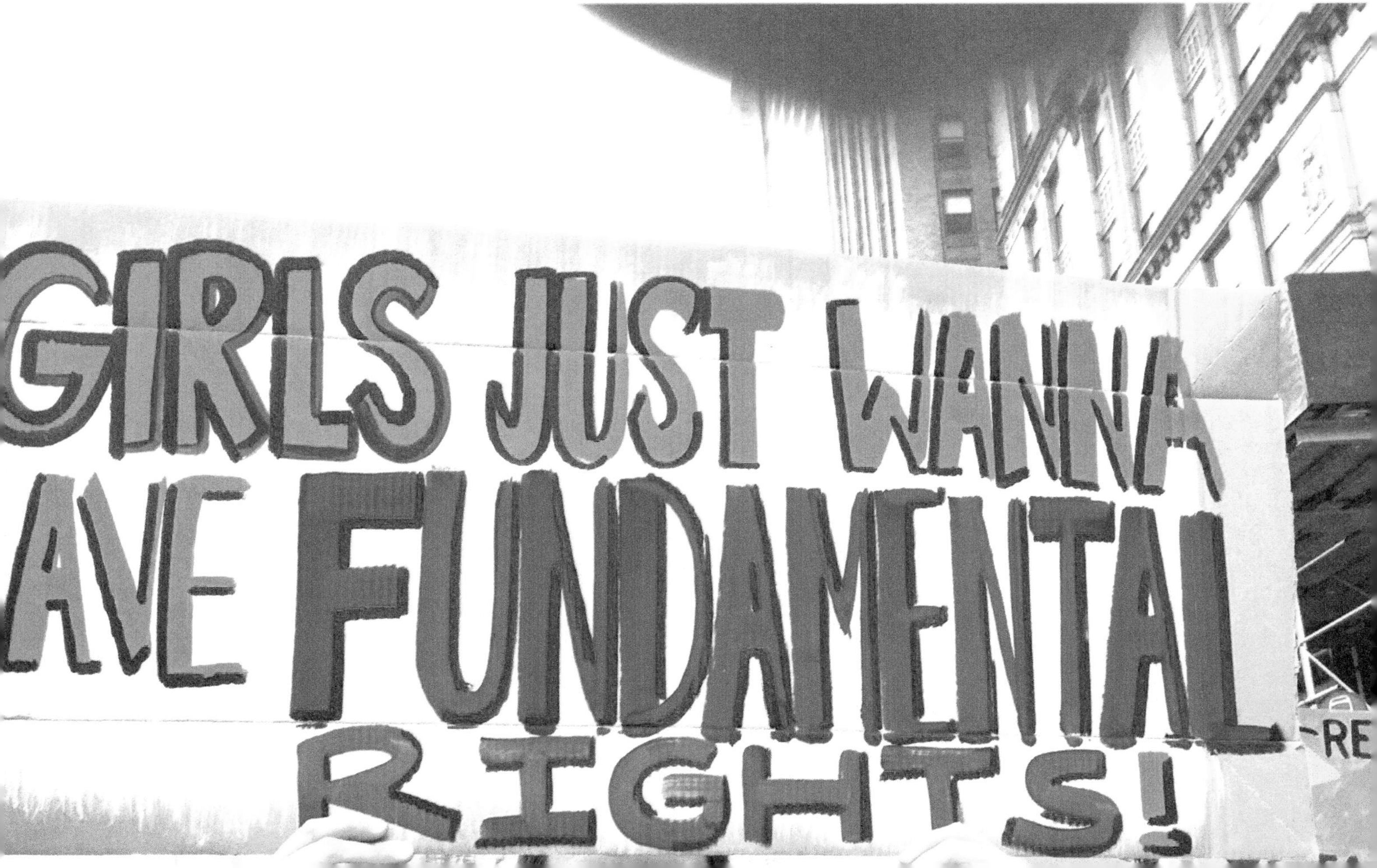
GIRLS JUST WANNA
AVE FUNDAMENTAL
RIGHTS!

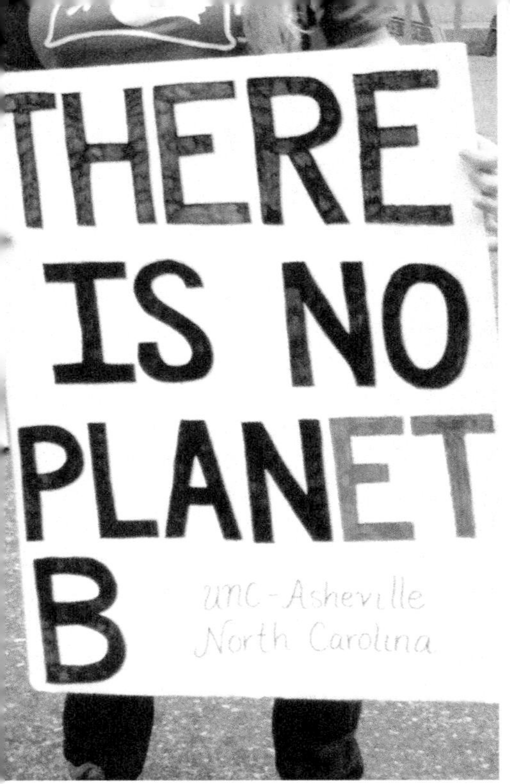
THERE IS NO PLANET B
UNC-Asheville North Carolina

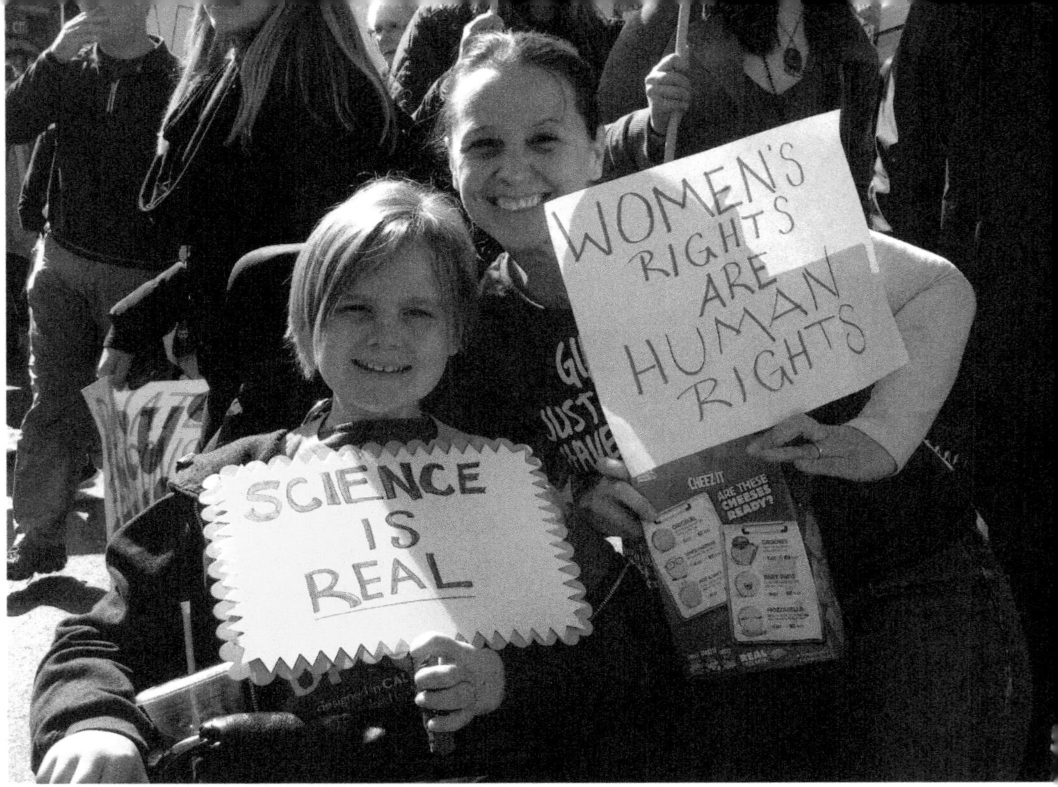
WOMEN'S RIGHTS ARE HUMAN RIGHTS
SCIENCE IS REAL

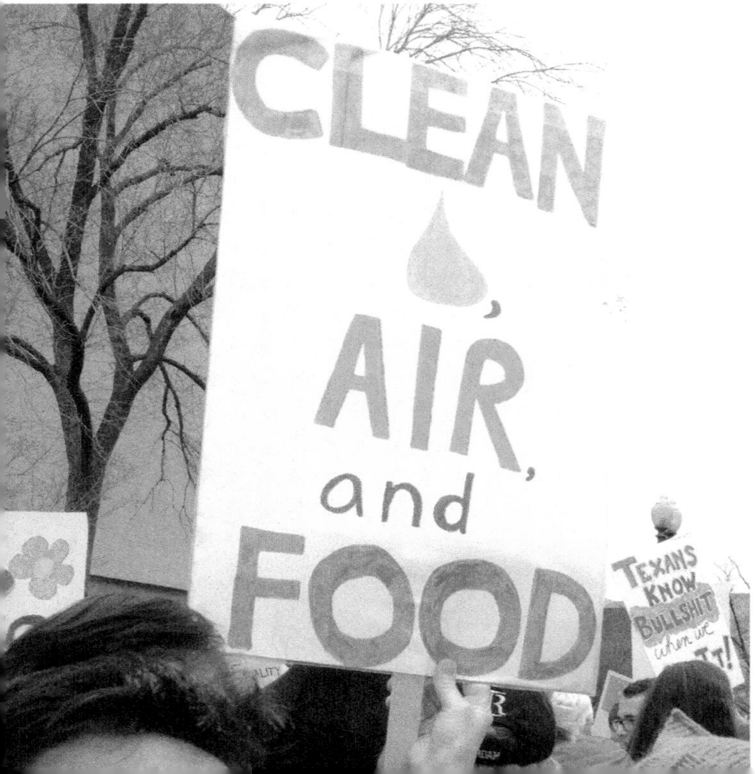
CLEAN , AIR, and FOOD
TEXANS KNOW BULLSHIT

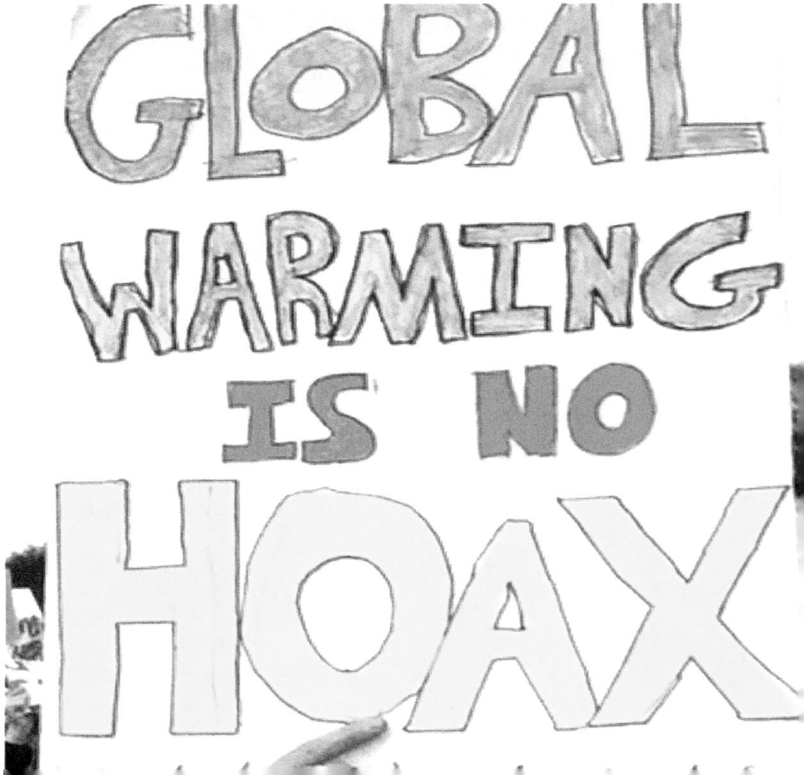
GLOBAL WARMING IS NO HOAX

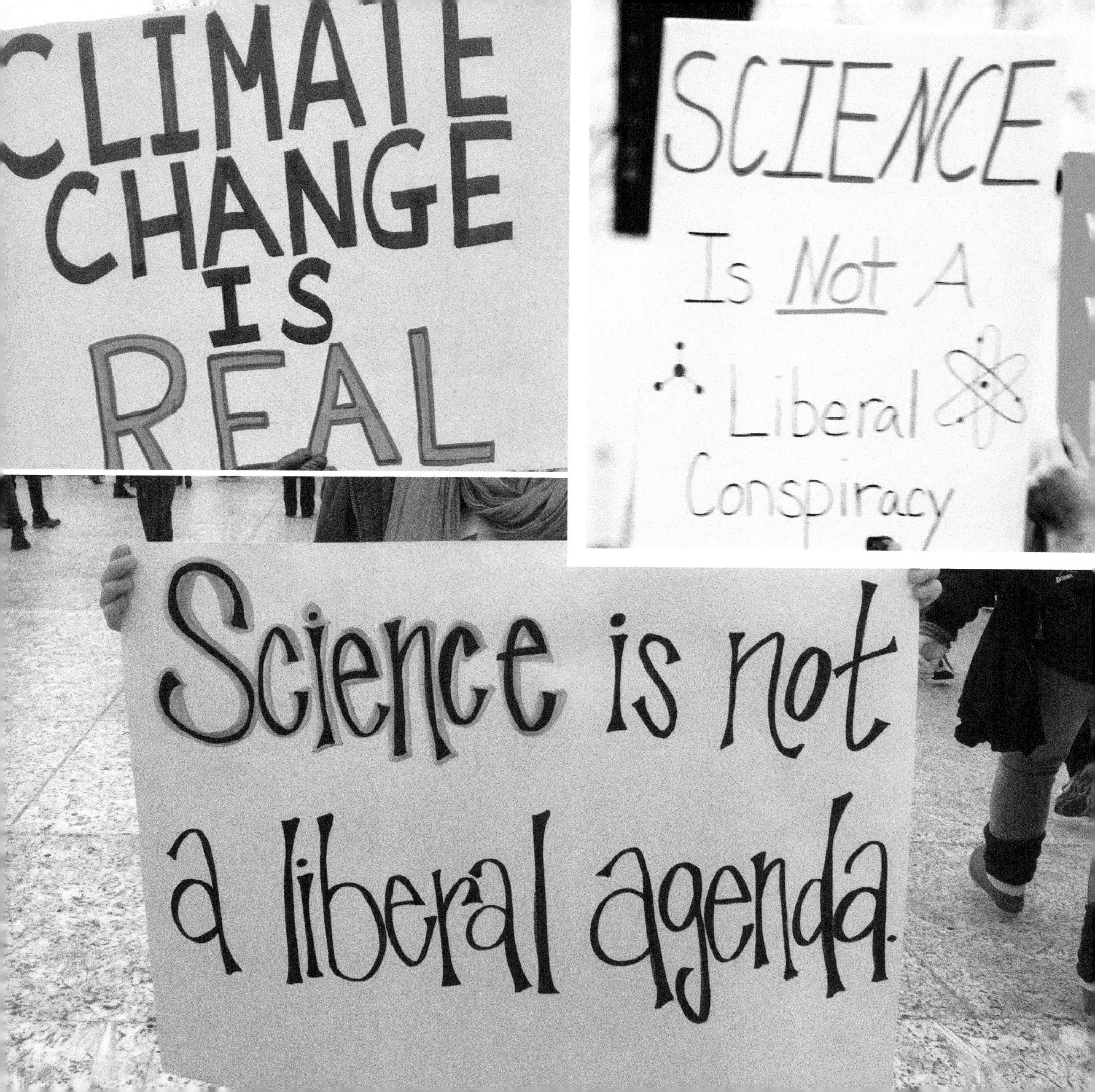
CLIMATE CHANGE IS REAL
SCIENCE Is Not A Liberal Conspiracy
Science is not a liberal agenda.

RESPECT
TO GET IT,
YA GOTTA GIVE IT!!

OUR BODIES
OUR MINDS
OUR POWER

RESPETA MI
EXISTENCIA
O ESPER

@atchooleyra
@everseeforme

FUCK OFF
FUCK OFF
OFF

Do not go gentle into that good night.
Rage, Rage against
the Dying of our Rights.
Women Immigrant Muslim LGBTQI
BLM

THIS LAND
WAS MADE
FOR
YOU AND ME
Strength in Diversity

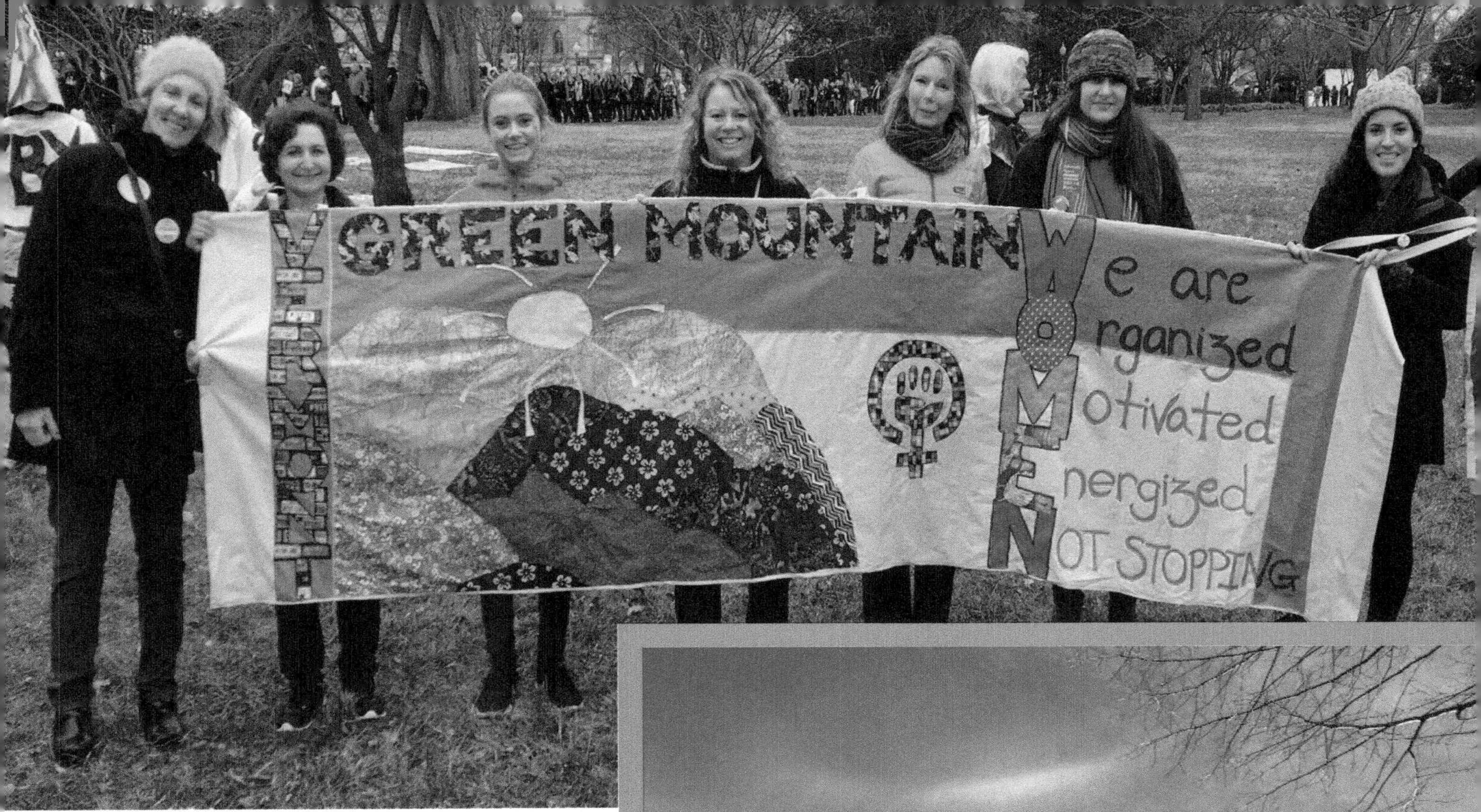
GREEN MOUNTAIN
We are
Organized
Motivated
Energized
NOT STOPPING

How can we teach our children well?

Karen Gross

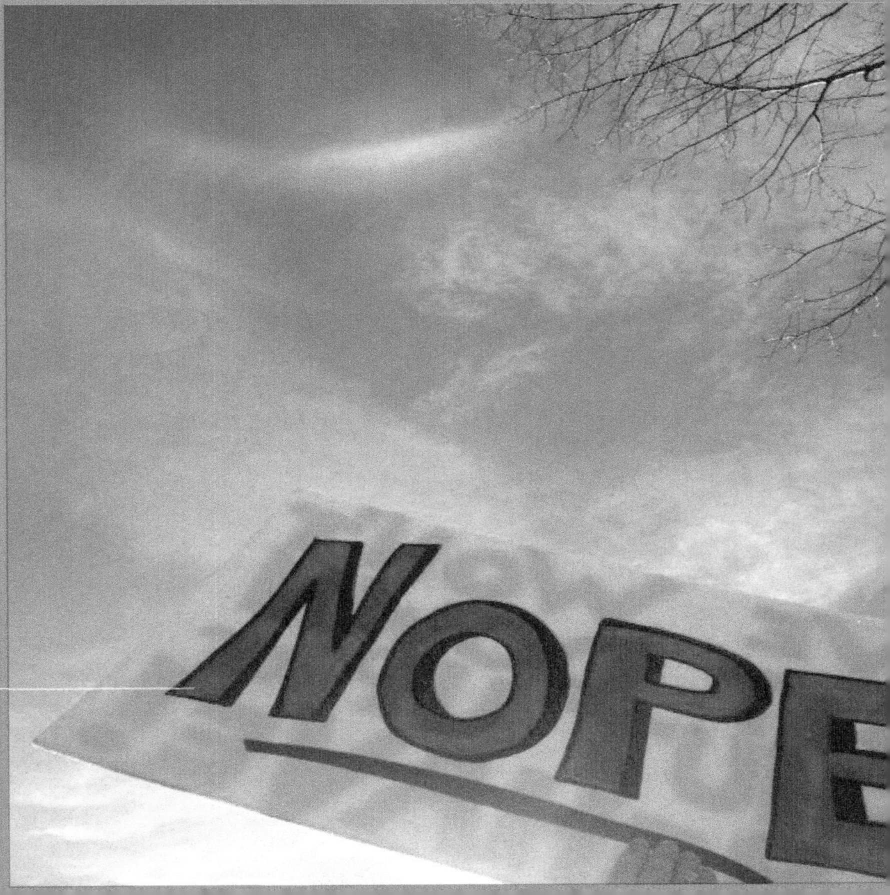
NOPE

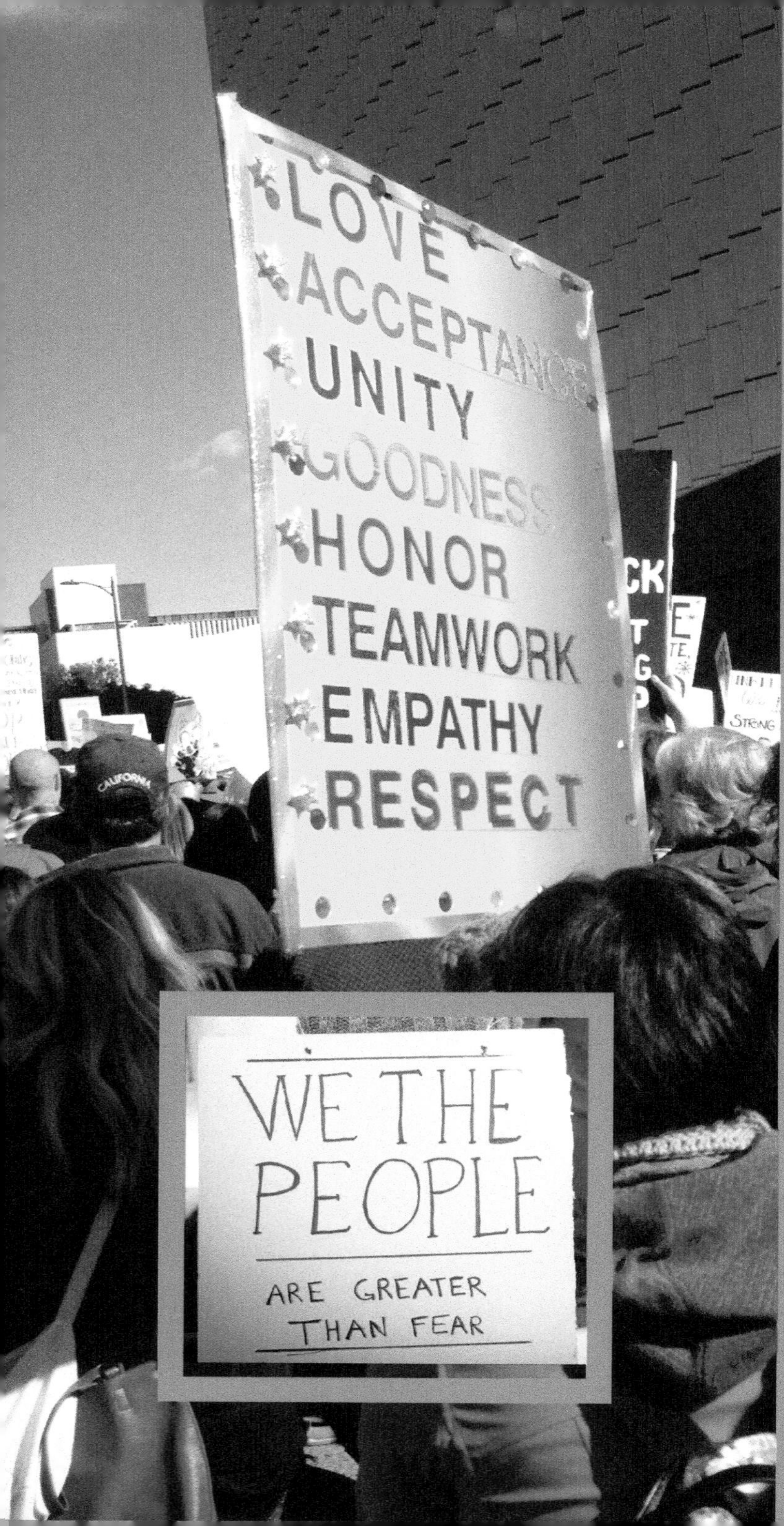
LOVE
ACCEPTANCE
UNITY
GOODNESS
HONOR
TEAMWORK
EMPATHY
RESPECT
WE THE PEOPLE
ARE GREATER THAN FEAR

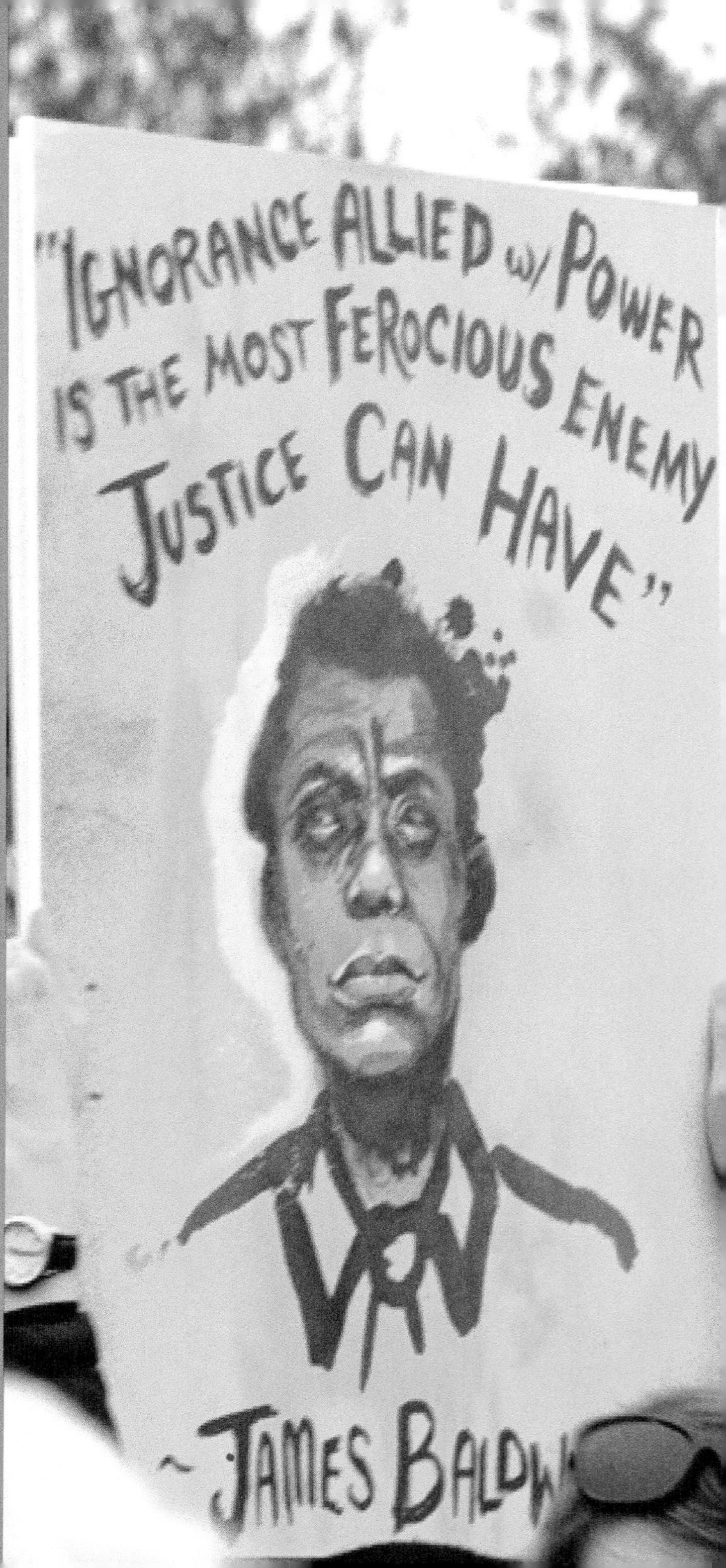
"IGNORANCE ALLIED w/ POWER IS THE MOST FEROCIOUS ENEMY JUSTICE CAN HAVE"
~JAMES BALDW

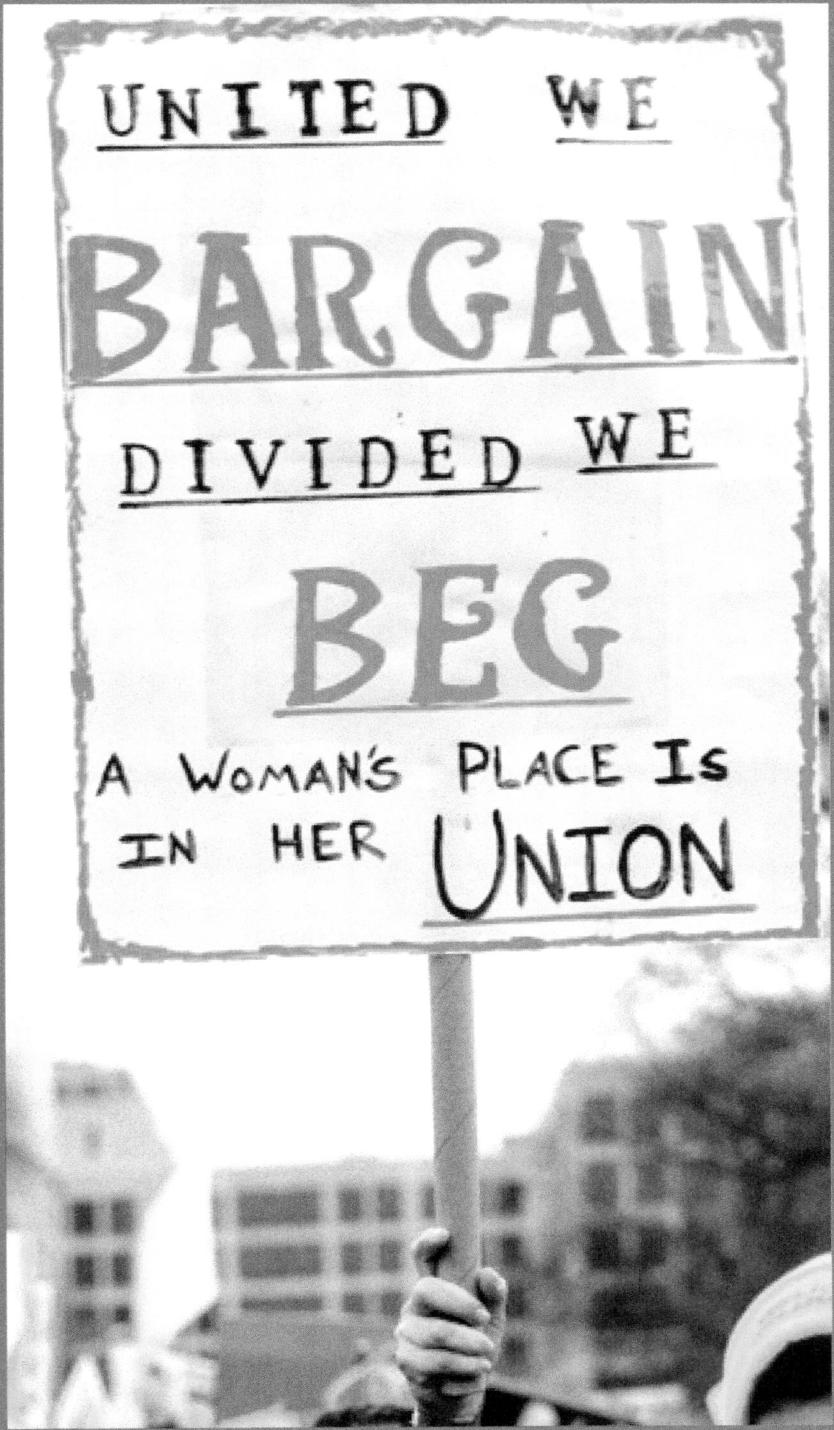
UNITED WE
BARGAIN
DIVIDED WE
BEG
A WOMAN'S PLACE IS
IN HER UNION

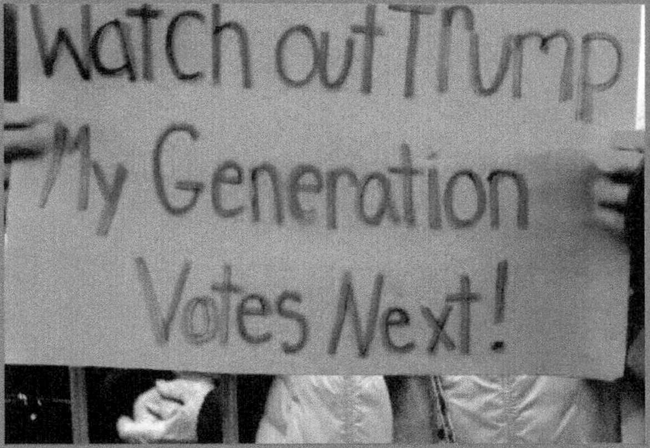
Watch out Trump
My Generation
Votes Next!

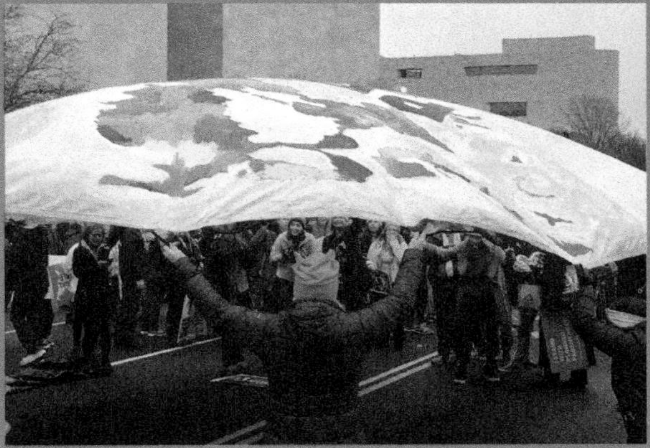

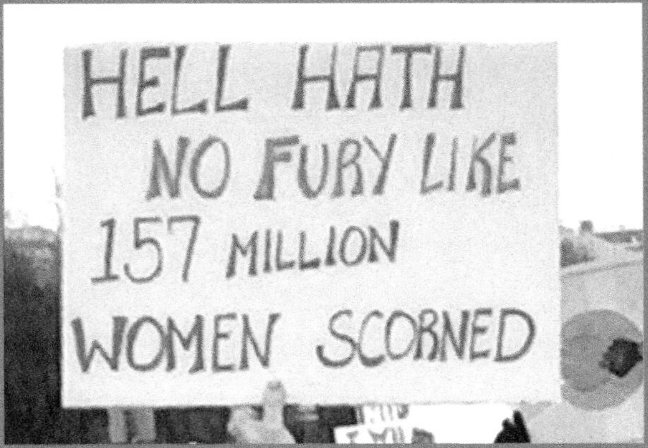
HELL HATH
NO FURY LIKE
157 MILLION
WOMEN SCORNED

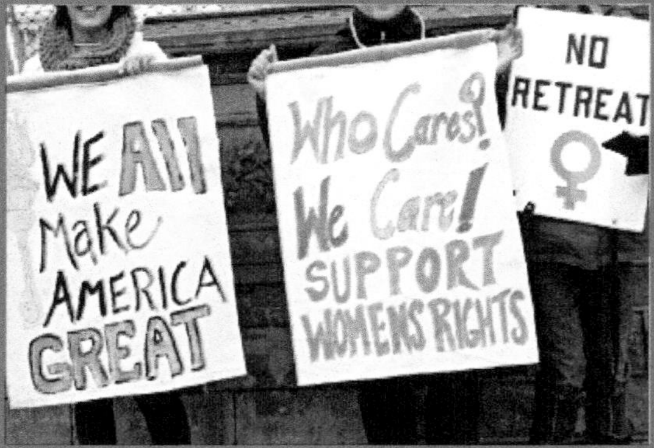
WE All Make AMERICA GREAT
Who Cares! We Care! SUPPORT WOMENS RIGHTS
NO RETREAT

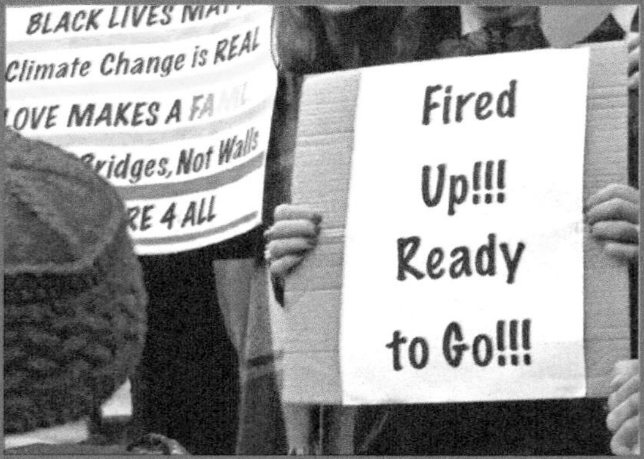
Climate Change is REAL
Fired Up!!! Ready to Go!!!

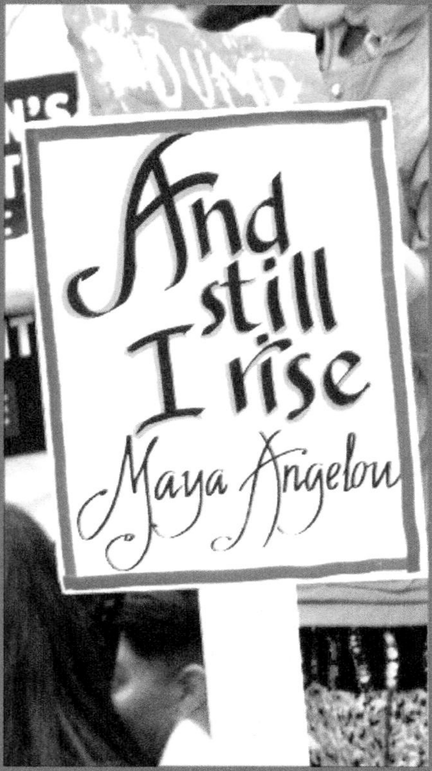
And still I rise
Maya Angelou

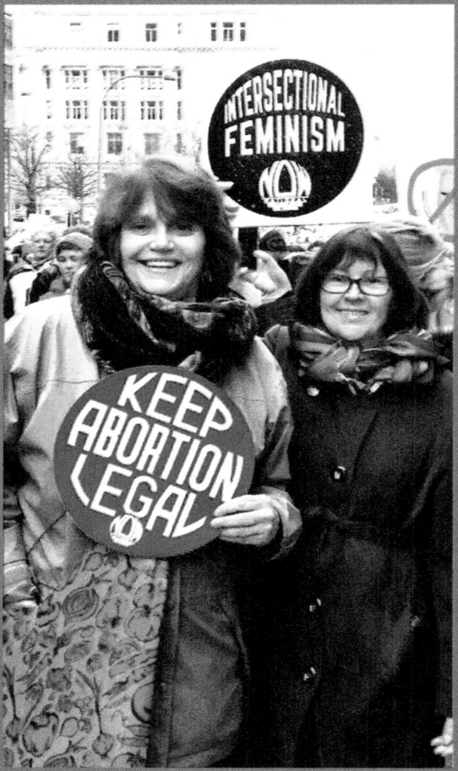
INTERSECTIONAL FEMINISM
KEEP ABORTION LEGAL

These signs – these plentiful and powerful signs – can serve as reminders of what we can do for our children, with our children and on behalf of our world.

Karen Gross

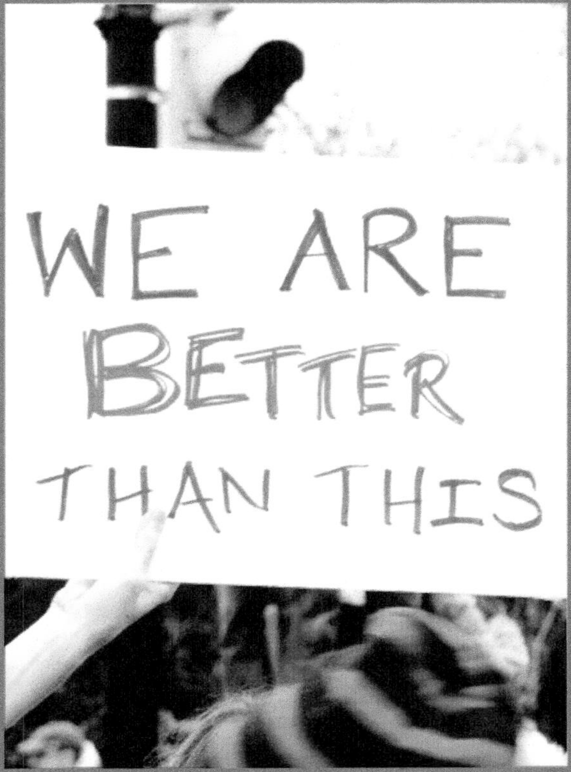
WE ARE
BETTER
THAN THIS

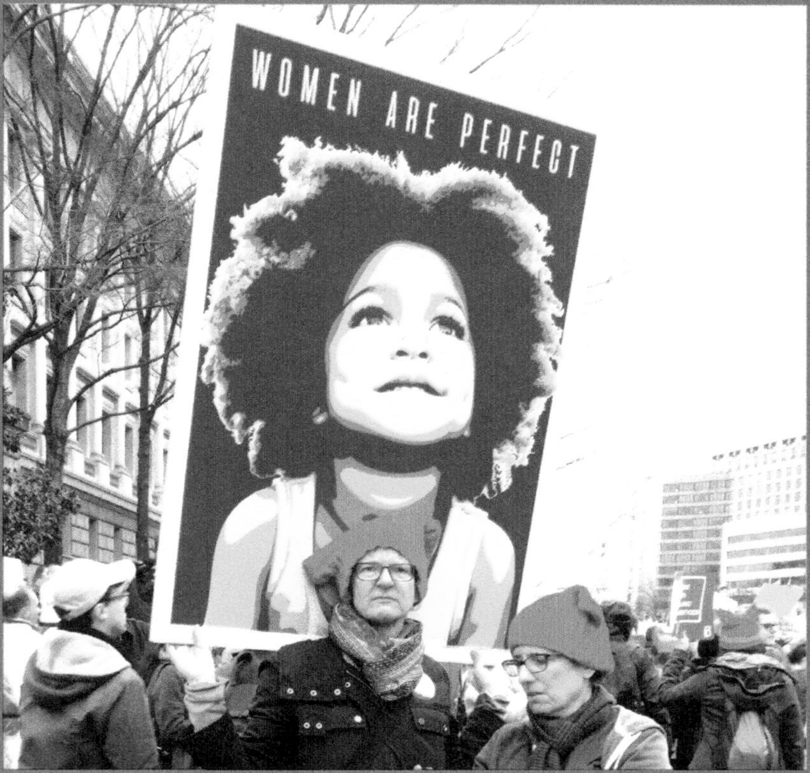
WOMEN ARE PERFECT

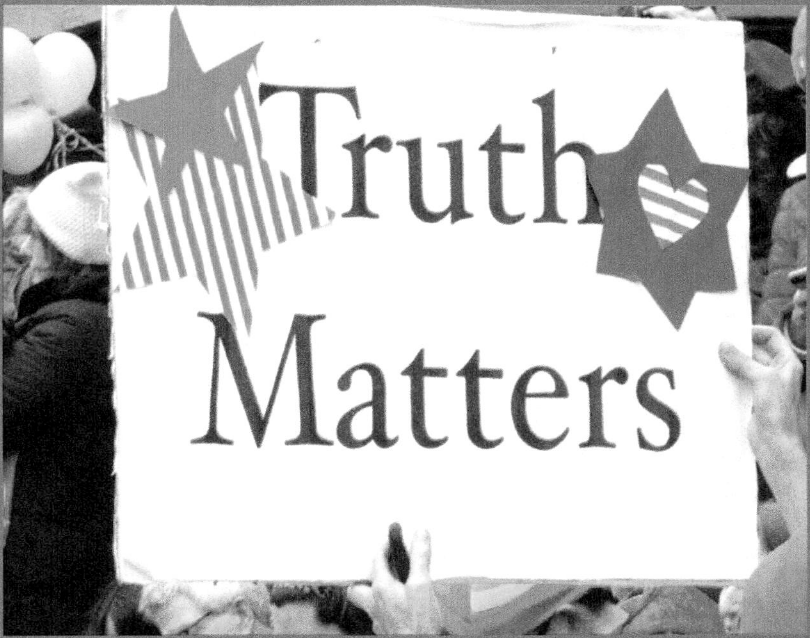
Truth
Matters

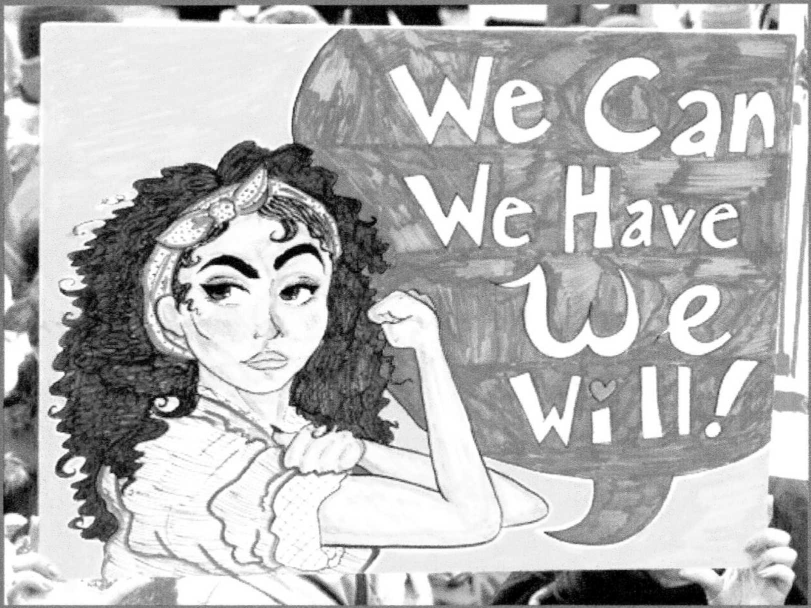
We Can
We Have
We
Will!

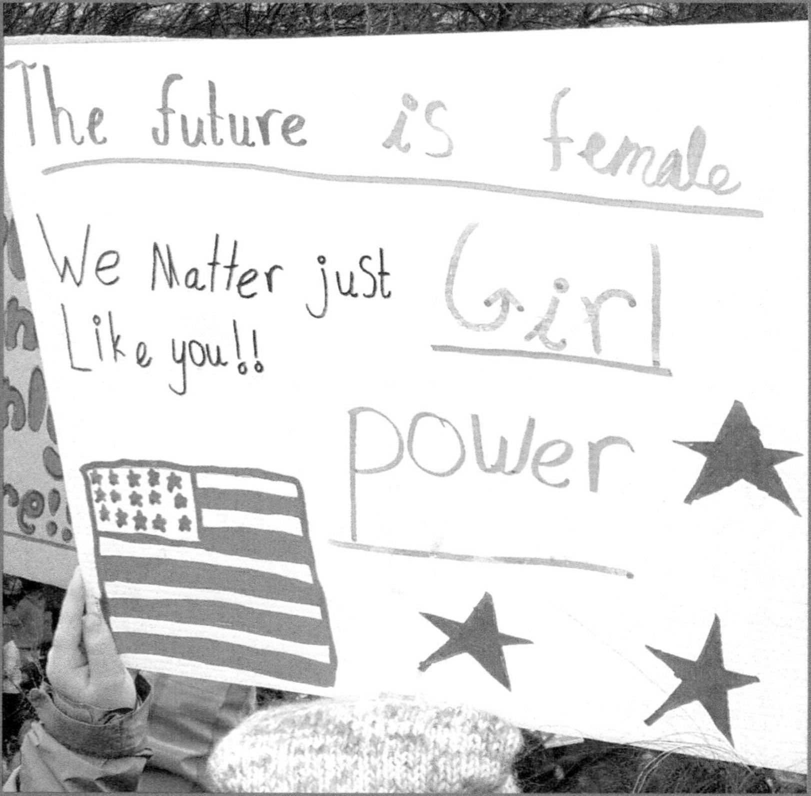
The future is female
We Matter just Like you!!
Girl
power

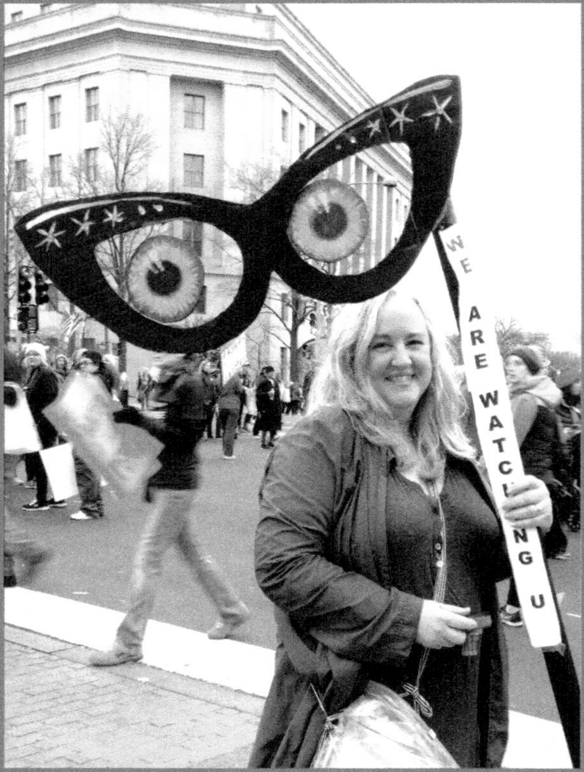
WE
ARE
WATC
NG
U

We all can contribute to being a Patriot but in our own way, using our own talents, recognizing the marked diversity among us as women, as workers, as thinkers, as mothers, as people.

Karen Gross

...then they came
for me,
and there was
no one left
to SPEAK UP"

WE THE PEOPLE

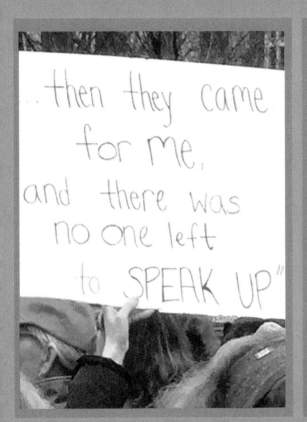

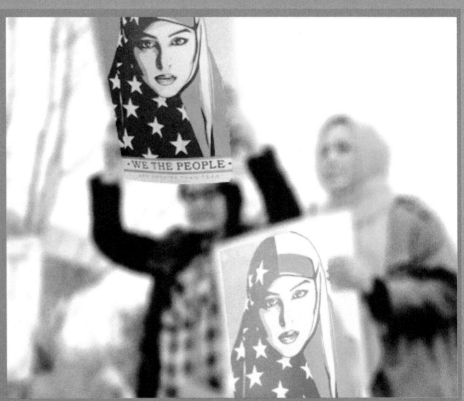

Others can push for change within their families; some can write books and essays that promote change; others can make art whether that is painting or music or dance.

Karen Gross

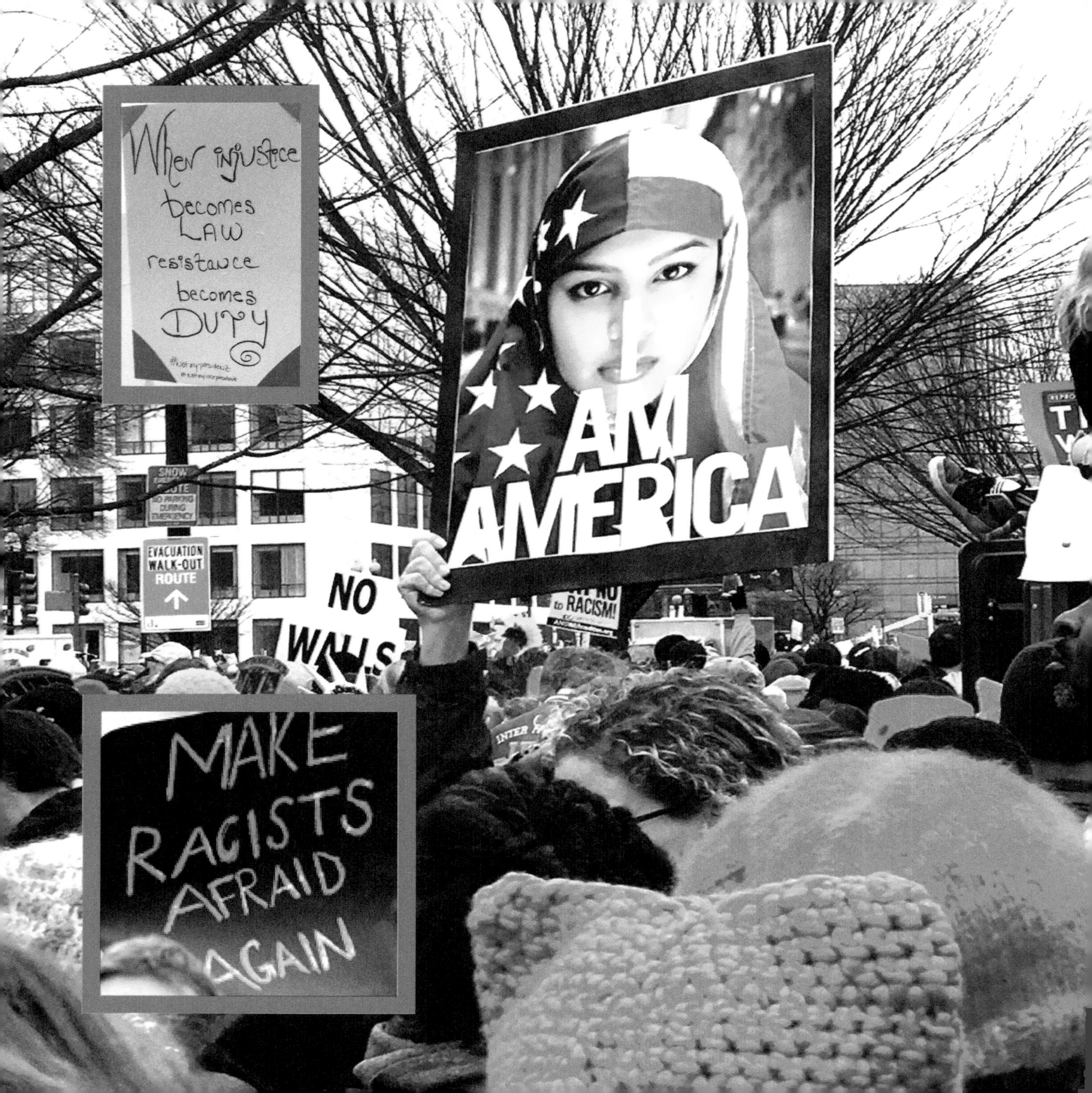
When injustice becomes LAW resistance becomes DUTY
AM AMERICA
EVACUATION WALK-OUT ROUTE
NO
to RACISM!
MAKE RACISTS AFRAID AGAIN

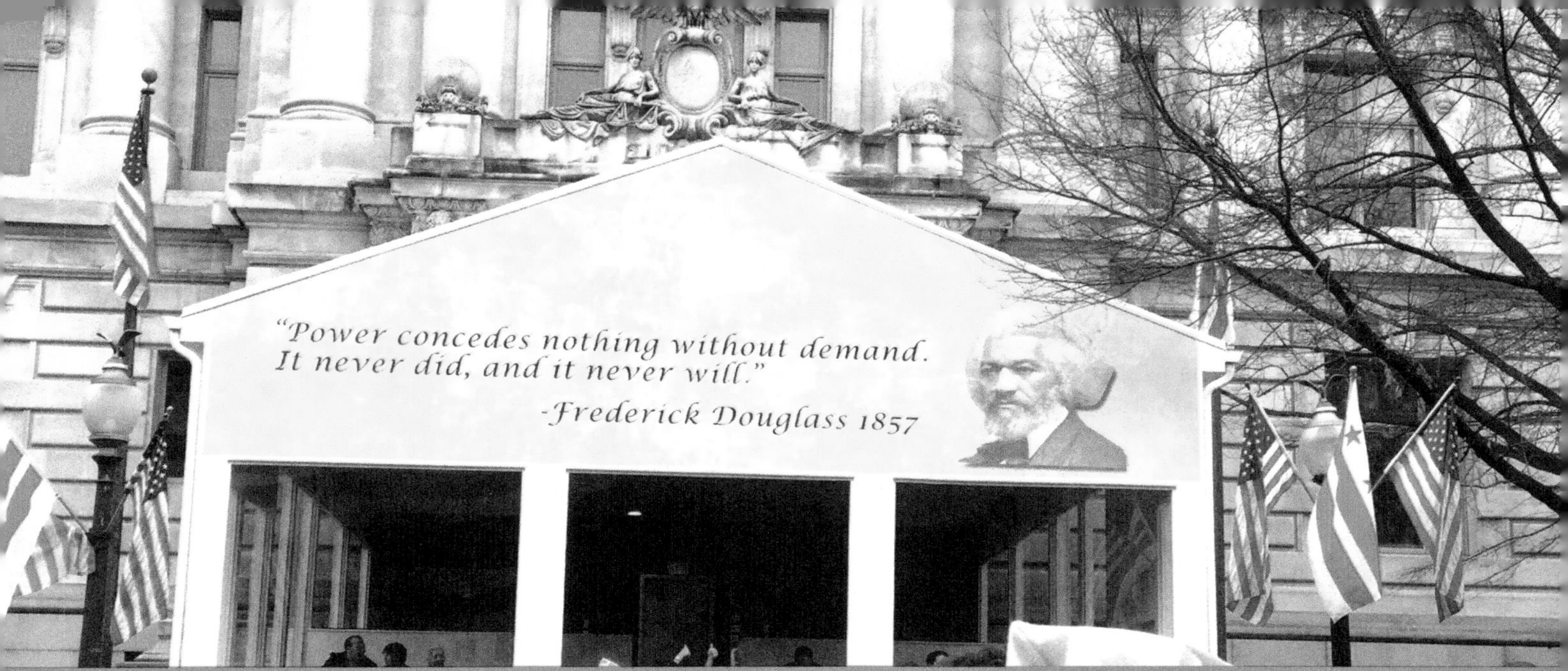
"Power concedes nothing without demand.
It never did, and it never will."
-Frederick Douglass 1857

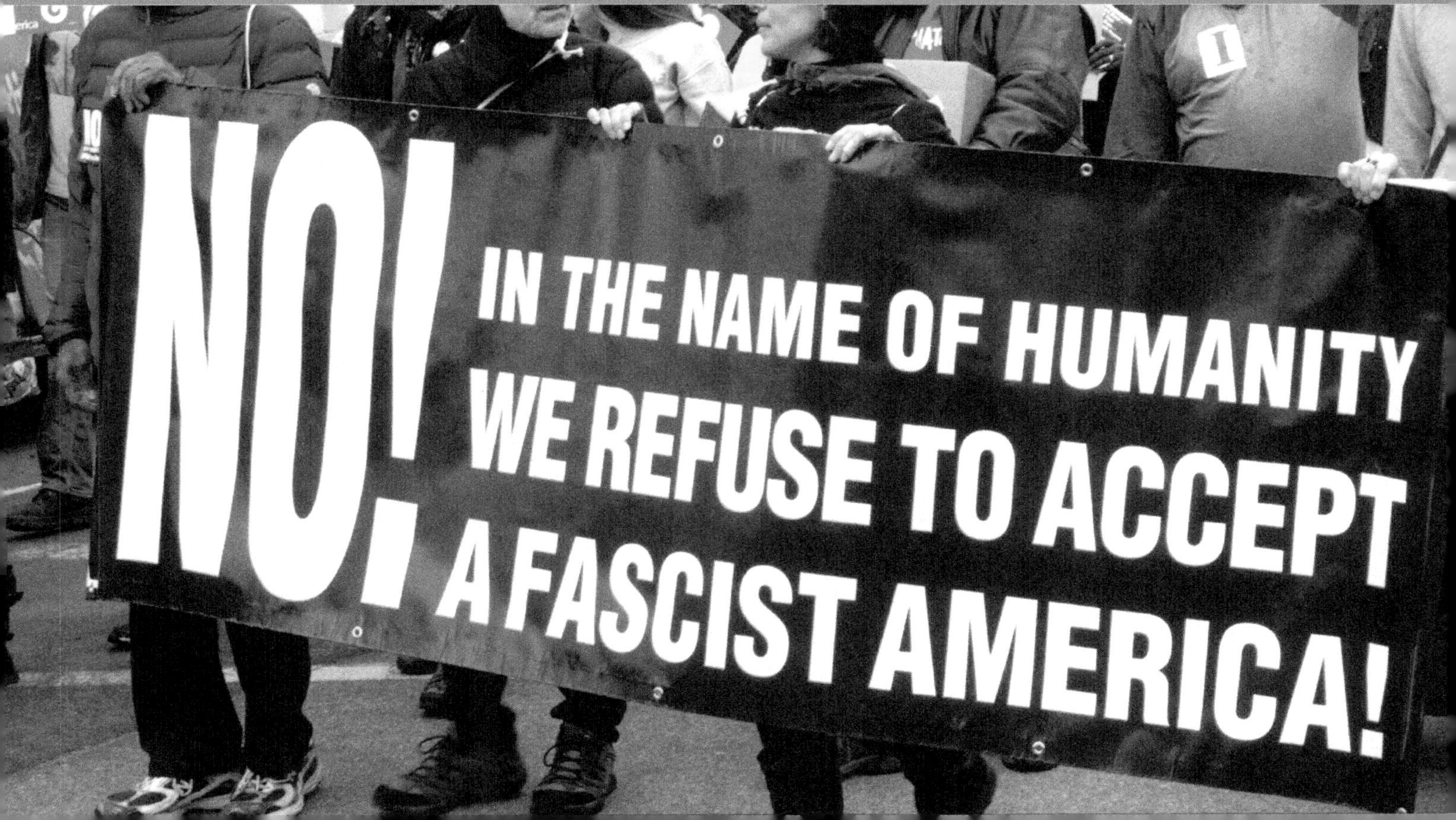
NO!
IN THE NAME OF HUMANITY
WE REFUSE TO ACCEPT
A FASCIST AMERICA!

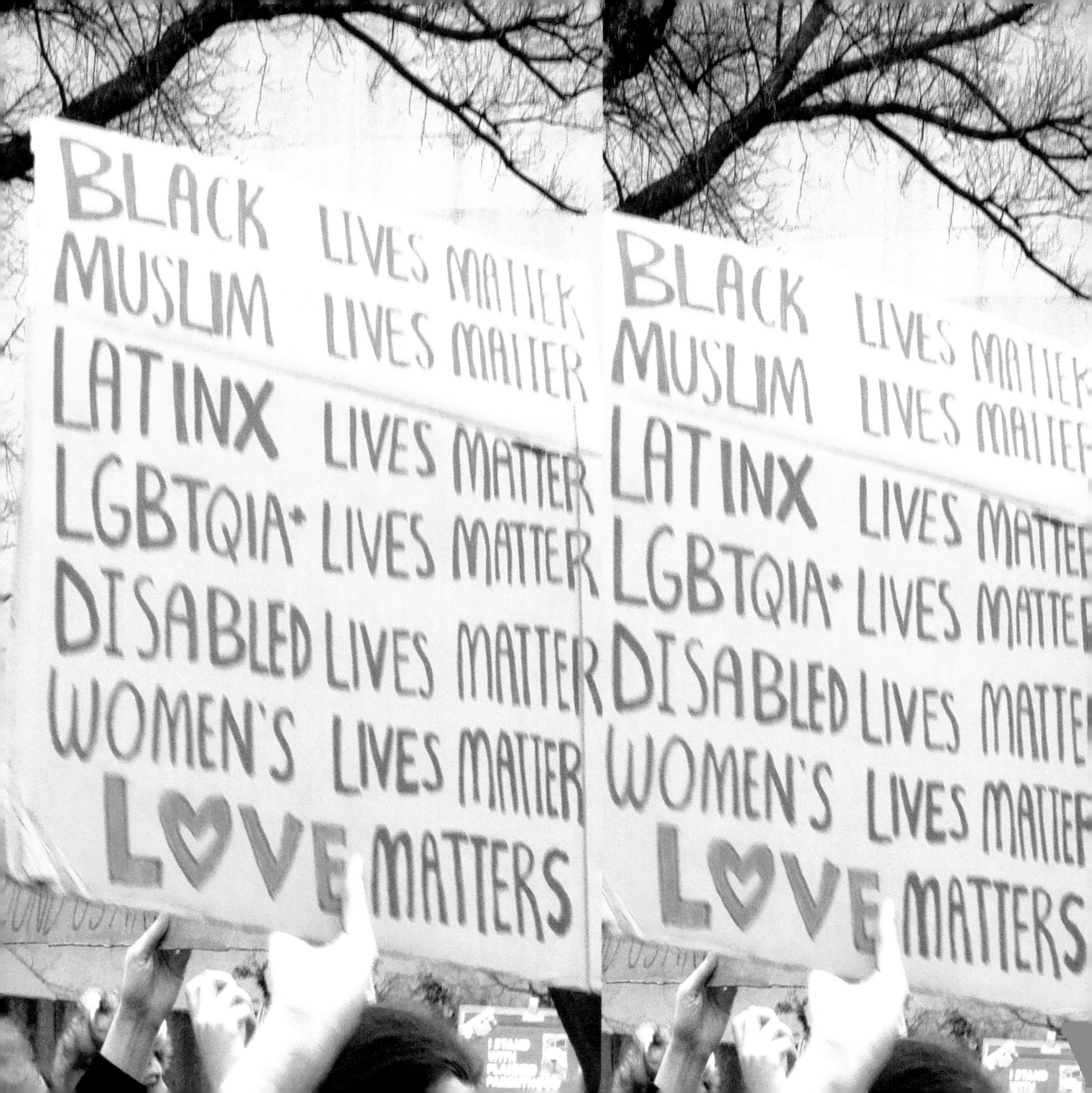
BLACK LIVES MATTER
MUSLIM LIVES MATTER
LATINX LIVES MATTER
LGBTQIA+ LIVES MATTER
DISABLED LIVES MATTER
WOMEN'S LIVES MATTER
LOVE MATTERS

BLACK LIVES MATTER
MUSLIM LIVES MATTER
LATINX LIVES MATTER
LGBTQIA+ LIVES MATTER
DISABLED LIVES MATTER
WOMEN'S LIVES MATTER
LOVE MATTERS

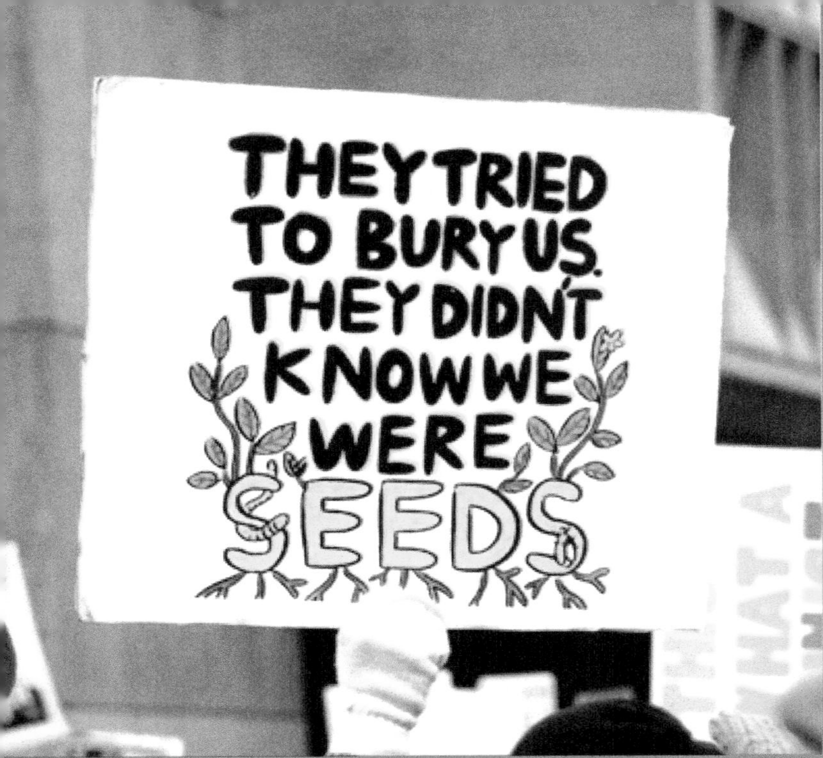
THEY TRIED
TO BURY US.
THEY DIDN'T
KNOW WE
WERE
SEEDS

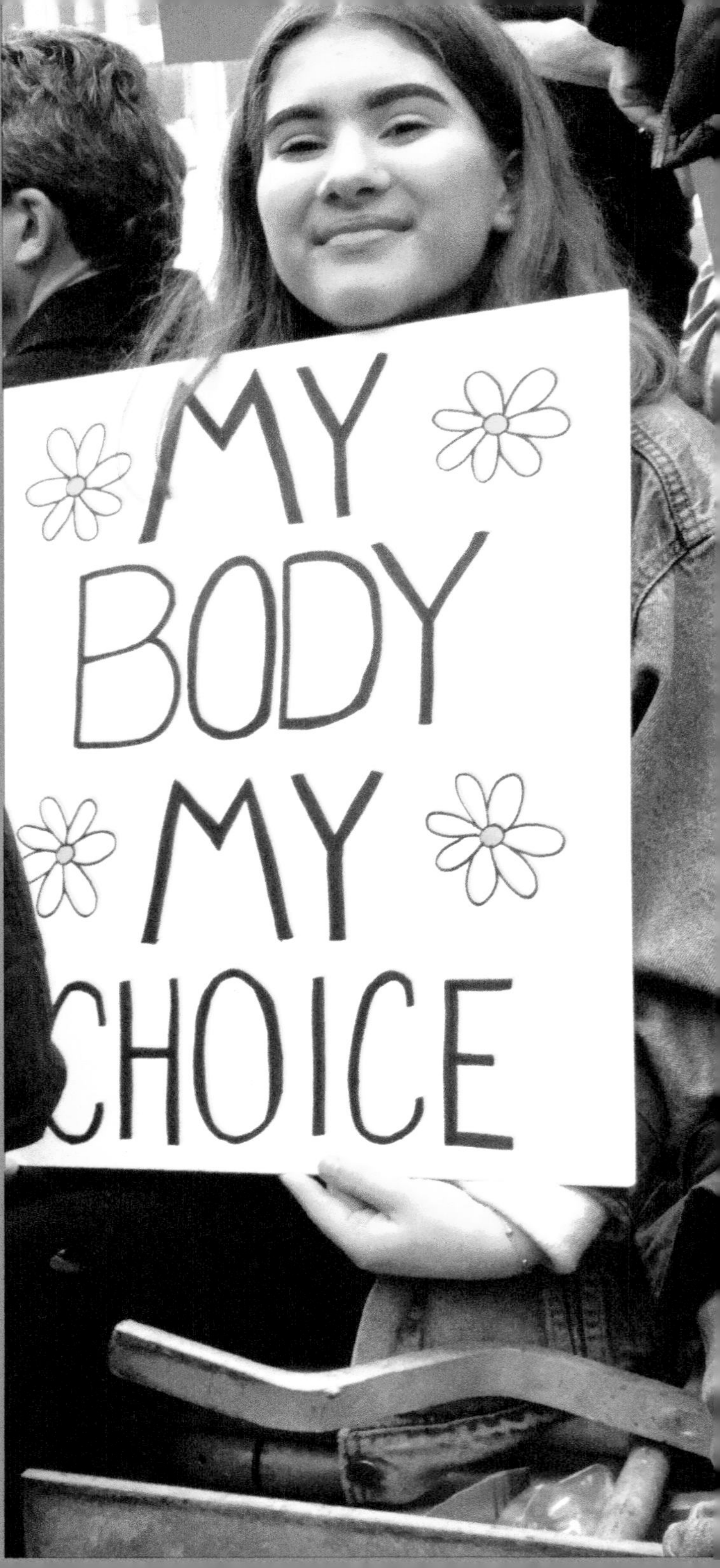
MY
BODY
MY
CHOICE

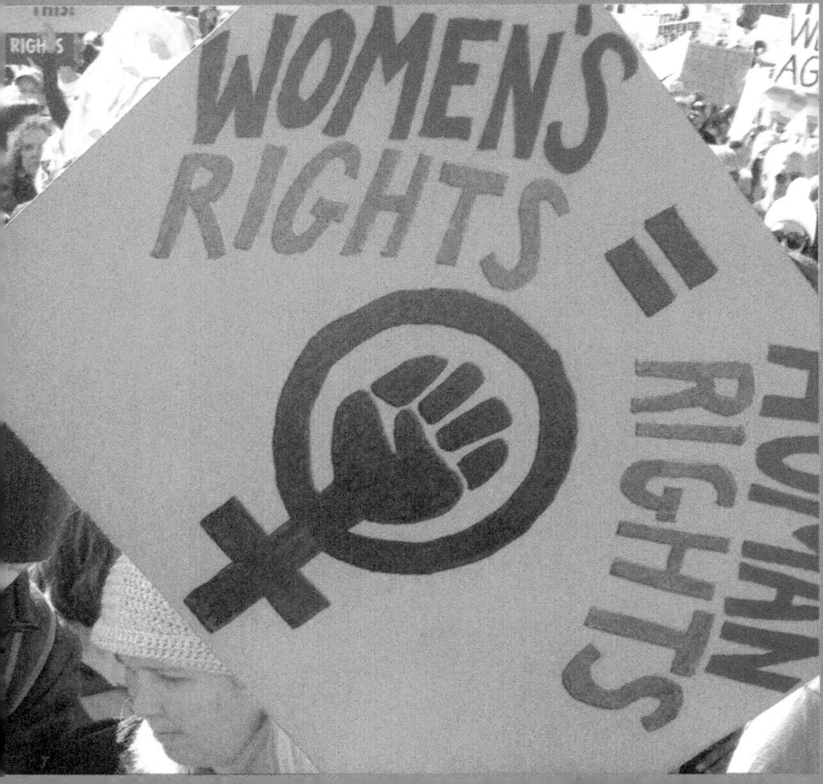
WOMEN'S
RIGHTS
=
RIGHTS

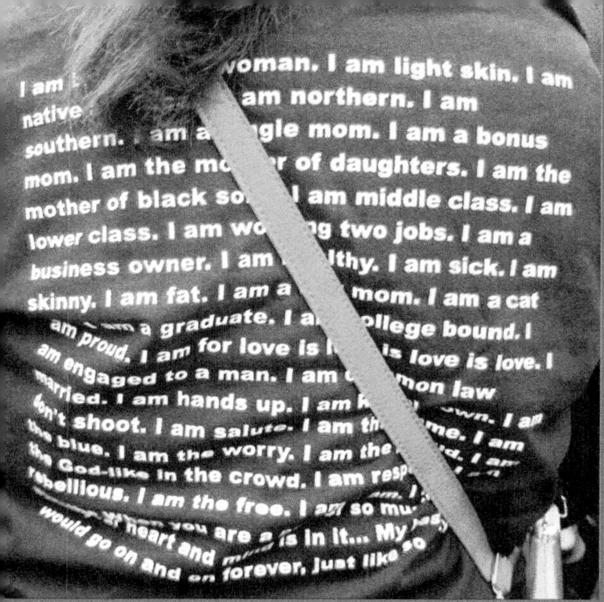
woman. I am light skin. I am
am northern. I am
southern.
mom. I am the
of daughters. I am the
mother of black
am middle class. I am
lower class. I am
two jobs. I am a
business owner. I am
I am sick. I am
skinny. I am fat. I am a
mom. I am a cat
a graduate. I
college bound. I
am proud. I am for love is
is love is love. I
am engaged to a man. I am
married. I am hands up. I am
don't shoot. I am
I am
the blue. I am the worry. I am the
the God-like in the crowd. I am
rebellious. I am the free. I
you are a
is in it... My
would go on and on forever, just like

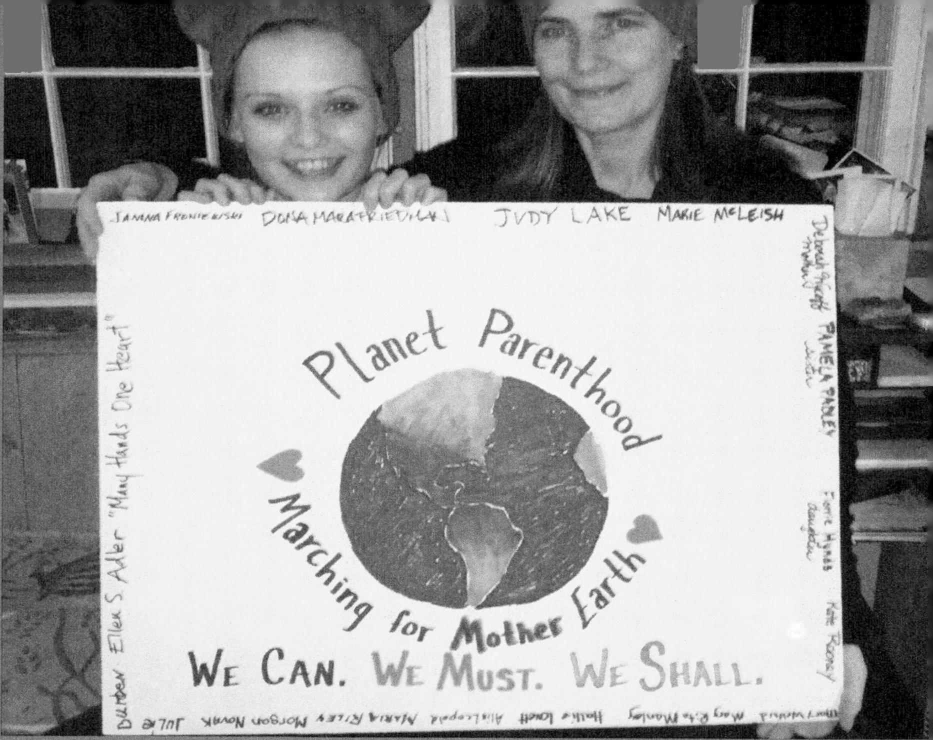
JUDY LAKE
MARIE McLEISH
PAMELA PADLEY
Planet Parenthood
Marching for Mother Earth
WE CAN. WE MUST. WE SHALL.
Ellen S. Adler "Many Hands One Heart"
Kate Rooney
MARIA RILEY
Morgan Novak

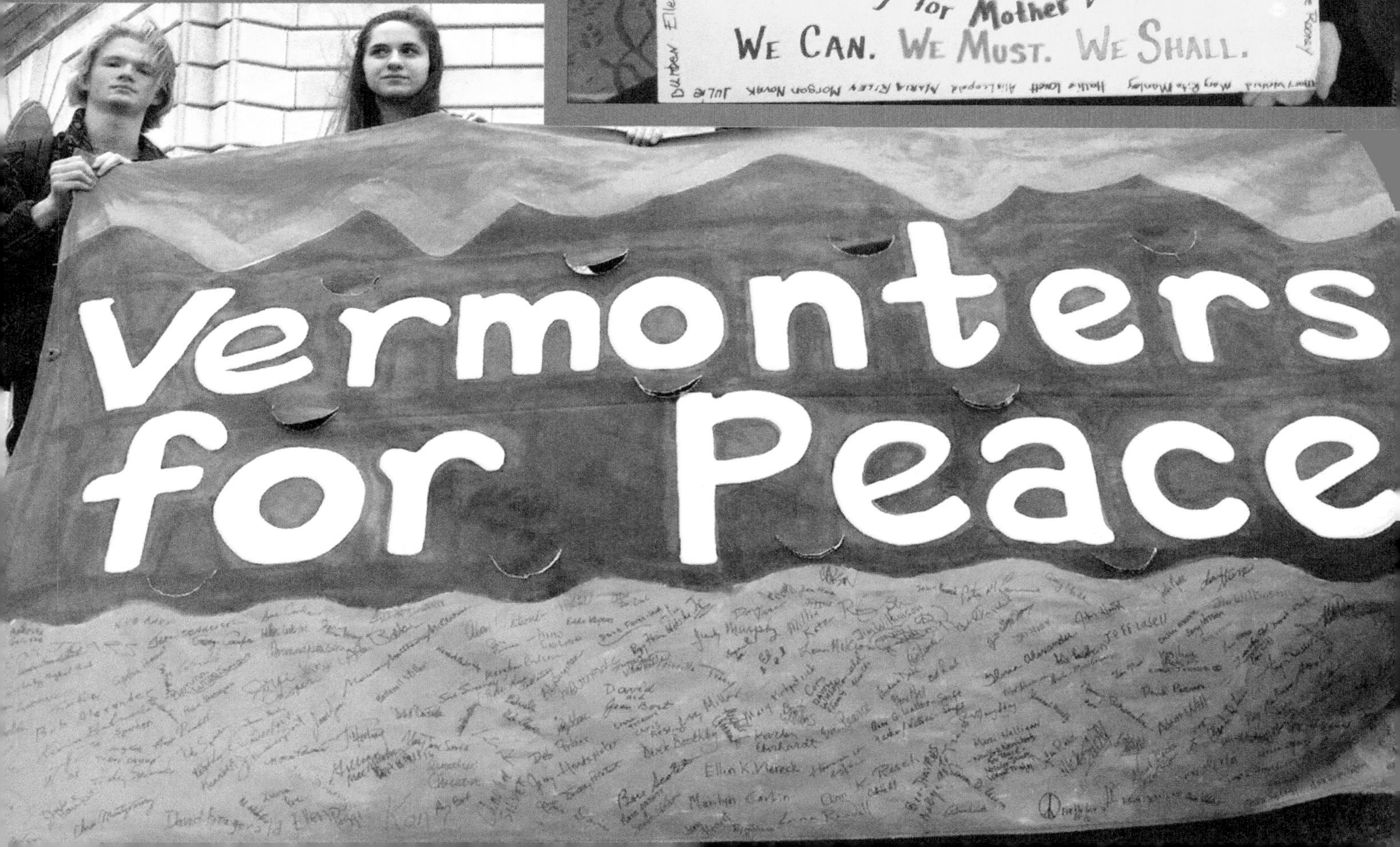
Vermonters
for Peace

IN OUR AMERICA
ALL PEOPLE ARE EQUAL
LOVE WINS
BLACK LIVES MATTER
IMMIGRANTS & REFUGEES ARE WELCOME
DISABILITIES ARE RESPECTED
WOMEN ARE IN CHARGE OF THEIR BODIES
PEOPLE & PLANET ARE VALUED OVER PROFIT
DIVERSITY IS CELEBRATED

LOVE WINS

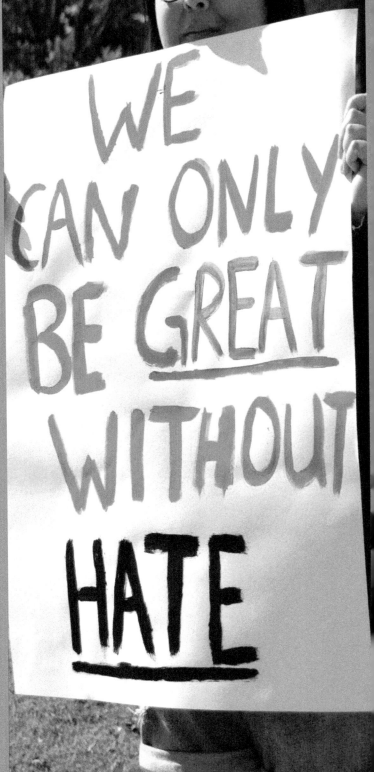

WE CAN ONLY BE GREAT WITHOUT HATE

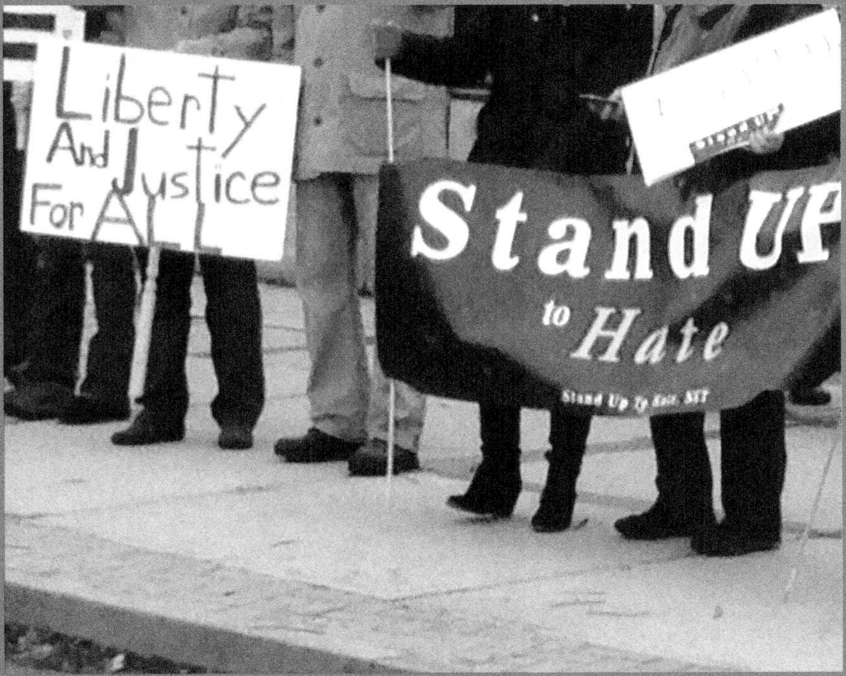
Liberty And Justice For ALL
Stand UP
to Hate

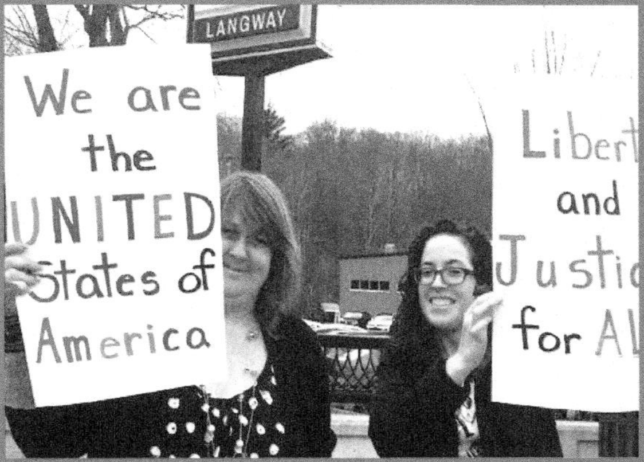
LANGWAY
We are the UNITED States of America

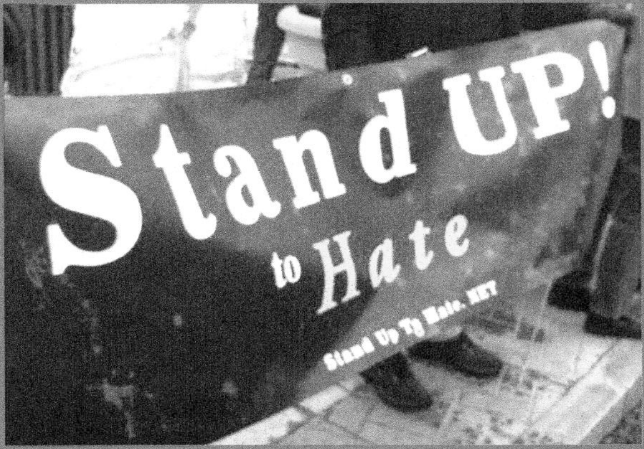
Stand UP!
to Hate

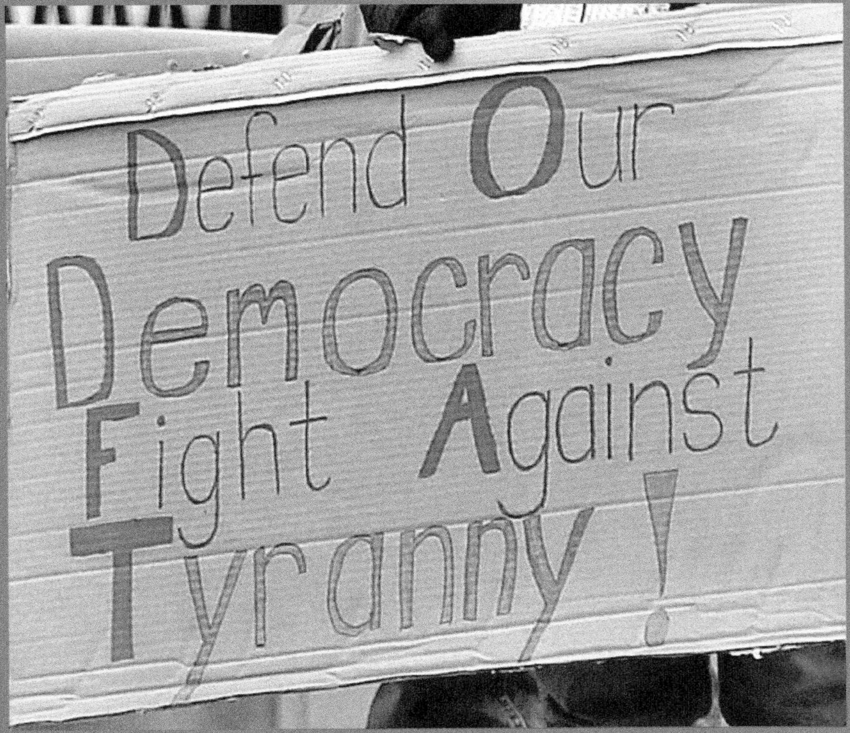
Defend Our Democracy Fight Against Tyranny!

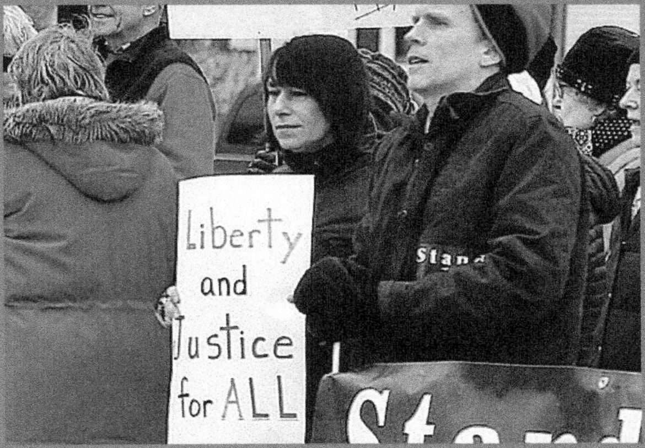
Liberty and Justice for ALL

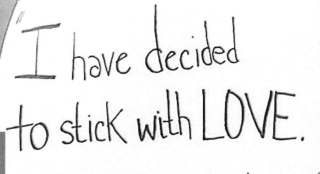

"I have decided to stick with LOVE. Hate is too great a burden to bear."

Martin Luther King Jr.

It's Easier to hate Without listening

WHAT HAPPENS NEXT IS UP TO ALL OF US

You Don't OWN ME!

WE THE PEOPLE

•STAND UNITED•
•WILL RESIST•
•WILL NOT BE SILENT•
•WILL PROTECT ONE ANOTHER•
•WITH INTELLIGENCE and COMPASSION•
•OUR LOVE IS STRONGER THAN HATE

NO ROOM FOR HATE IN OUR BRAVE LITTLE STATE

Yes We Can!

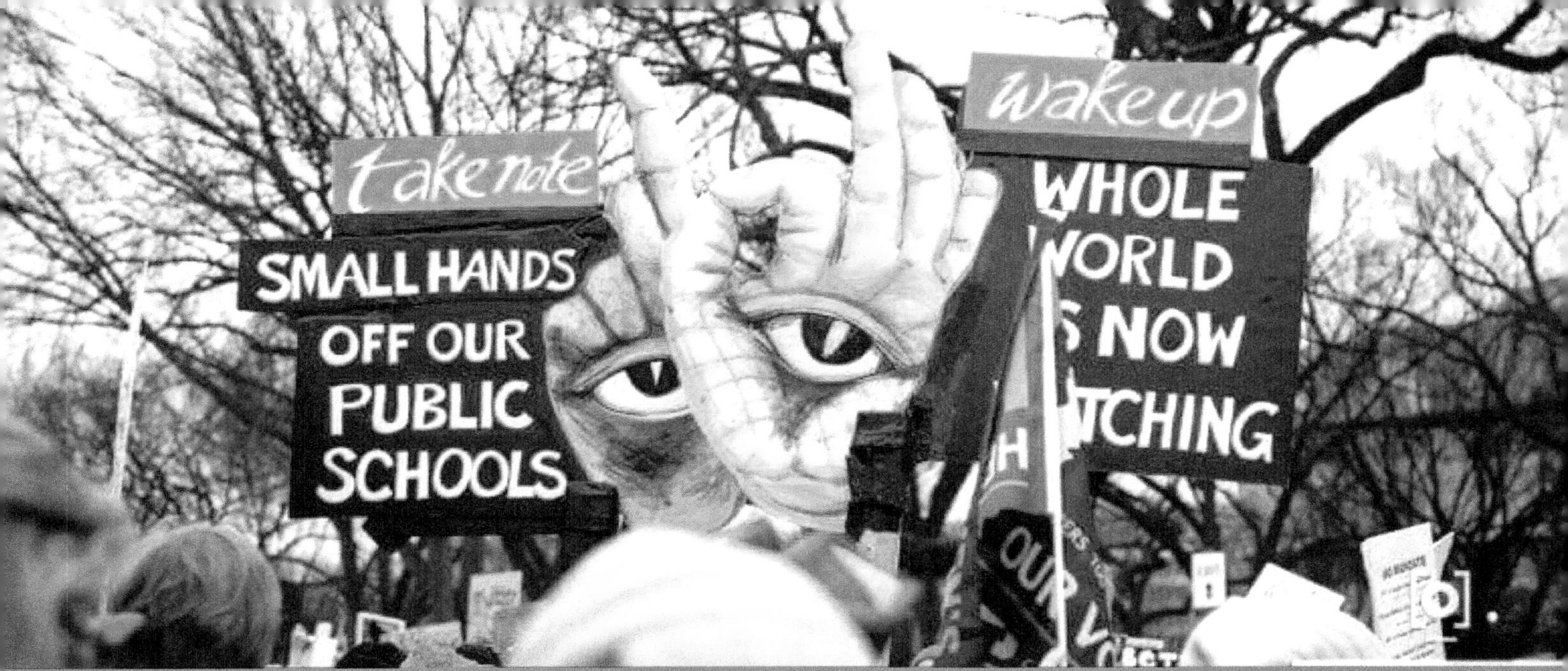
take note
SMALL HANDS
OFF OUR
PUBLIC
SCHOOLS
wake up
WHOLE

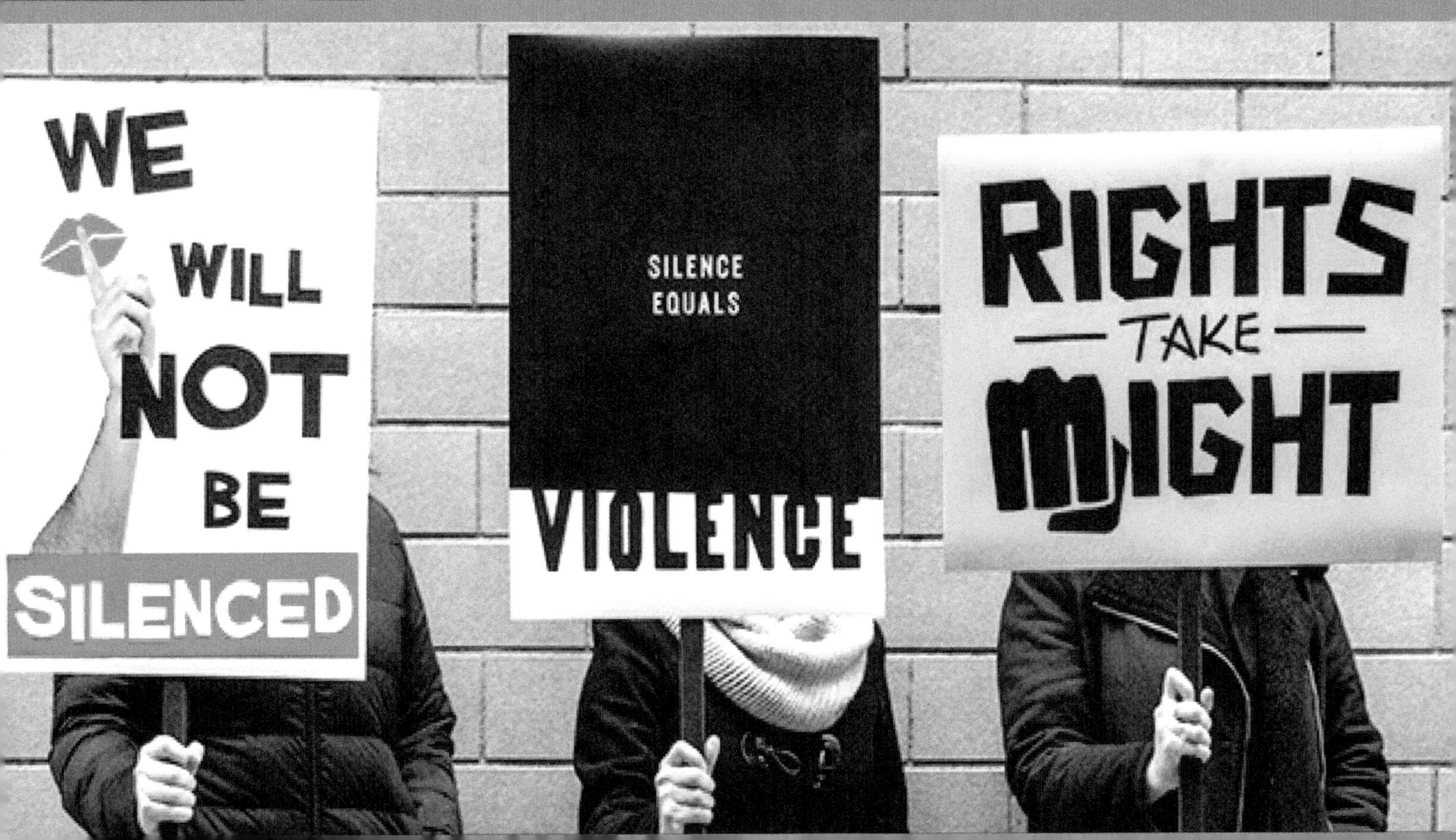
WE WILL NOT BE SILENCED
SILENCE
EQUALS
VIOLENCE
RIGHTS
TAKE
MIGHT

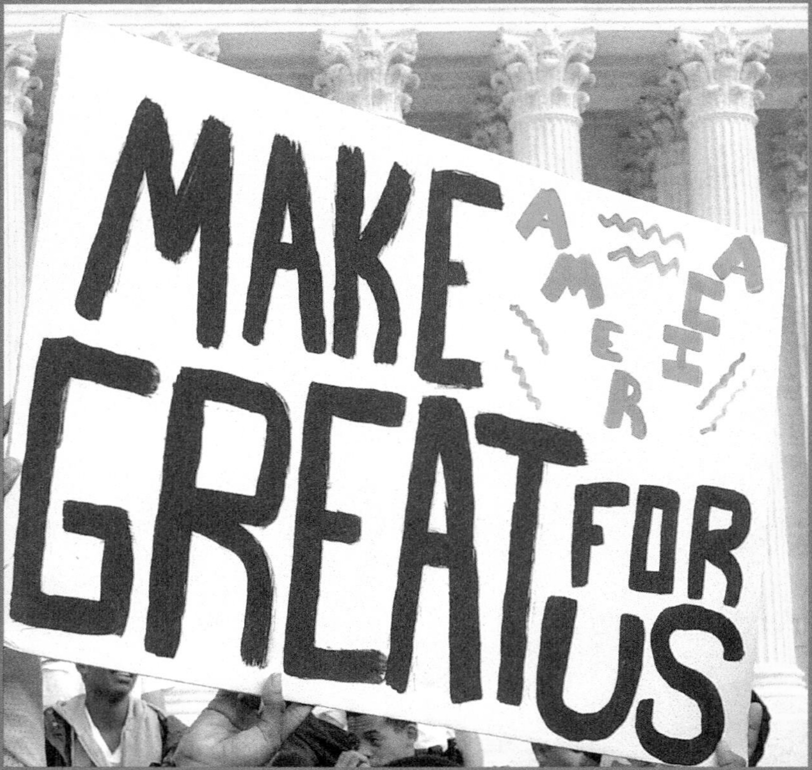
MAKE
AMERICA
GREAT
FOR
US

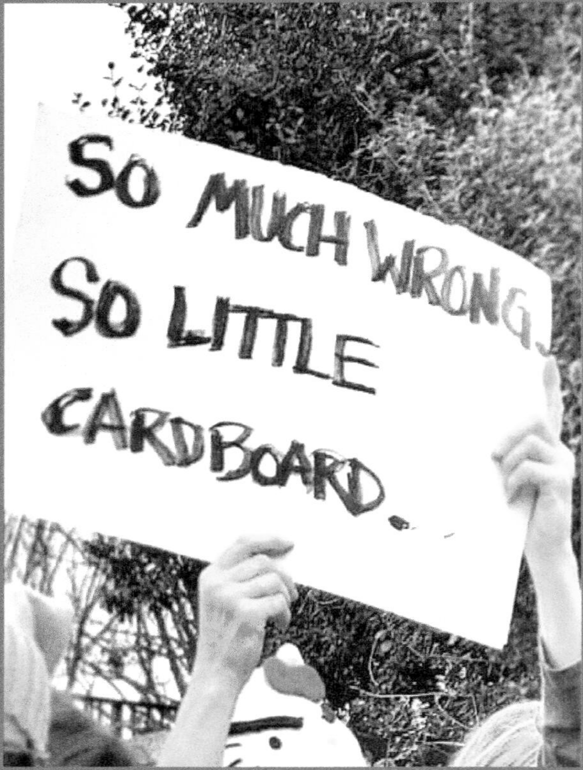
SO MUCH WRONG..
SO LITTLE
CARDBOARD.

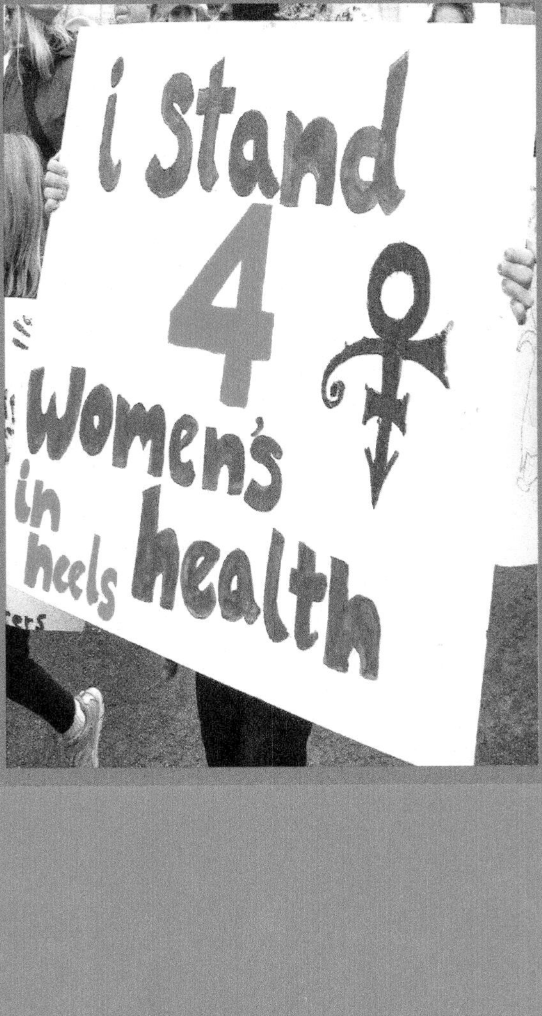
i Stand
4
Women's
health
in
heels

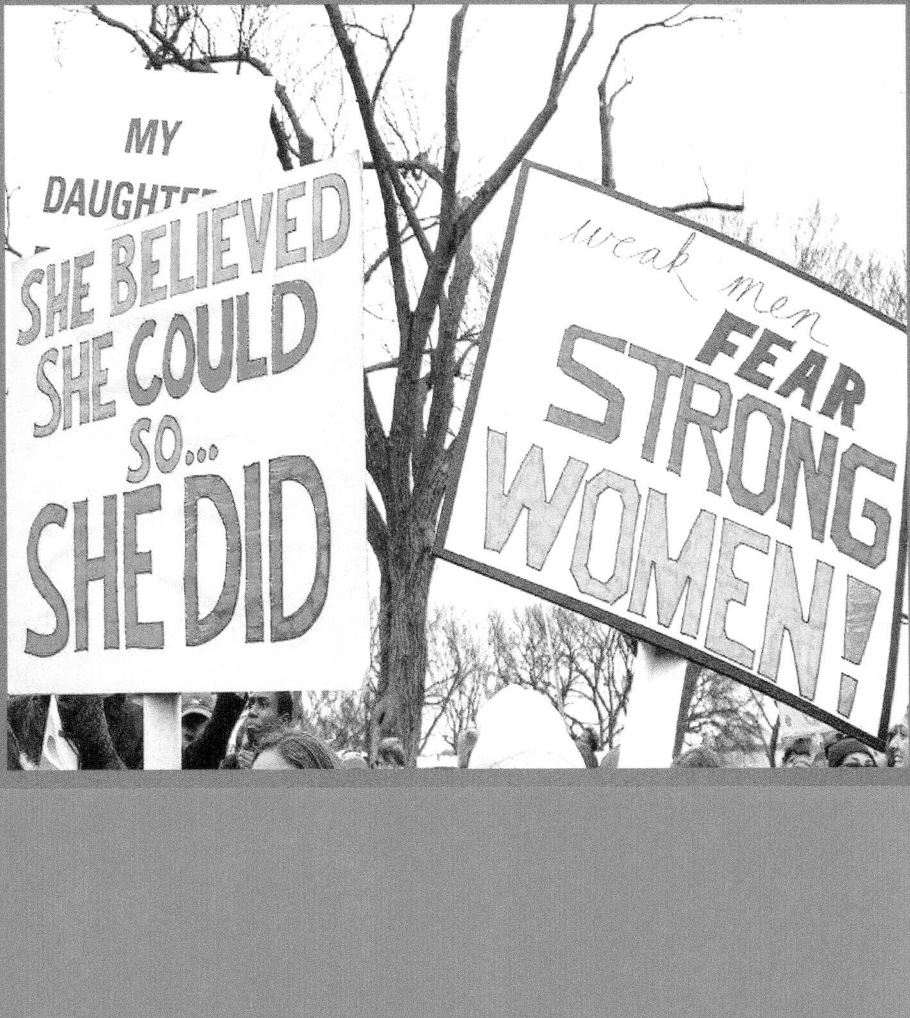
MY
DAUGHTE
SHE BELIEVED
SHE COULD
SO...
SHE DID
weak men
FEAR
STRONG
WOMEN!

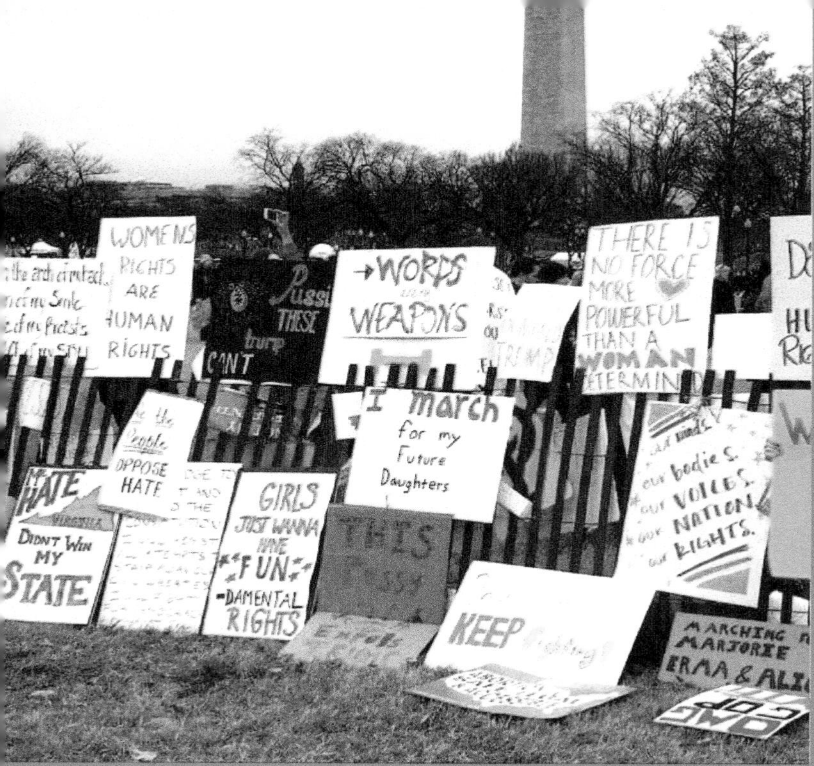
WOMENS RIGHTS ARE HUMAN RIGHTS
WORDS
WEAPONS
THERE IS NO FORCE MORE POWERFUL THAN A WOMAN
I march for my Future Daughters
OPPOSE HATE
GIRLS JUST WANNA HAVE *FUN* -DAMENTAL RIGHTS
DIDN'T WIN MY STATE
our bodies. our voices. our NATION. our RIGHTS.
KEEP

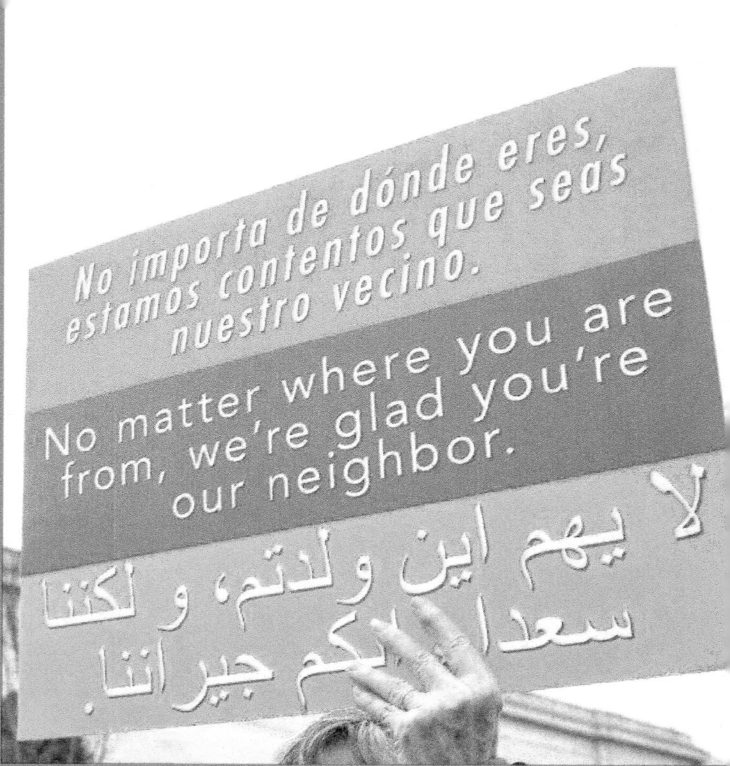
No importa de dónde eres, estamos contentos que seas nuestro vecino.
No matter where you are from, we're glad you're our neighbor.
لا يهم اين ولدتم، و لكننا

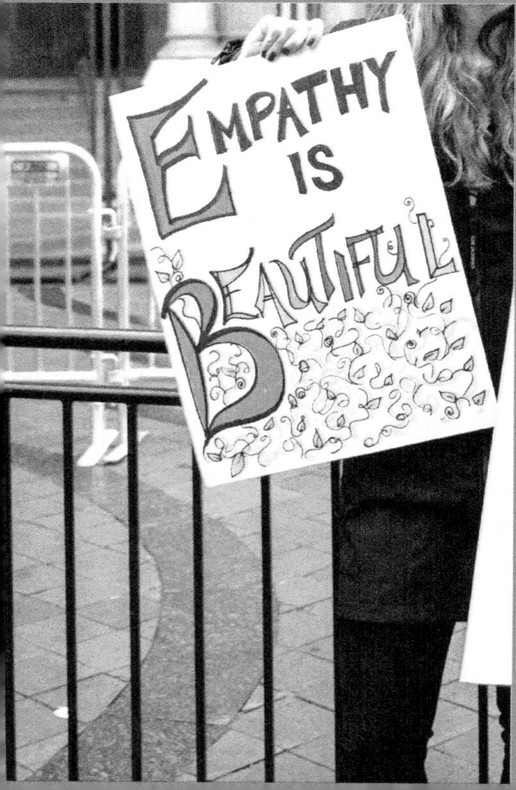
EMPATHY IS BEAUTIFUL

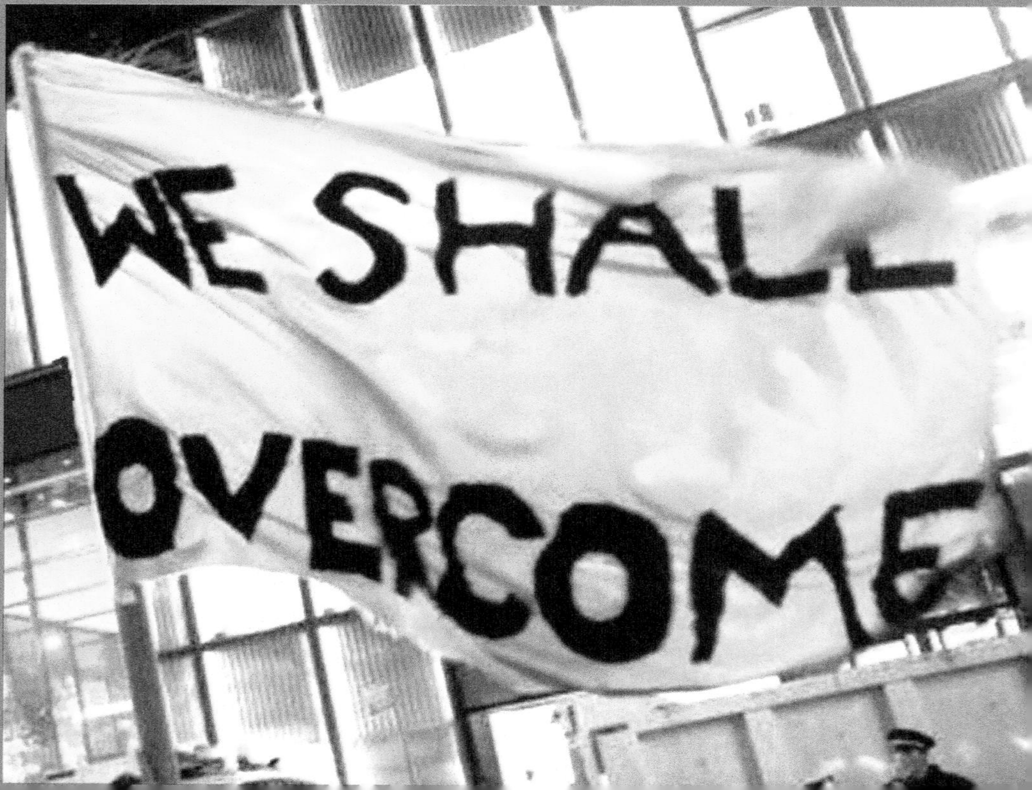
WE SHALL OVERCOME

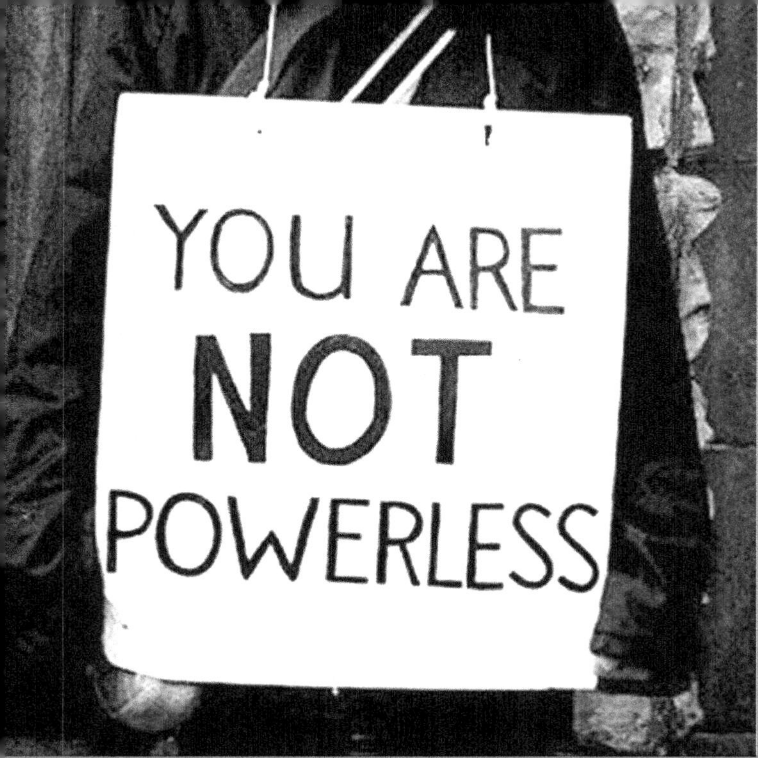
YOU ARE
NOT
POWERLESS

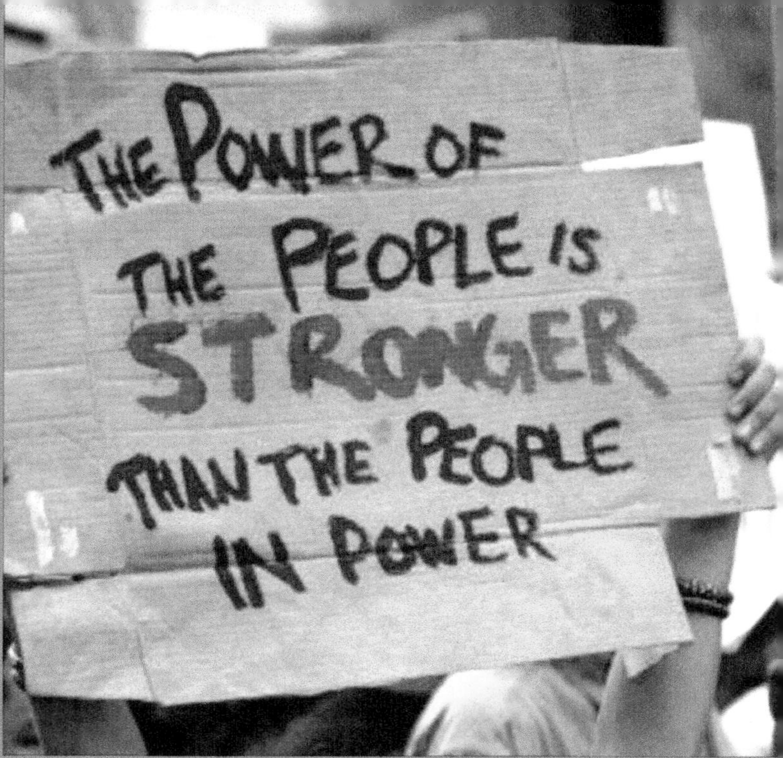
THE POWER OF
THE PEOPLE IS
STRONGER
THAN THE PEOPLE
IN POWER

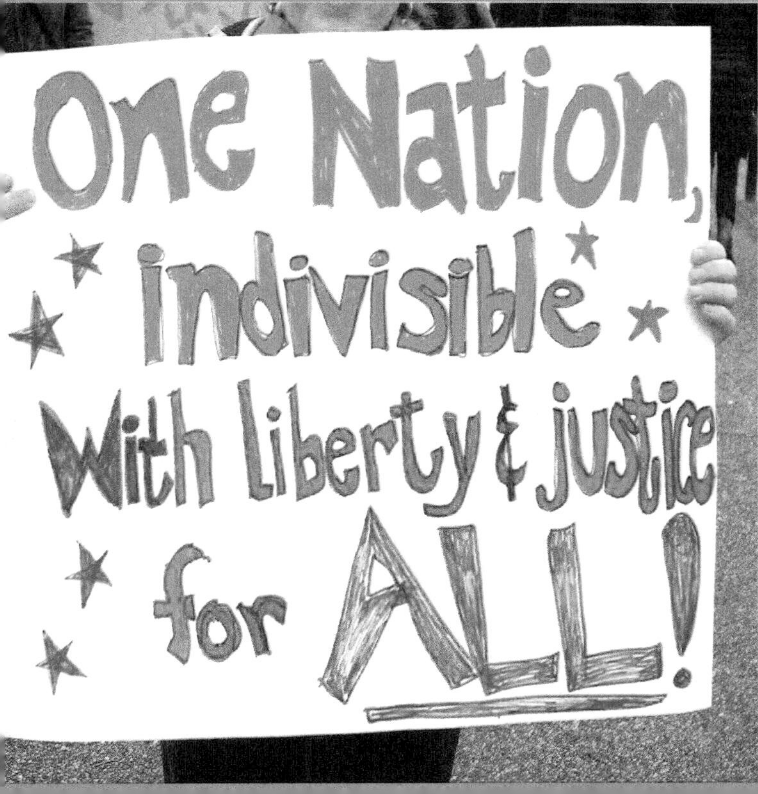
One Nation,
indivisible
With liberty & justice
for ALL!

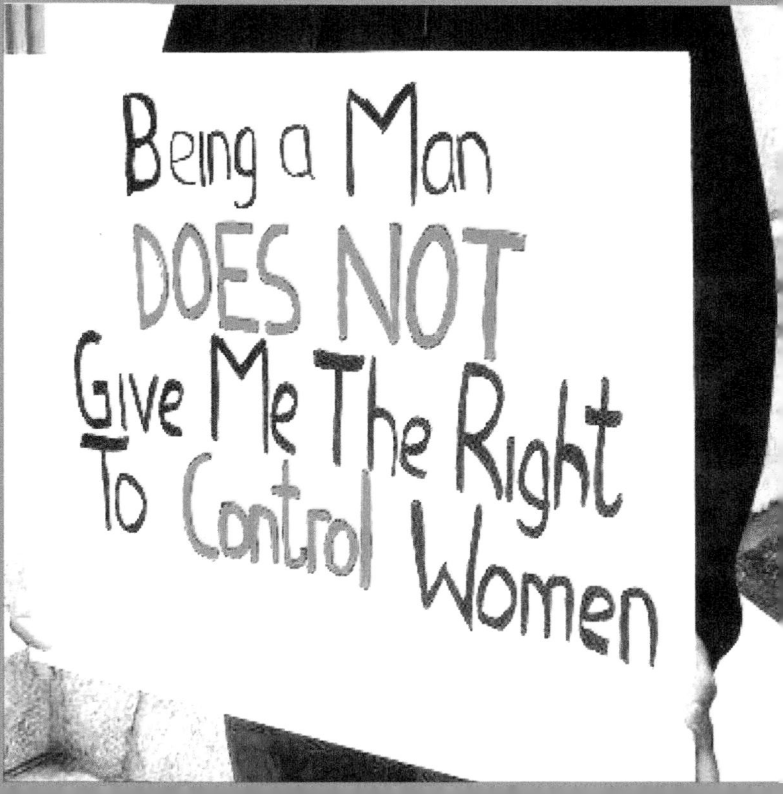
Being a Man
DOES NOT
Give Me The Right
To Control Women

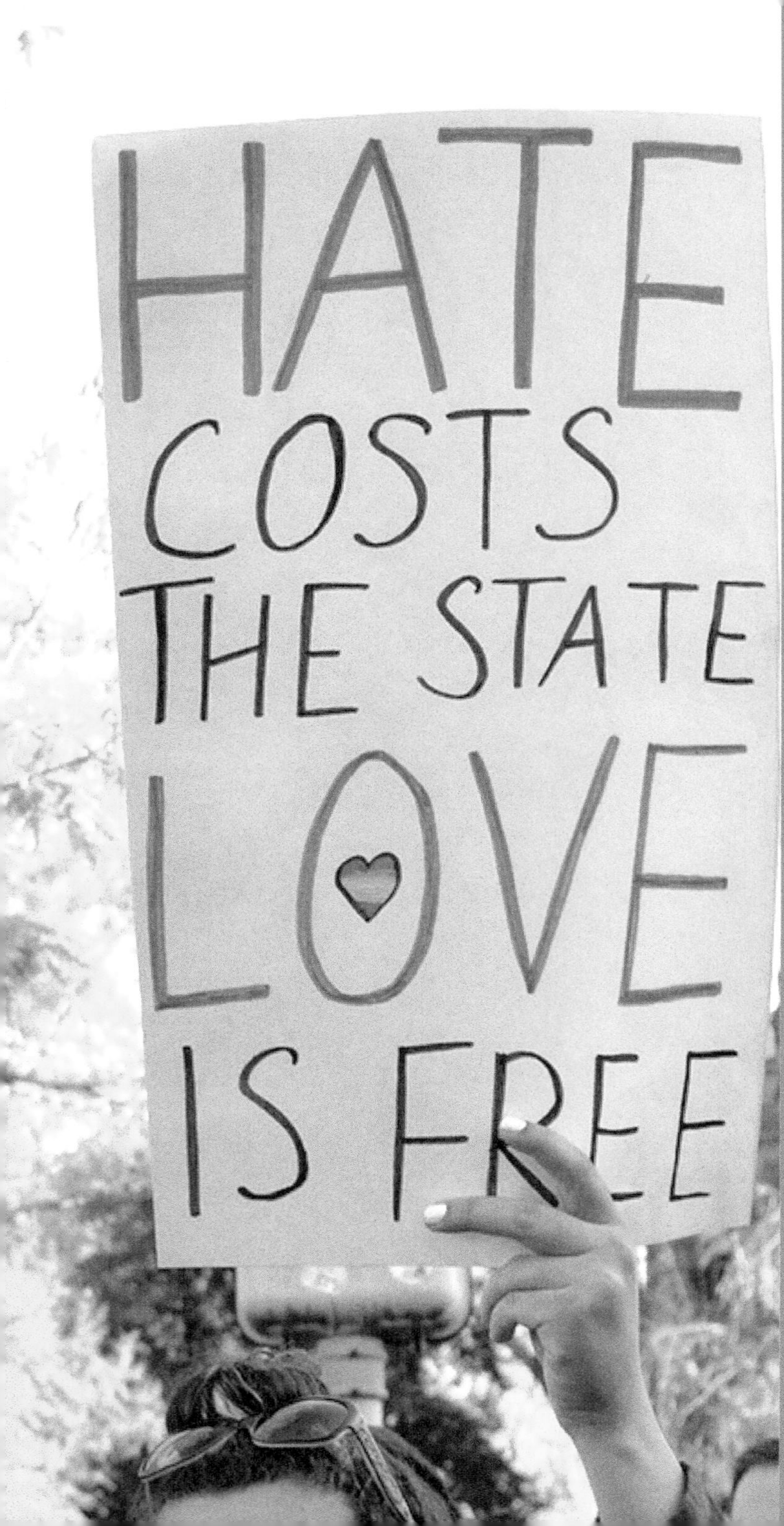
HATE
COSTS
THE STATE
LOVE
IS FREE

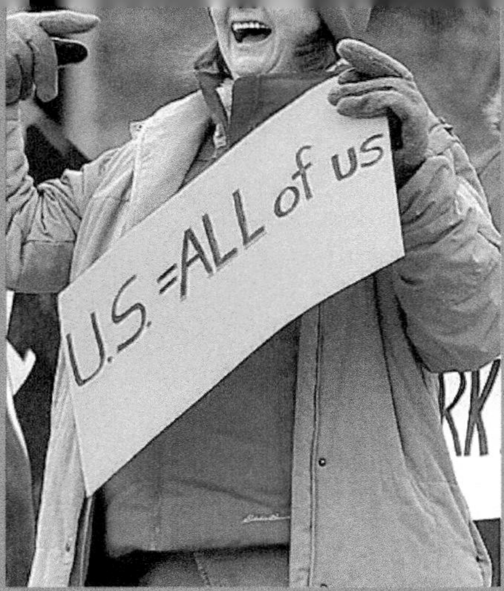
U.S. =ALL of us

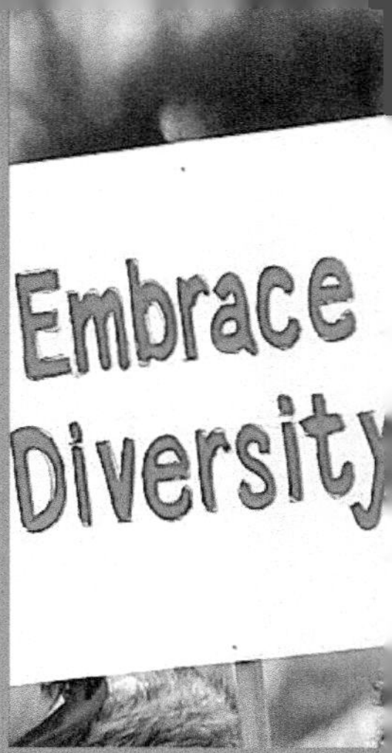
Embrace
Diversity

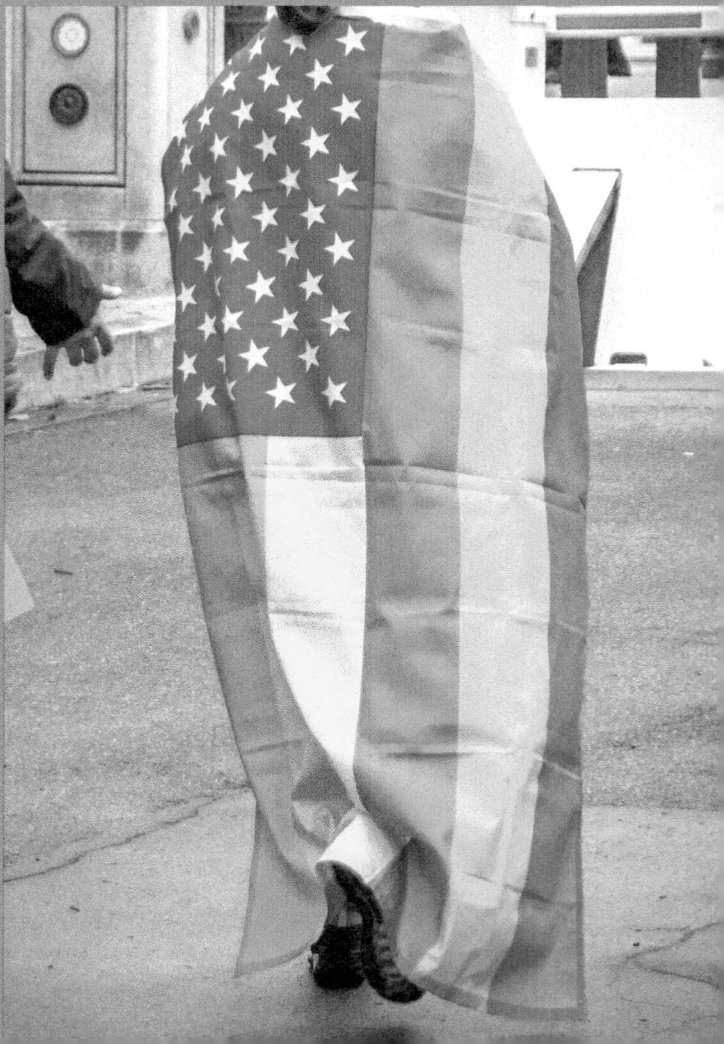

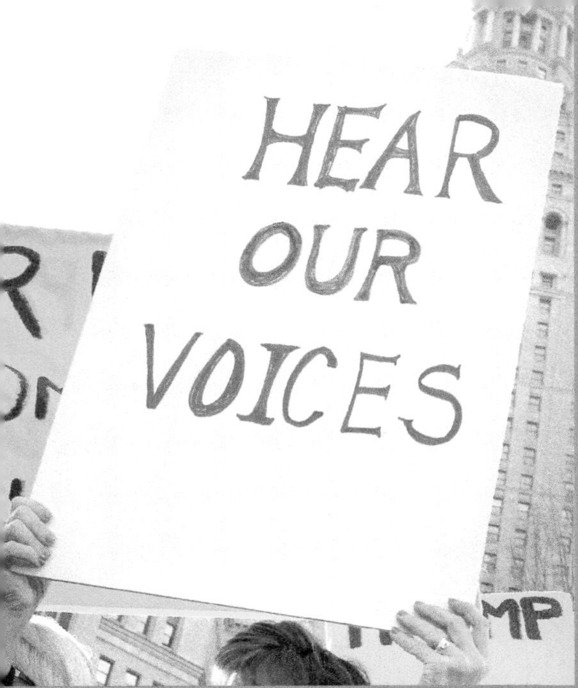
HEAR
OUR
VOICES

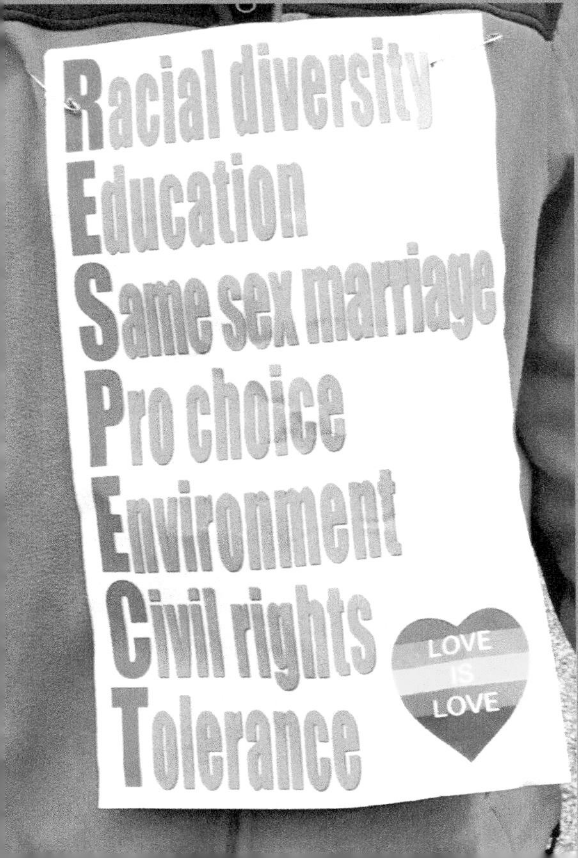
Racial diversity
Education
Same sex marriage
Pro choice
Environment
Civil rights
Tolerance
LOVE
IS
LOVE

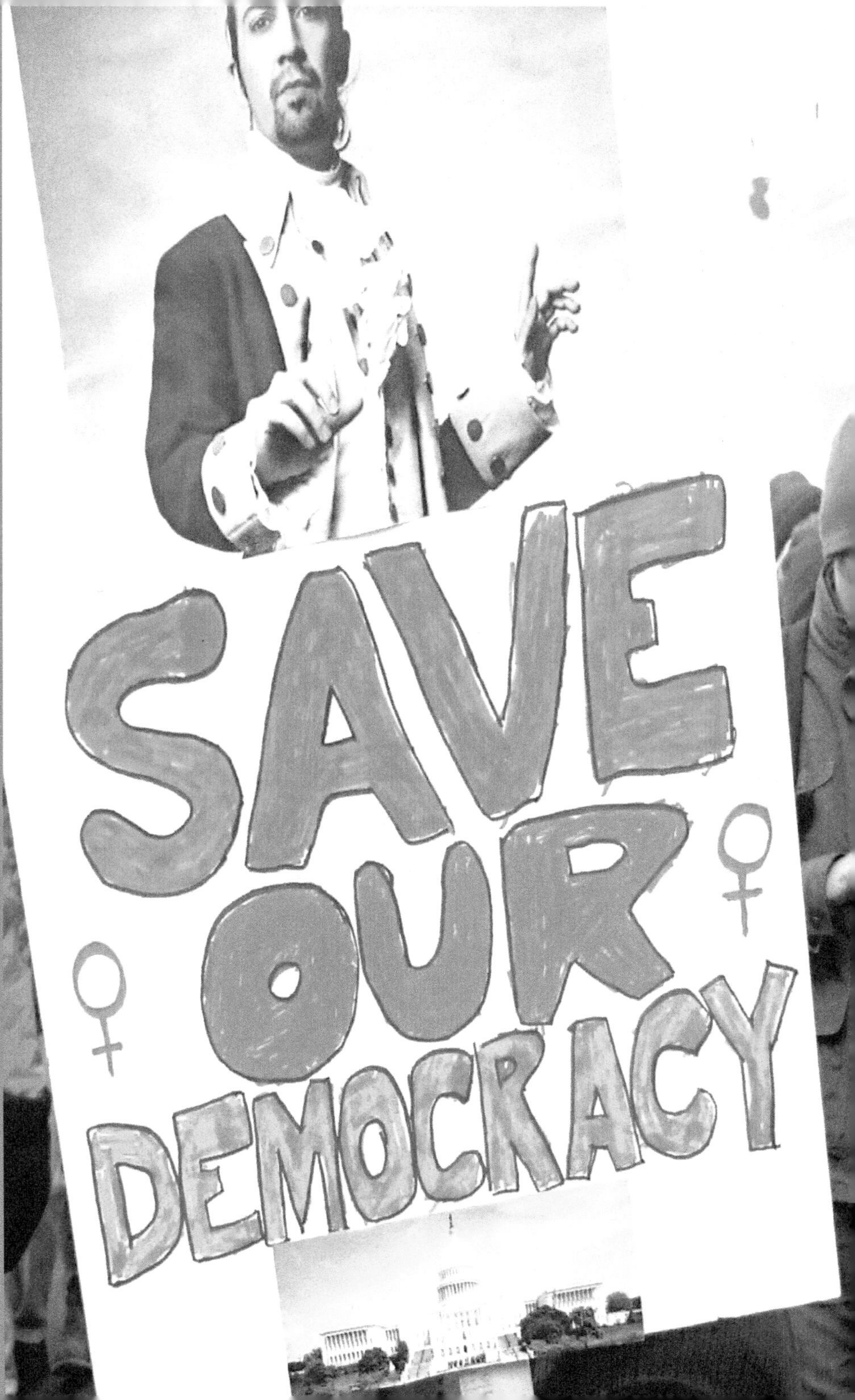
SAVE
OUR
DEMOCRACY

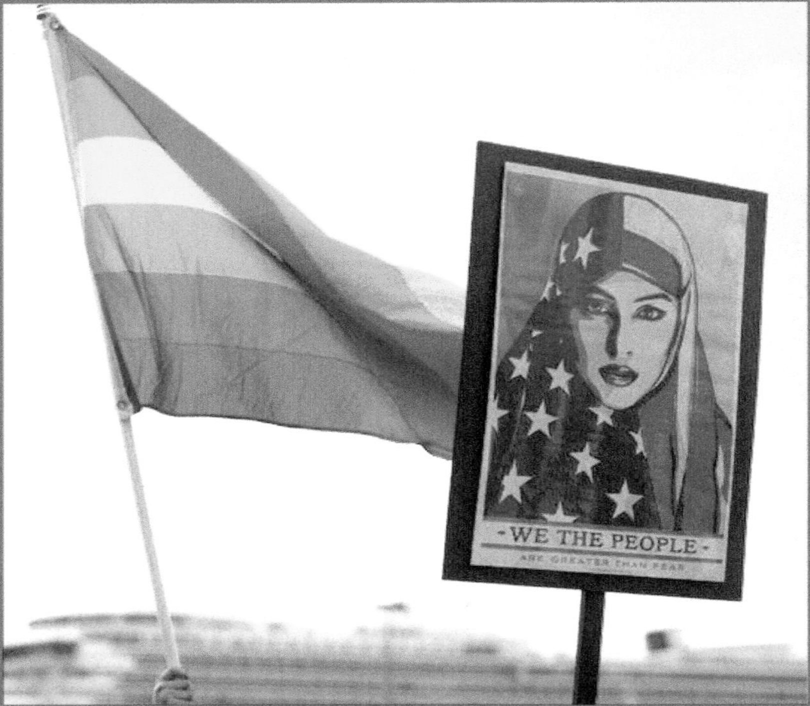
WE THE PEOPLE
ARE GREATER THAN FEAR

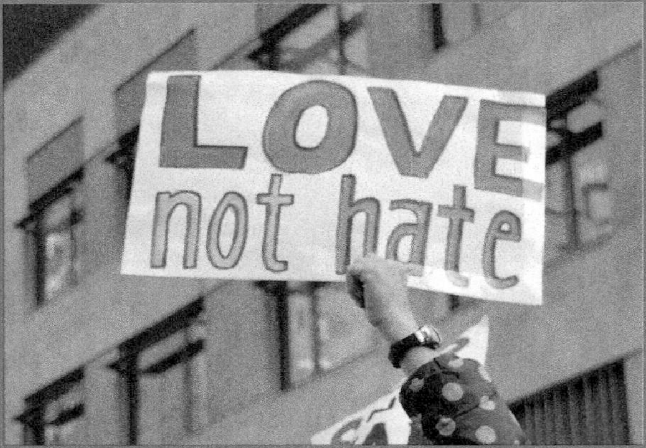
LOVE
not hate

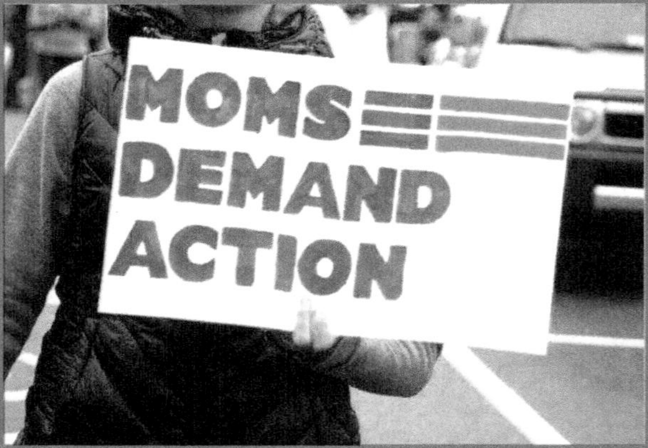
MOMS
DEMAND
ACTION

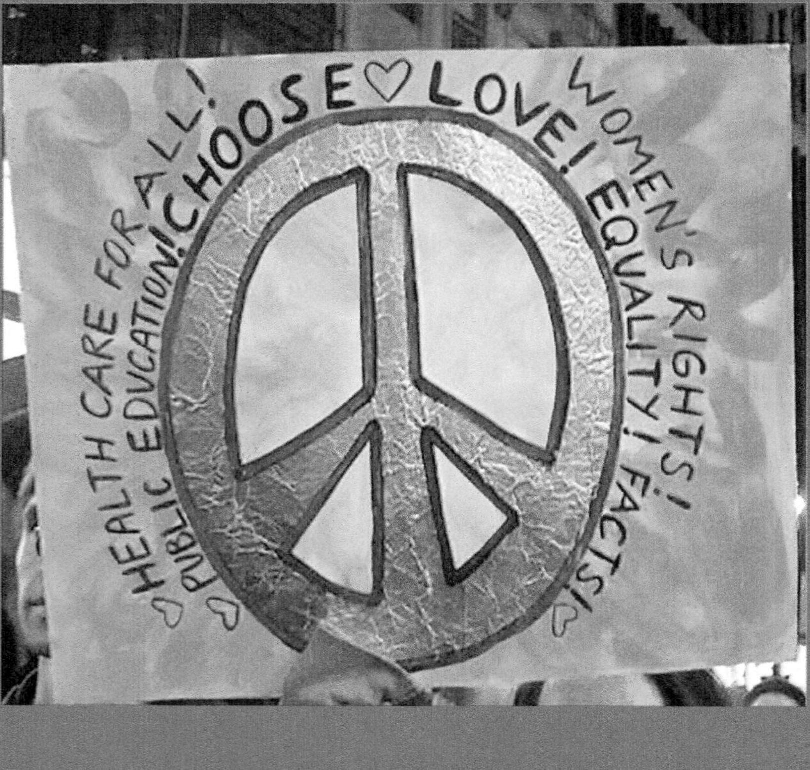
HEALTH CARE FOR ALL!
PUBLIC EDUCATION!
CHOOSE ♡ LOVE!
EQUALITY!
FACTS!
WOMEN'S RIGHTS!

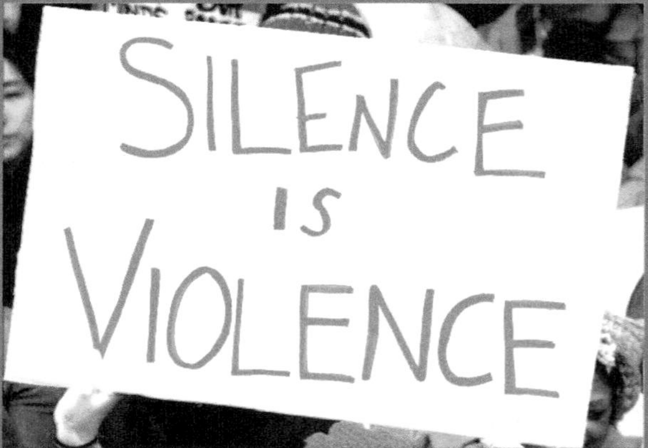
SILENCE
IS
VIOLENCE

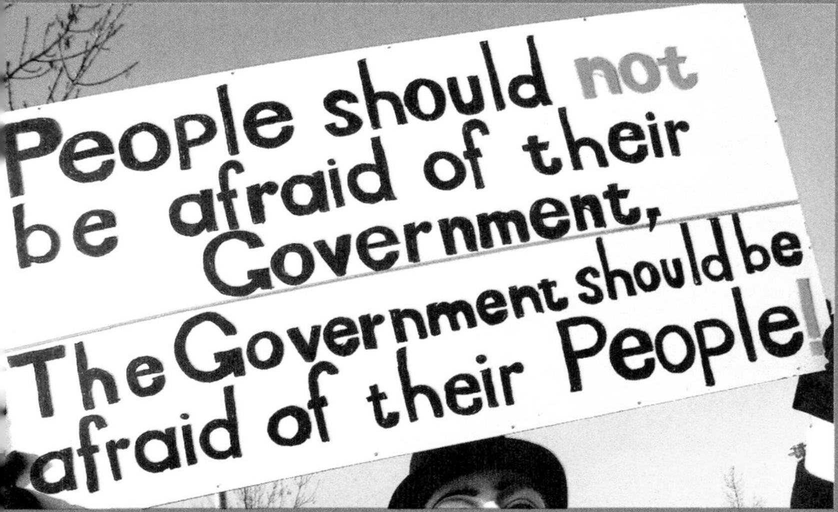
People should not be afraid of their Government,
The Government should be afraid of their People!

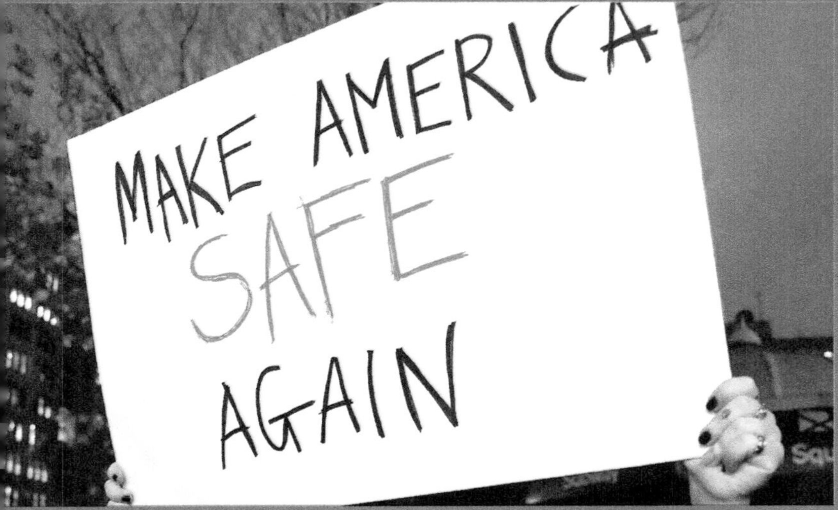
MAKE AMERICA SAFE AGAIN

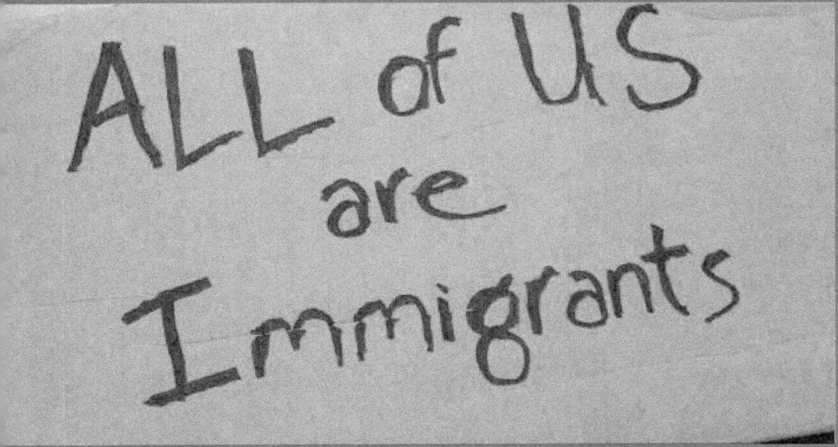
ALL of US are Immigrants

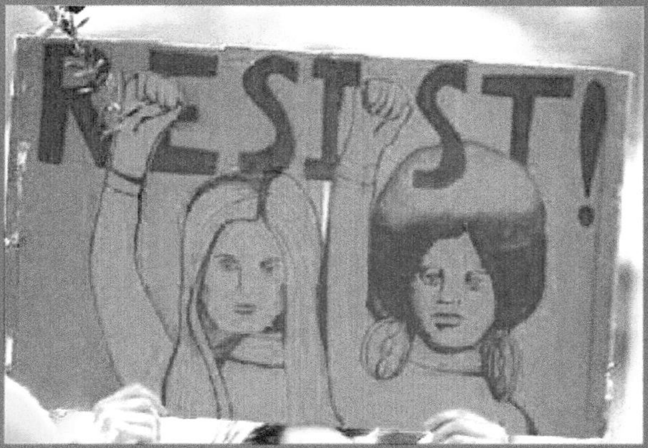
RESIST!

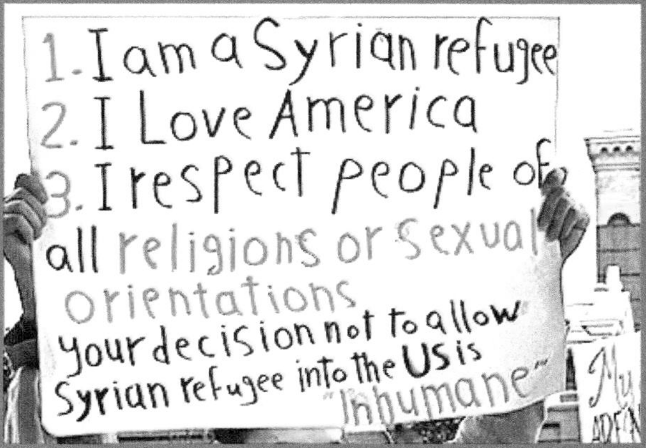
1. I am a Syrian refugee
2. I Love America
3. I respect people of all religions or sexual orientations
your decision not to allow Syrian refugee into the US is "Inhumane"

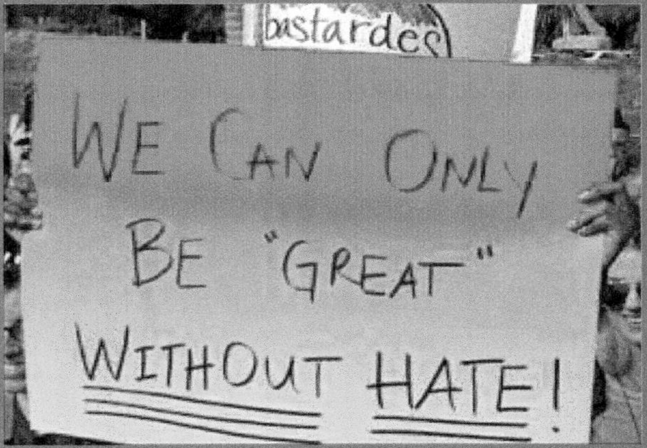
bastardes
WE CAN ONLY BE "GREAT" WITHOUT HATE!

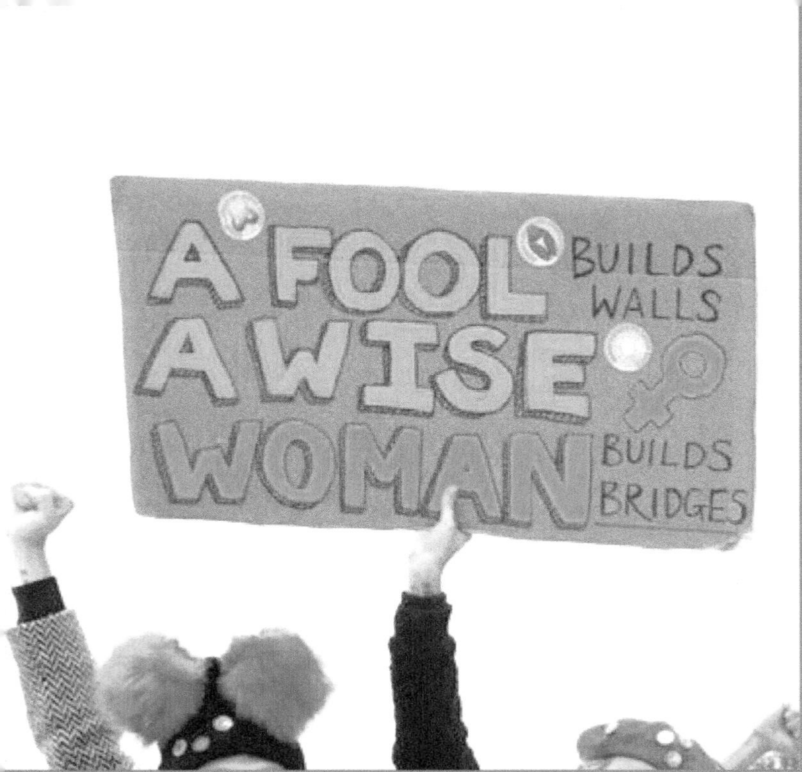
A FOOL BUILDS WALLS
A WISE WOMAN BUILDS BRIDGES

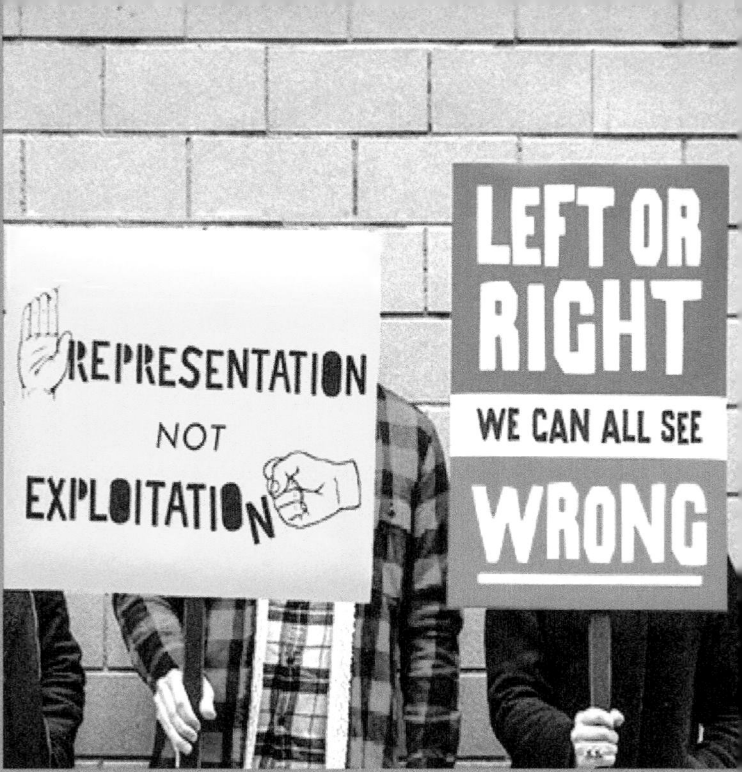
REPRESENTATION
NOT
EXPLOITATION
LEFT OR RIGHT
WE CAN ALL SEE
WRONG

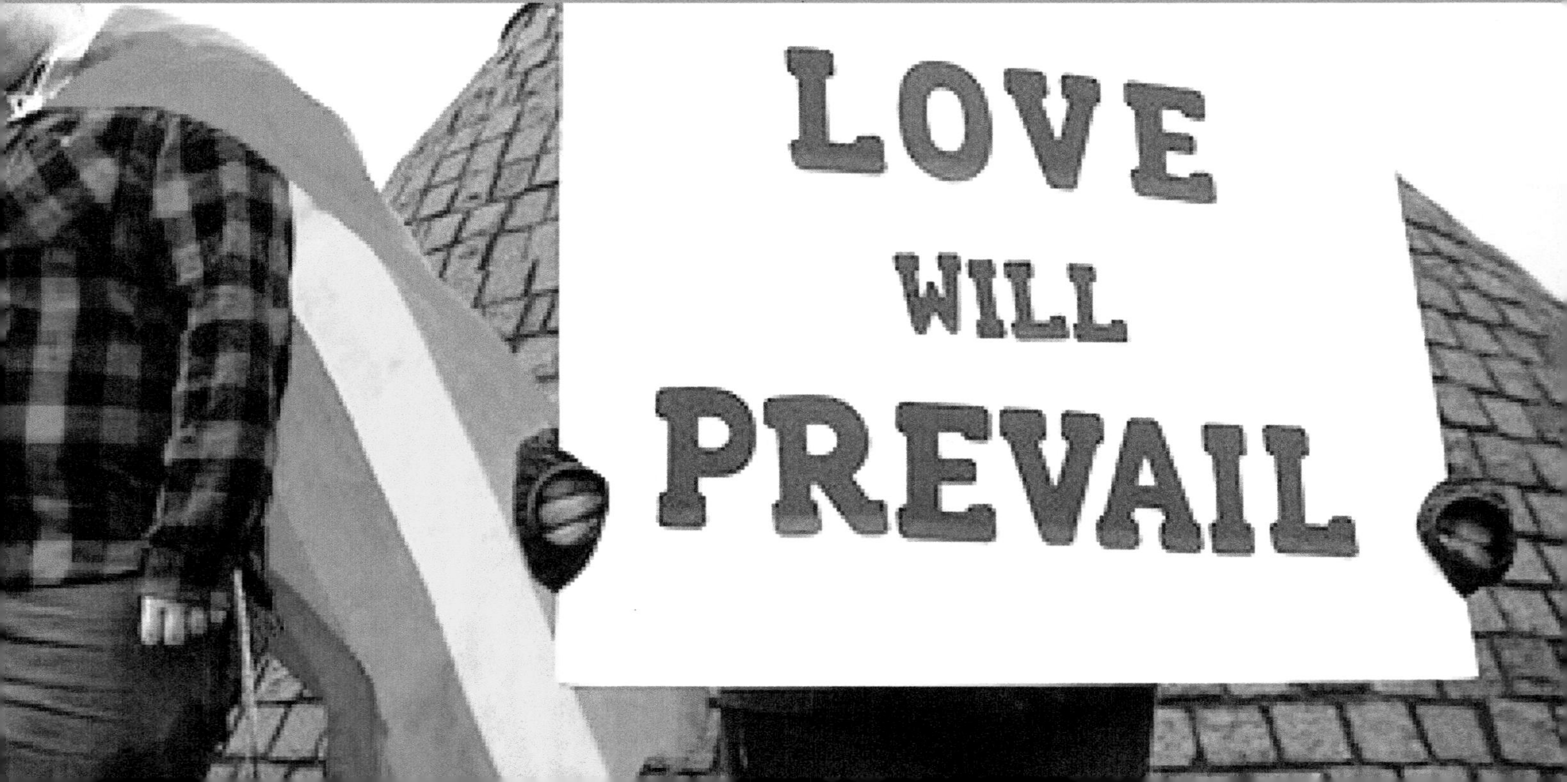
LOVE
WILL
PREVAIL

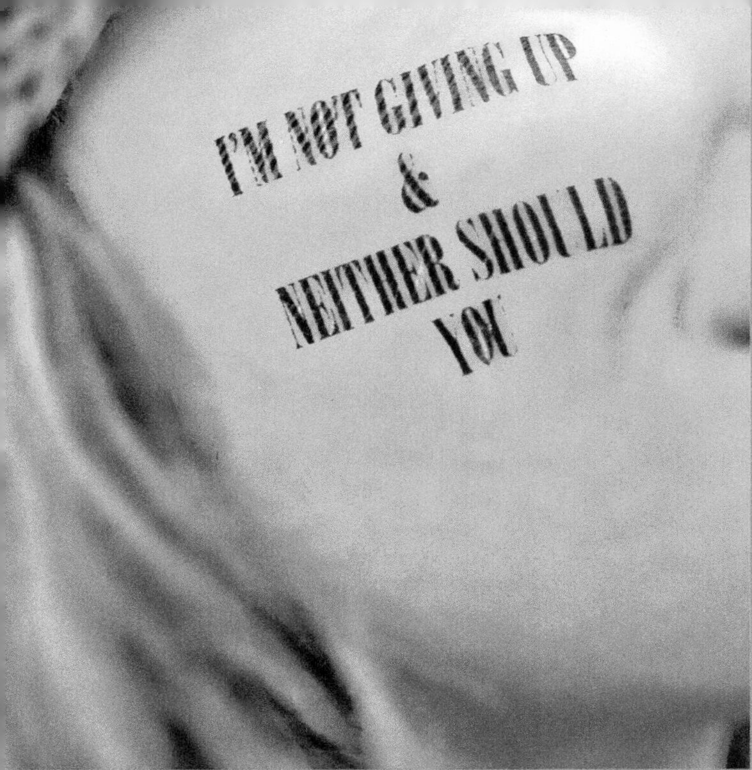
I'M NOT GIVING UP
&
NEITHER SHOULD
YOU
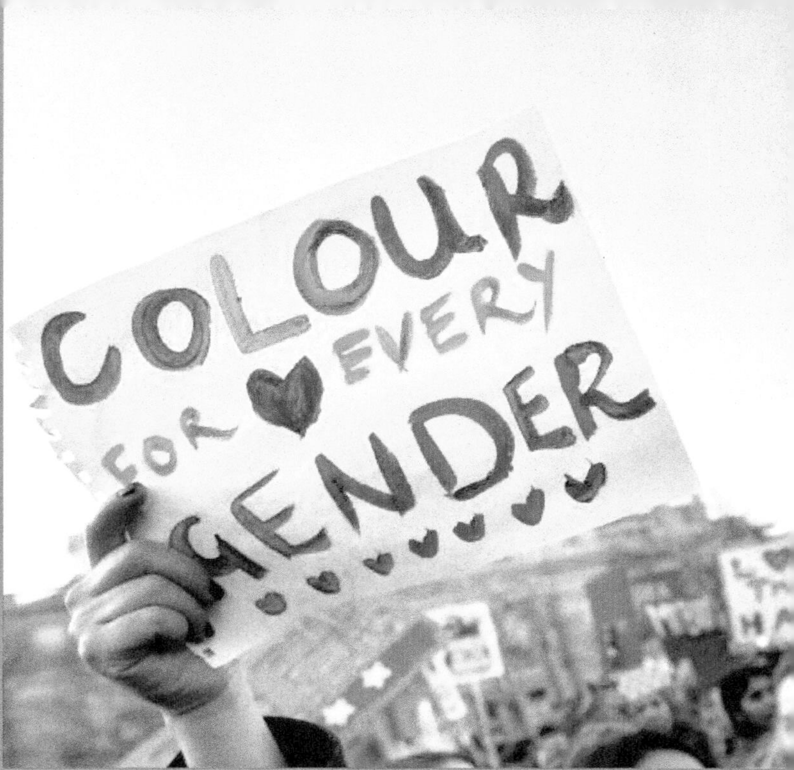
COLOUR
FOR EVERY
GENDER
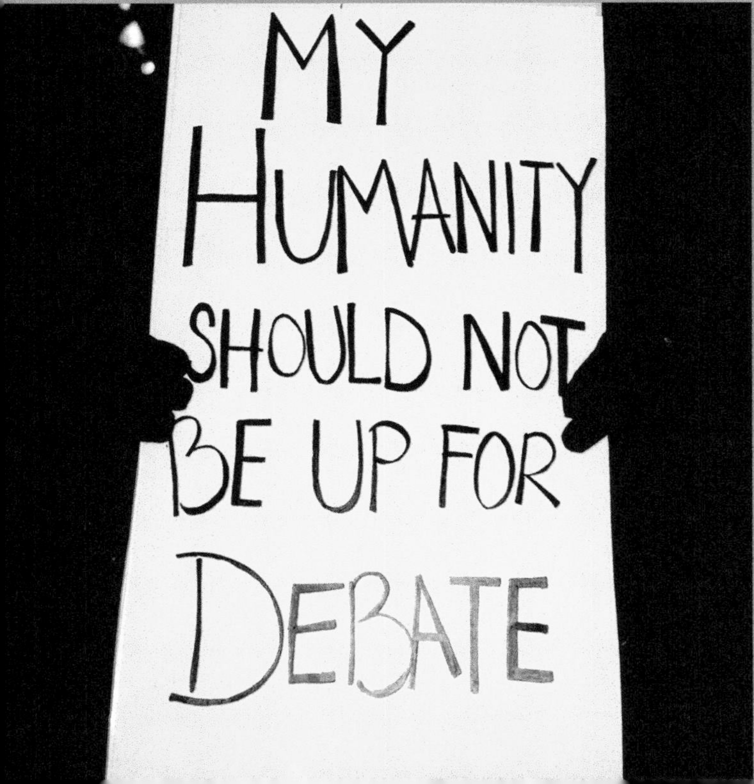
MY
HUMANITY
SHOULD NOT
BE UP FOR
DEBATE
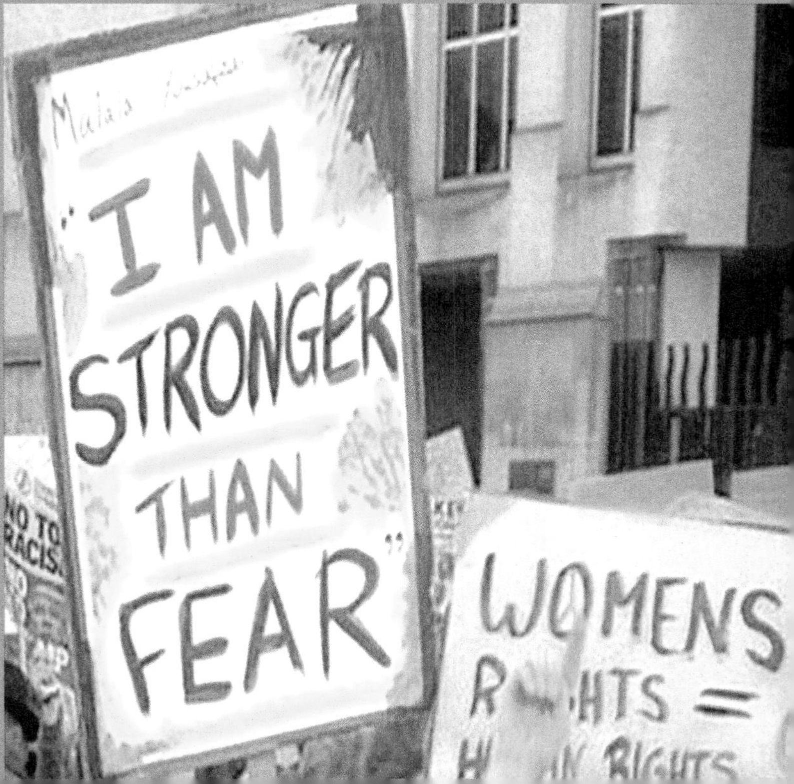
"I AM
STRONGER
THAN
FEAR"
WOMENS

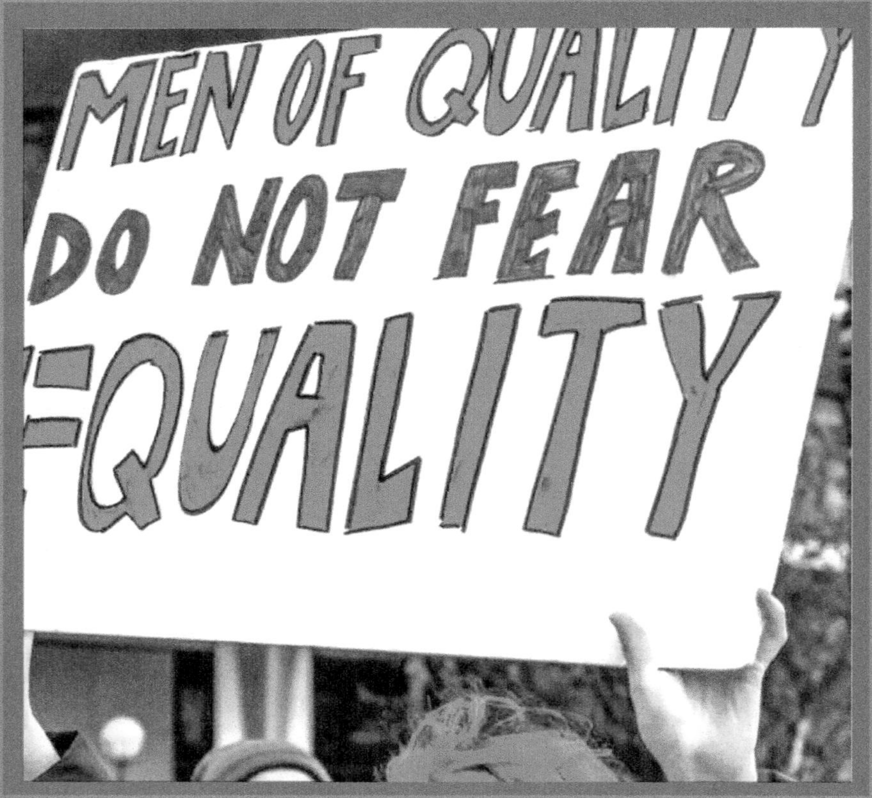
MEN OF QUALITY
DO NOT FEAR
EQUALITY

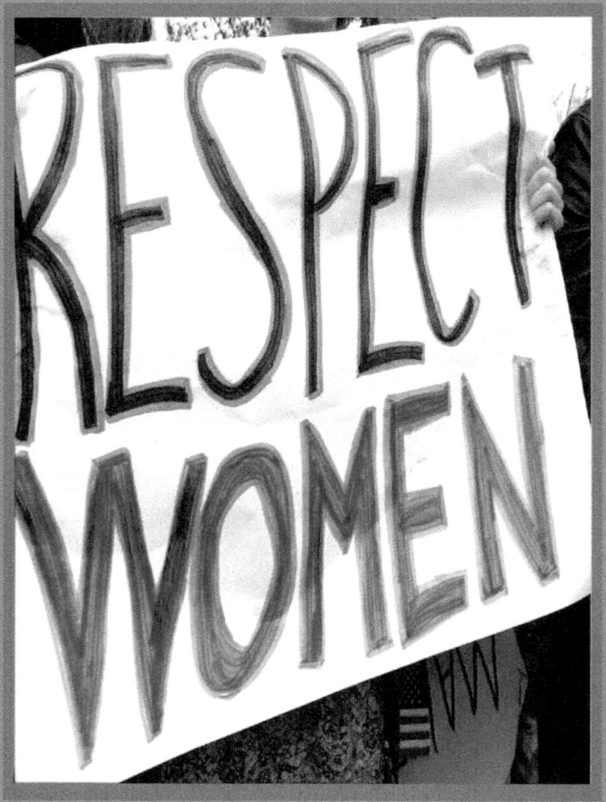
RESPECT
WOMEN

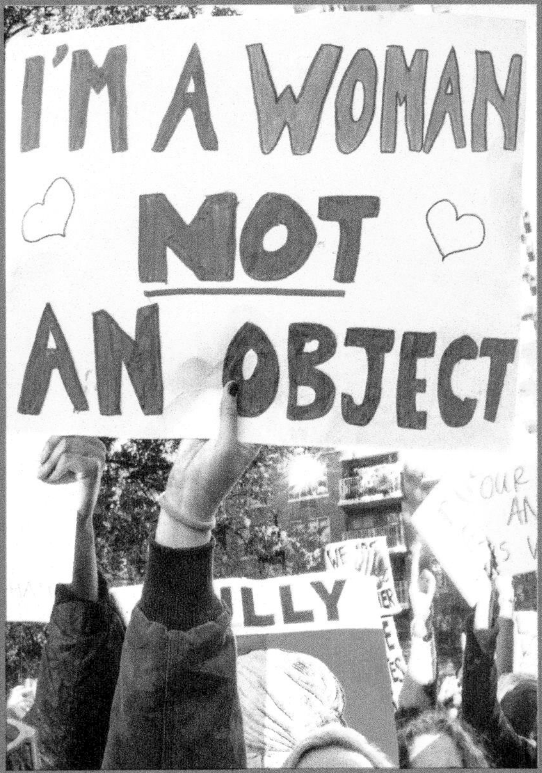
I'M A WOMAN
NOT
AN OBJECT

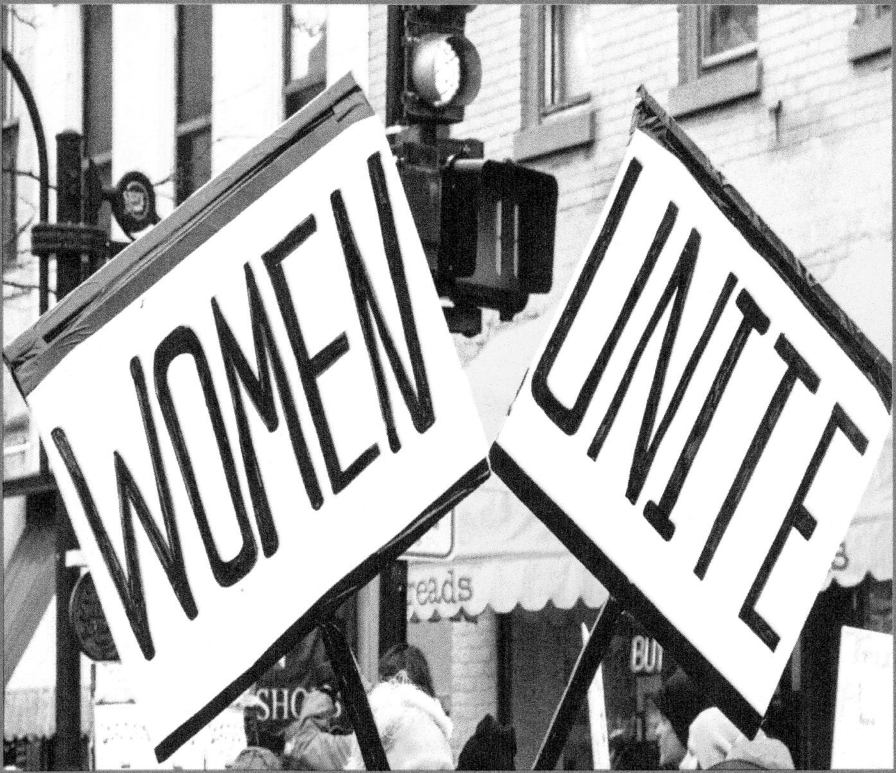
WOMEN
UNITE

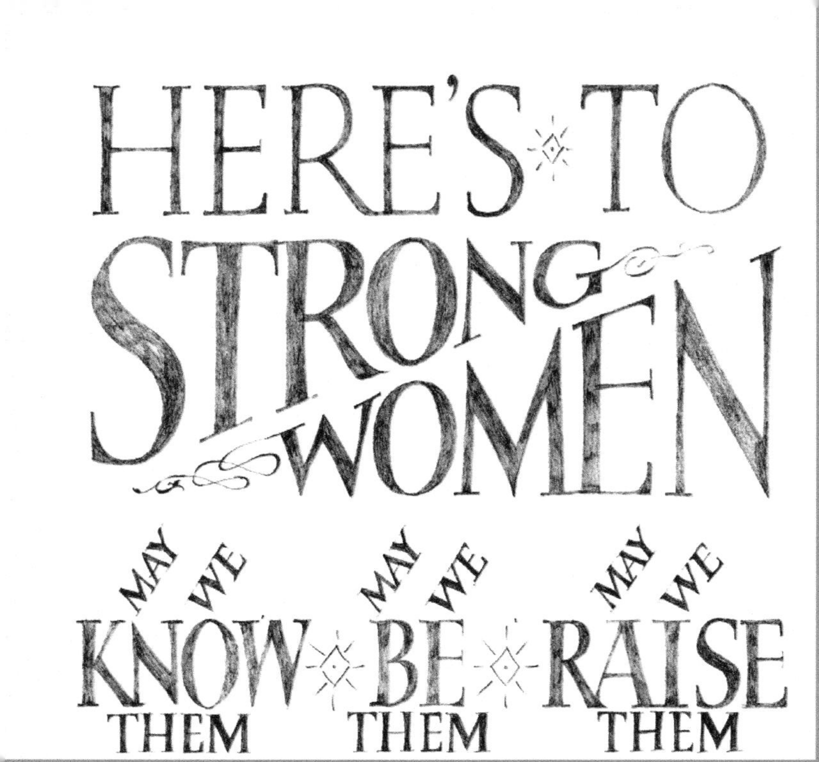
HERE'S TO
STRONG
WOMEN
MAY WE KNOW THEM
MAY WE BE THEM
MAY WE RAISE THEM

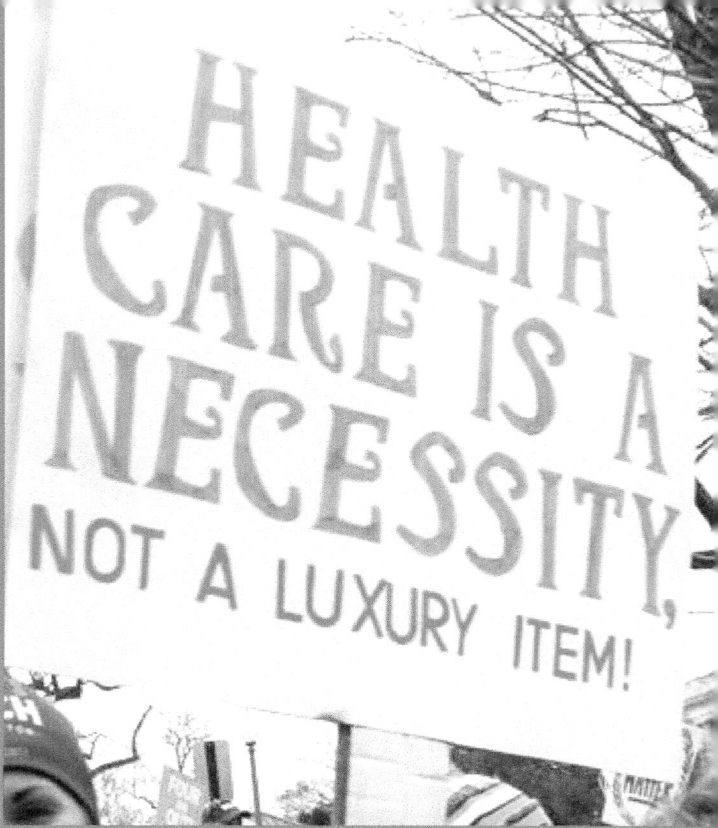
HEALTH
CARE IS A
NECESSITY,
NOT A LUXURY ITEM!

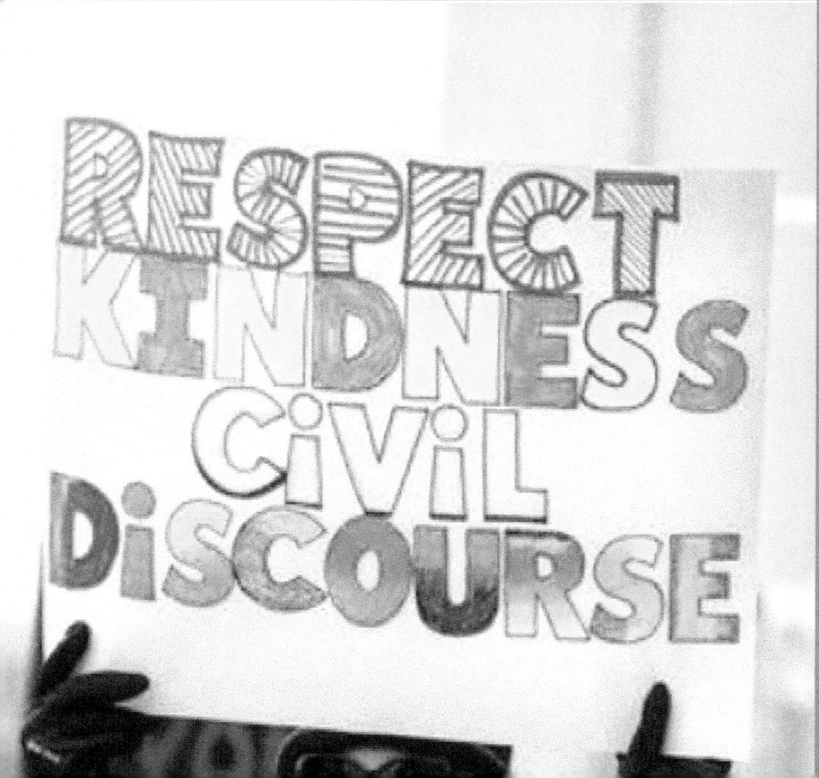
RESPECT
KINDNESS
CiViL
DiSCOURSE

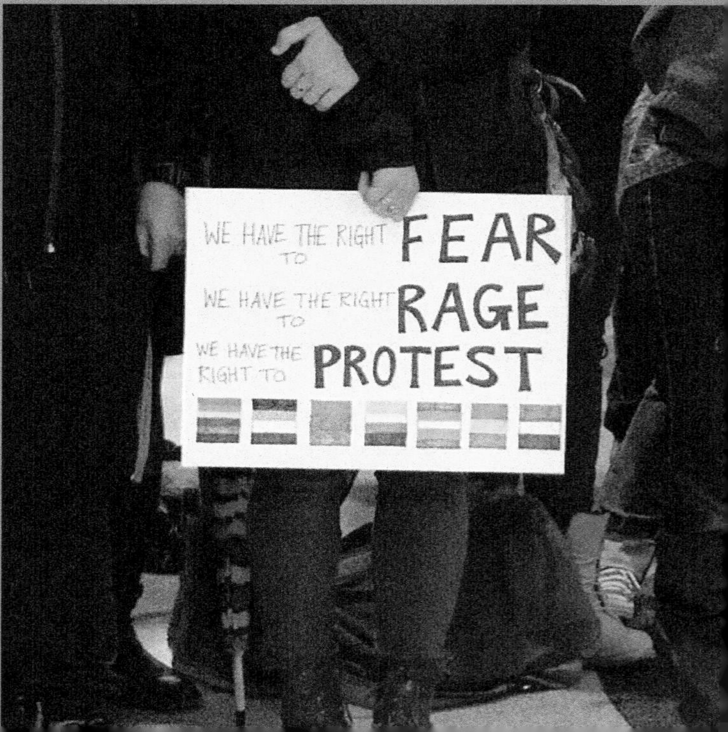
WE HAVE THE RIGHT TO FEAR
WE HAVE THE RIGHT TO RAGE
WE HAVE THE RIGHT TO PROTEST

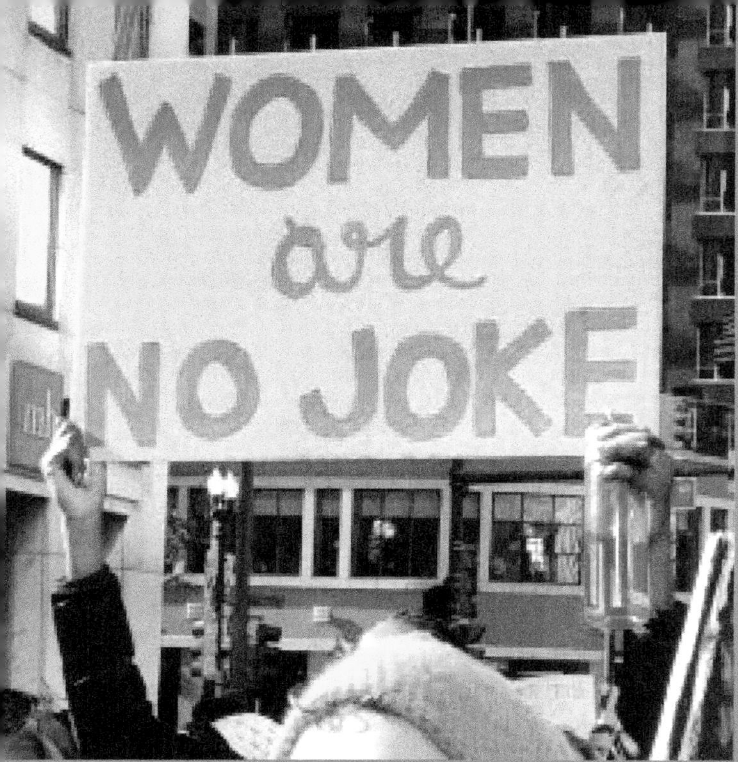
WOMEN are NO JOKE

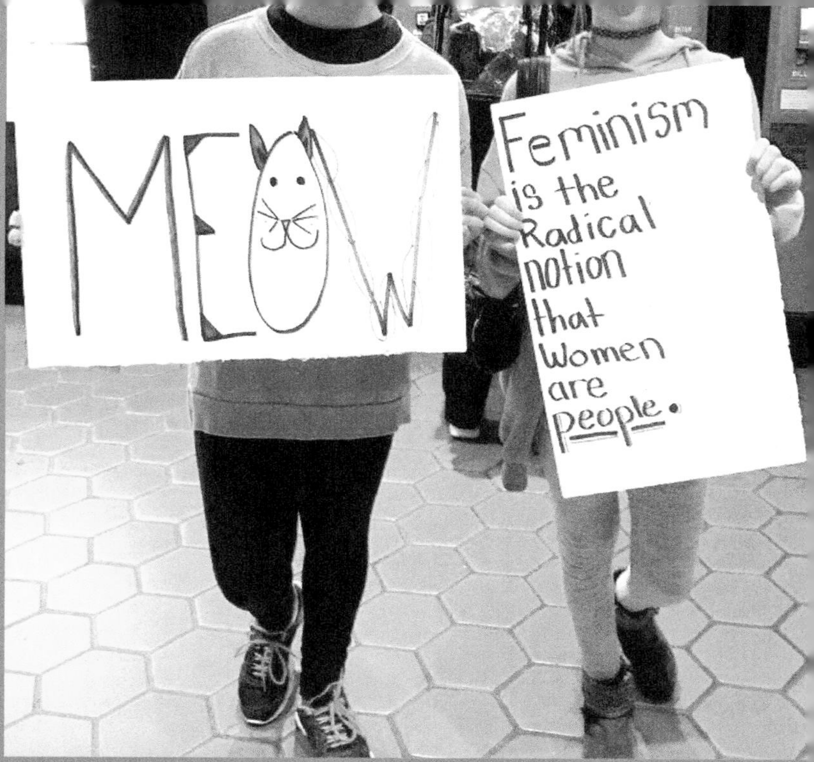
MEOW
Feminism is the Radical notion that Women are people.

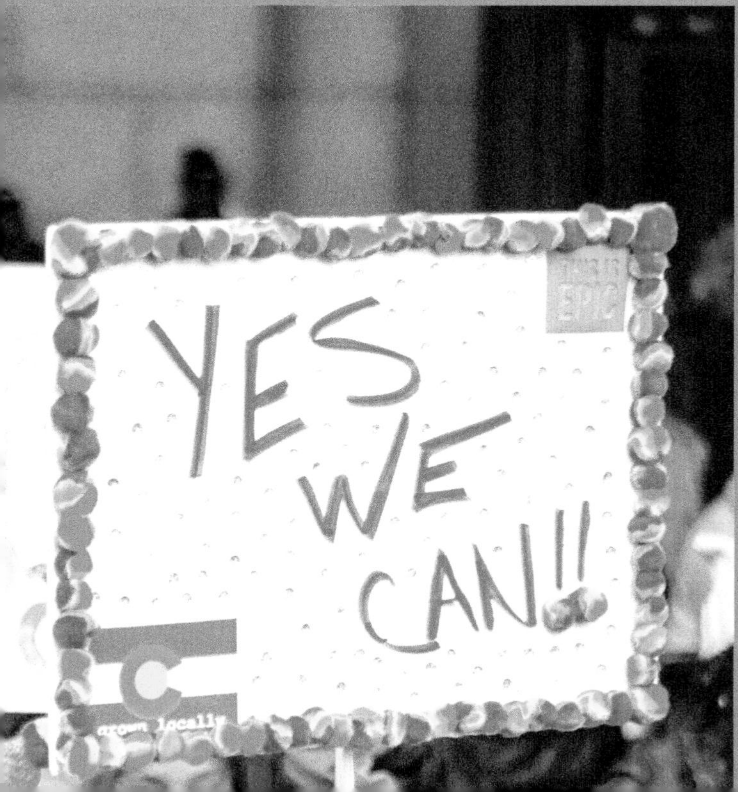
YES WE CAN!!

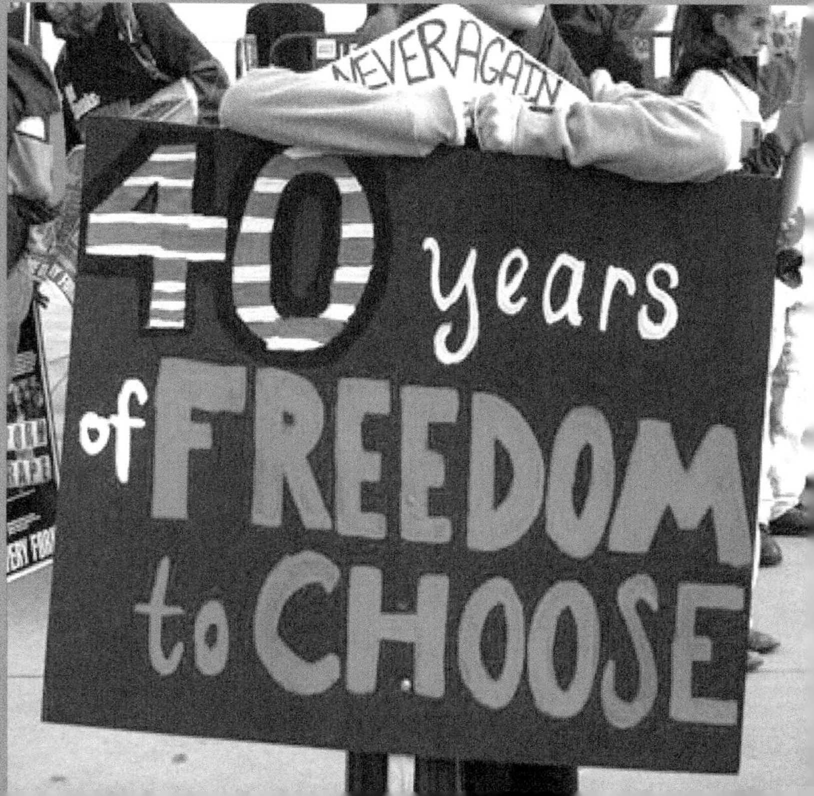
NEVERAGAIN
40 years of FREEDOM to CHOOSE

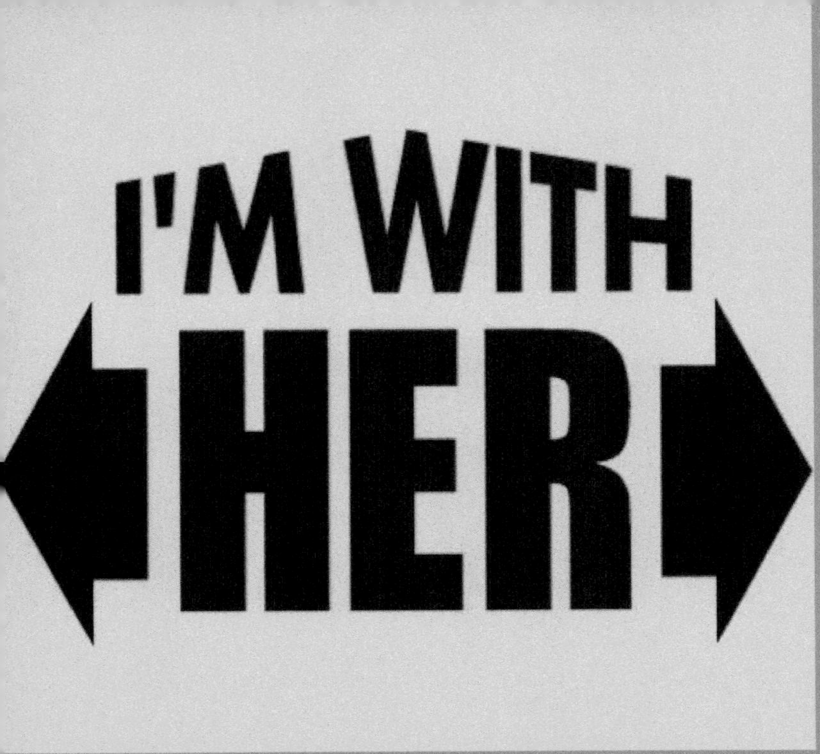
I'M WITH
HER

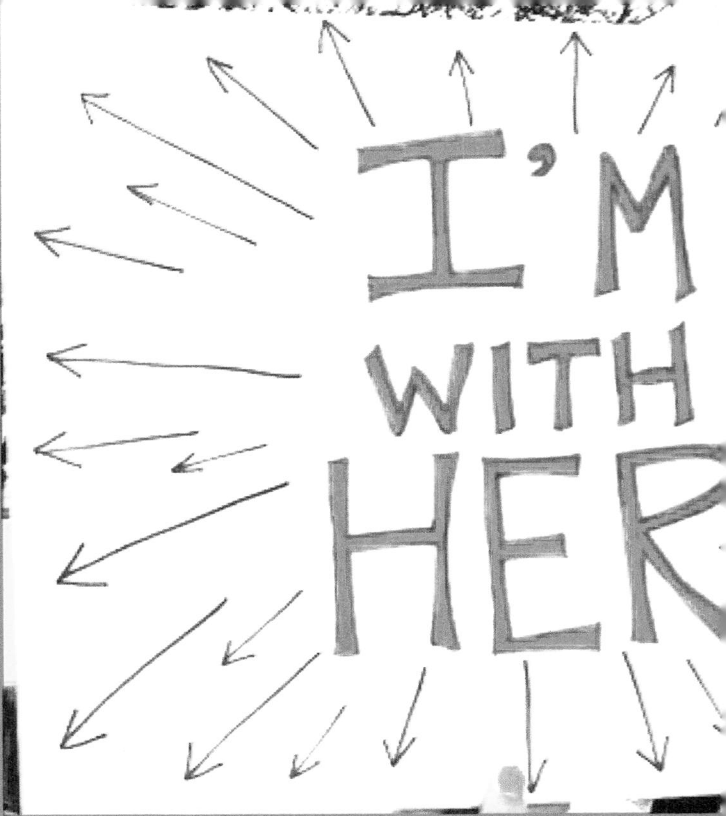
I'M
WITH
HER

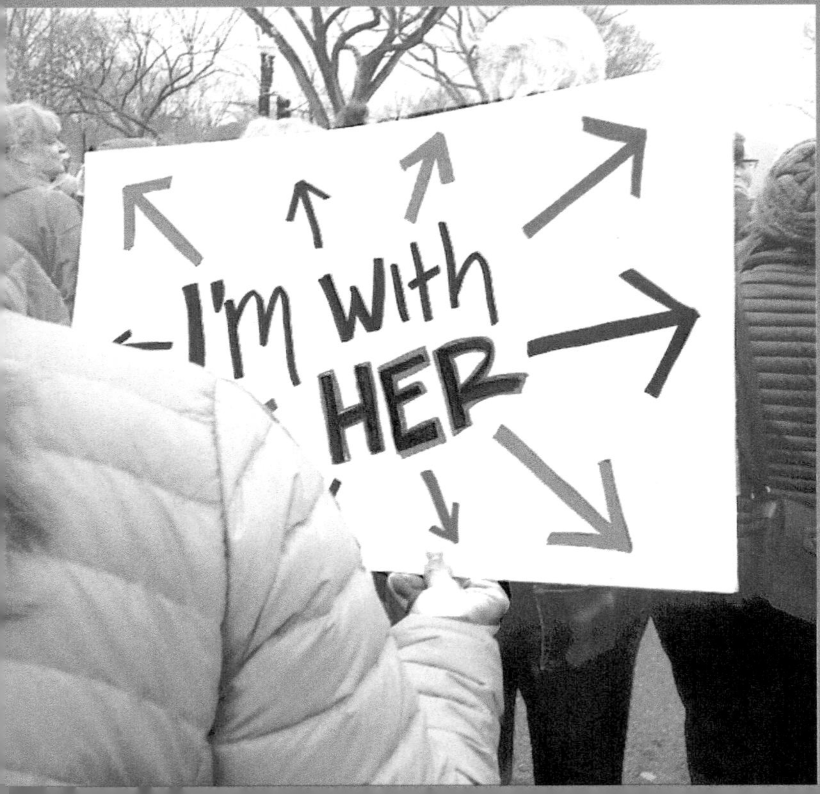
I'm with
HER

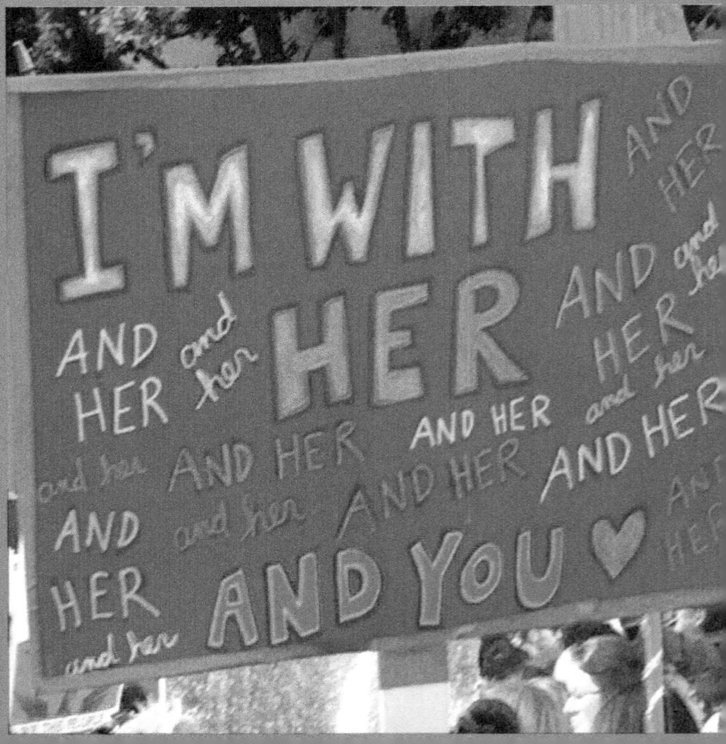
I'M WITH
HER
AND HER
and her
AND HER
and her
AND HER
AND HER
AND HER
AND HER
AND HER
AND YOU ♥

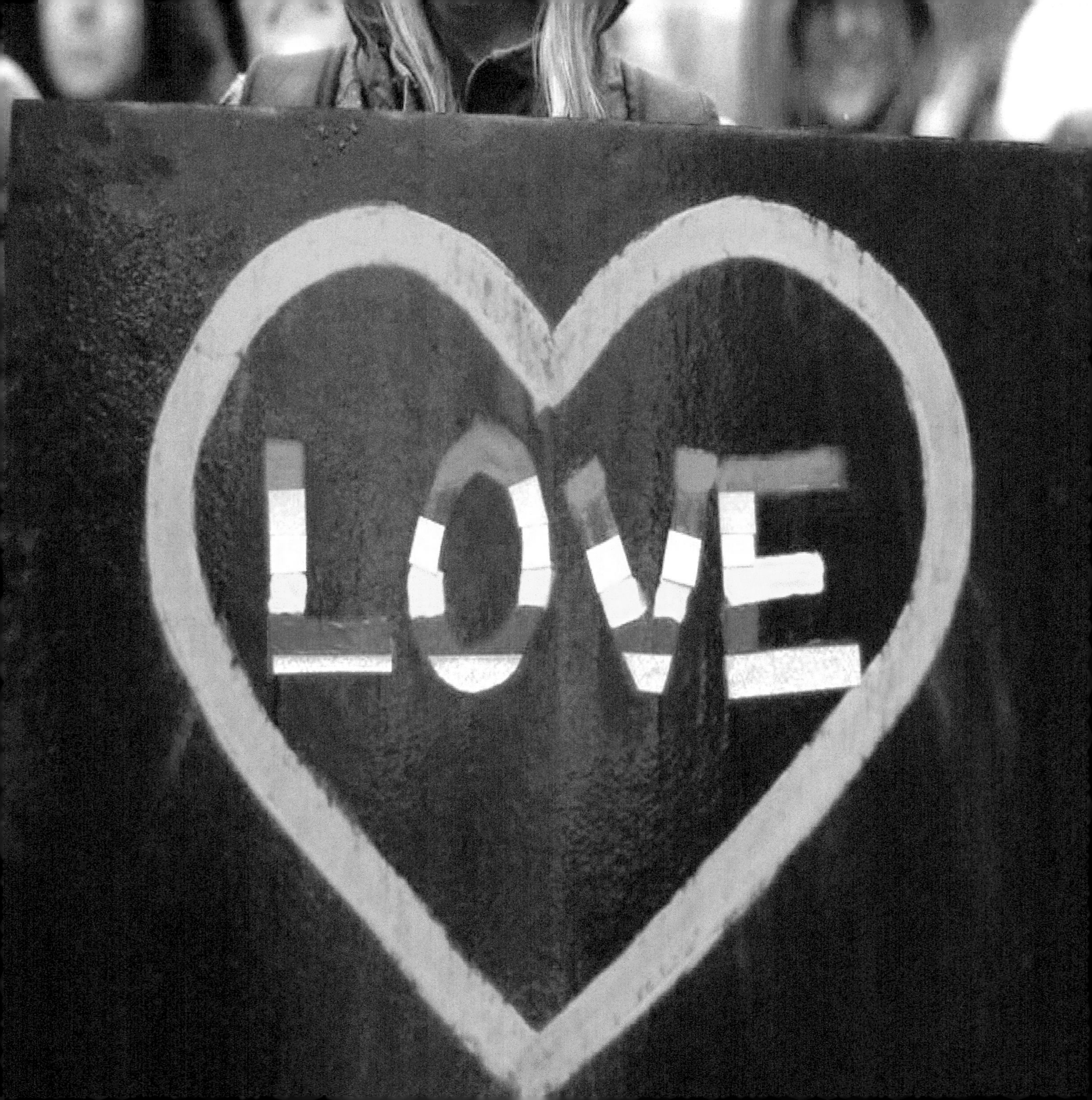
LOVE

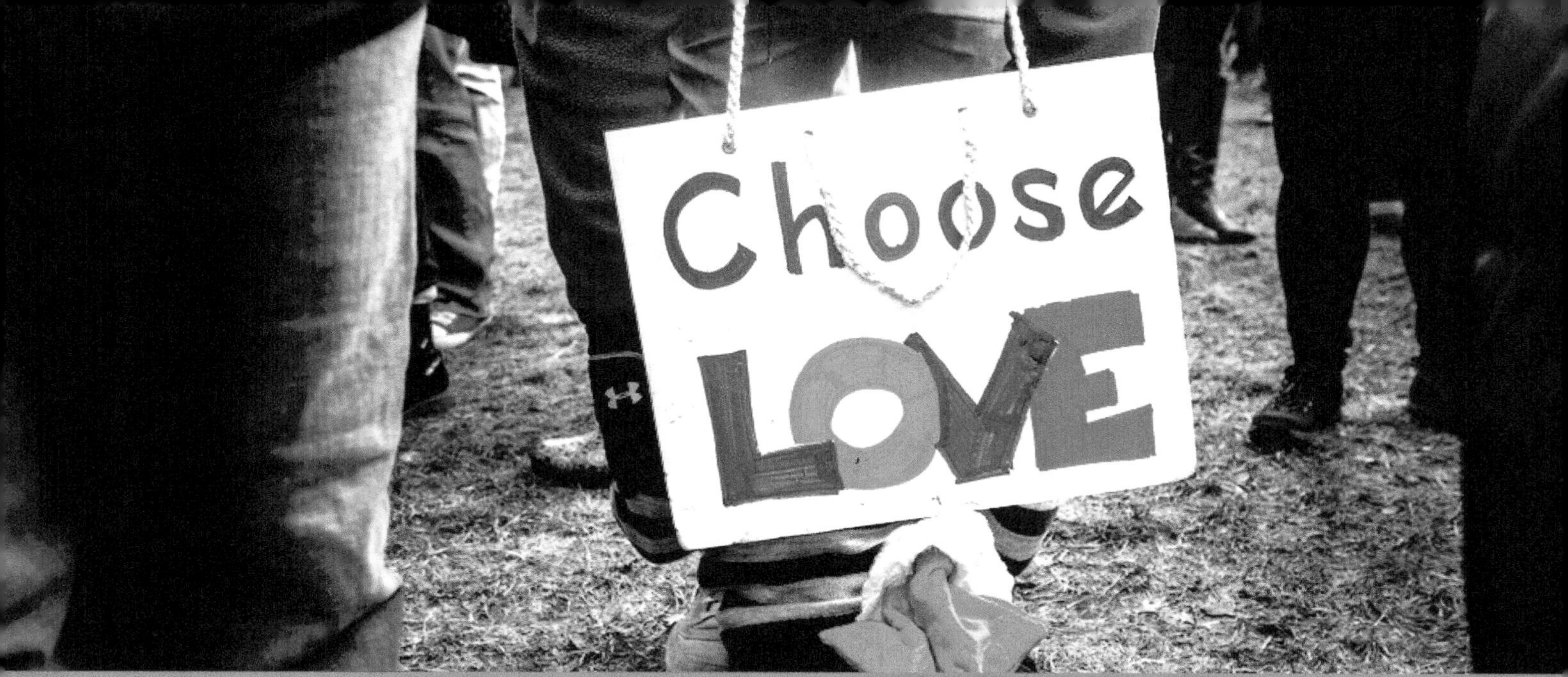
Choose
LOVE

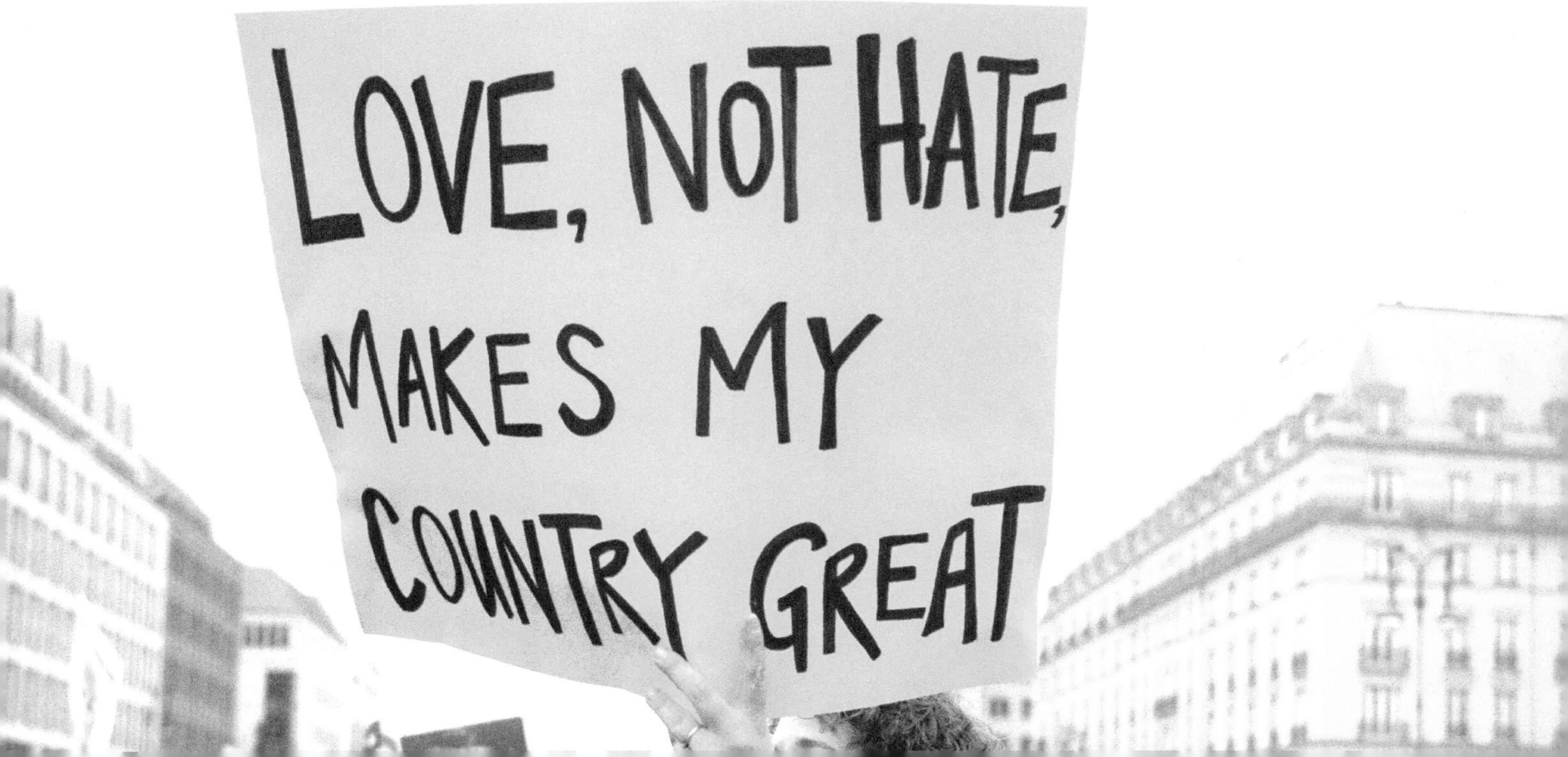
LOVE, NOT HATE,
MAKES MY
COUNTRY GREAT

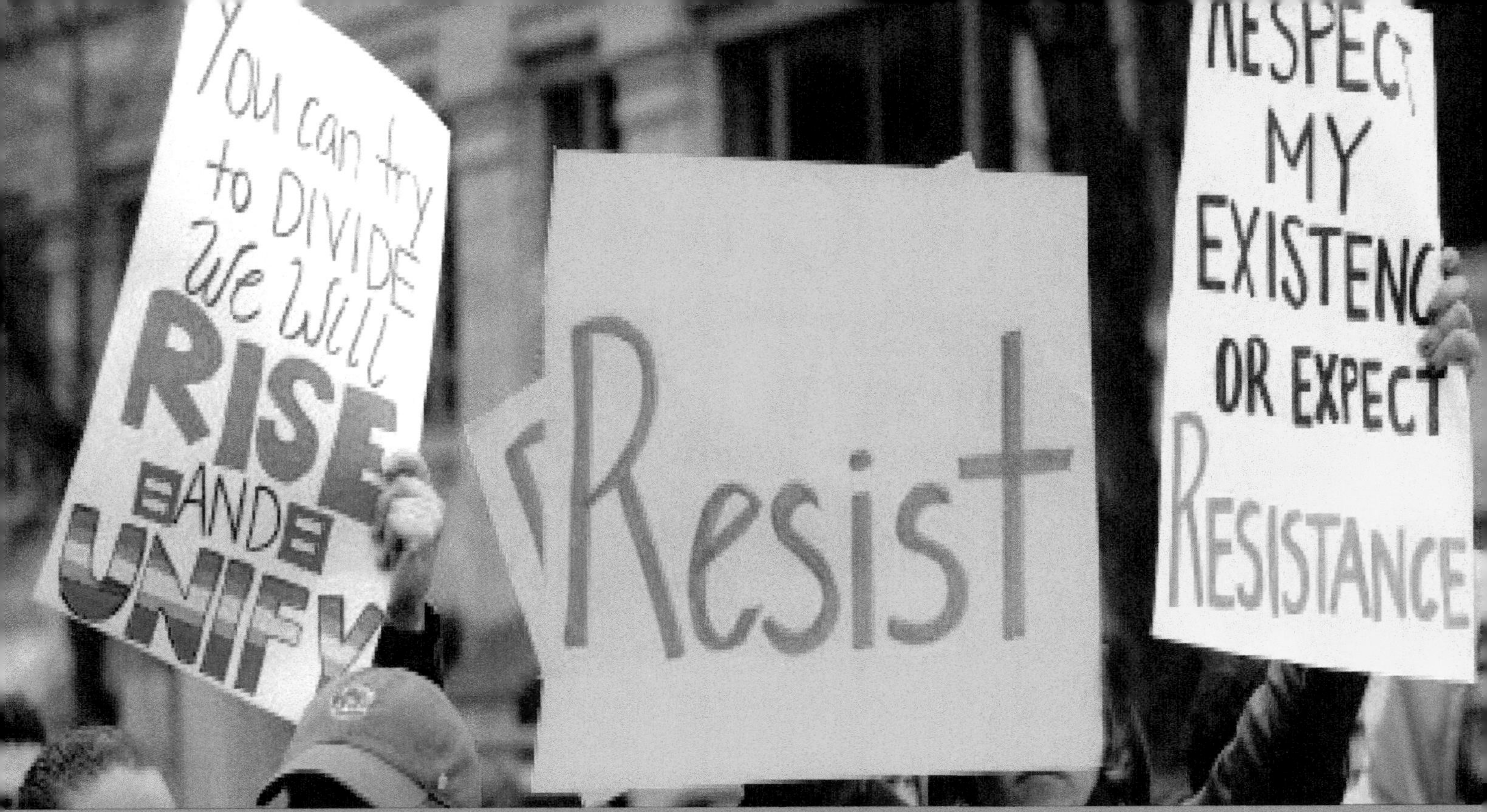
You can try
to DIVIDE
We will
RISE
AND
UNIFY
Resist
RESPECT
MY
EXISTENC
OR EXPECT
RESISTANCE

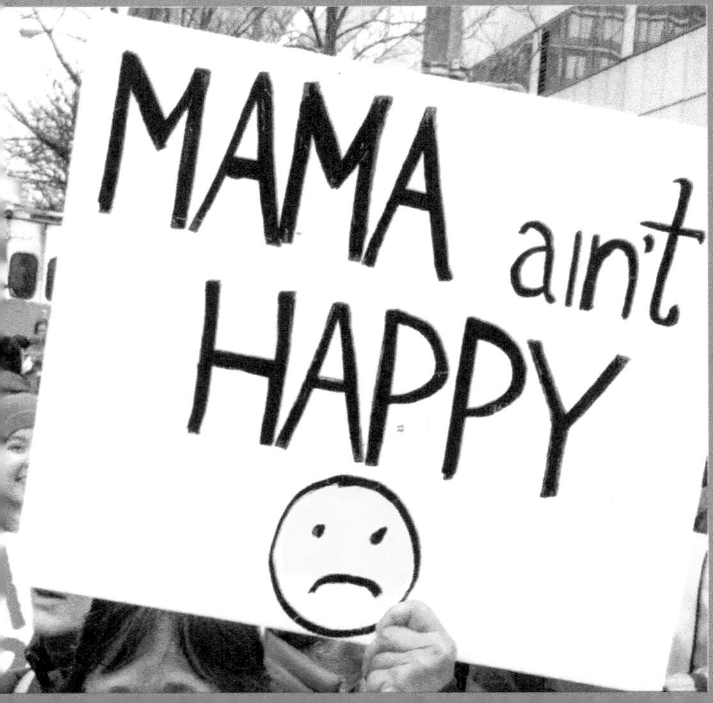
MAMA ain't
HAPPY

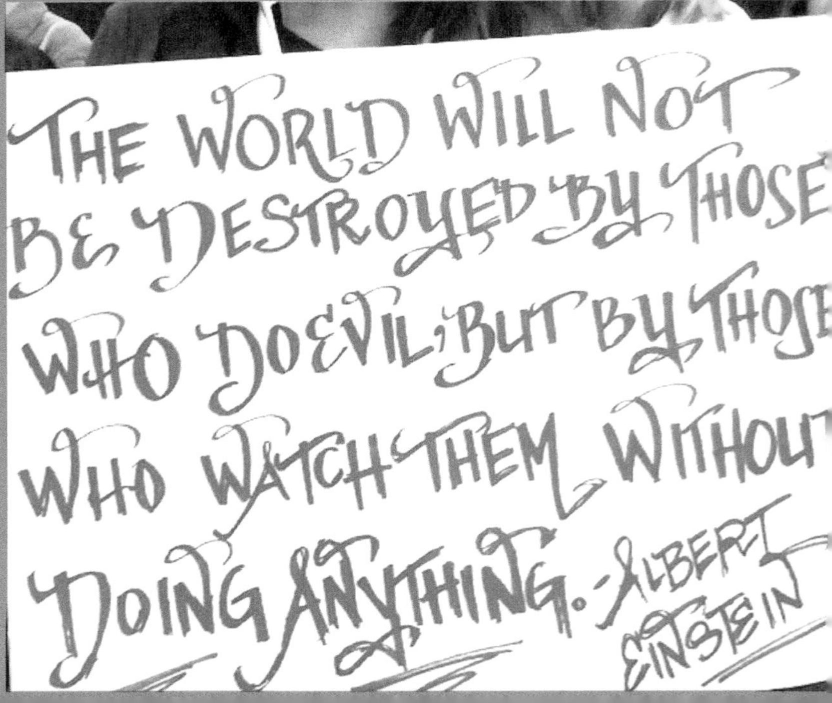
THE WORLD WILL NOT
BE DESTROYED BY THOSE
WHO DO EVIL, BUT BY THOSE
WHO WATCH THEM WITHOUT
DOING ANYTHING. - ALBERT
EINSTEIN

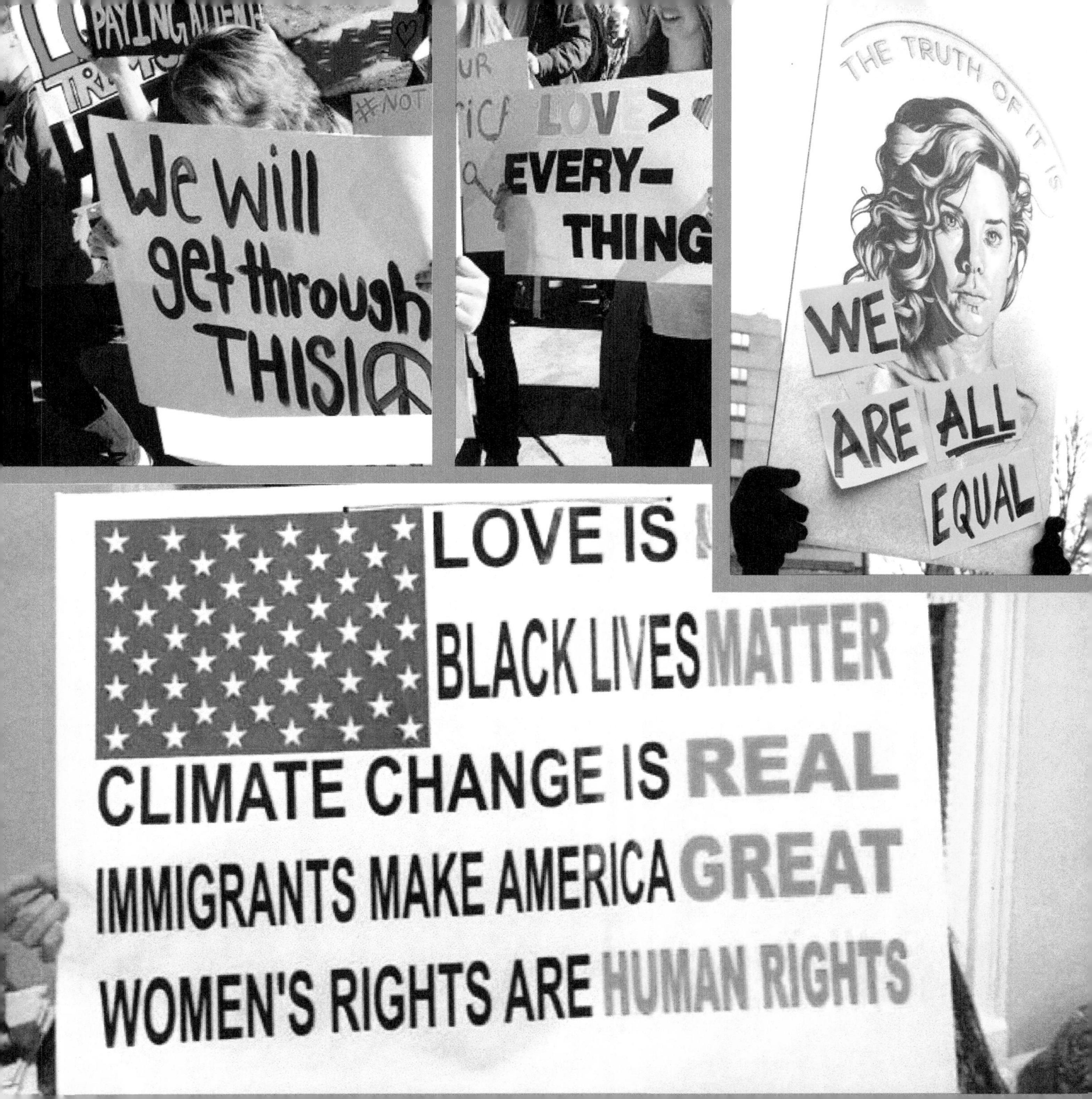
We will get through THIS!
EVERY-THING
THE TRUTH OF IT IS
WE ARE ALL EQUAL
LOVE IS
BLACK LIVES MATTER
CLIMATE CHANGE IS REAL
IMMIGRANTS MAKE AMERICA GREAT
WOMEN'S RIGHTS ARE HUMAN RIGHTS

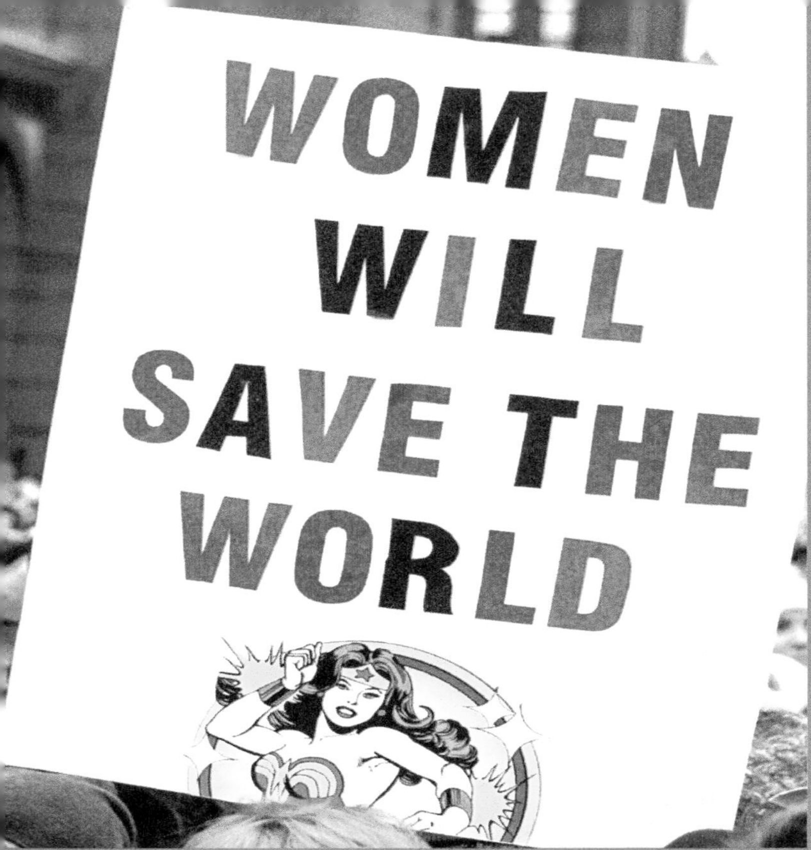
WOMEN
WILL
SAVE THE
WORLD

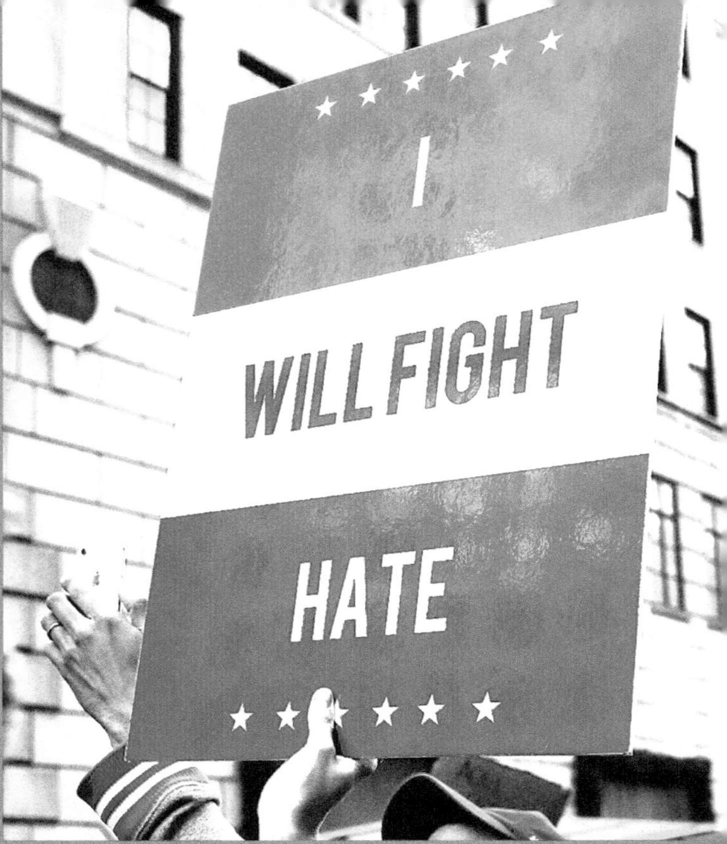
I
WILL FIGHT
HATE

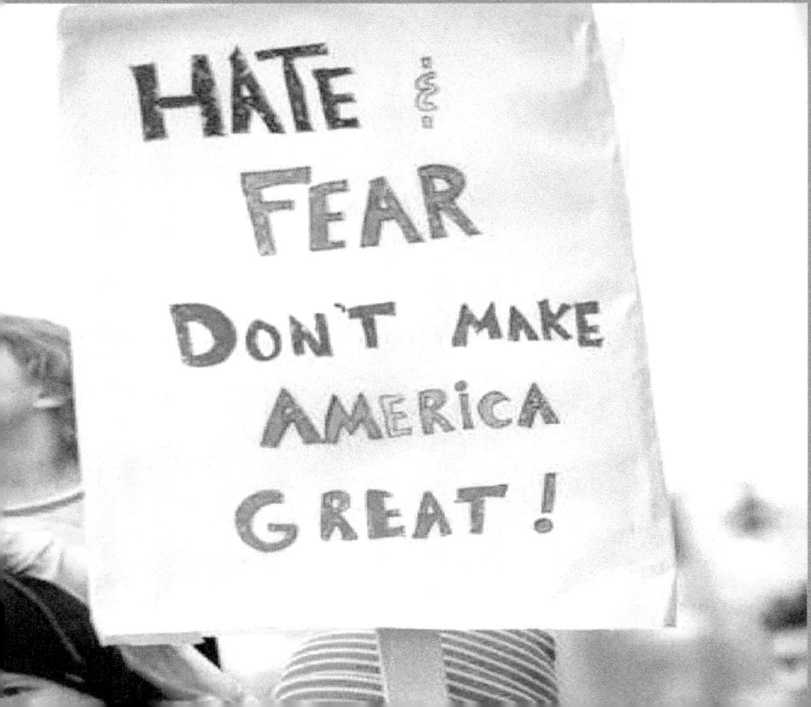
HATE &
FEAR
DON'T MAKE
AMERICA
GREAT!

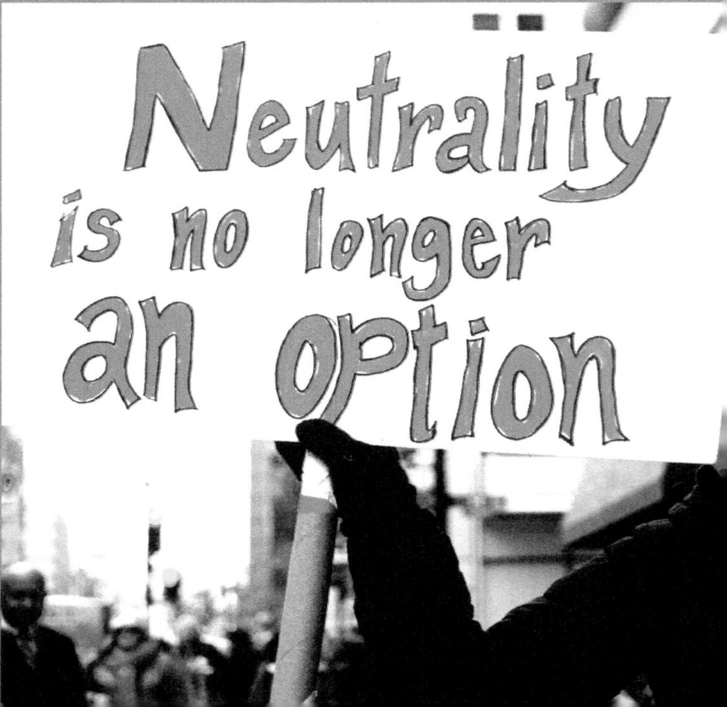
Neutrality
is no longer
an option

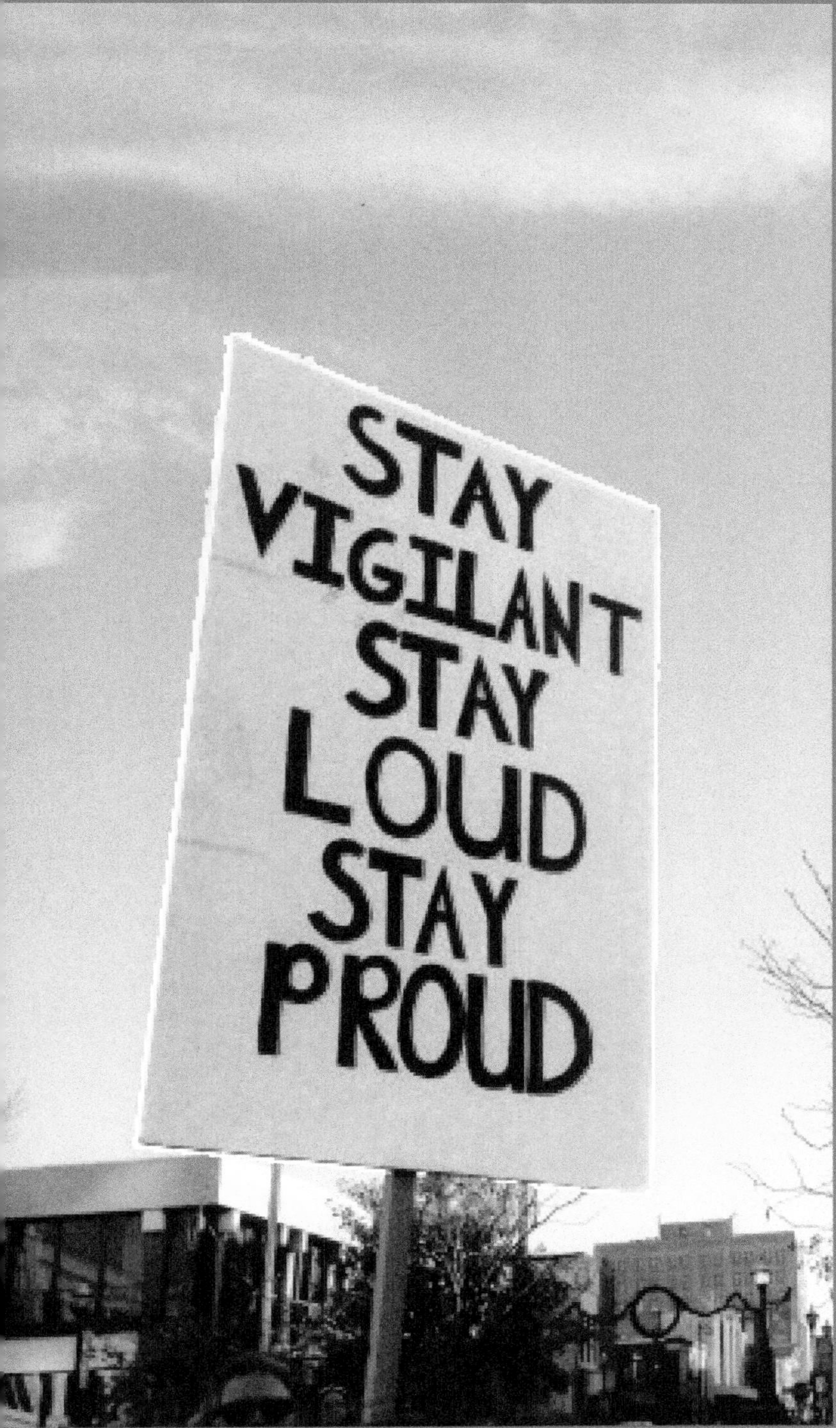
STAY
VIGILANT
STAY
LOUD
STAY
PROUD

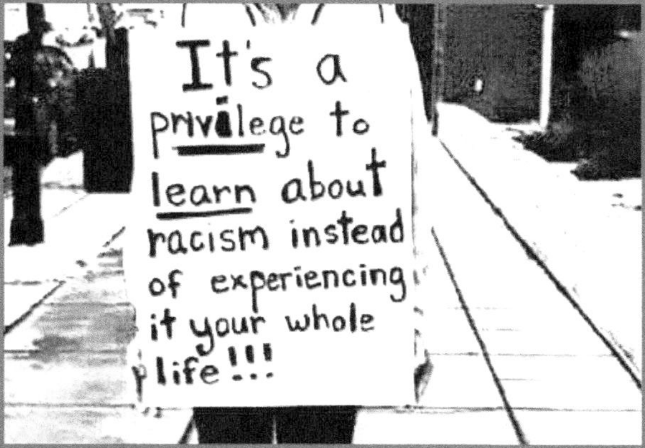
It's a privilege to learn about racism instead of experiencing it your whole life!!!

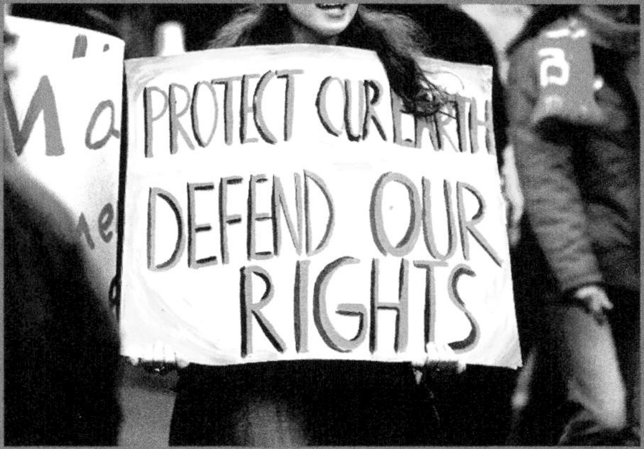
PROTECT OUR EARTH
DEFEND OUR RIGHTS

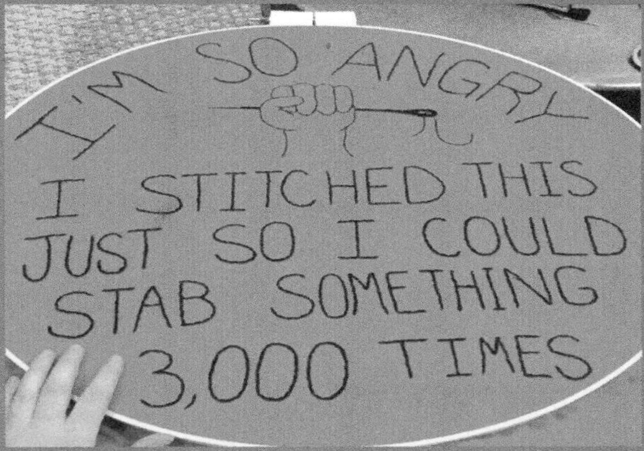
I'M SO ANGRY
I STITCHED THIS JUST SO I COULD STAB SOMETHING 3,000 TIMES

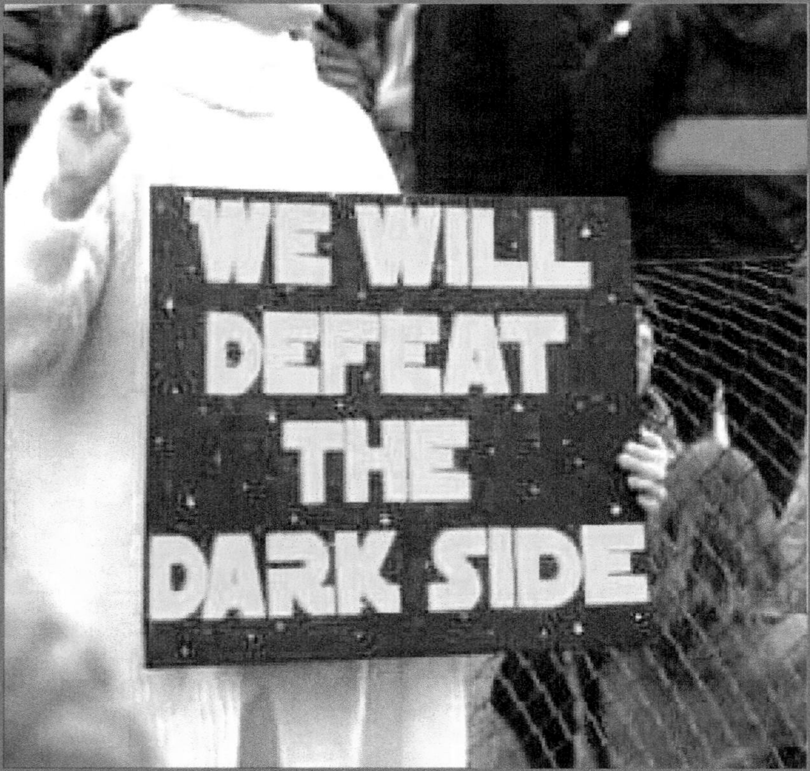
WE WILL
DEFEAT
THE
DARK SIDE

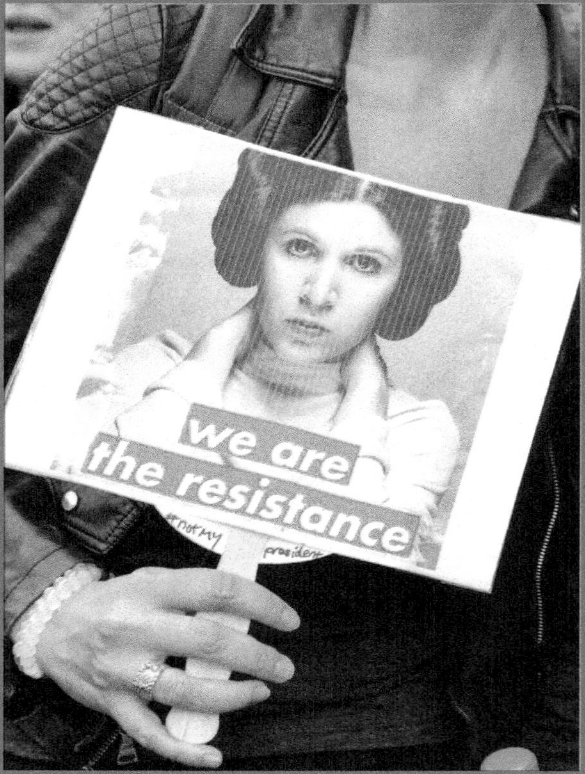
we are
the resistance

You may say that
I'm a DREAMER
But I'm not the
only one...
LOVE IS THE ANSWER

INJUSTICE
ANYWHERE IS A
THREAT TO
JUSTICE EVERYWHERE

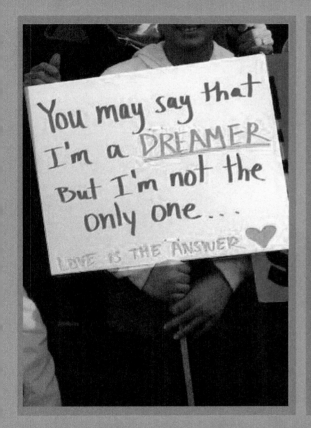

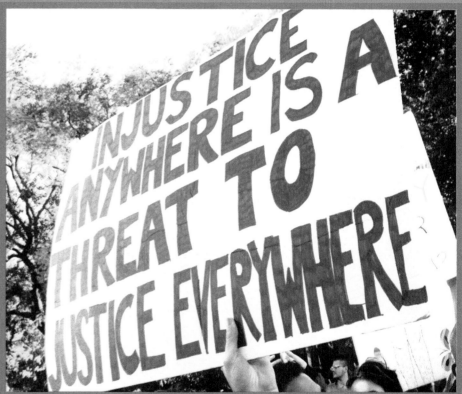

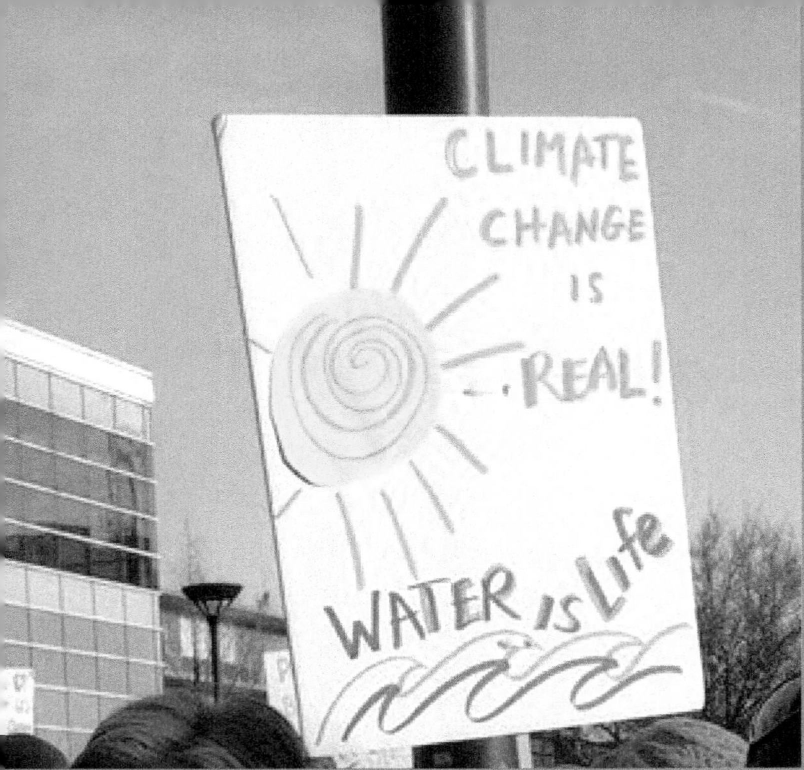
CLIMATE CHANGE IS REAL!
WATER IS LIFE

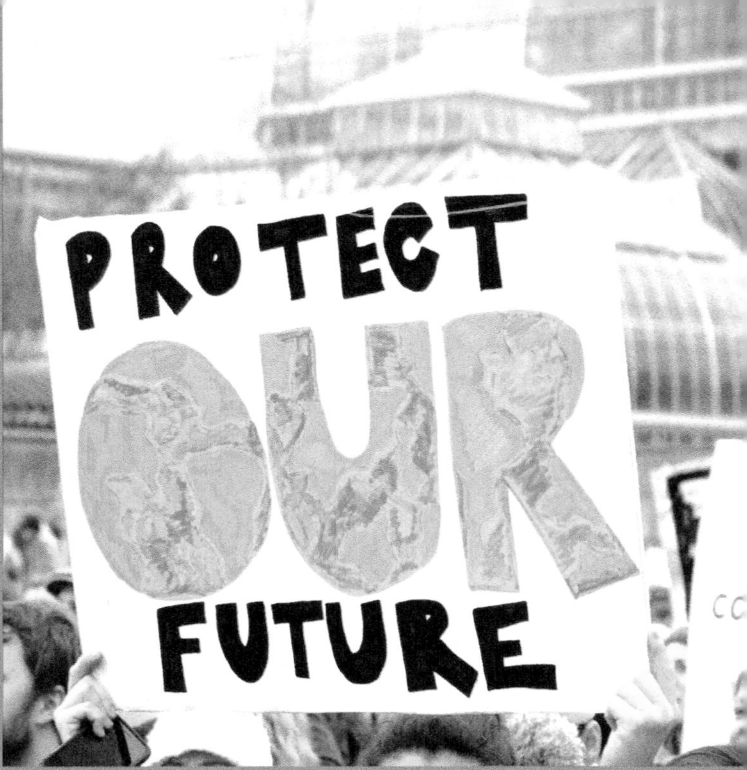
PROTECT OUR FUTURE

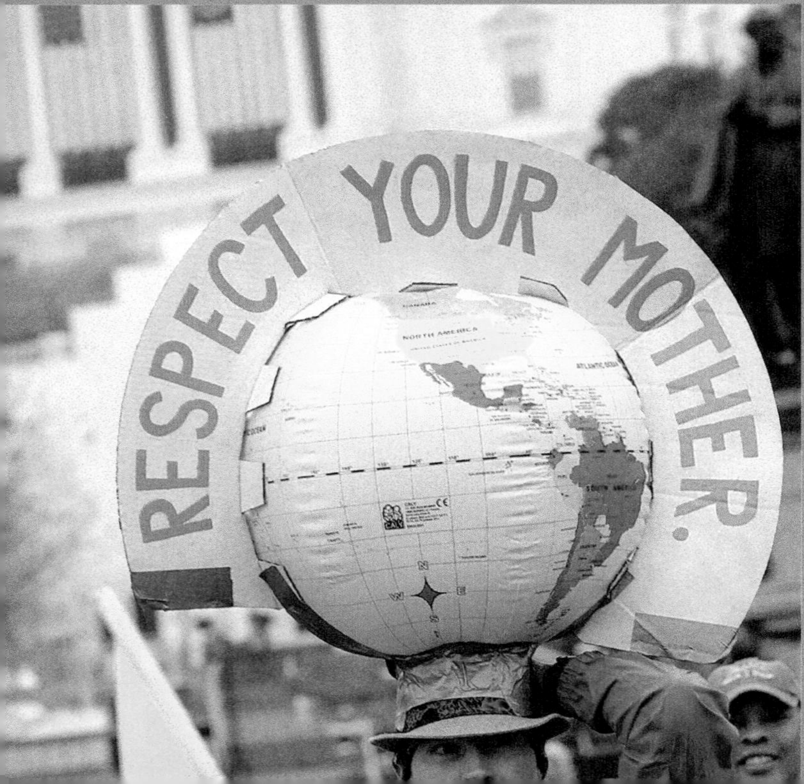
RESPECT YOUR MOTHER.

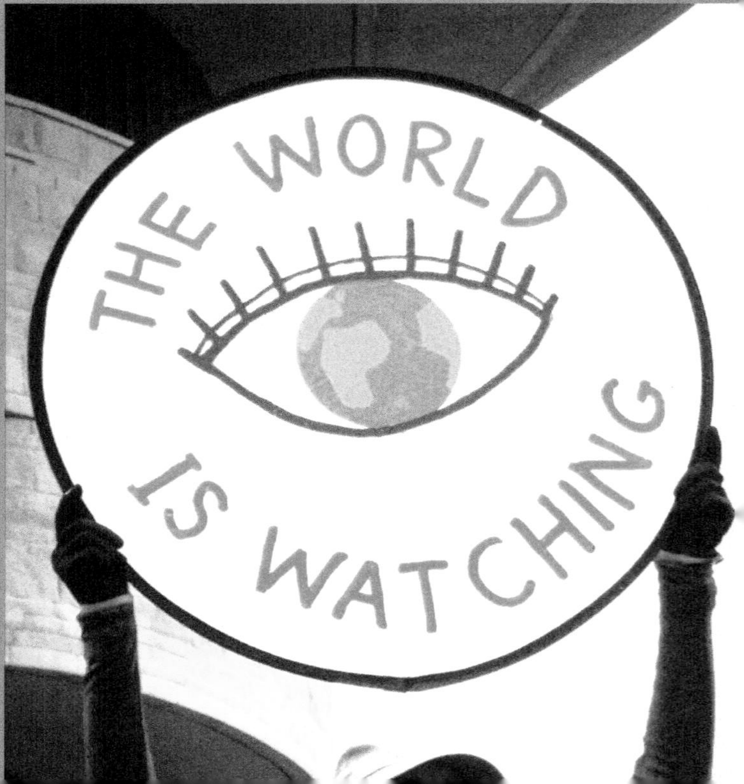
THE WORLD IS WATCHING

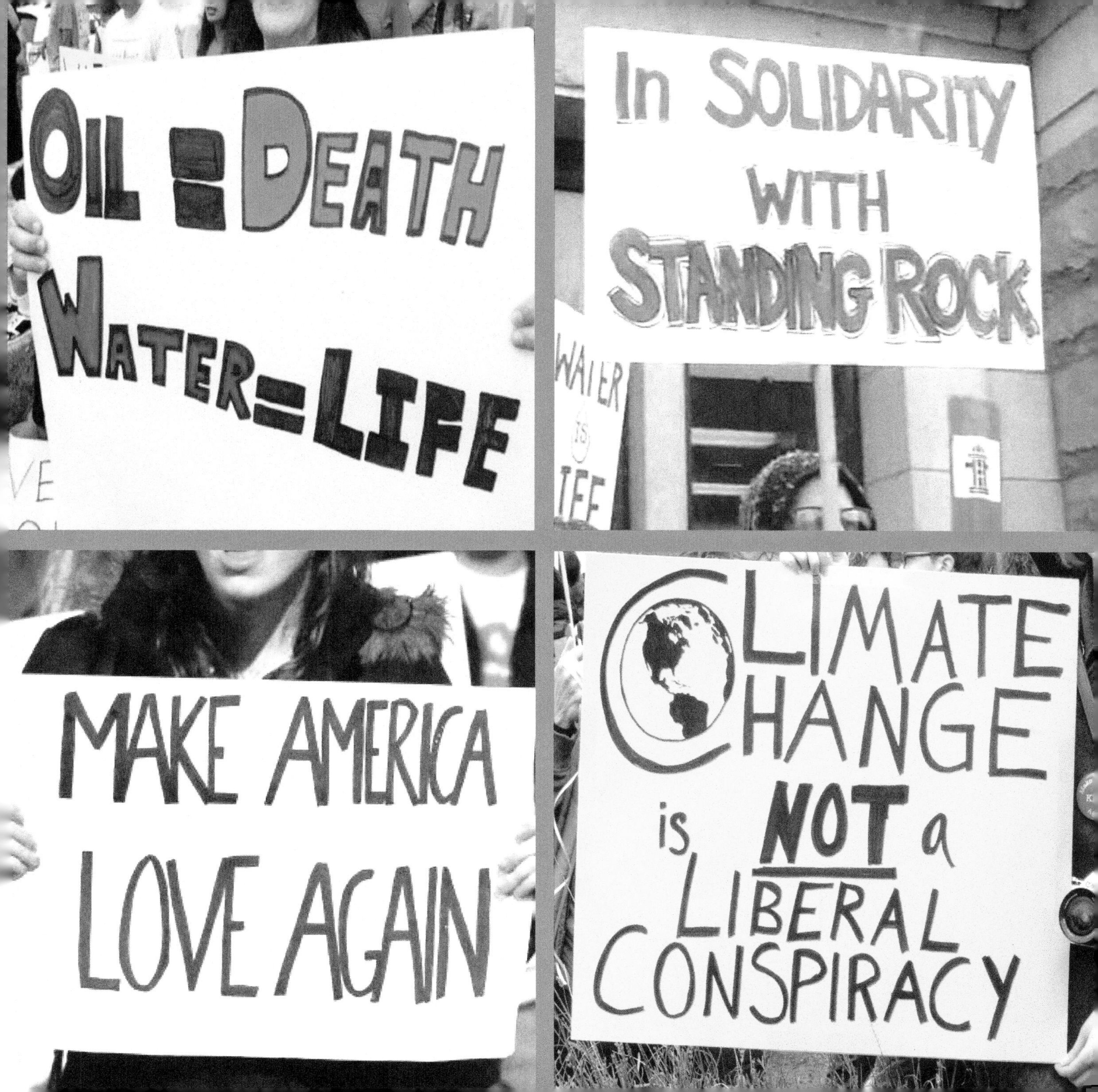
OIL = DEATH
WATER = LIFE
In SOLIDARITY
WITH
STANDING ROCK
MAKE AMERICA
LOVE AGAIN
CLIMATE
CHANGE
is NOT a
LIBERAL
CONSPIRACY

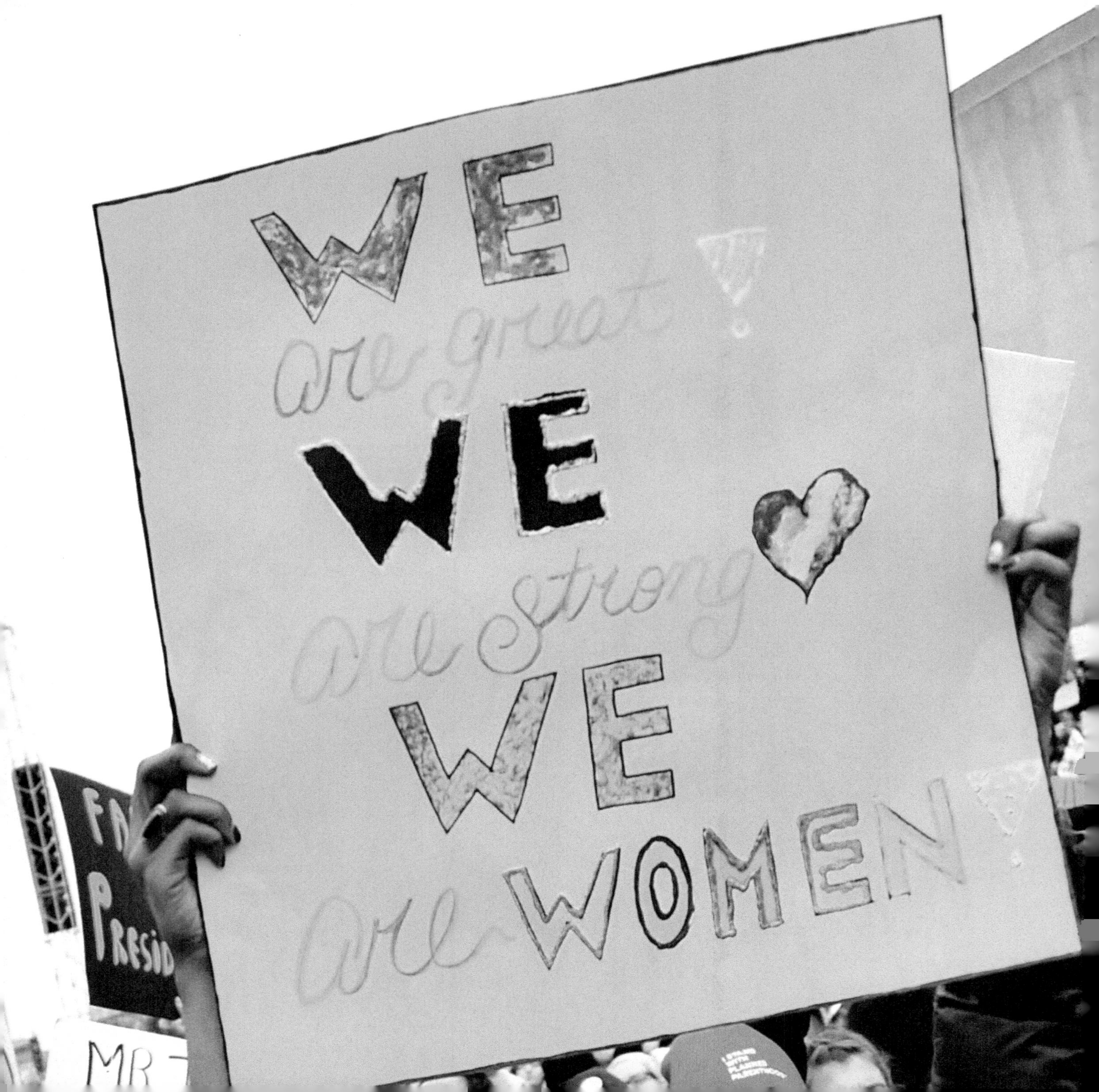
WE
are great!
WE
are strong
WE
are WOMEN!

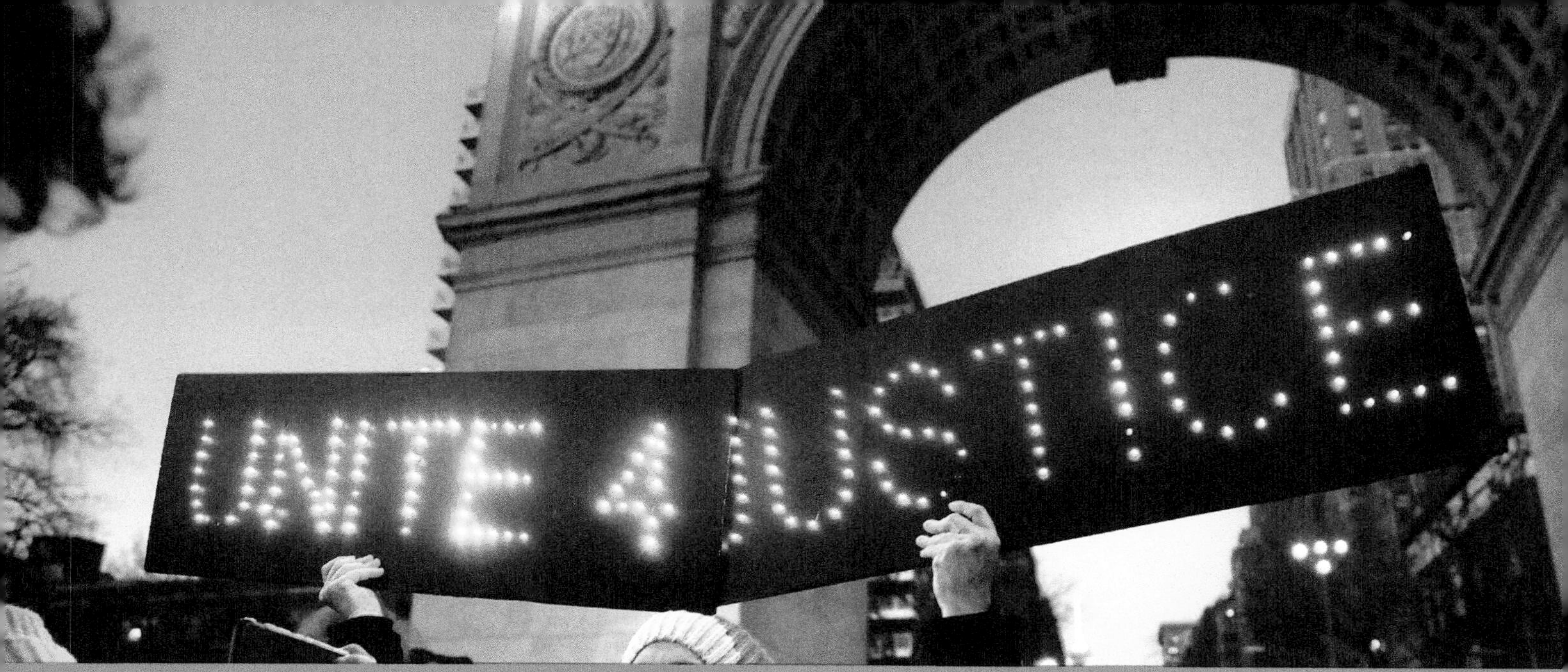
UNITE 4 JUSTICE

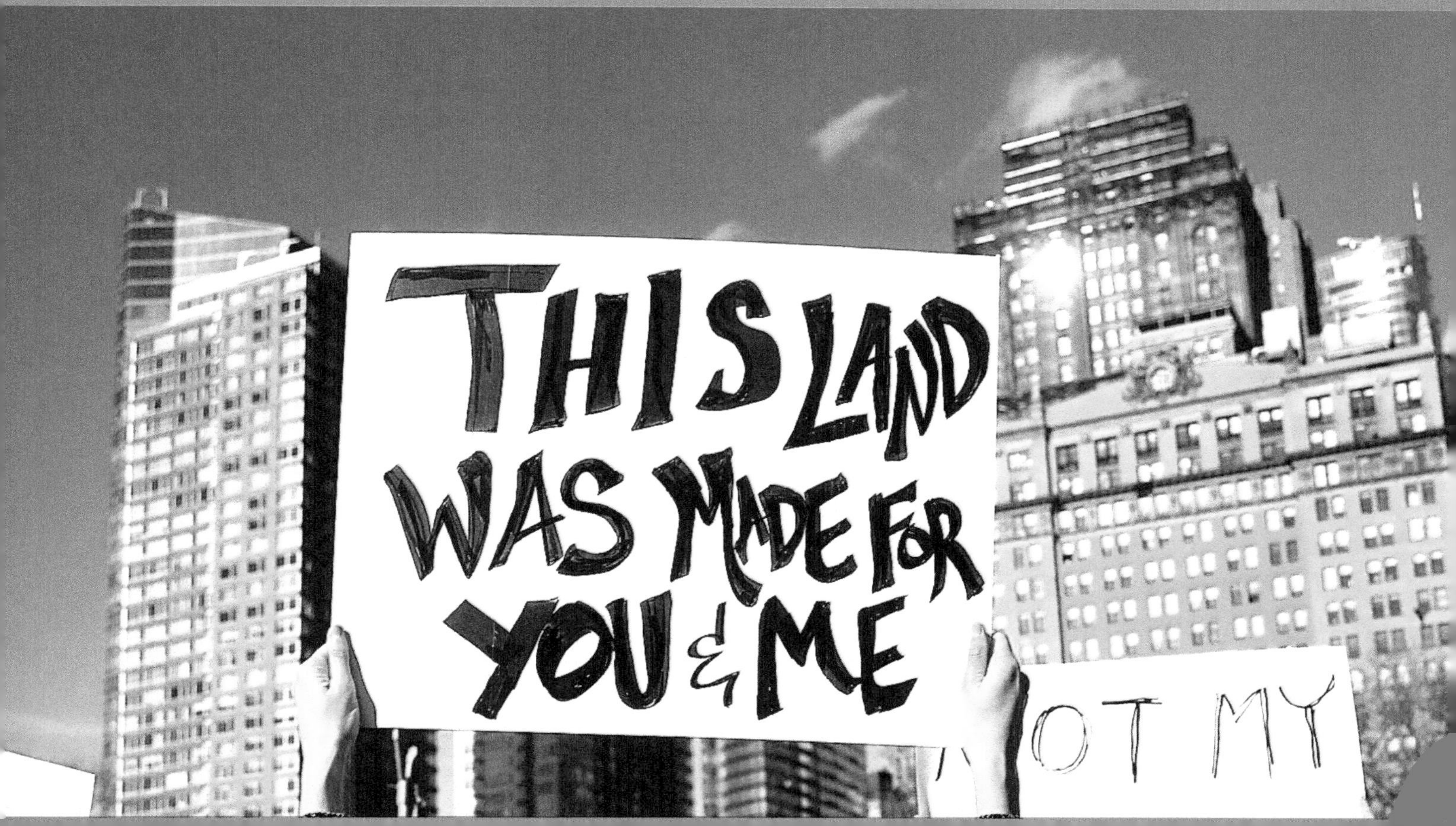
THIS LAND
WAS MADE FOR
YOU & ME
OT MY

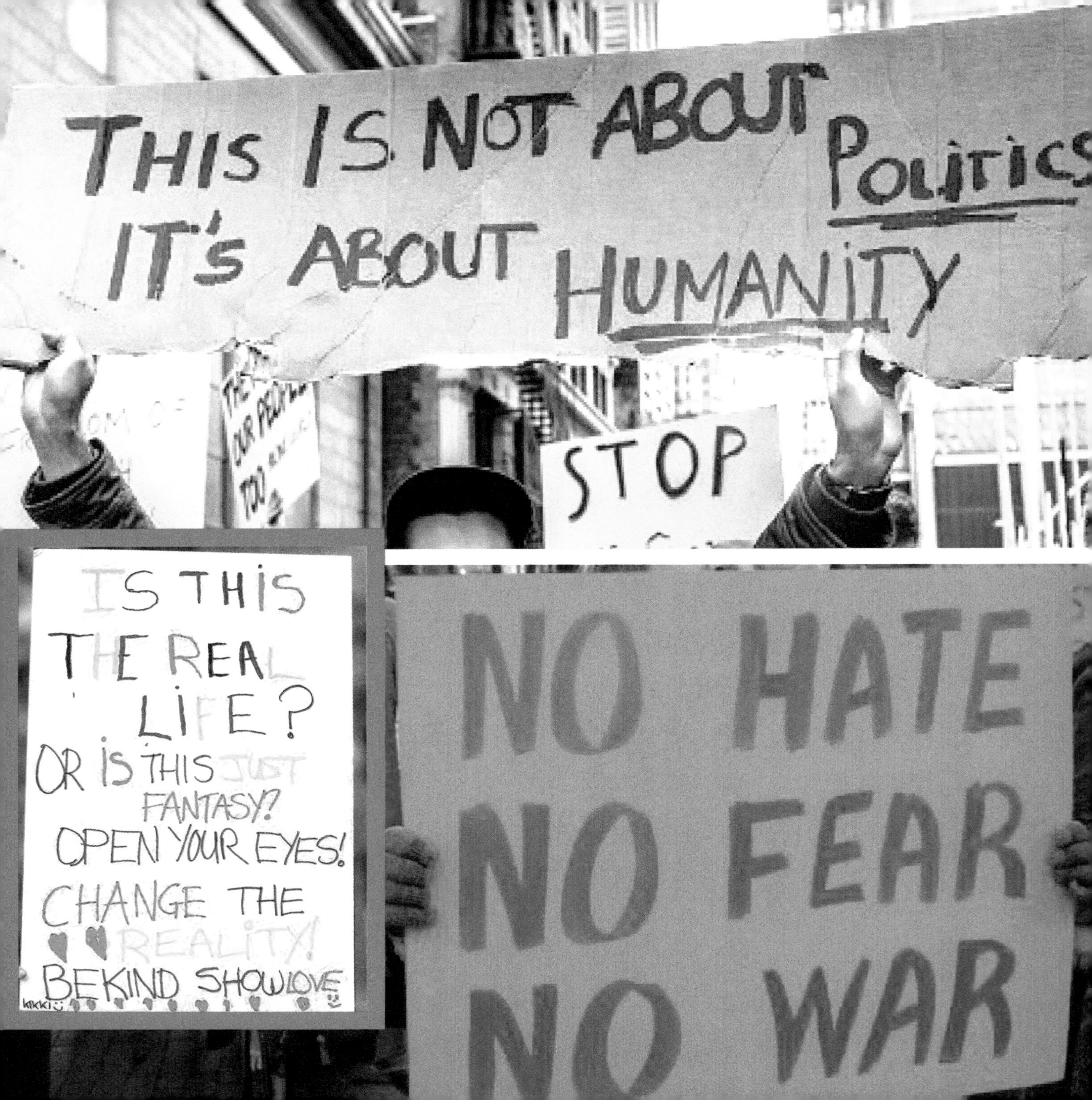
THIS IS NOT ABOUT POLITICS
IT'S ABOUT HUMANITY
STOP
IS THIS THE REAL LIFE? OR IS THIS JUST FANTASY?
OPEN YOUR EYES!
CHANGE THE REALITY!
BE KIND SHOW LOVE
NO HATE
NO FEAR
NO WAR

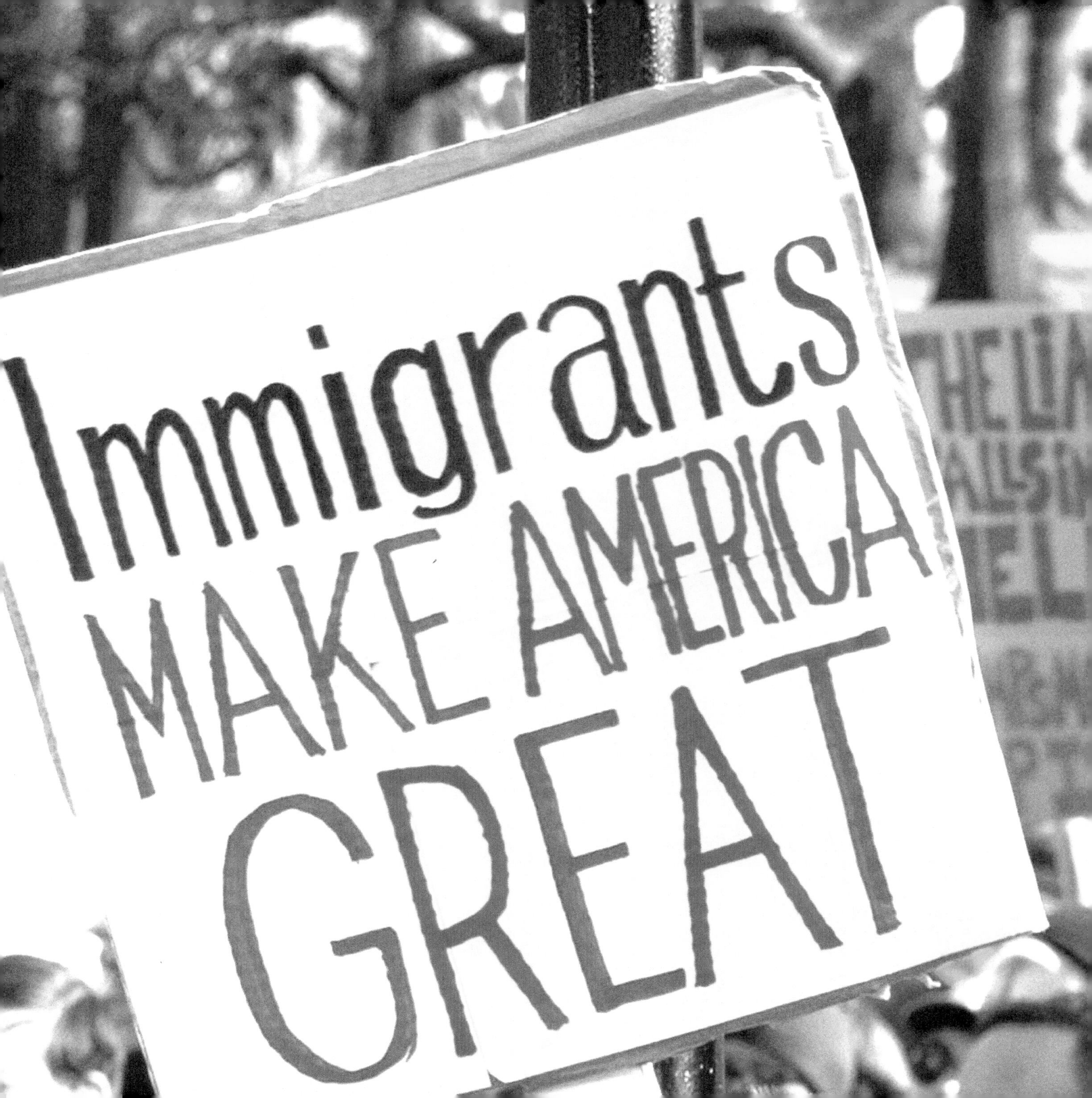
Immigrants
MAKE AMERICA
GREAT

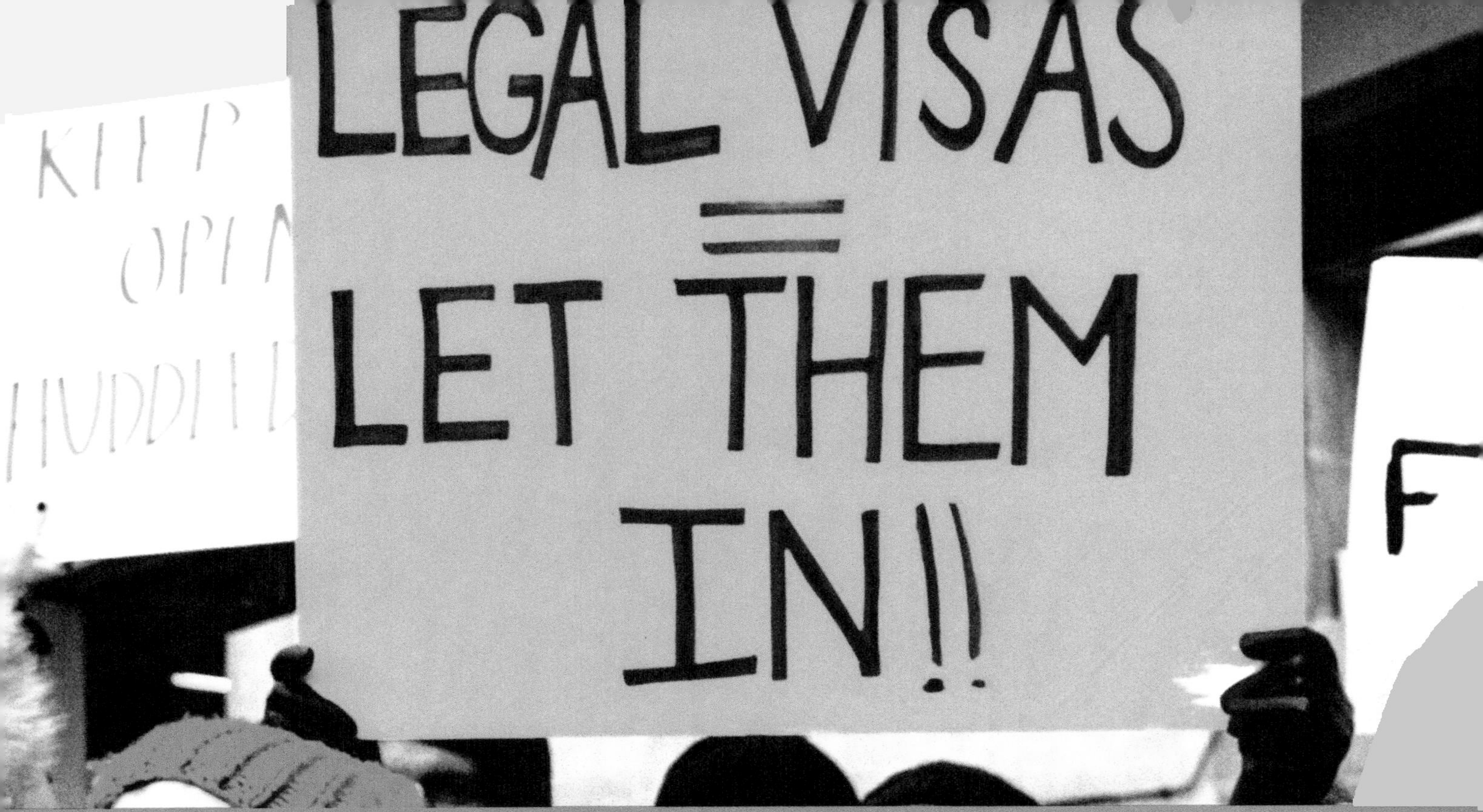
LEGAL VISAS
=
LET THEM
IN!!

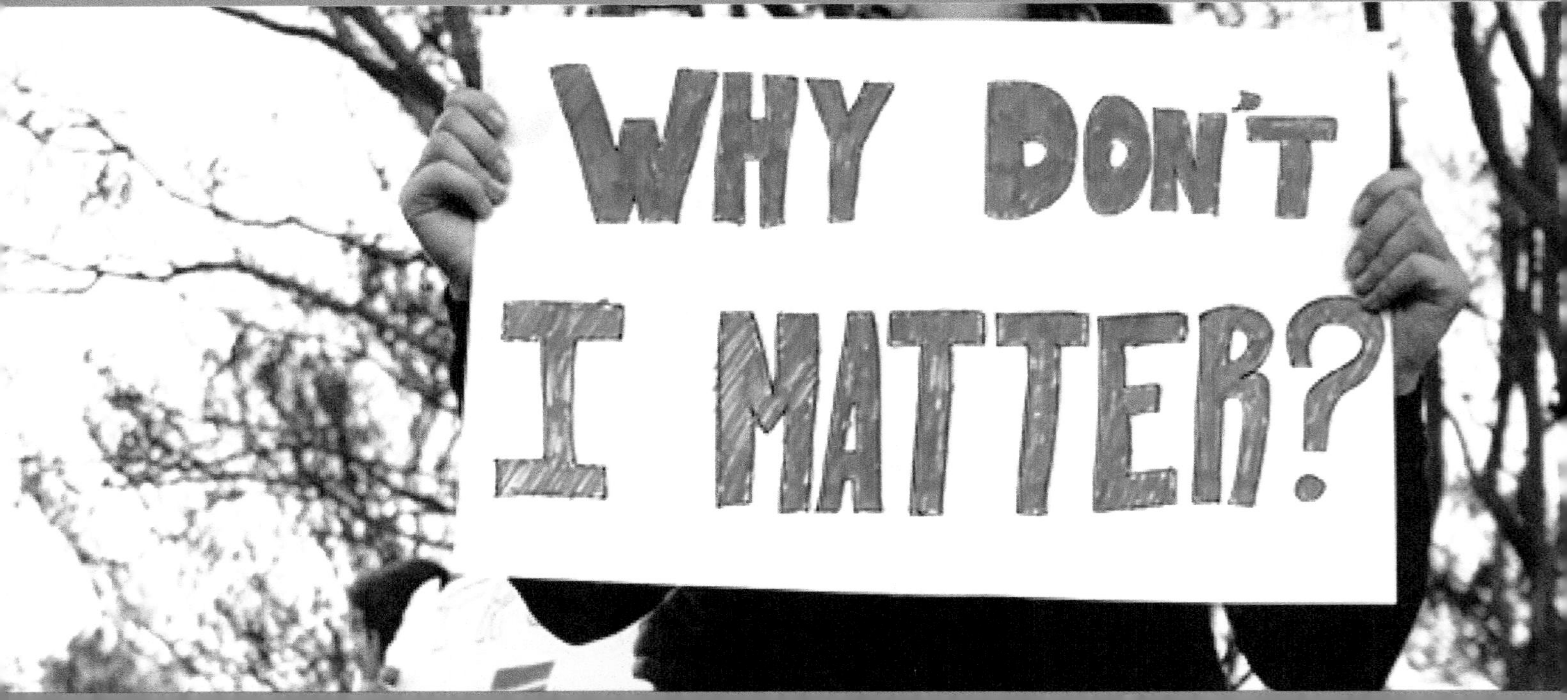
WHY DON'T
I MATTER?

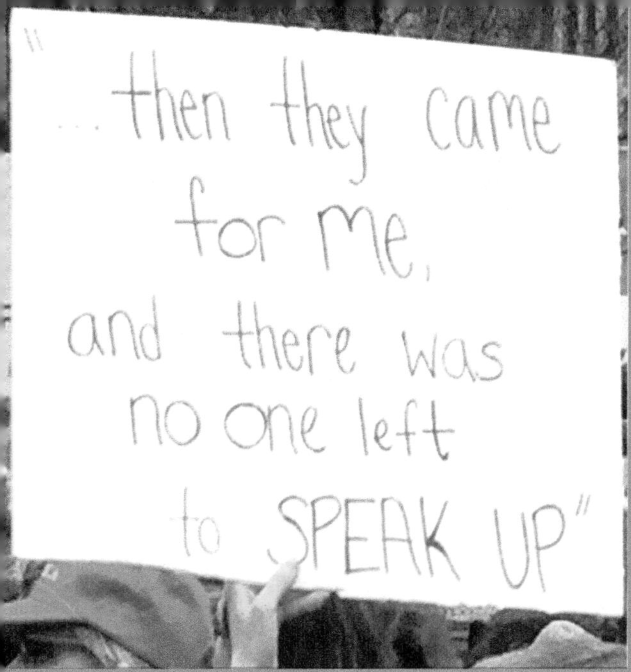
"...then they came
for me,
and there was
no one left
to SPEAK UP"

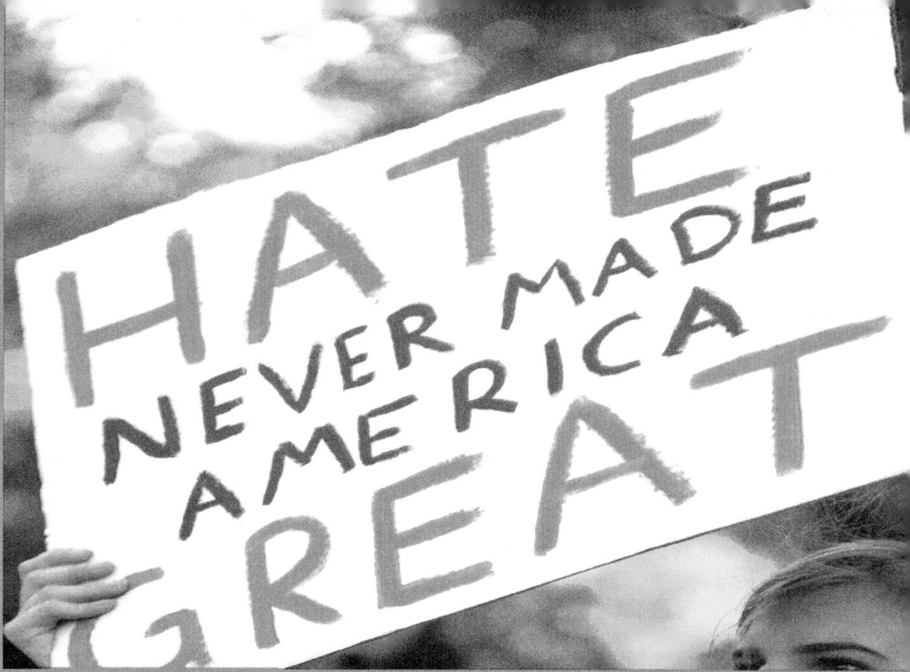
HATE
NEVER MADE
AMERICA
GREAT

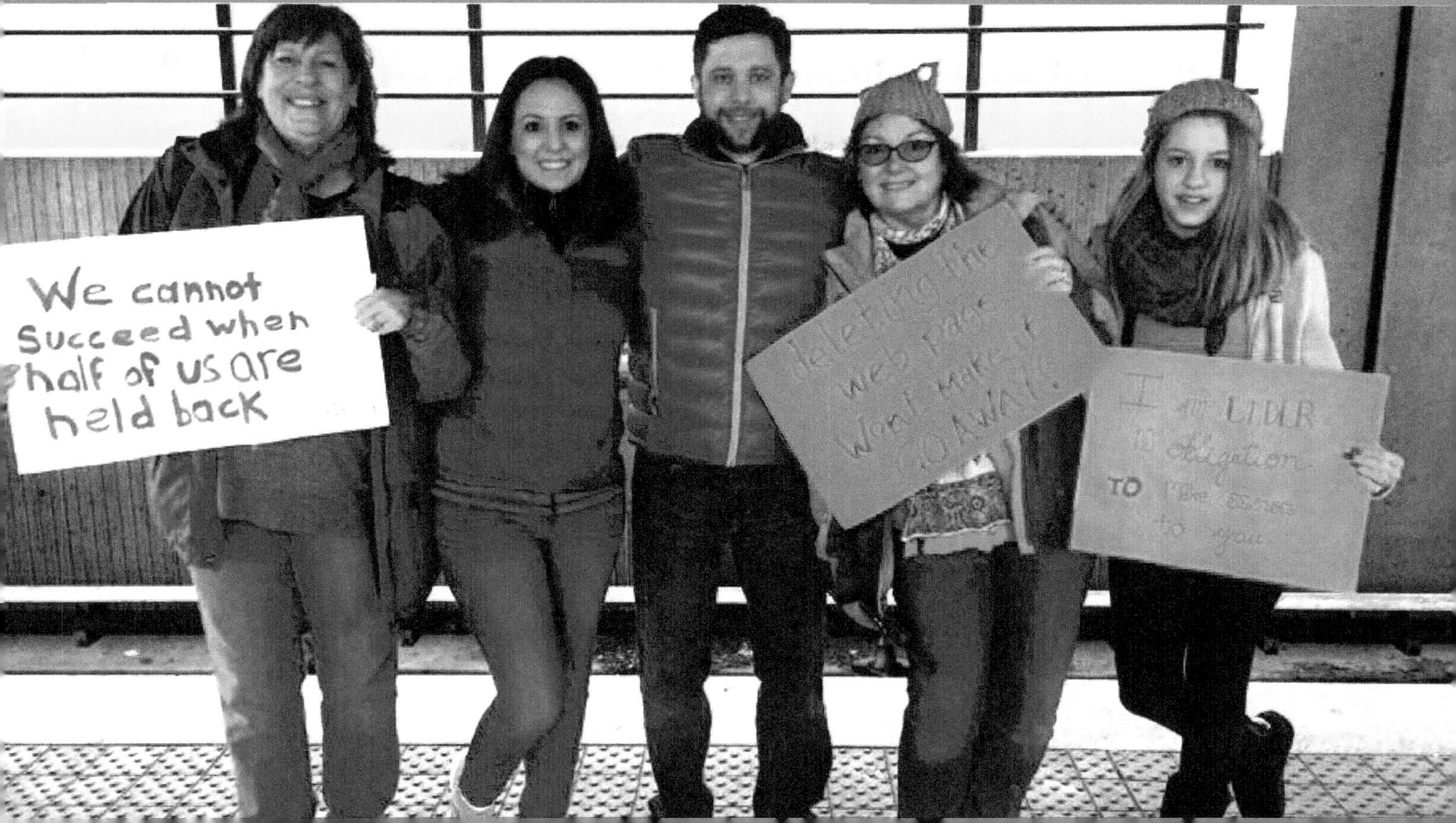
We cannot
succeed when
half of us are
held back
deleting the
web page
won't make it
go away!

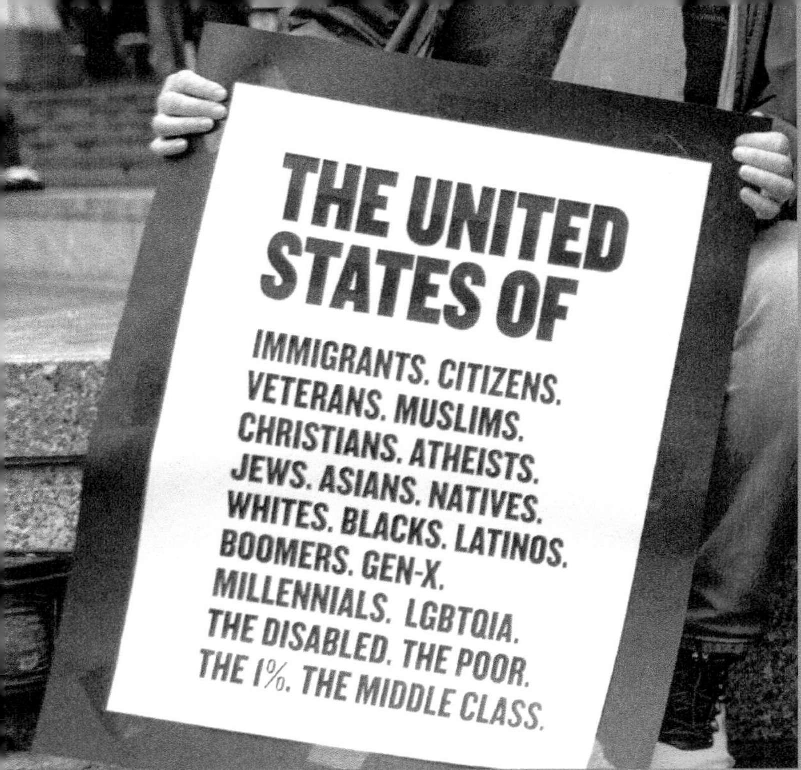
THE UNITED
STATES OF
IMMIGRANTS. CITIZENS.
VETERANS. MUSLIMS.
CHRISTIANS. ATHEISTS.
JEWS. ASIANS. NATIVES.
WHITES. BLACKS. LATINOS.
BOOMERS. GEN-X.
MILLENNIALS. LGBTQIA.
THE DISABLED. THE POOR.
THE 1%. THE MIDDLE CLASS.

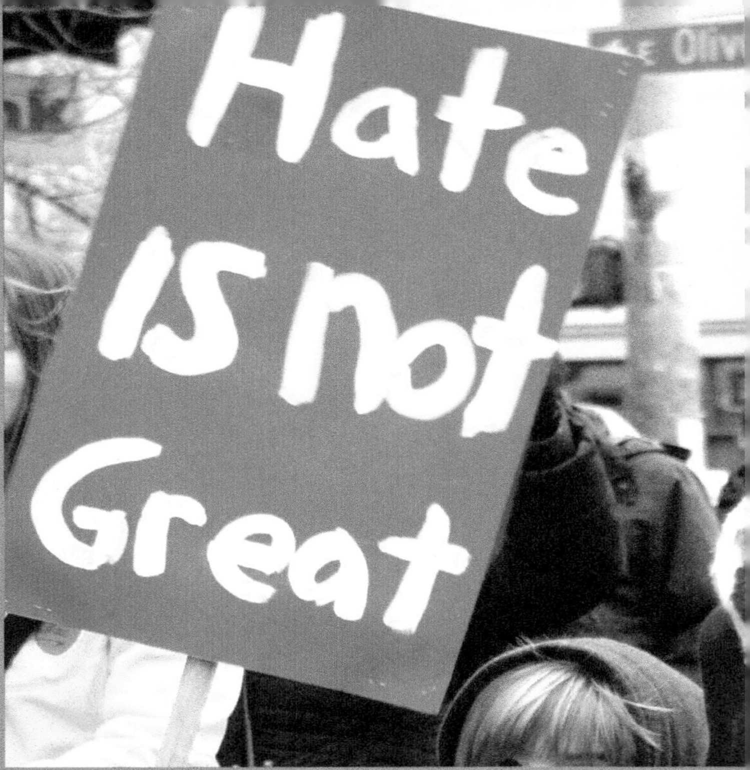
Hate
is not
Great

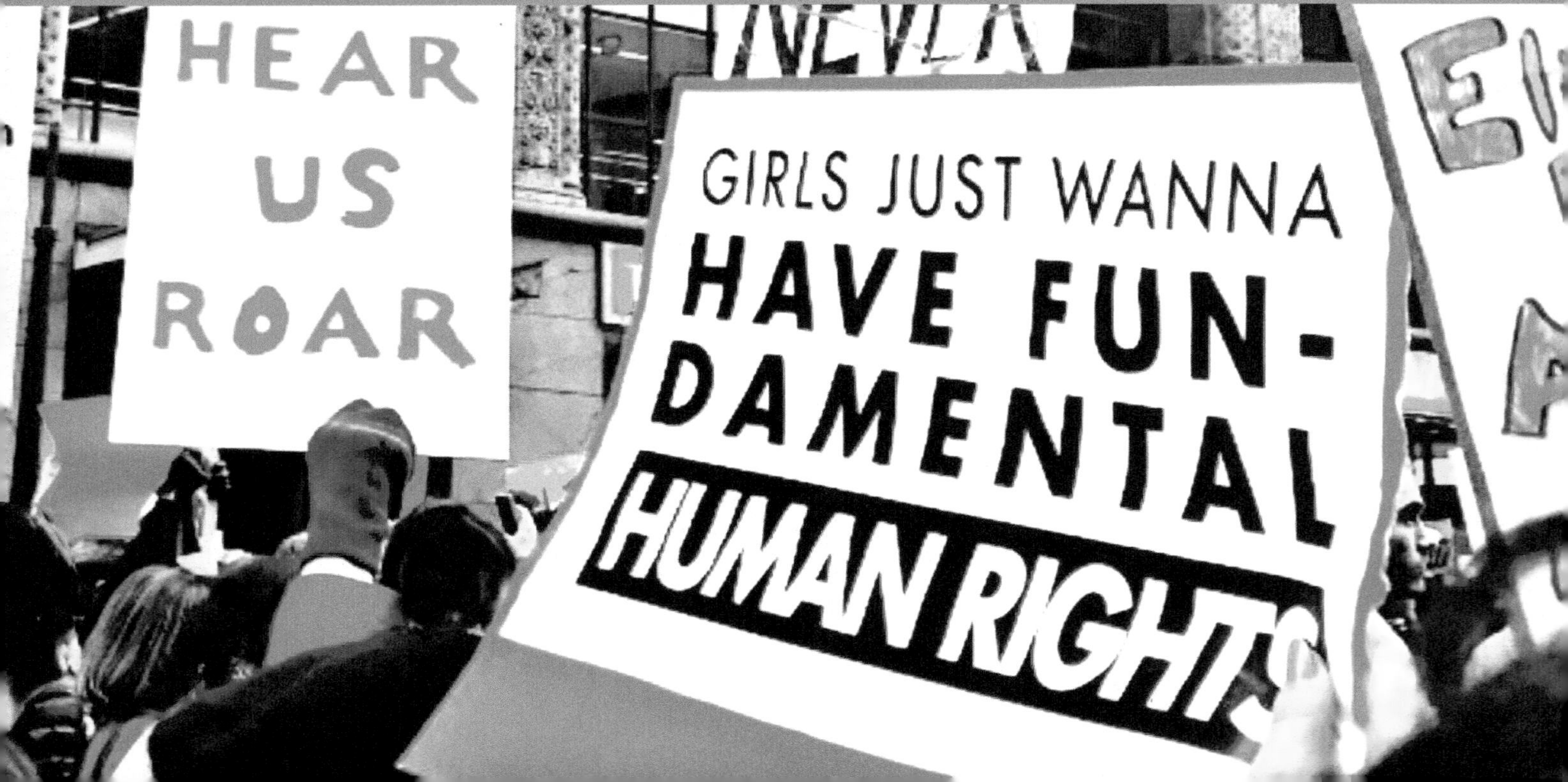
HEAR
US
ROAR
GIRLS JUST WANNA
HAVE FUN-
DAMENTAL
HUMAN RIGHTS

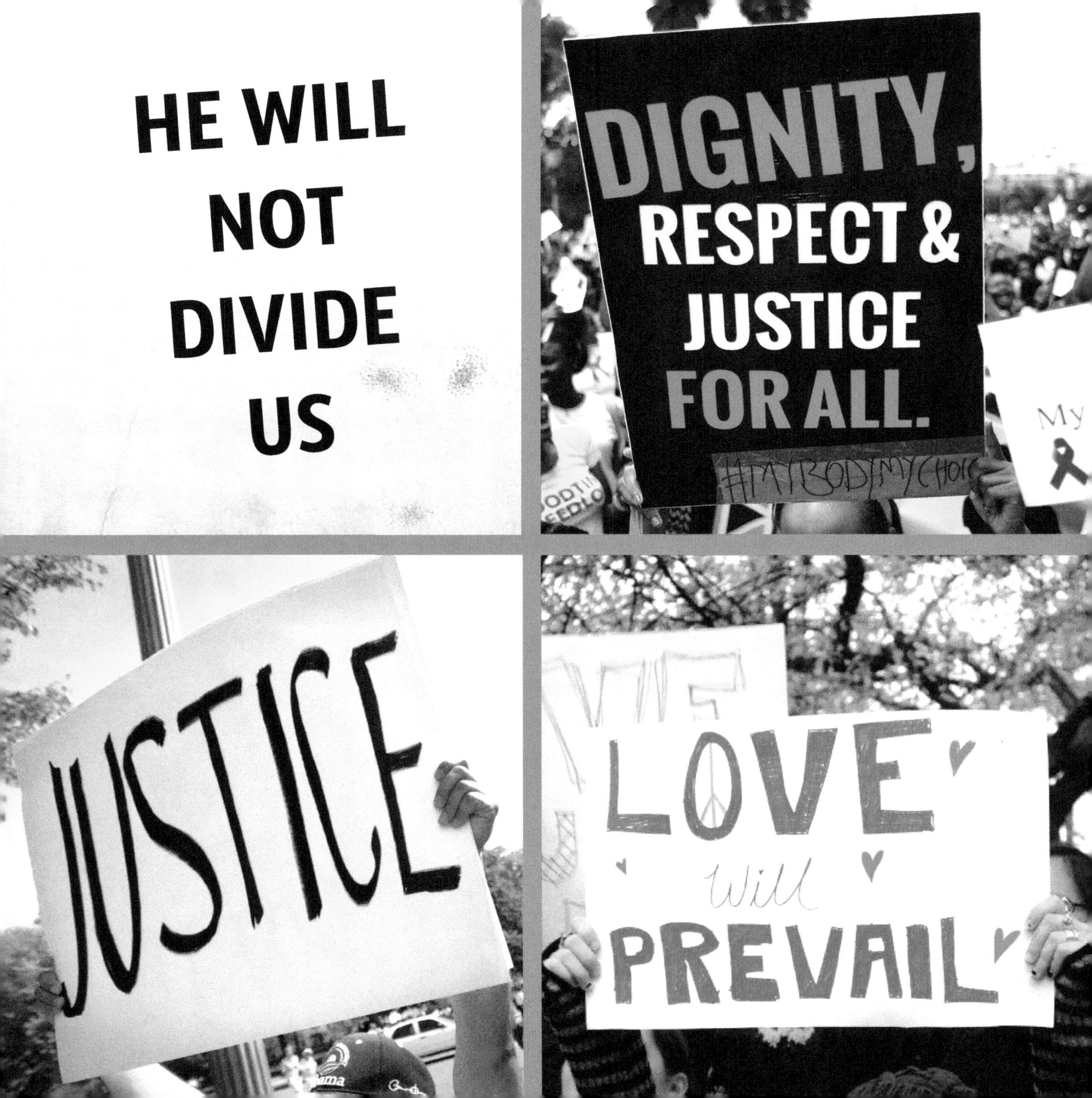
HE WILL NOT DIVIDE US
DIGNITY, RESPECT & JUSTICE FOR ALL.
My
JUSTICE
LOVE will PREVAIL

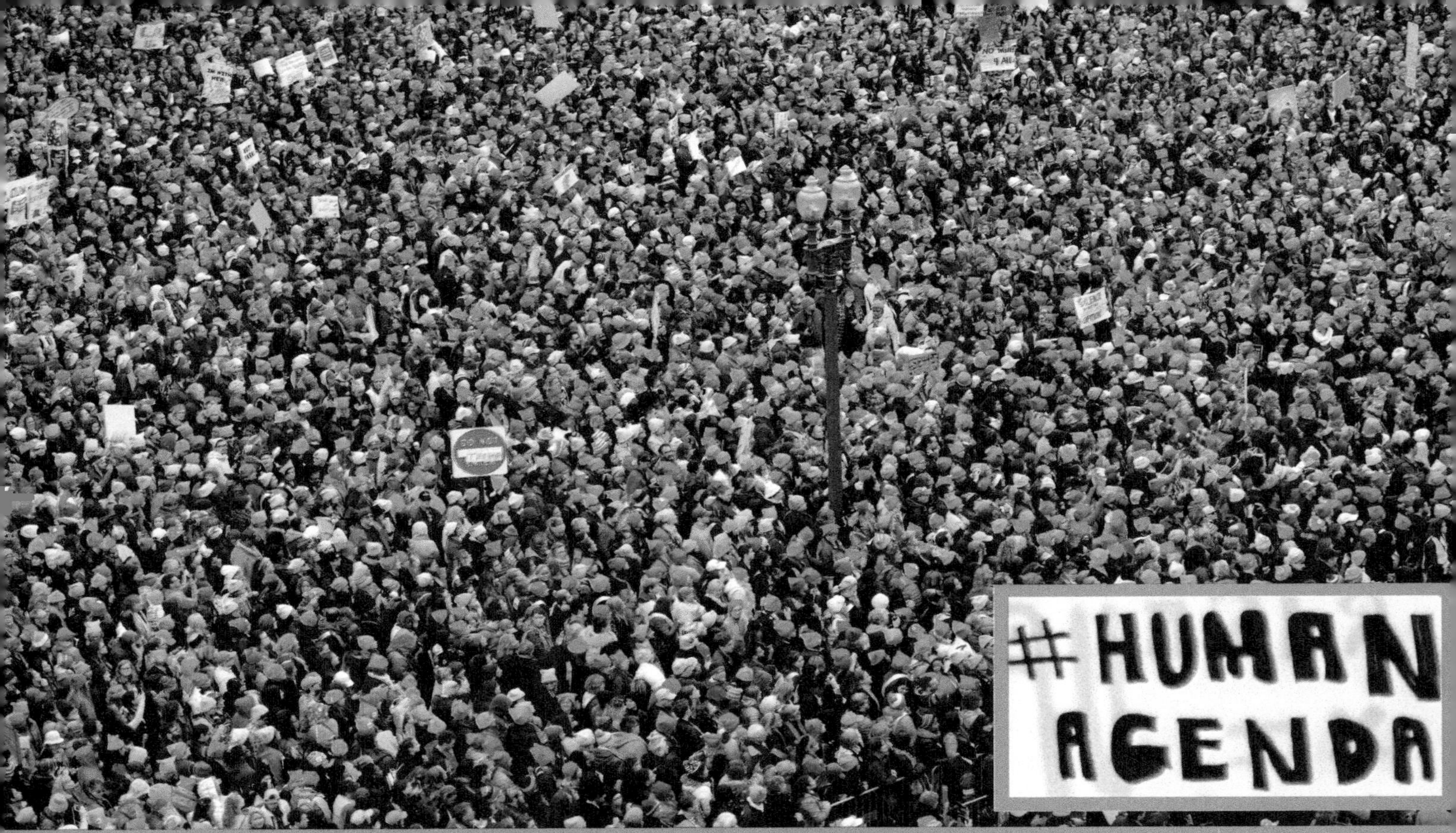
#HUMAN
AGENDA

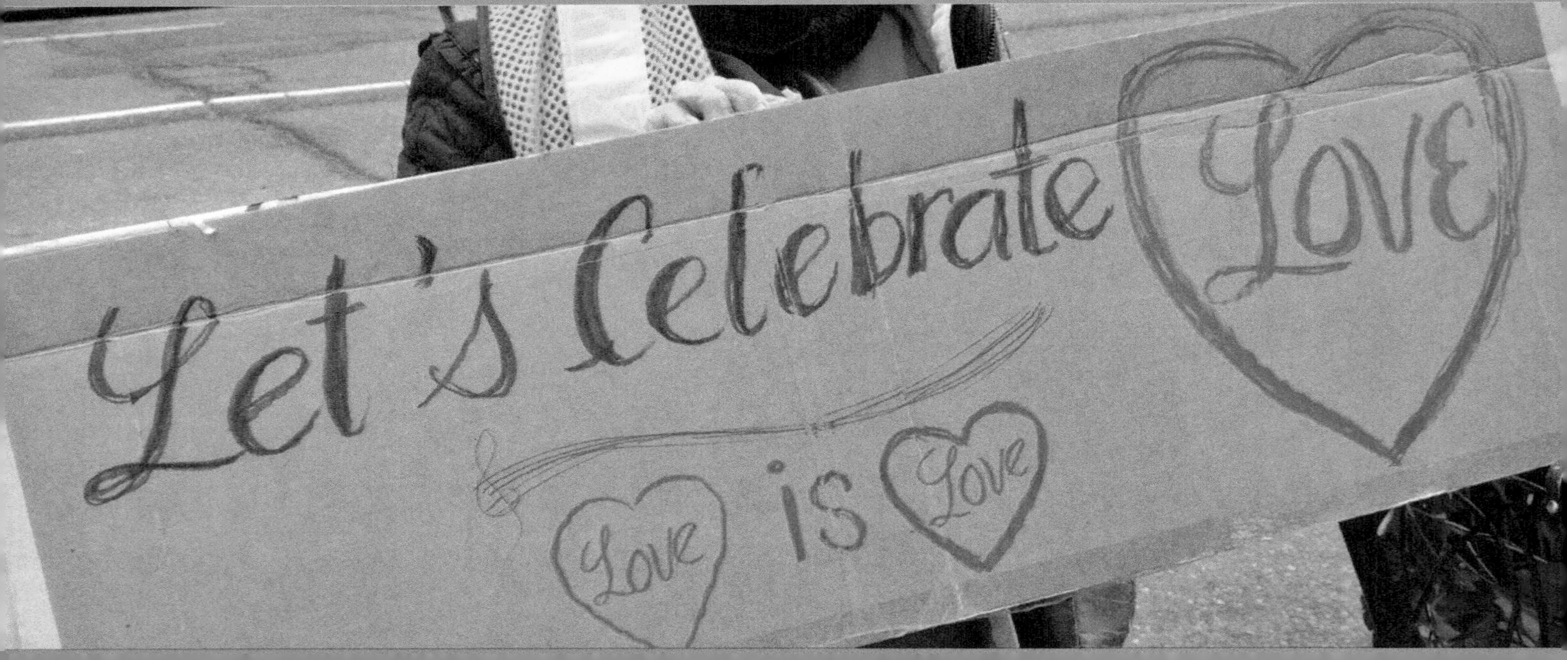
Let's Celebrate Love
Love is Love

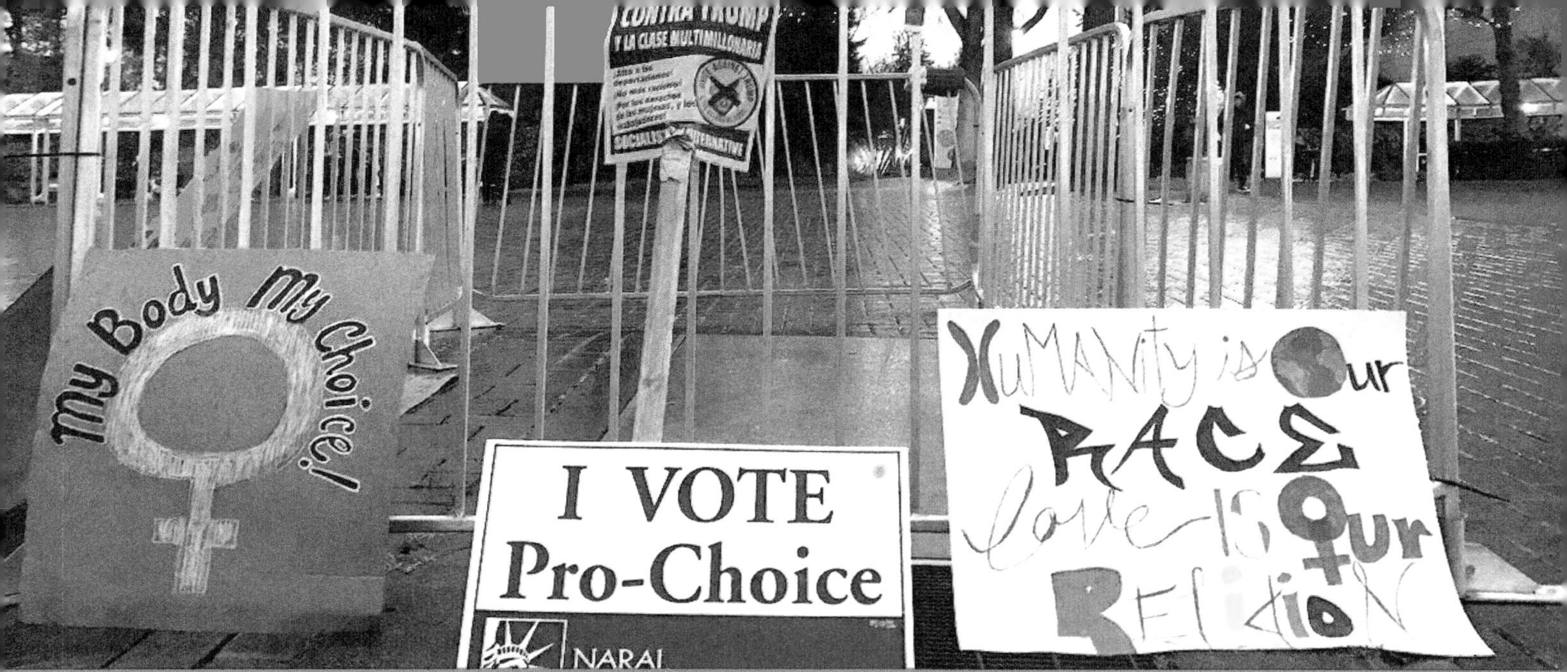
CONTRA TRUMP
Y LA CLASE MULTIMILLONARIA
My Body My Choice!
I VOTE
Pro-Choice
NARAL
HUMANITY is Our
RACE
love IS Our

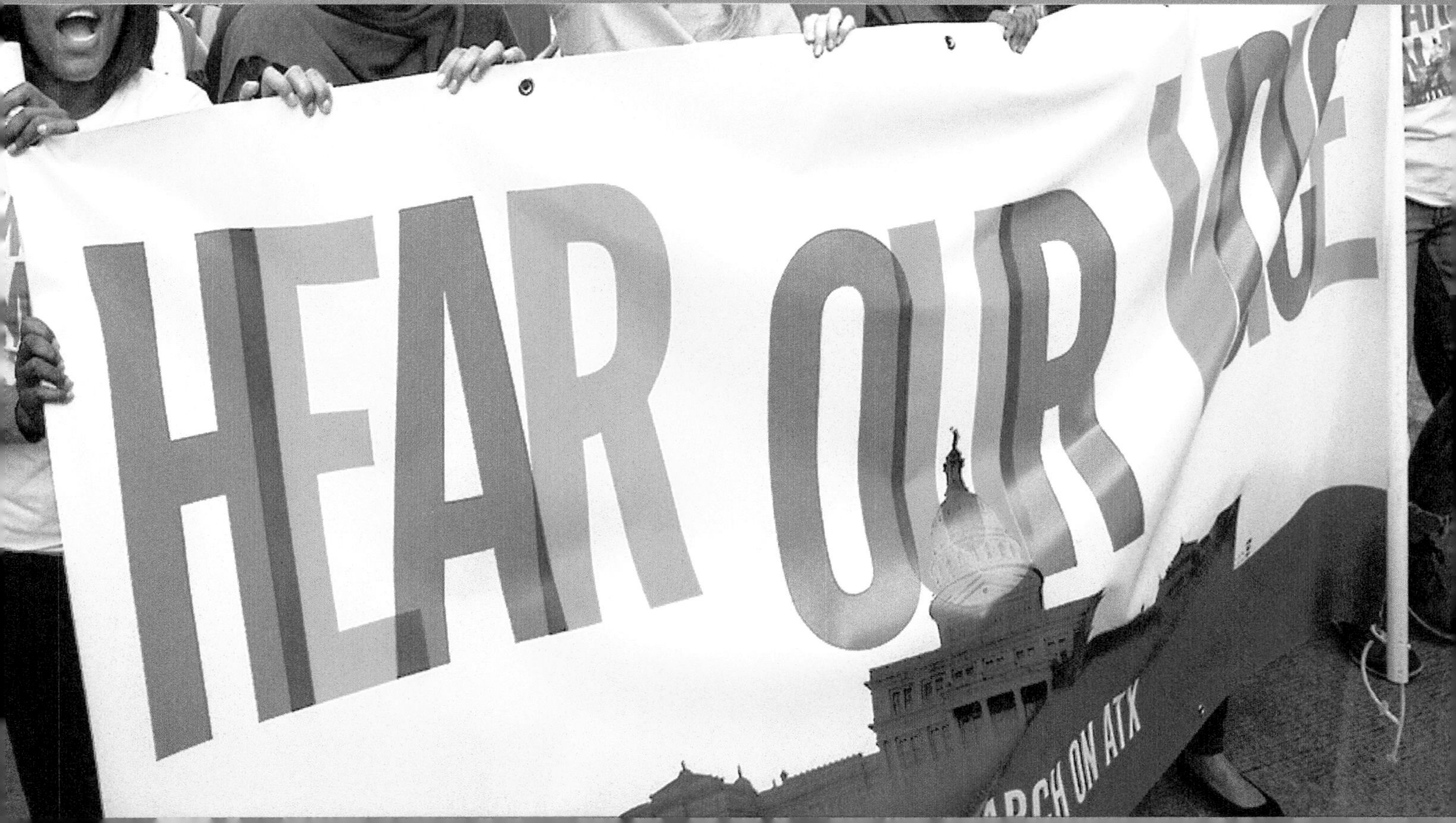
HEAR OUR

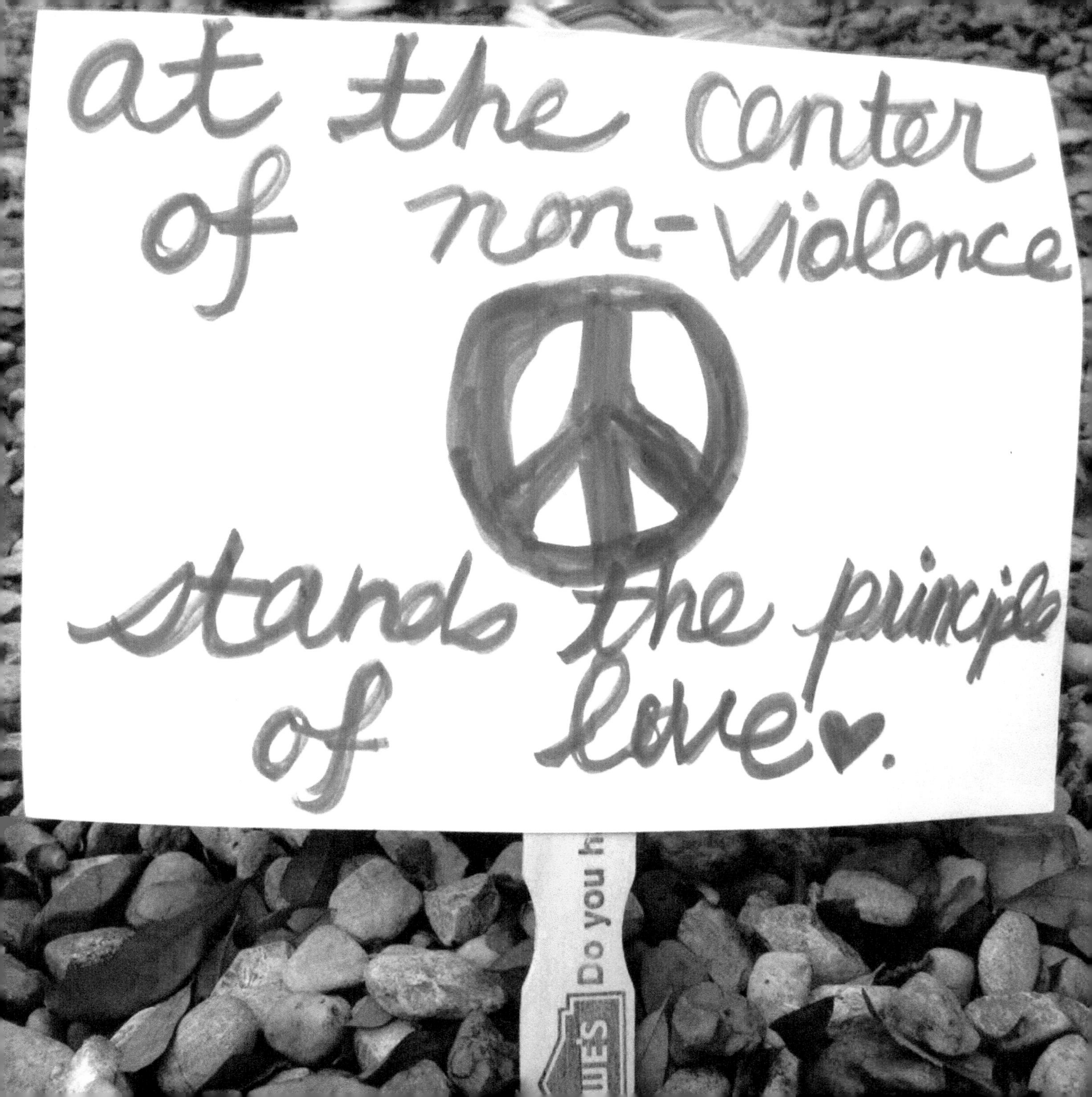
at the center
of non-violence
stands the principle
of love.

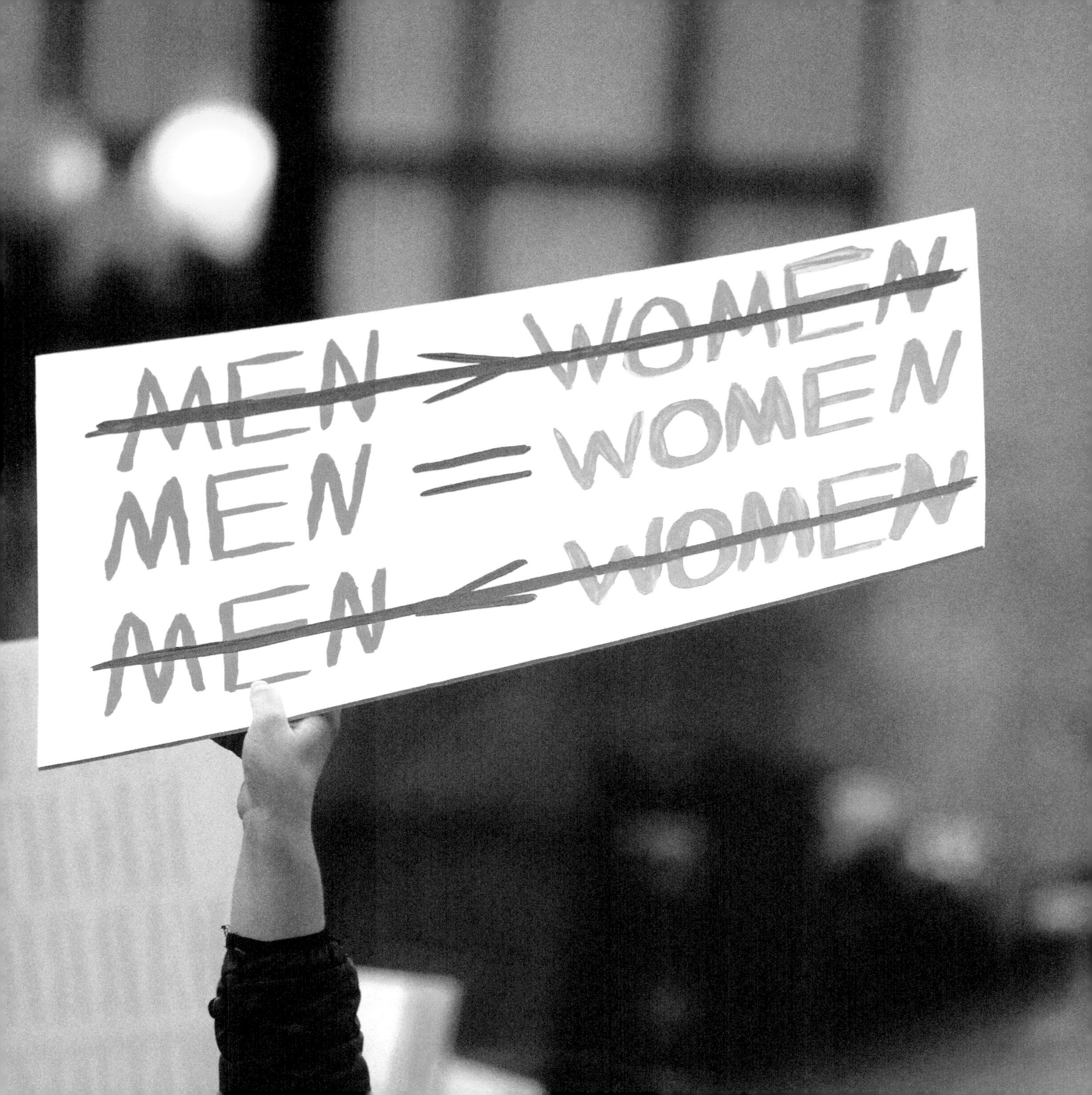
MEN > WOMEN
MEN = WOMEN
MEN < WOMEN

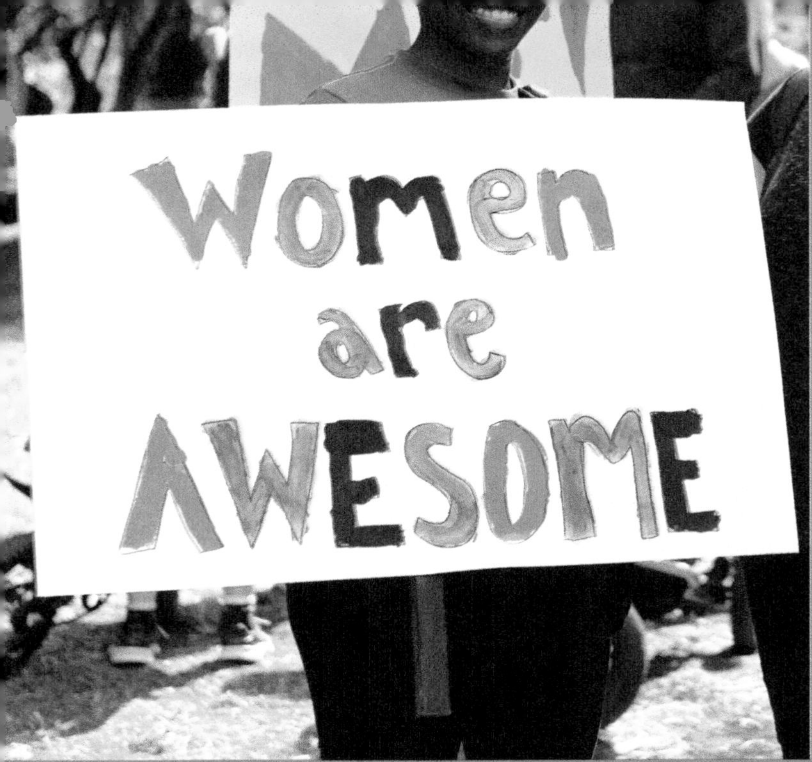
Women
are
AWESOME

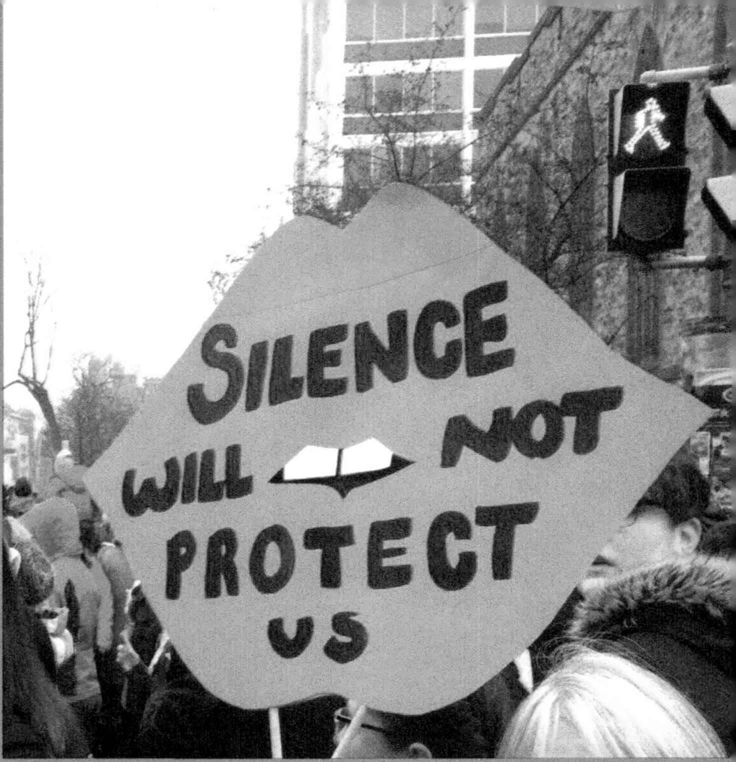
SILENCE
WILL NOT
PROTECT
US

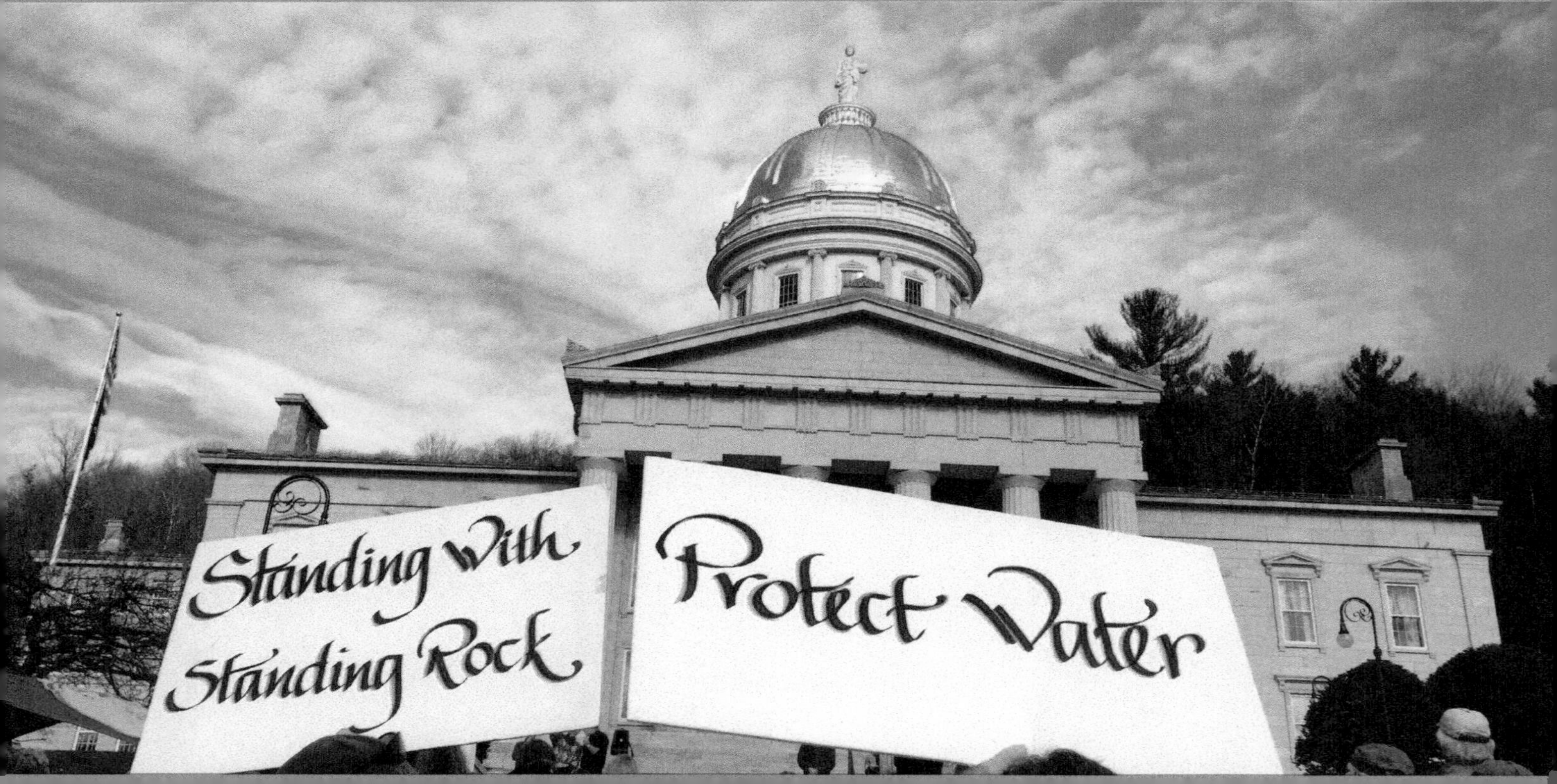
Standing with
Standing Rock
Protect Water

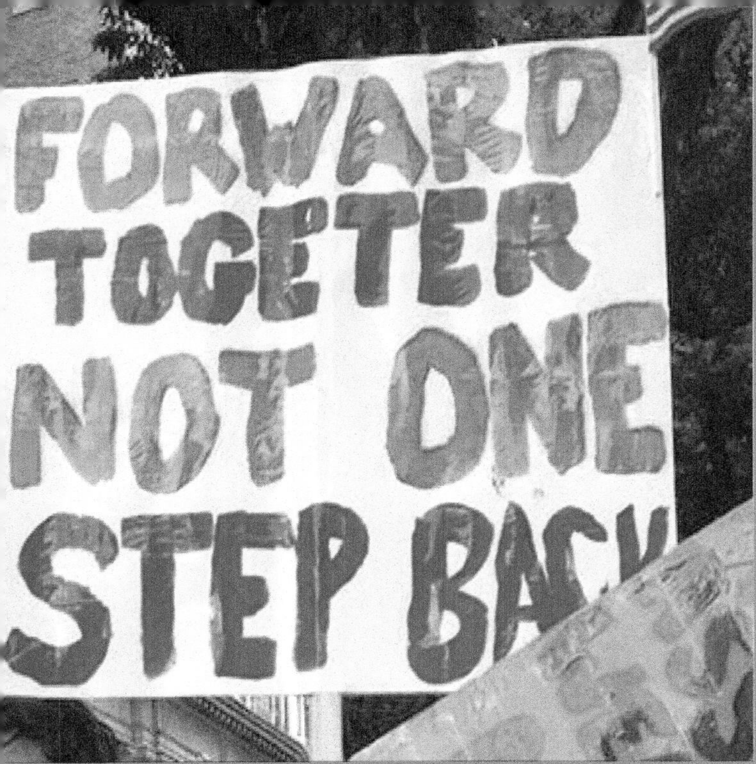
FORWARD
TOGETER
NOT ONE
STEP BAC

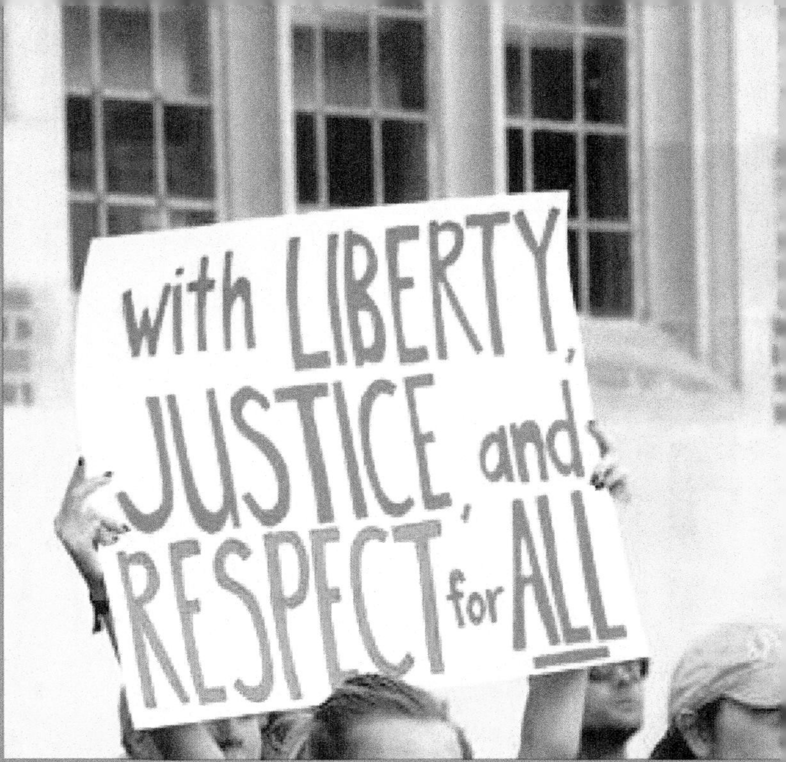
with LIBERTY,
JUSTICE, and
RESPECT for ALL

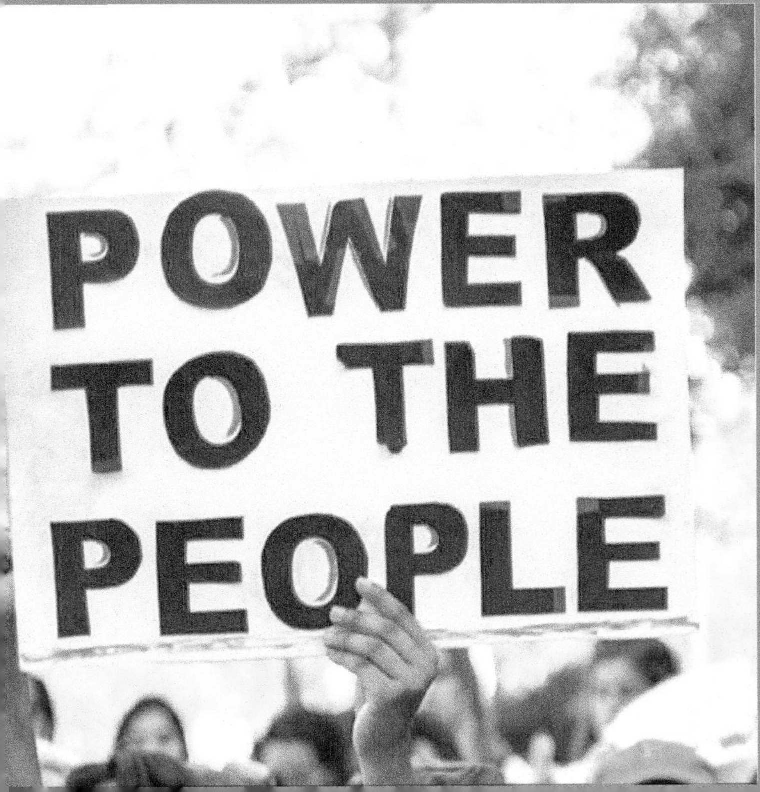
POWER
TO THE
PEOPLE

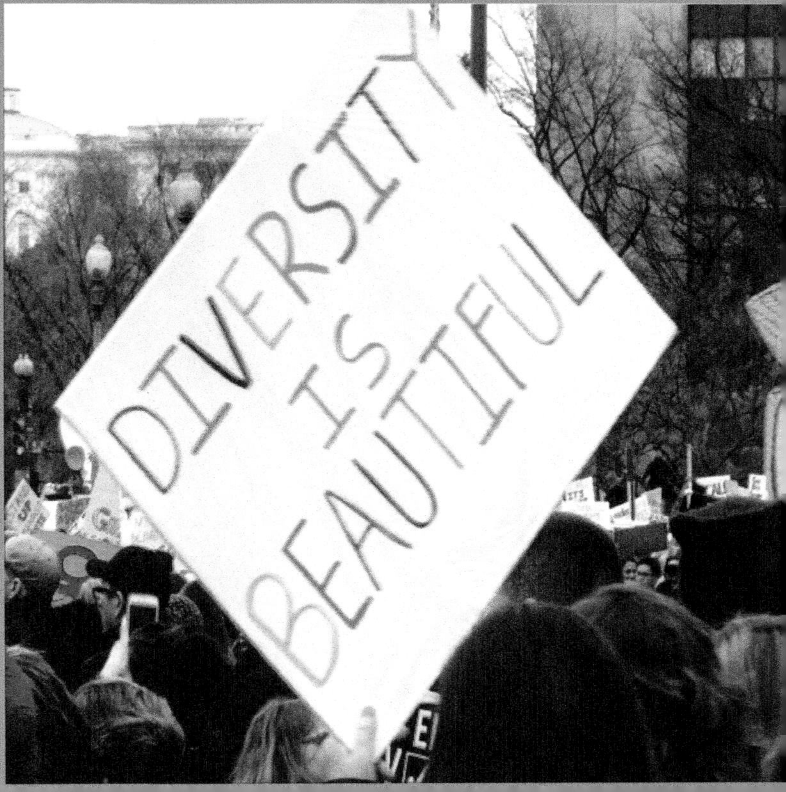
DIVERSITY
IS
BEAUTIFUL

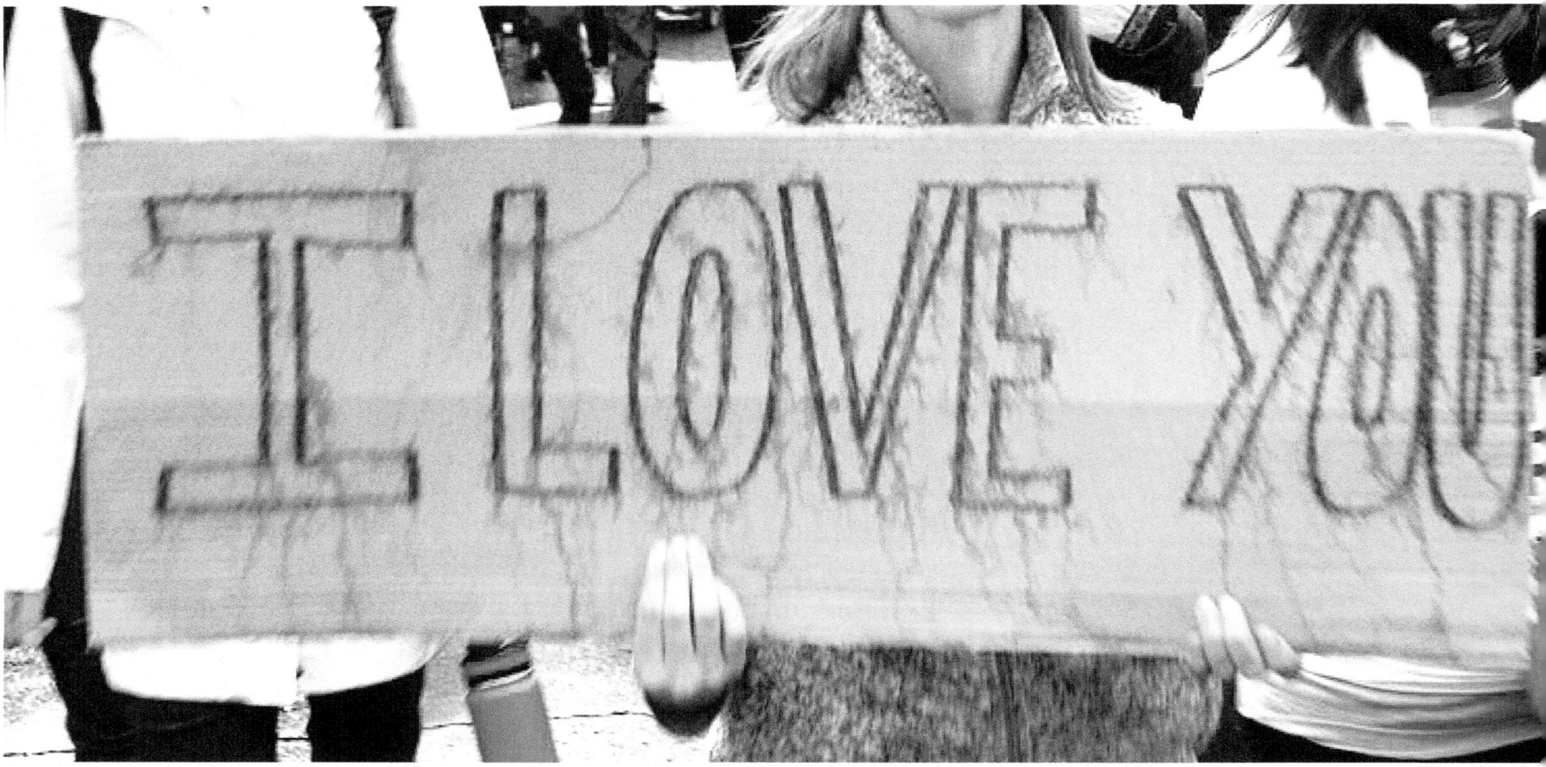
I LOVE YOU

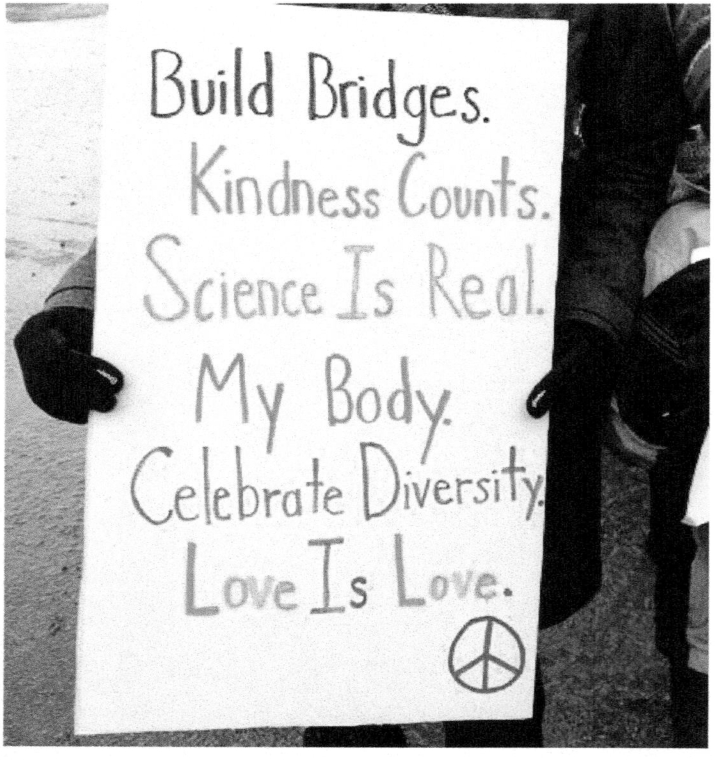
Build Bridges.
Kindness Counts.
Science Is Real.
My Body.
Celebrate Diversity.
Love Is Love.

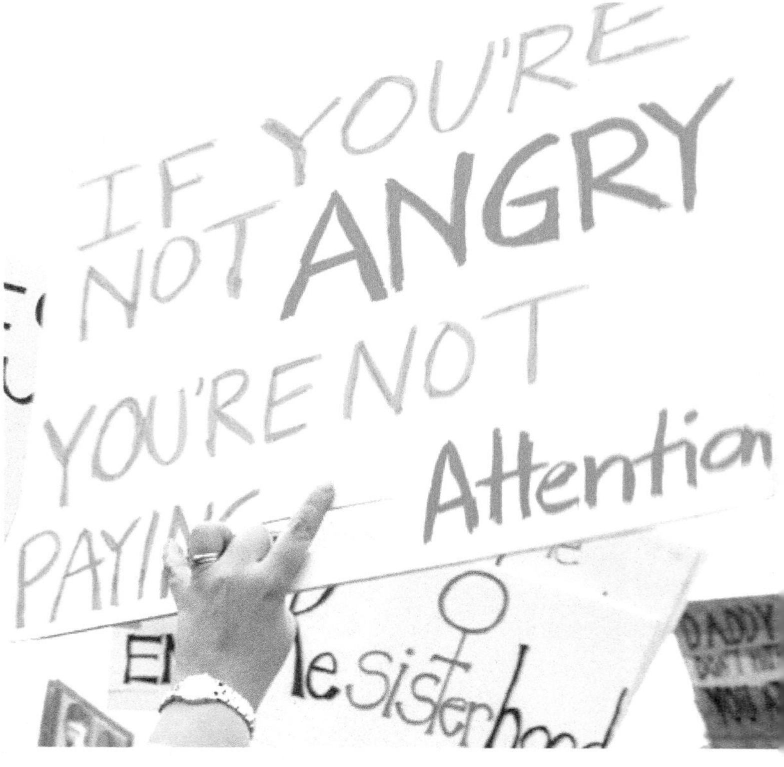
IF YOU'RE
NOT ANGRY
YOU'RE NOT
PAYIN
Attention

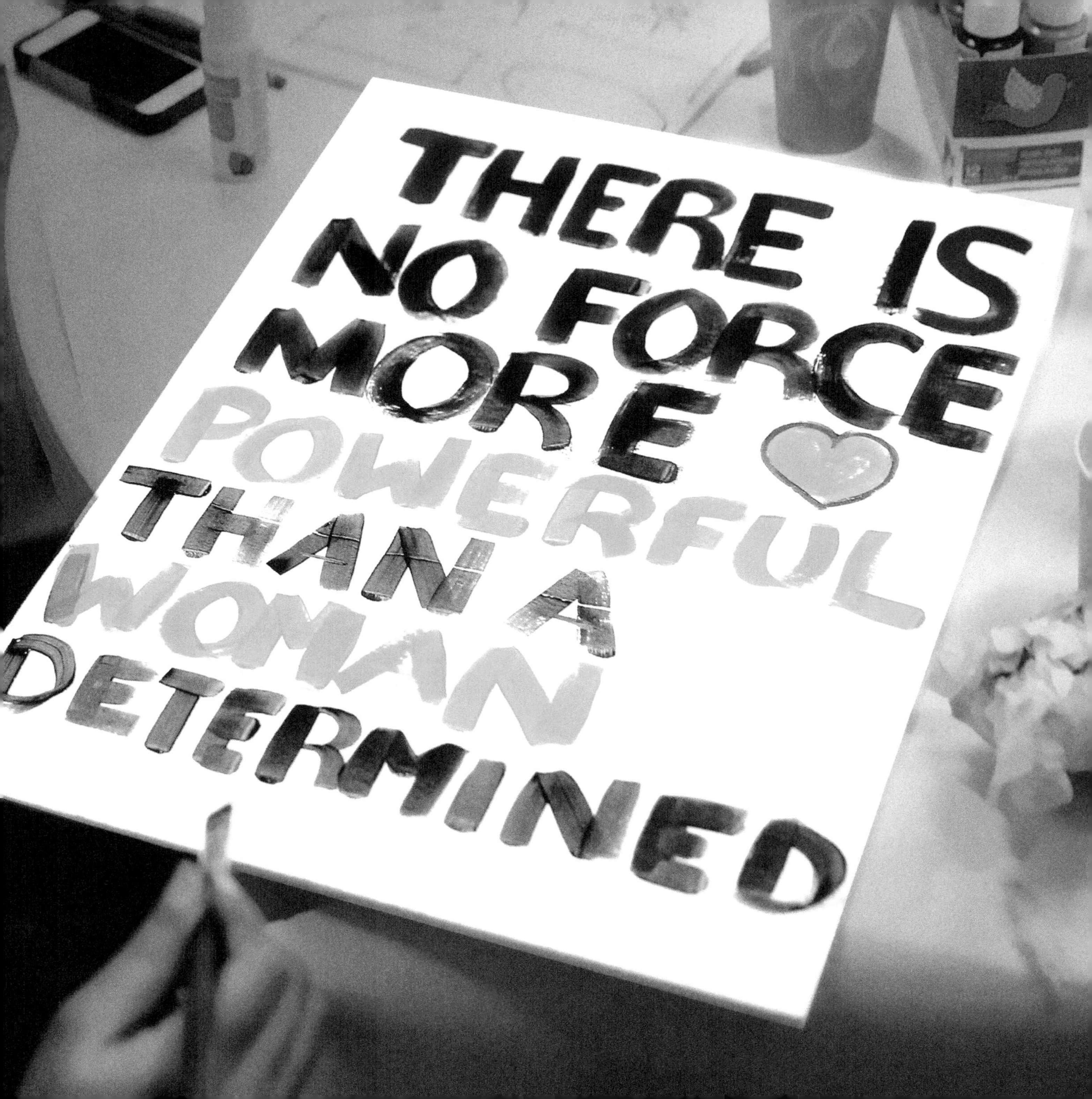
THERE IS
NO FORCE
MORE
POWERFUL
THAN A
WOMAN
DETERMINED

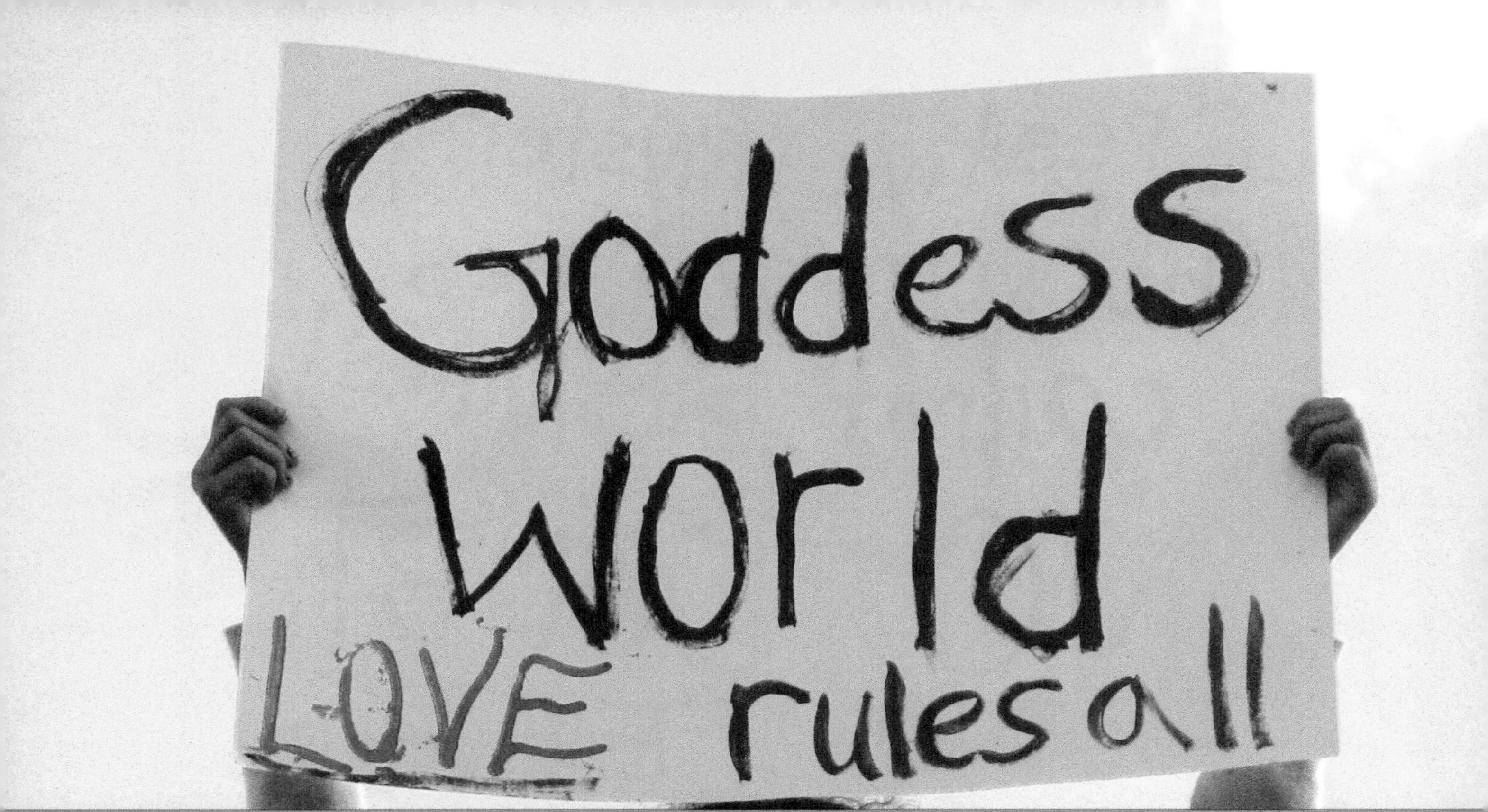
Goddess
World
LOVE rules all

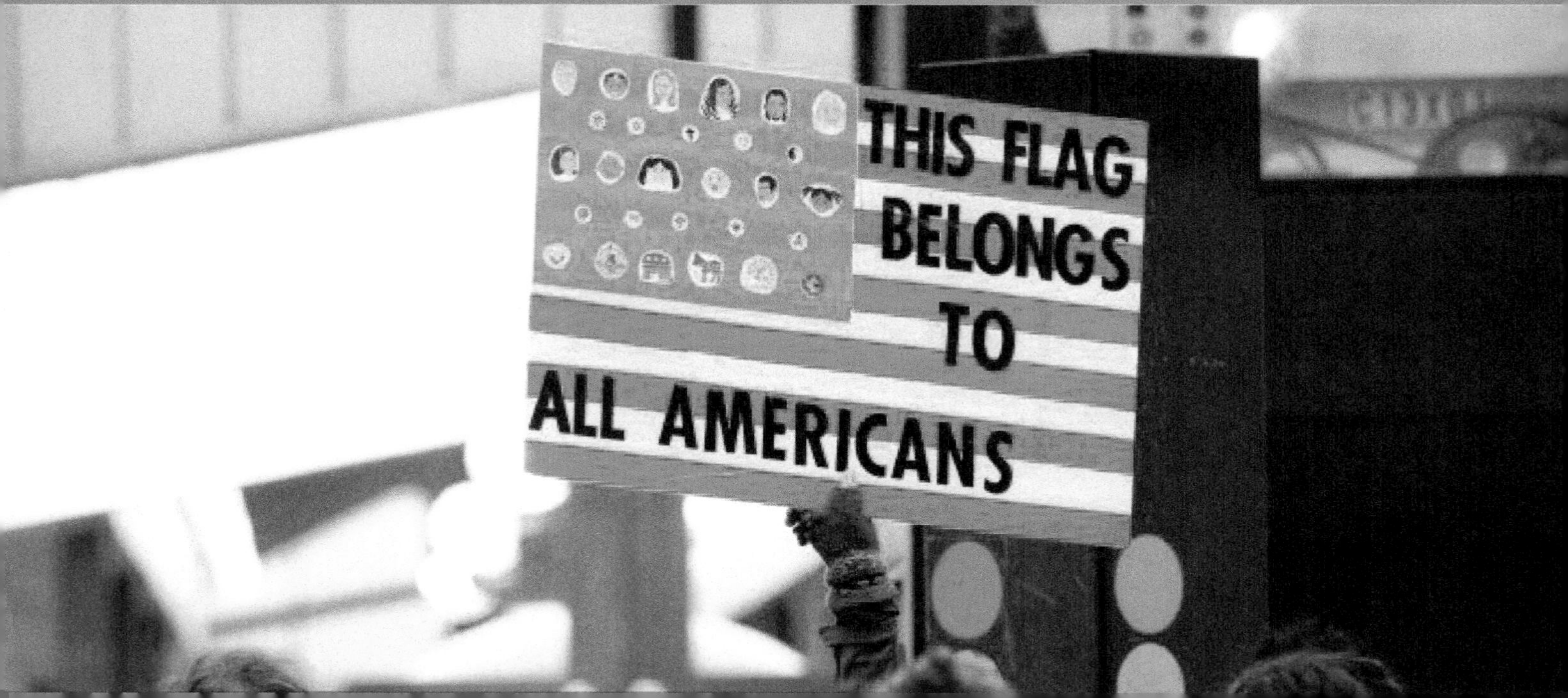
THIS FLAG
BELONGS
TO
ALL AMERICANS

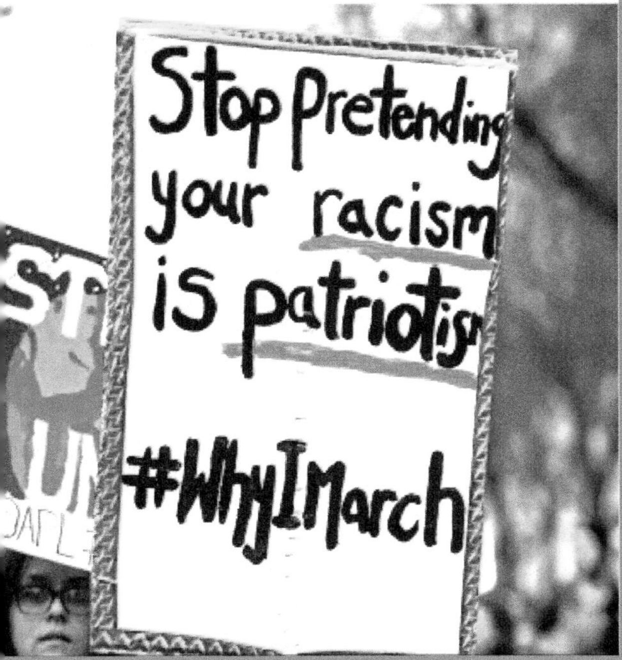
Stop Pretending
your racism
is patriotism
#WhyIMarch

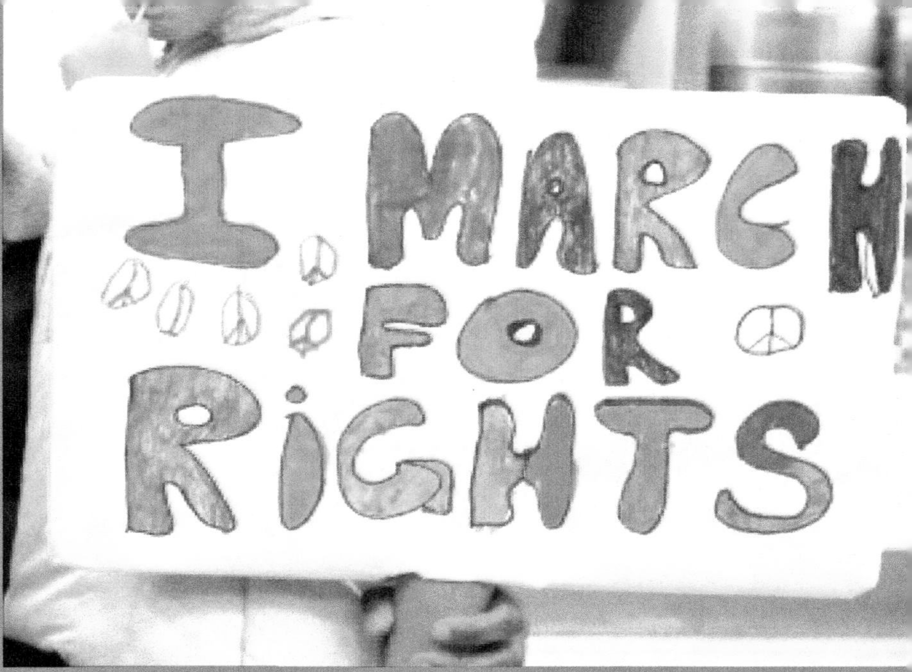
I MARCH
FOR
RIGHTS

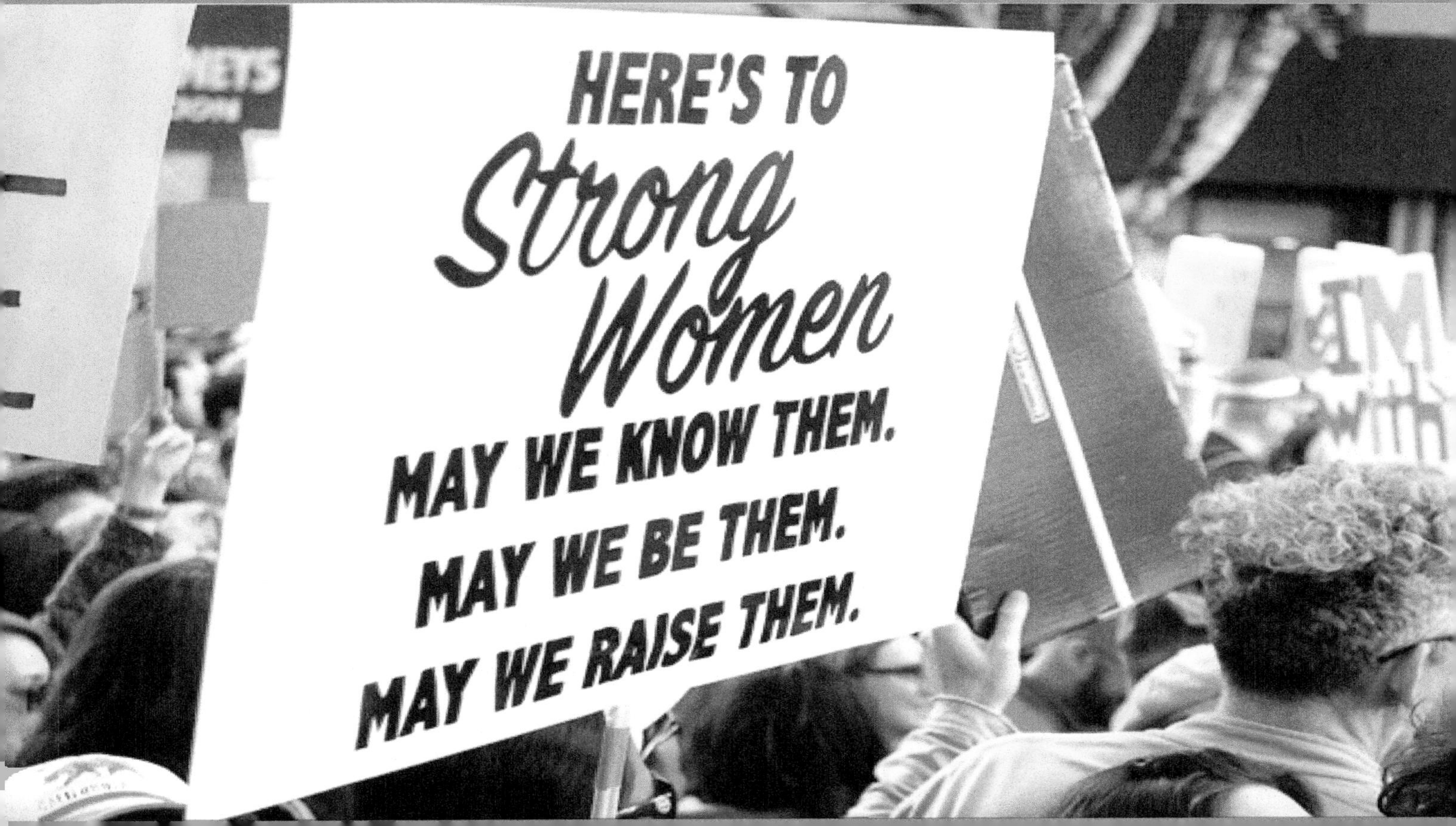
HERE'S TO
Strong
Women
MAY WE KNOW THEM.
MAY WE BE THEM.
MAY WE RAISE THEM.

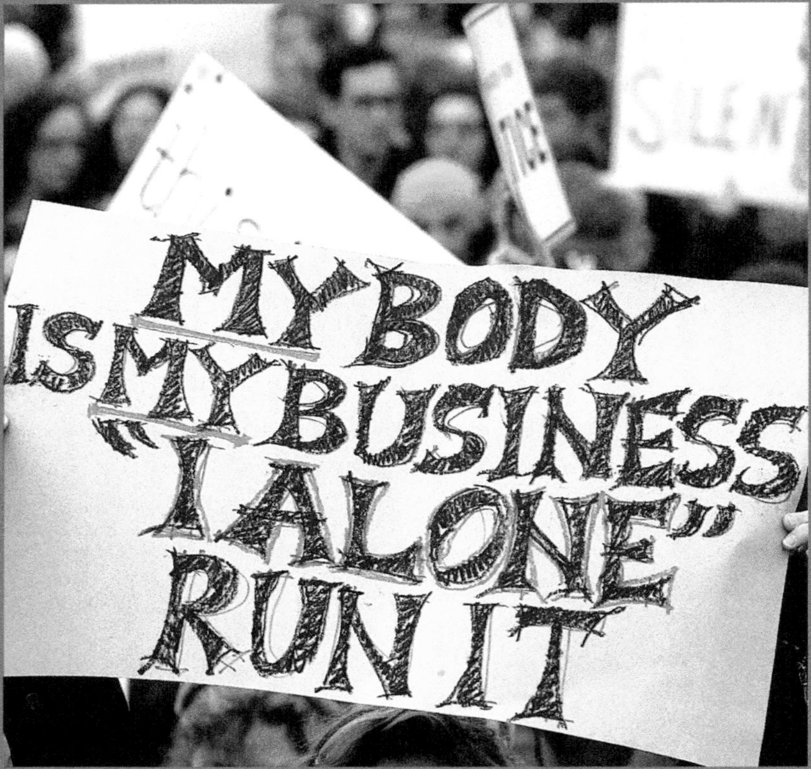
MY BODY
IS MY BUSINESS
"I ALONE"
RUN IT

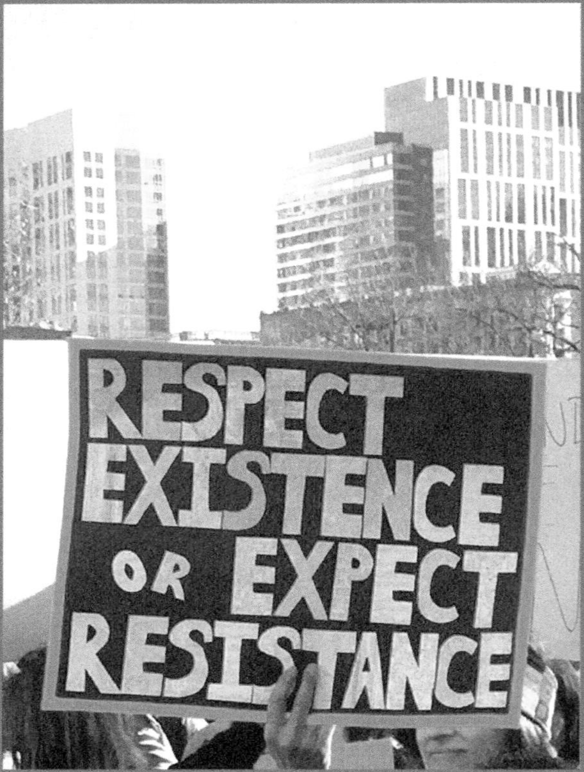
RESPECT
EXISTENCE
OR EXPECT
RESISTANCE

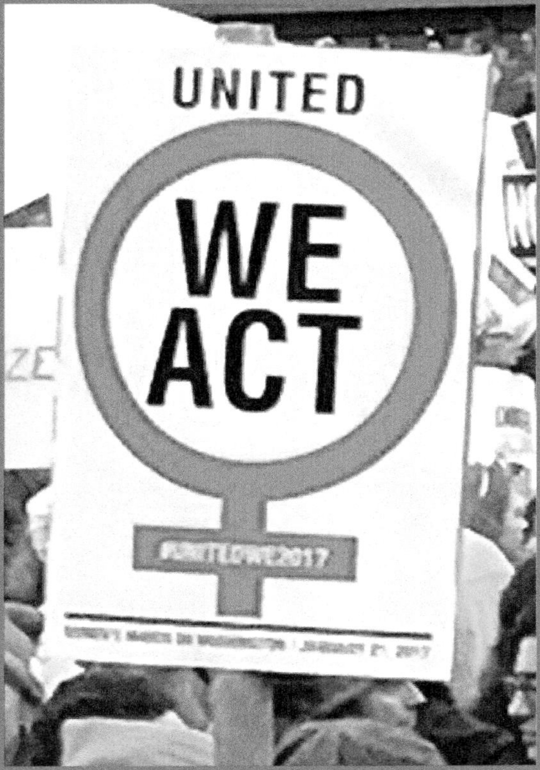
UNITED
WE
ACT

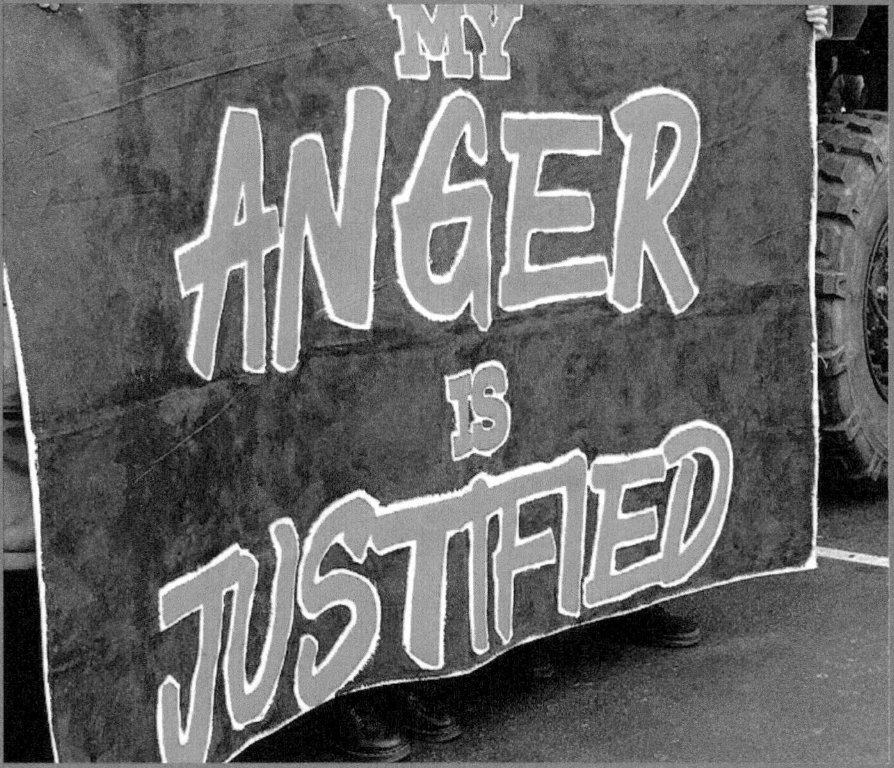
MY
ANGER
IS
JUSTIFIED

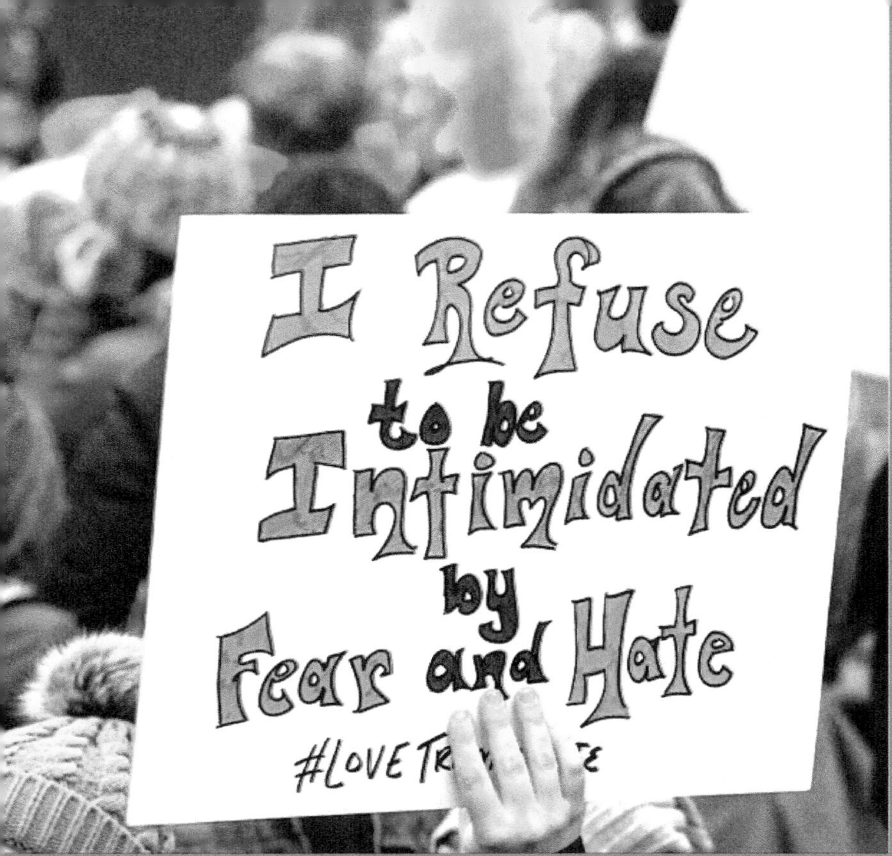
I Refuse
to be
Intimidated
by
Fear and Hate

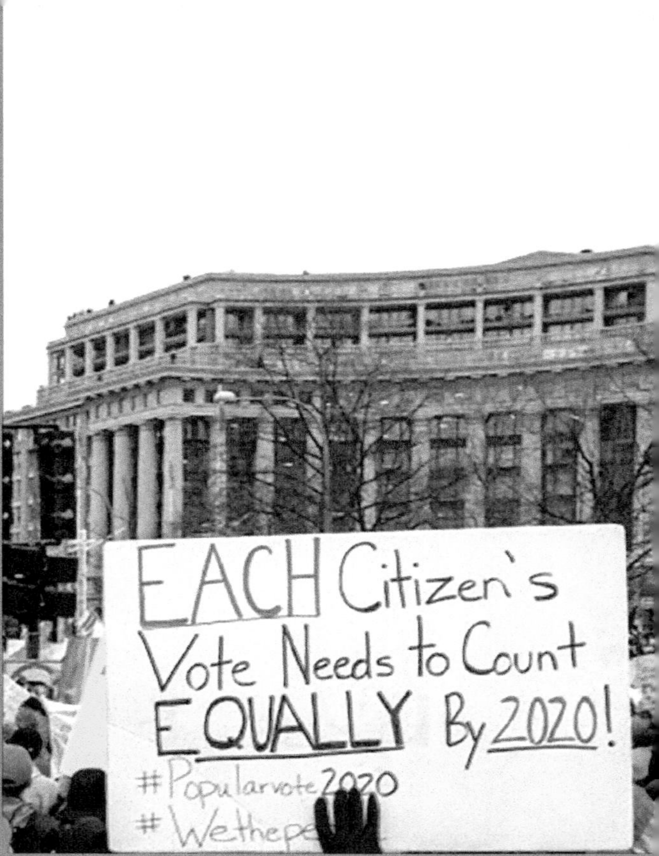
EACH Citizen's
Vote Needs to Count
EQUALLY By 2020!
#Popularvote2020

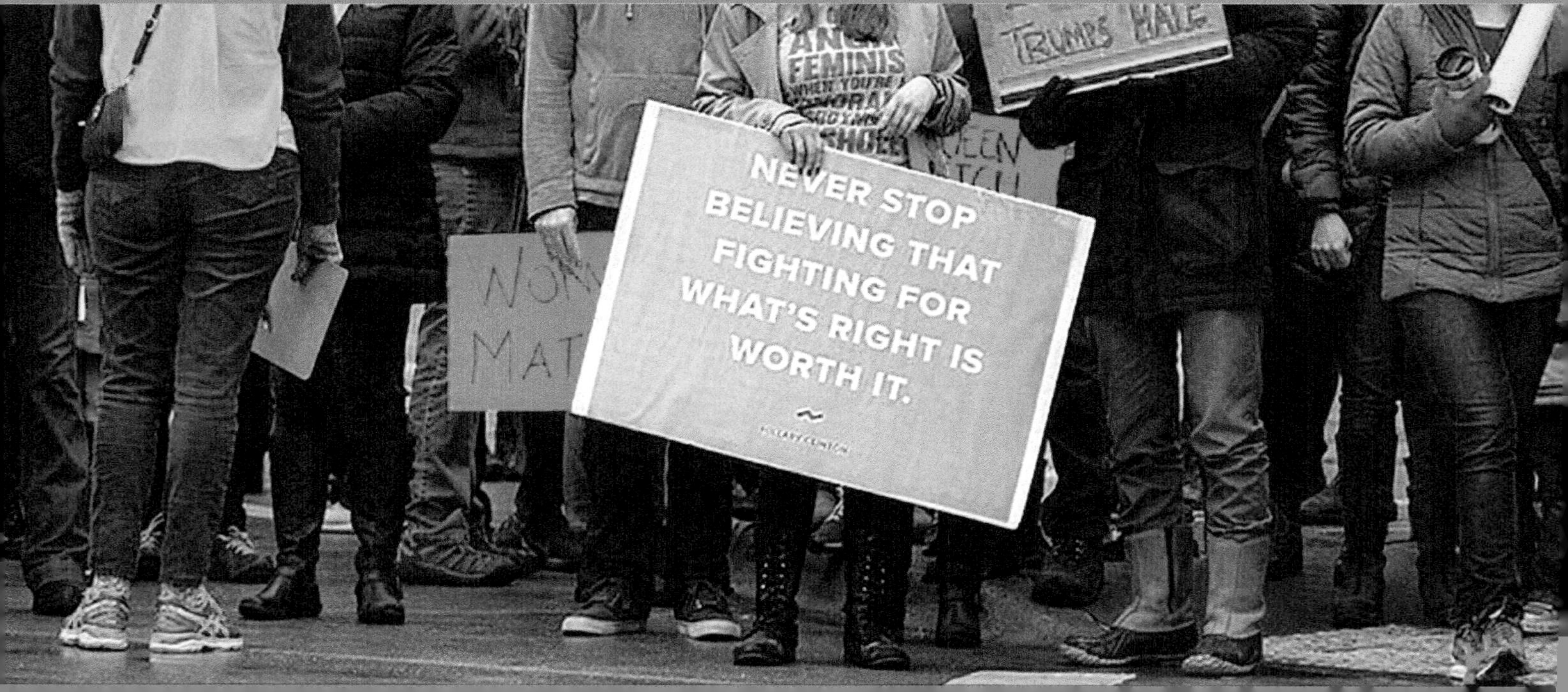
TRUMPS HATE
NEVER STOP
BELIEVING THAT
FIGHTING FOR
WHAT'S RIGHT IS
WORTH IT.

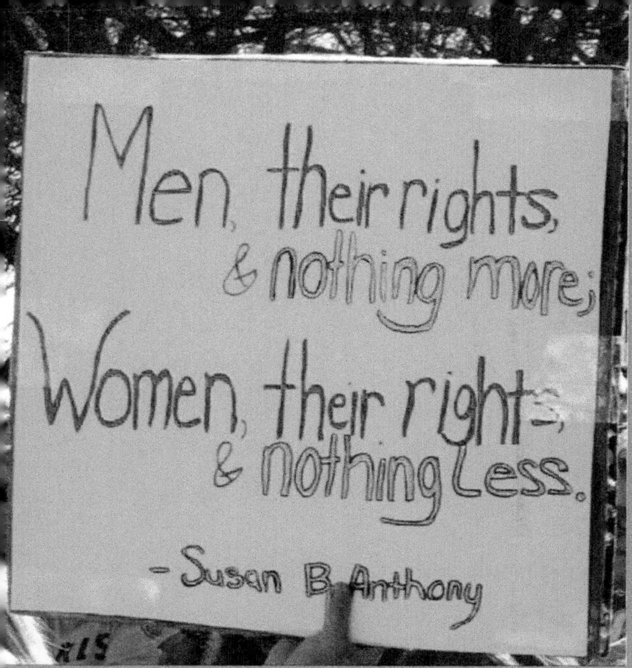
Men, their rights,
& nothing more;
Women, their rights,
& nothing Less.
- Susan B. Anthony

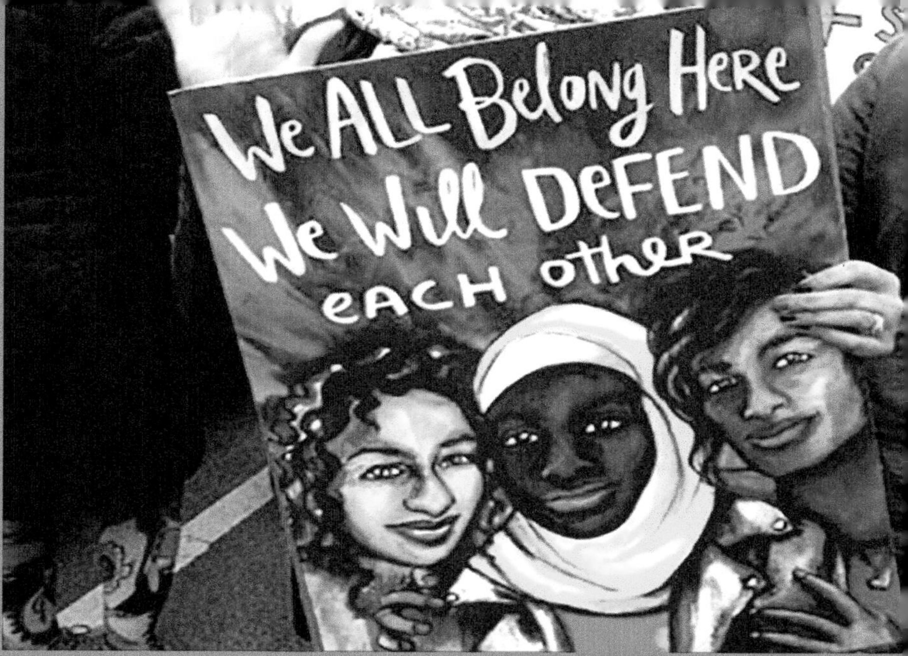
We ALL Belong Here
We Will DEFEND
EACH other

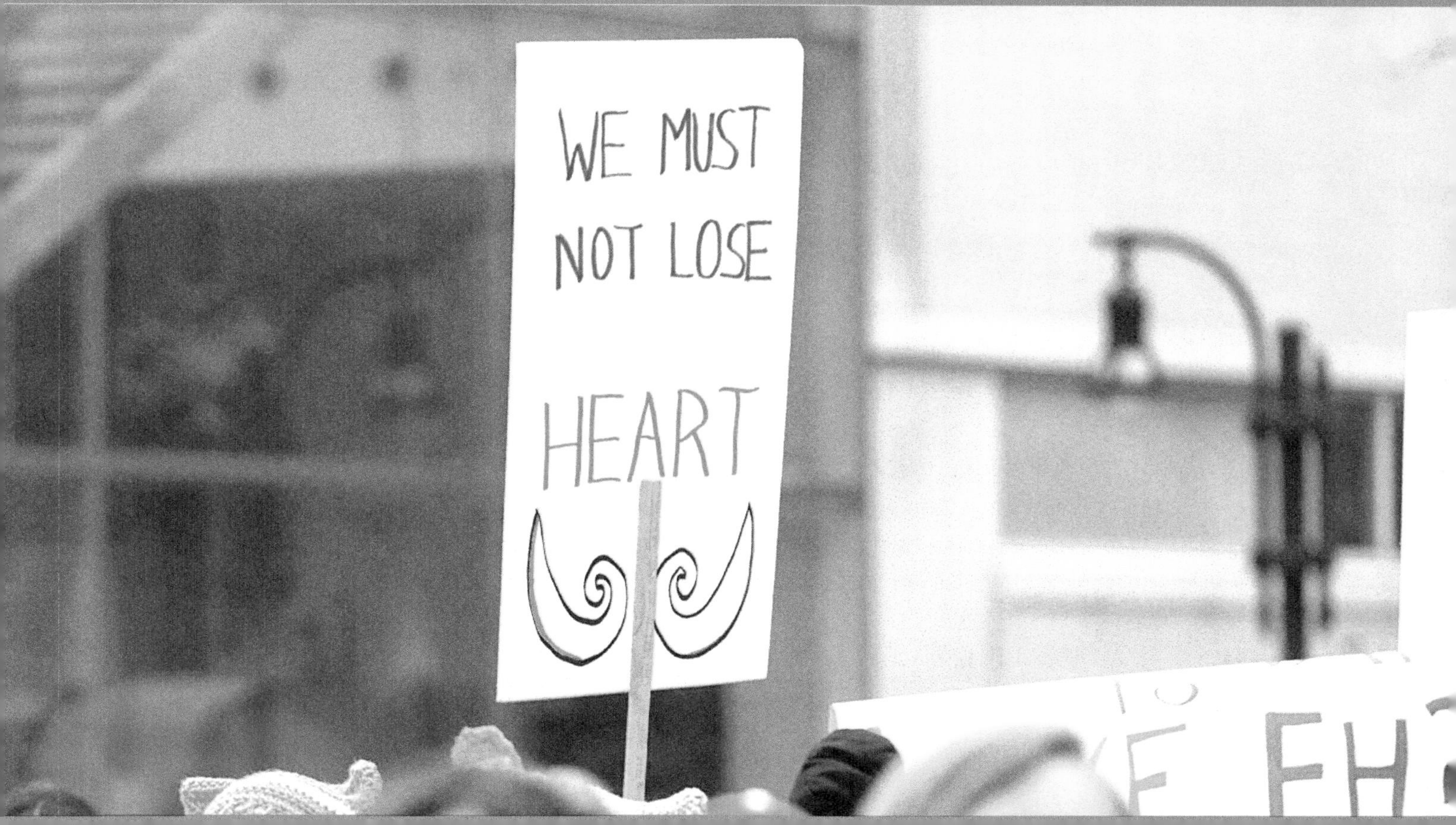
WE MUST
NOT LOSE
HEART

Teach Your Children Well

The title of this book was inspired by the now decades old song of Crosby, Stills, Nash & Young titled "Teach Your Children." It is a song that many of us who marched on January 21, 2017 remember from our college days. It was a part of a collection of music that might be characterized (with 20/20 hindsight for sure) as Rock and Roll protest music. It was music that tried to provide us guidance in an era of societal tumult as our friends were sent off to an unpopular war, as feminism grew and as change was in the air — hard fought change often accompanied, sadly, by violence and distrust.

In writing the song, Graham Nash (he wrote it when he was with the Hollies) made this prescient comment in a 1991-boxed set: "The idea is that you write something so personal that every single person on the planet can relate to it. Once it's there on vinyl it unfolds, outwards, so that it applies to almost any situation." While some have said the song was inspired by Nash's troubled relationship with his imprisoned father, Nash stated in an interview with Bob Edwards that, after the fact, the song reflected the message of non-violence in a 1962 famous photograph by Diane Arbus titled "Child with Toy Hand Grenade in Central Park." (Incidentally, Nash views himself as a photographer before he self-describes as a musician. https://www.youtube.com/watch?v=9M0B_V3VvSY)

At a 2013 interview at the Rock and Roll Hall of Fame (where Nash was previously inducted for his role in the Hollies and Crosby, Stills, Nash & Young), he referenced songs as "newspapers of the street." What an image — what a way to think about songs and their meaning. See: https://www.youtube.com/watch?v=9M0B_V3VvSY.

The signs of the post-Inaugural March are like Nash's description of the songs: these are telling the news on the ground -- delivered loudly, vibrantly, proudly and peacefully. To everyone and for everyone. We need to share the signs' messages with all our children and our children's children. And, we need to see, acknowledge, know and speak to the real "news" --- the values we hold dear, the values we want to preserve, the values that undergird who we are as individuals, as families, as a nation. We need to message the world: teach your children well.

We hope this book does just that.

— Karen Gross

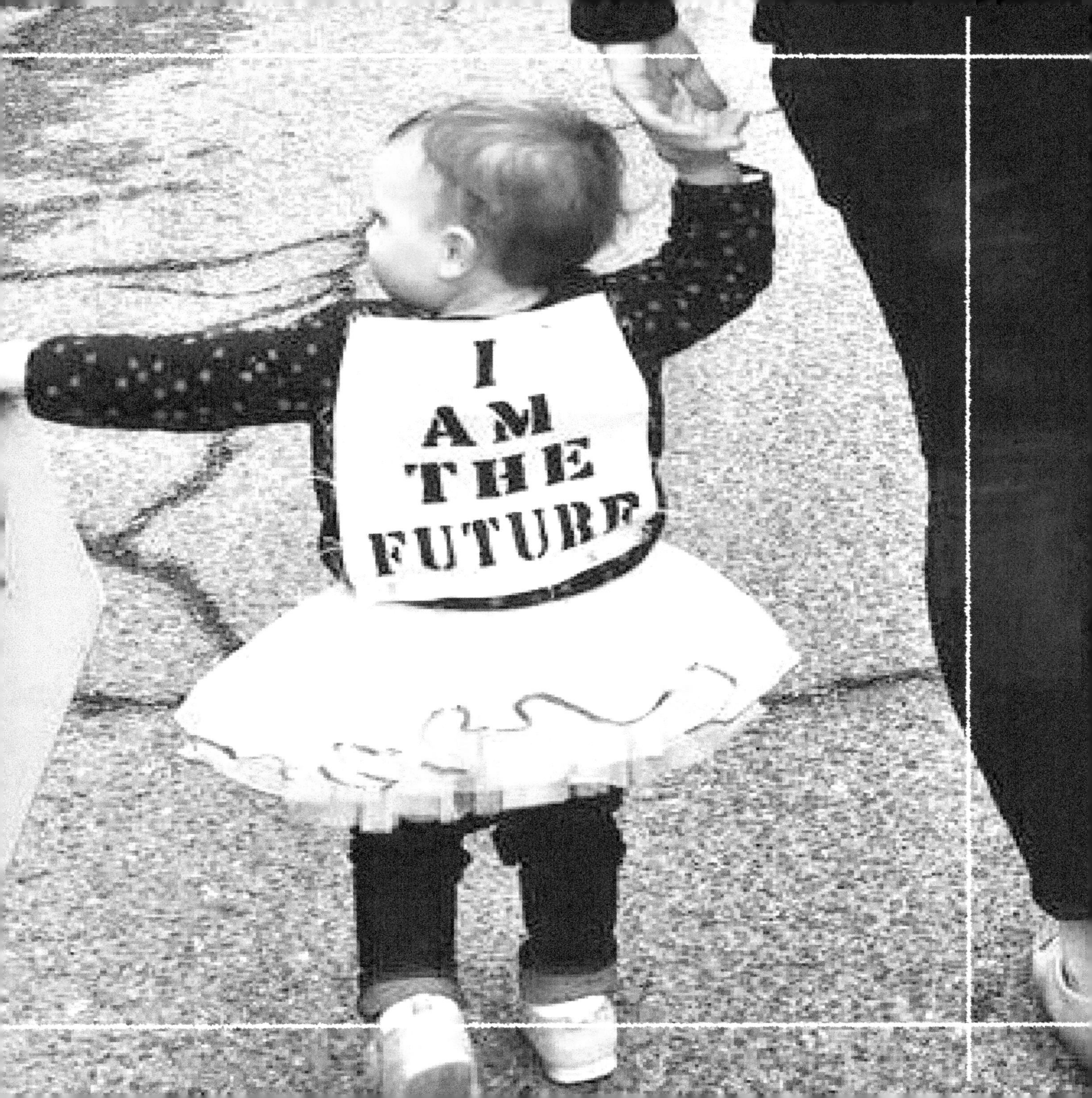
I
AM
THE
FUTURE

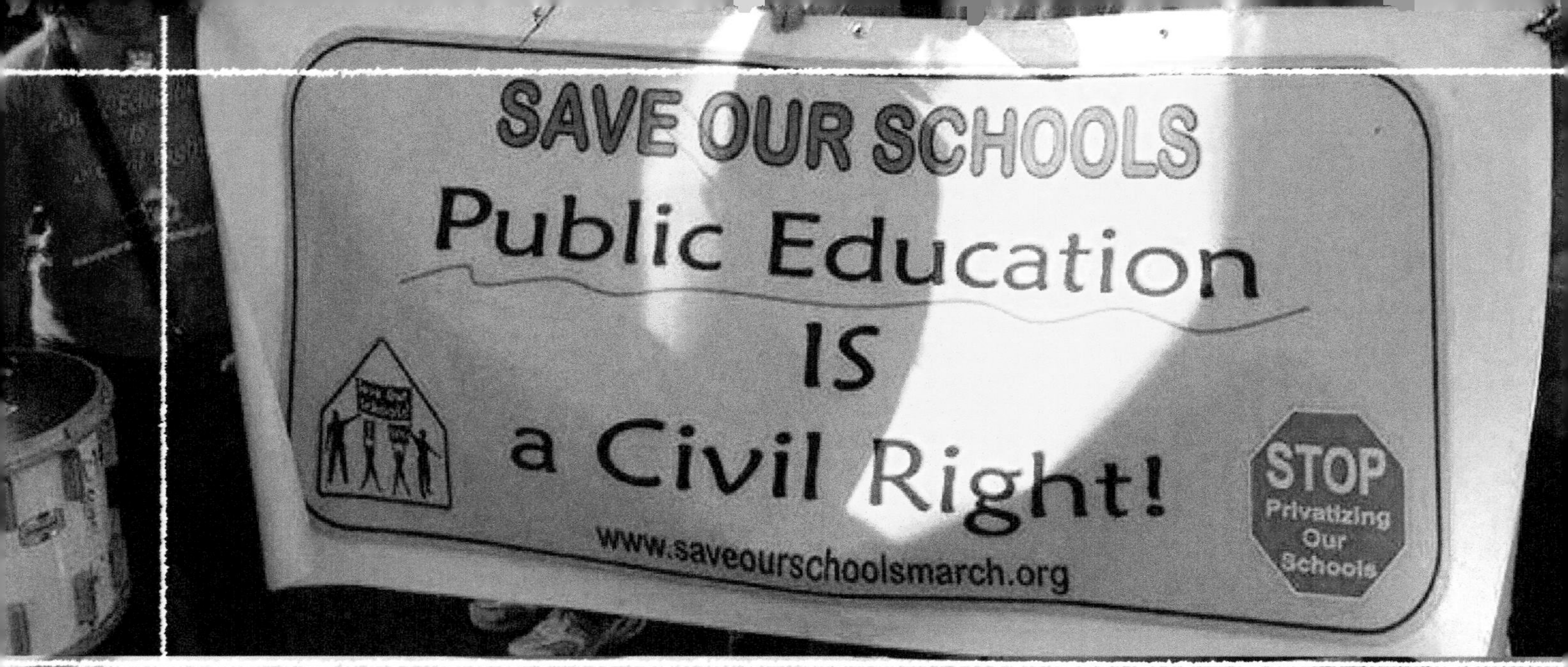
SAVE OUR SCHOOLS
Public Education
IS
a Civil Right!
STOP
Privatizing
Our
Schools
www.saveourschoolsmarch.org

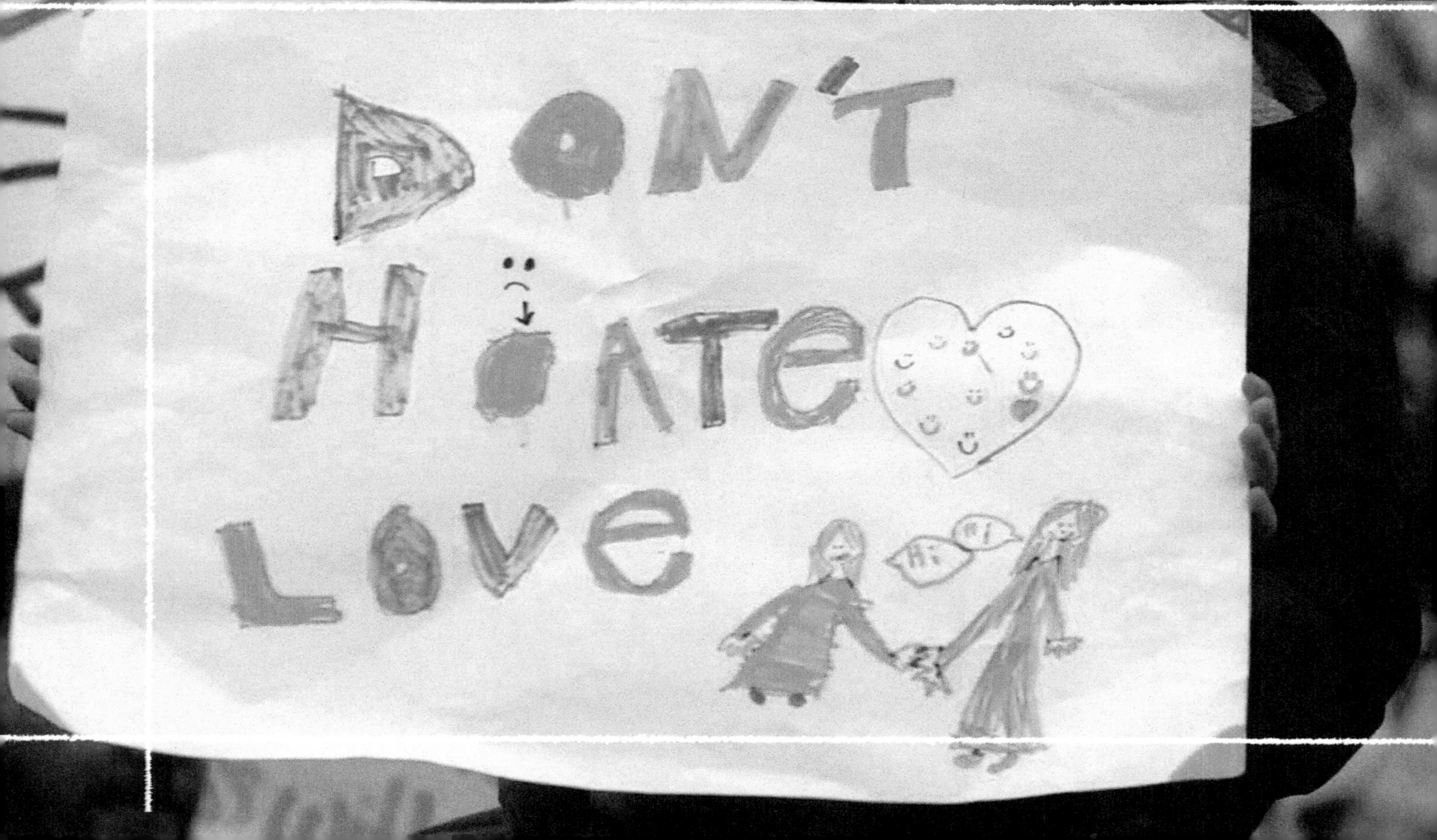
DON'T
HATE
LOVE
Hi
Hi

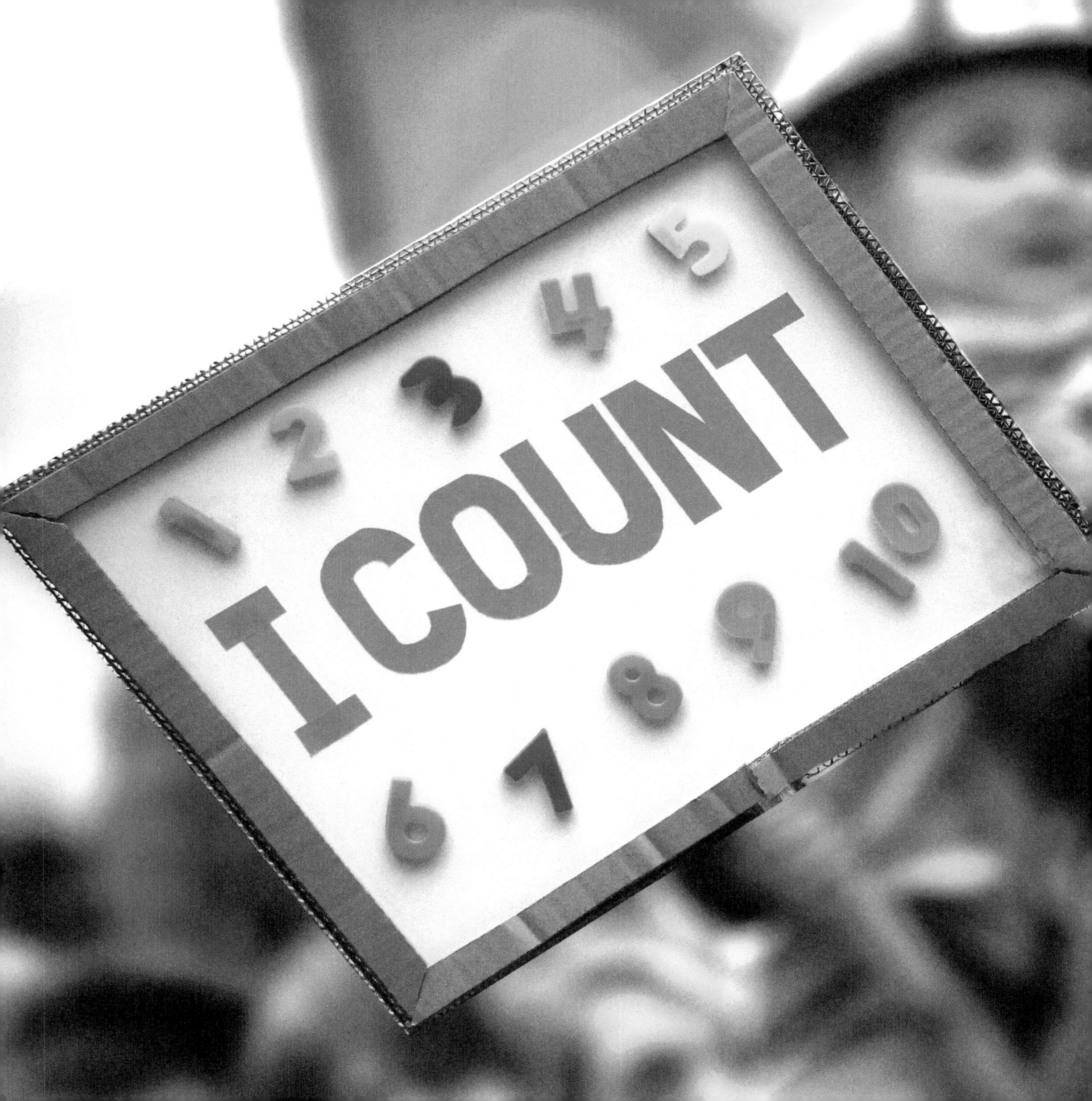

I COUNT
1 2 3 4 5
6 7 8 9 10

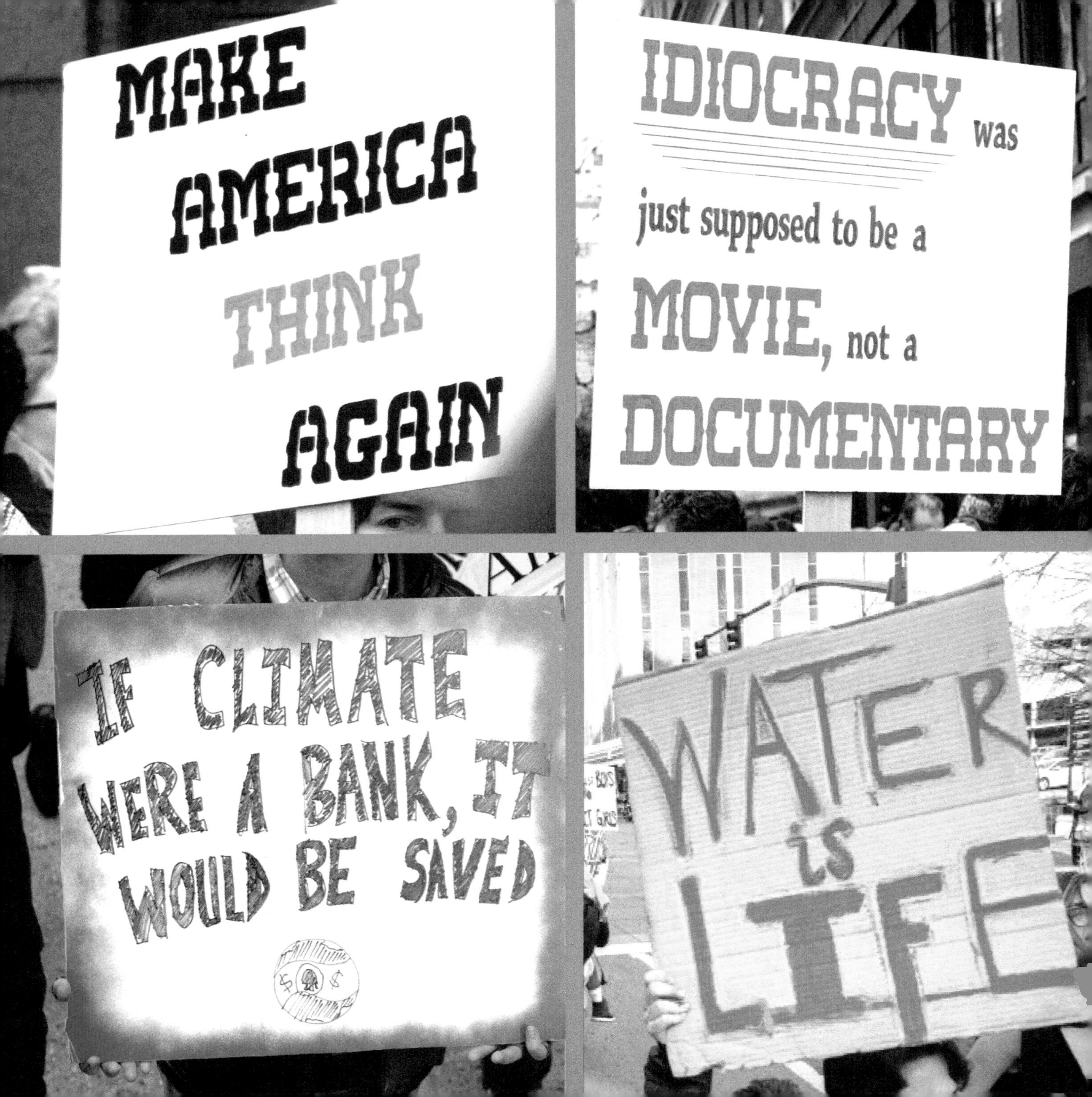
MAKE AMERICA THINK AGAIN
IDIOCRACY was just supposed to be a MOVIE, not a DOCUMENTARY
IF CLIMATE WERE A BANK, IT WOULD BE SAVED
WATER is LIFE

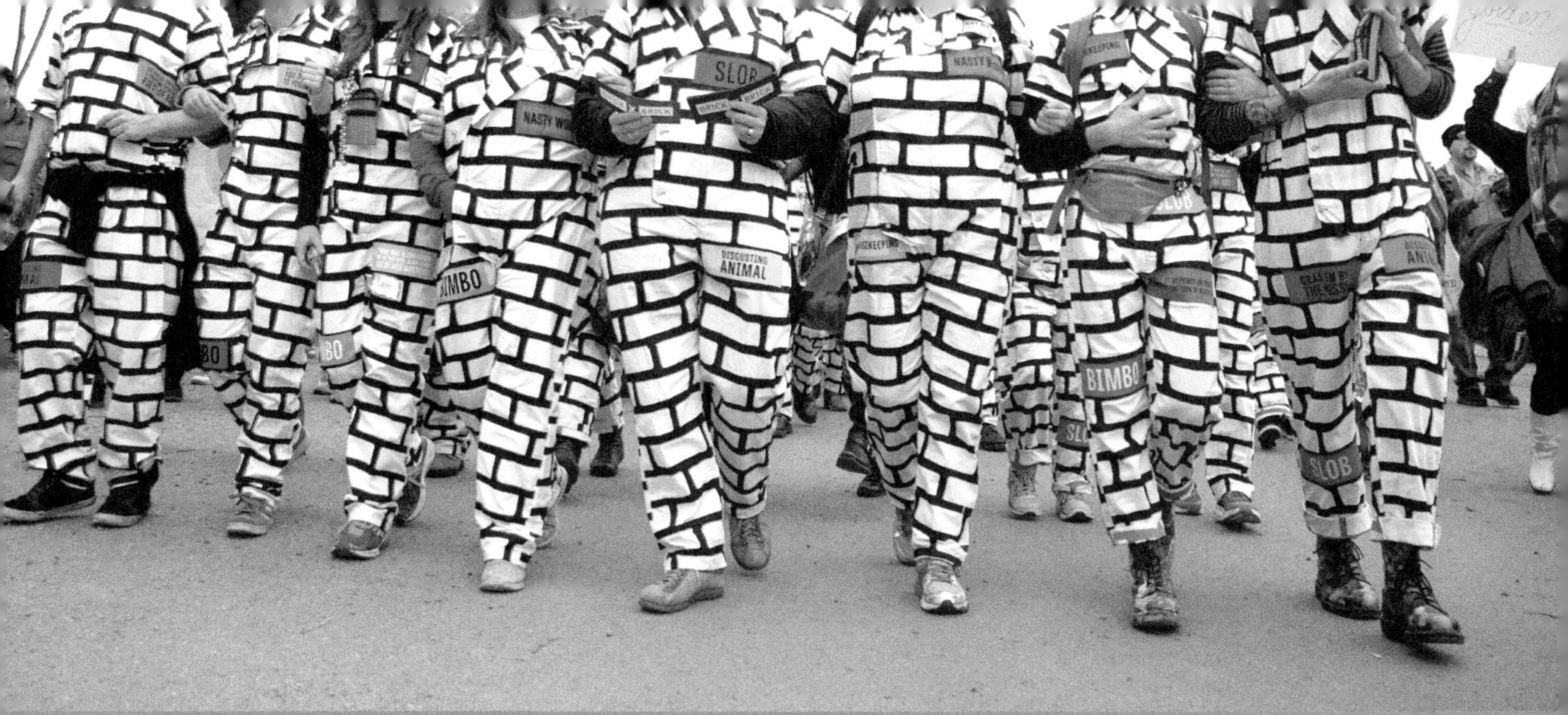
SLOB
BIMBO
DISGUSTING ANIMAL

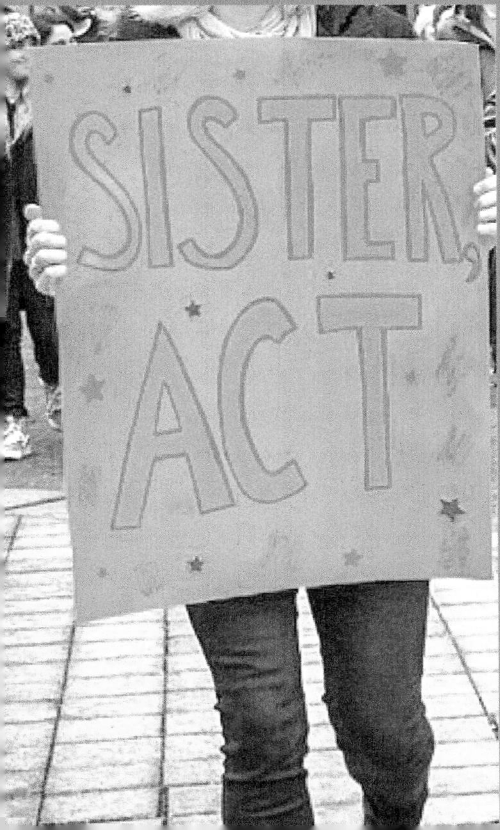
SISTER, ACT

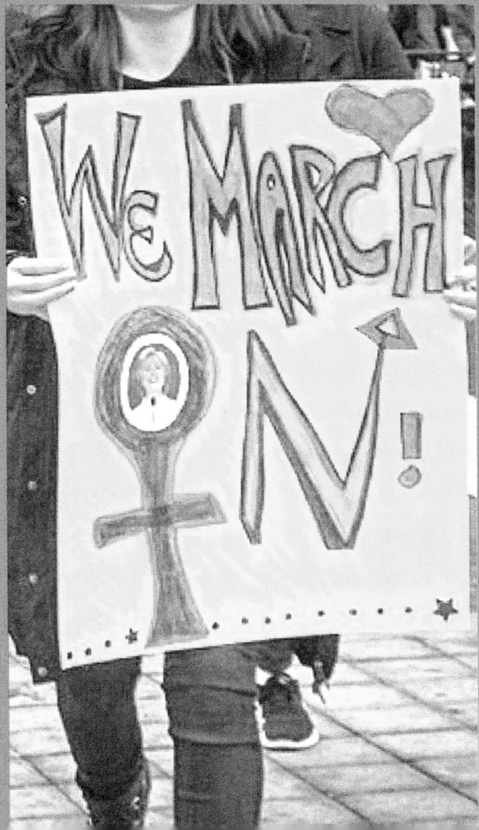
WE MARCH ON!

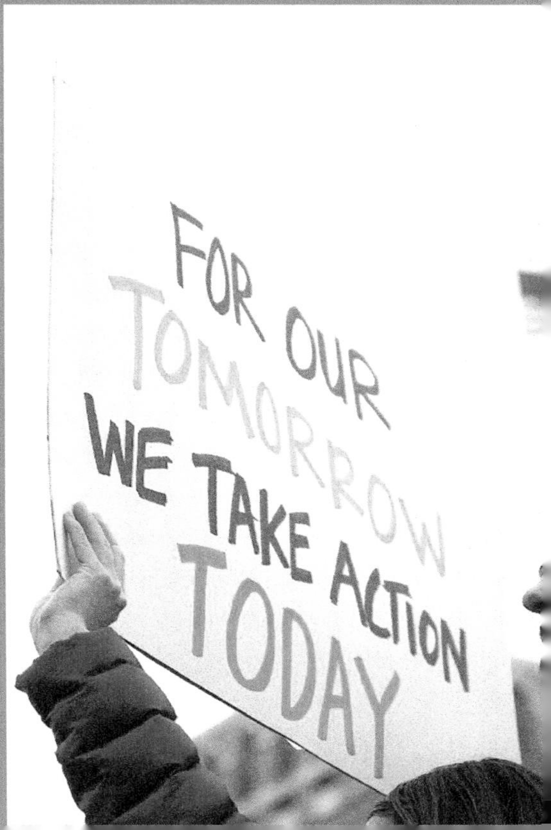
FOR OUR TOMORROW
WE TAKE ACTION
TODAY

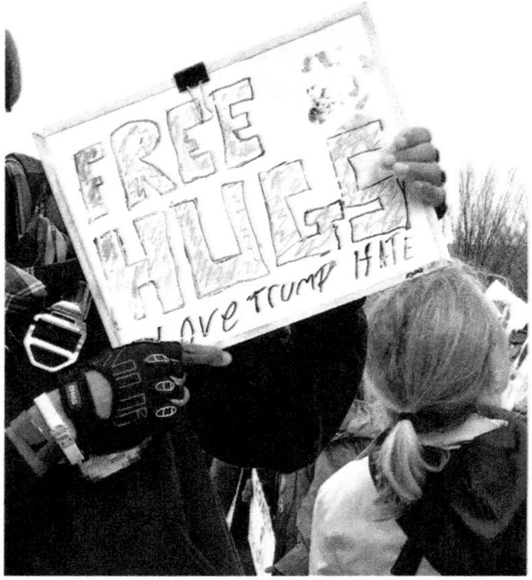
FREE HUGS

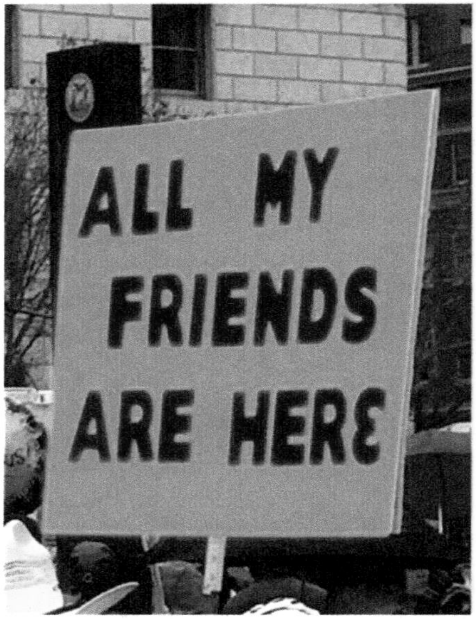
ALL MY FRIENDS ARE HERE

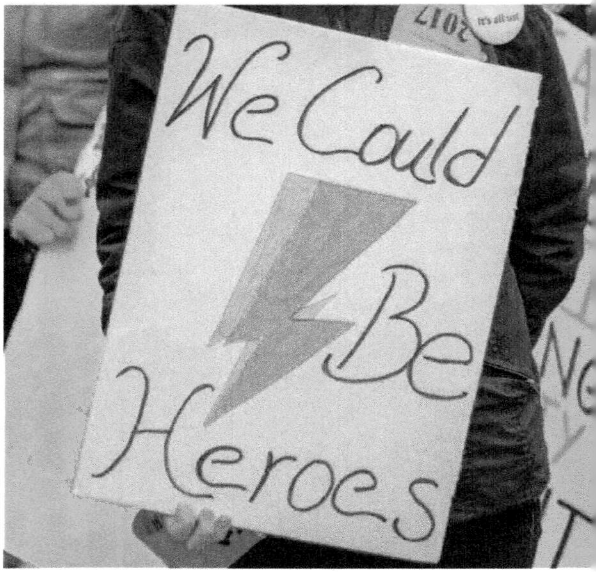
We Could Be Heroes

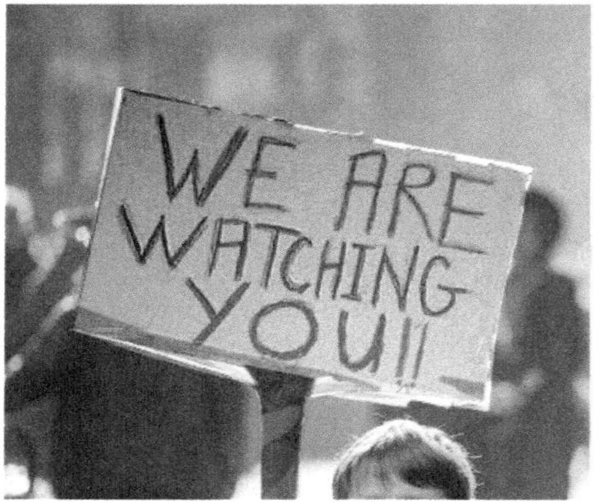
WE ARE WATCHING YOU!!

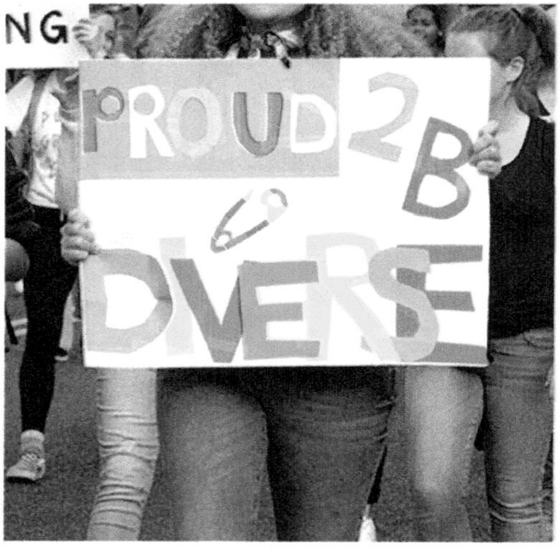
PROUD 2B DIVERSE

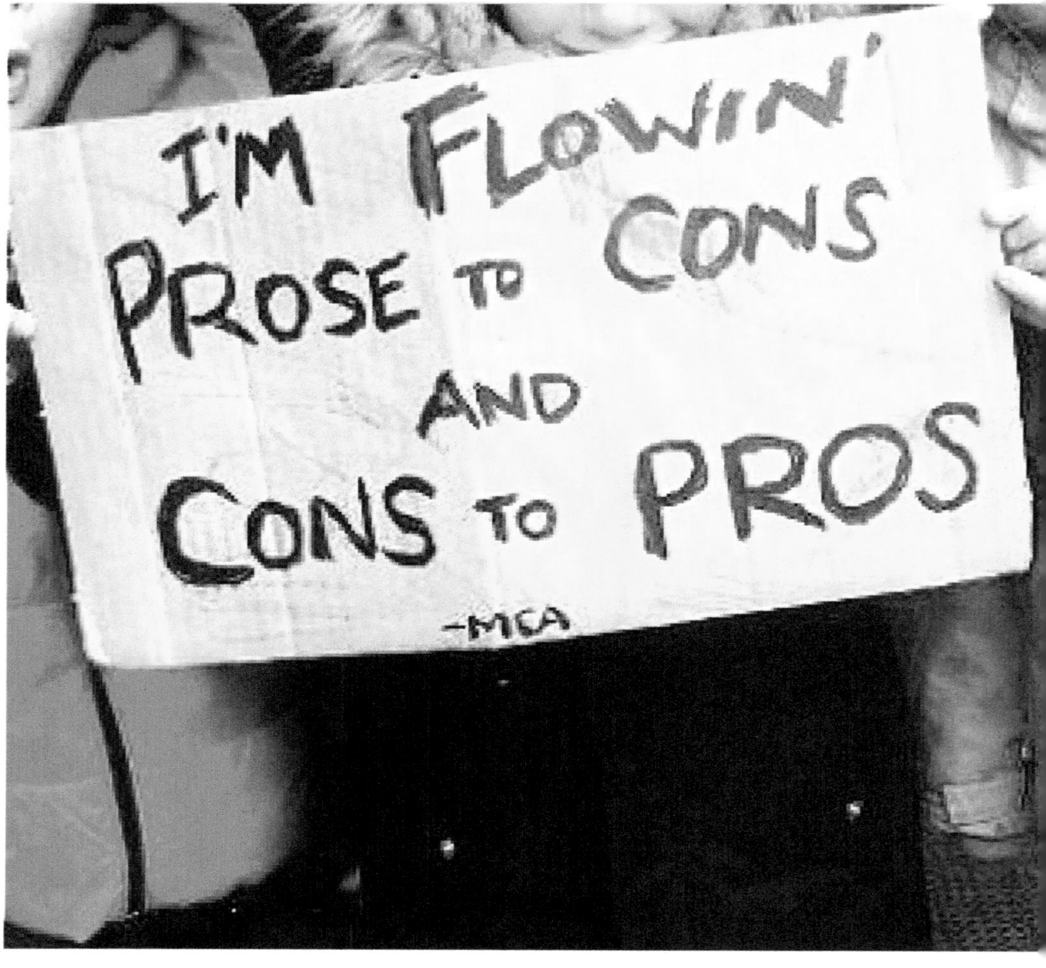
I'M FLOWIN' PROSE TO CONS AND CONS TO PROS
-MCA

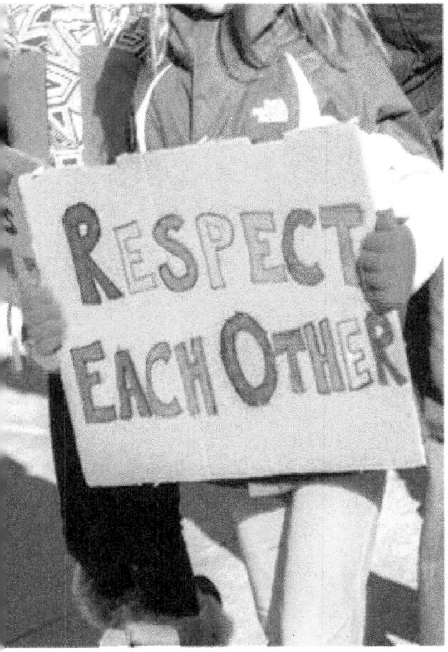
RESPECT
EACH OTHER

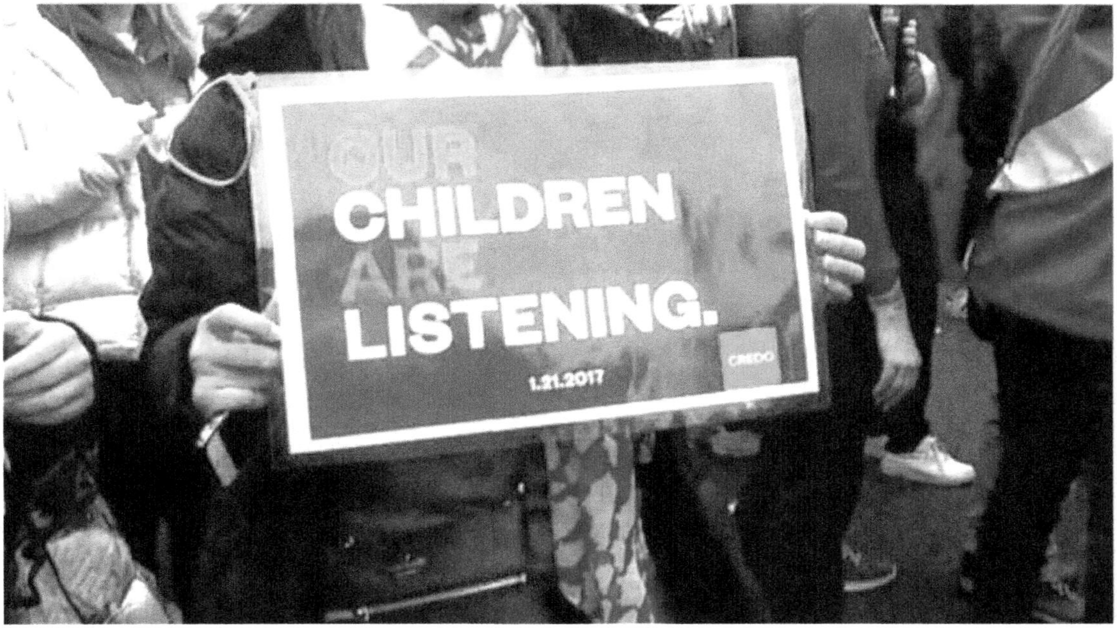
OUR
CHILDREN
ARE
LISTENING.
1.21.2017
CREDO

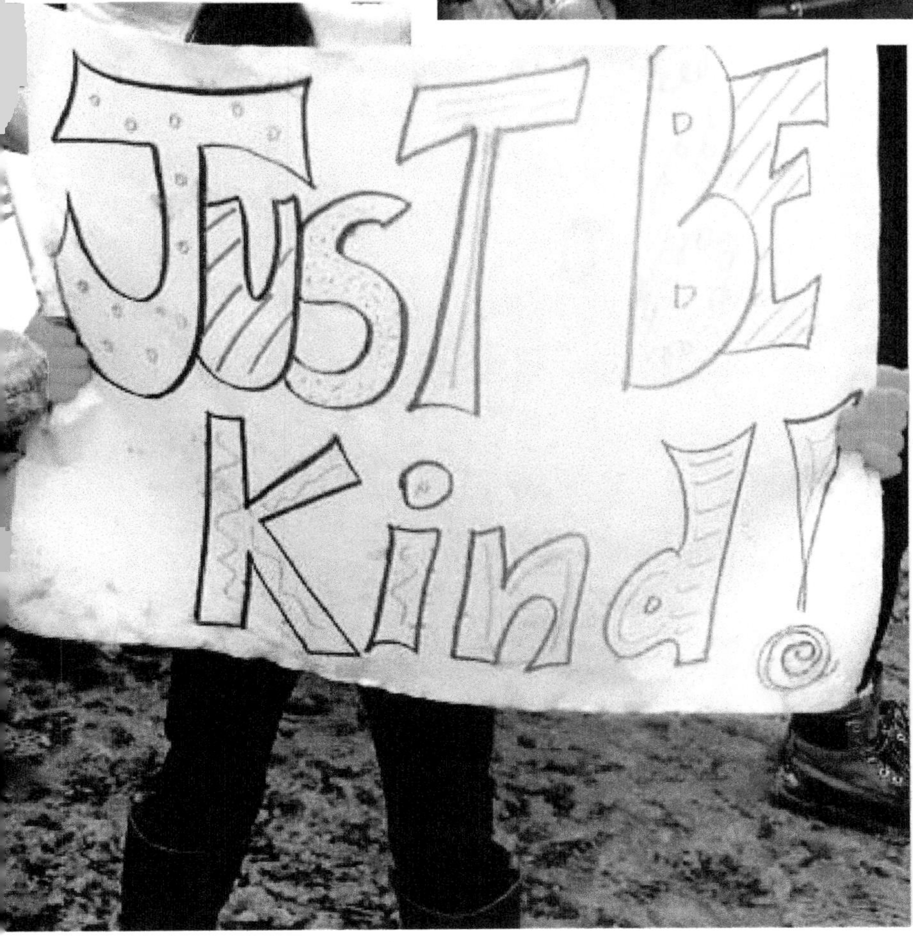
JUST BE
Kind!

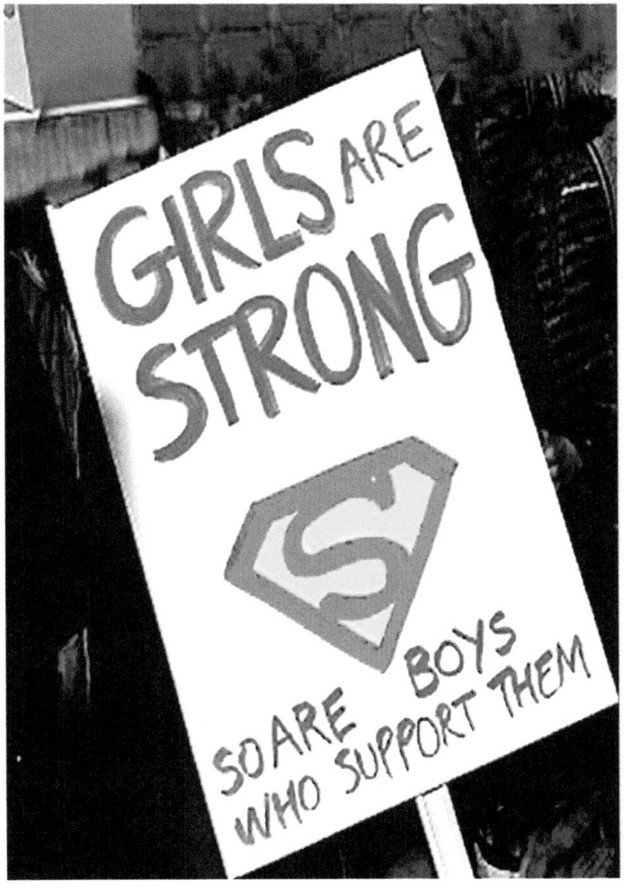
GIRLS ARE
STRONG
SO ARE BOYS
WHO SUPPORT THEM

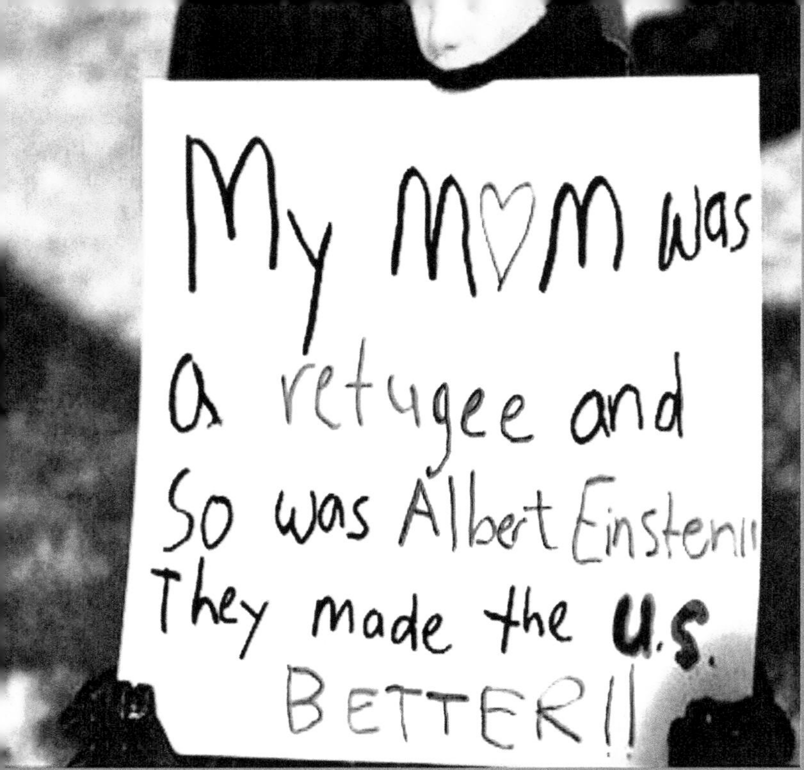
My Mom was
a refugee and
So was Albert Einstein!!
They made the U.S.
BETTER!!

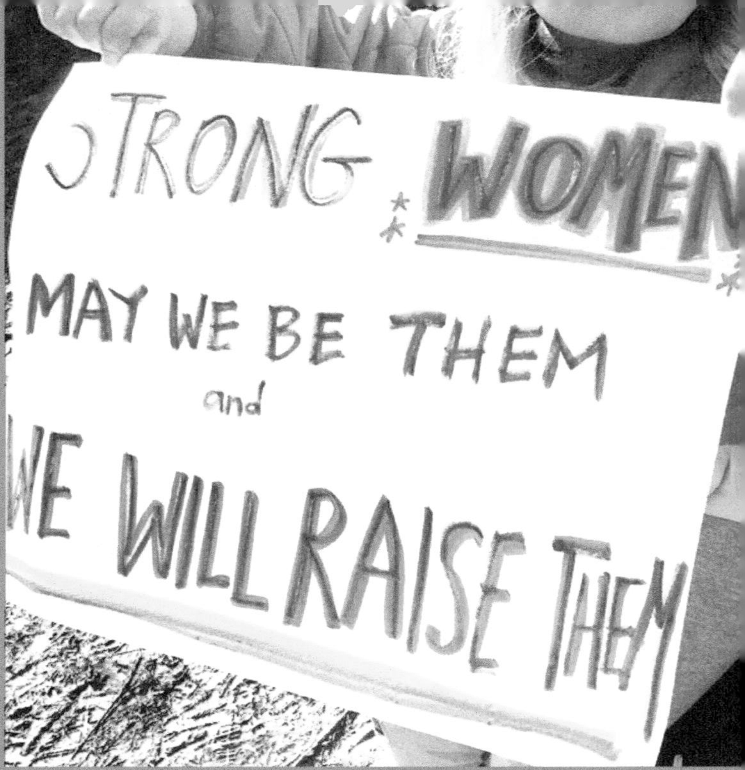
STRONG WOMEN
MAY WE BE THEM
and
WE WILL RAISE THEM

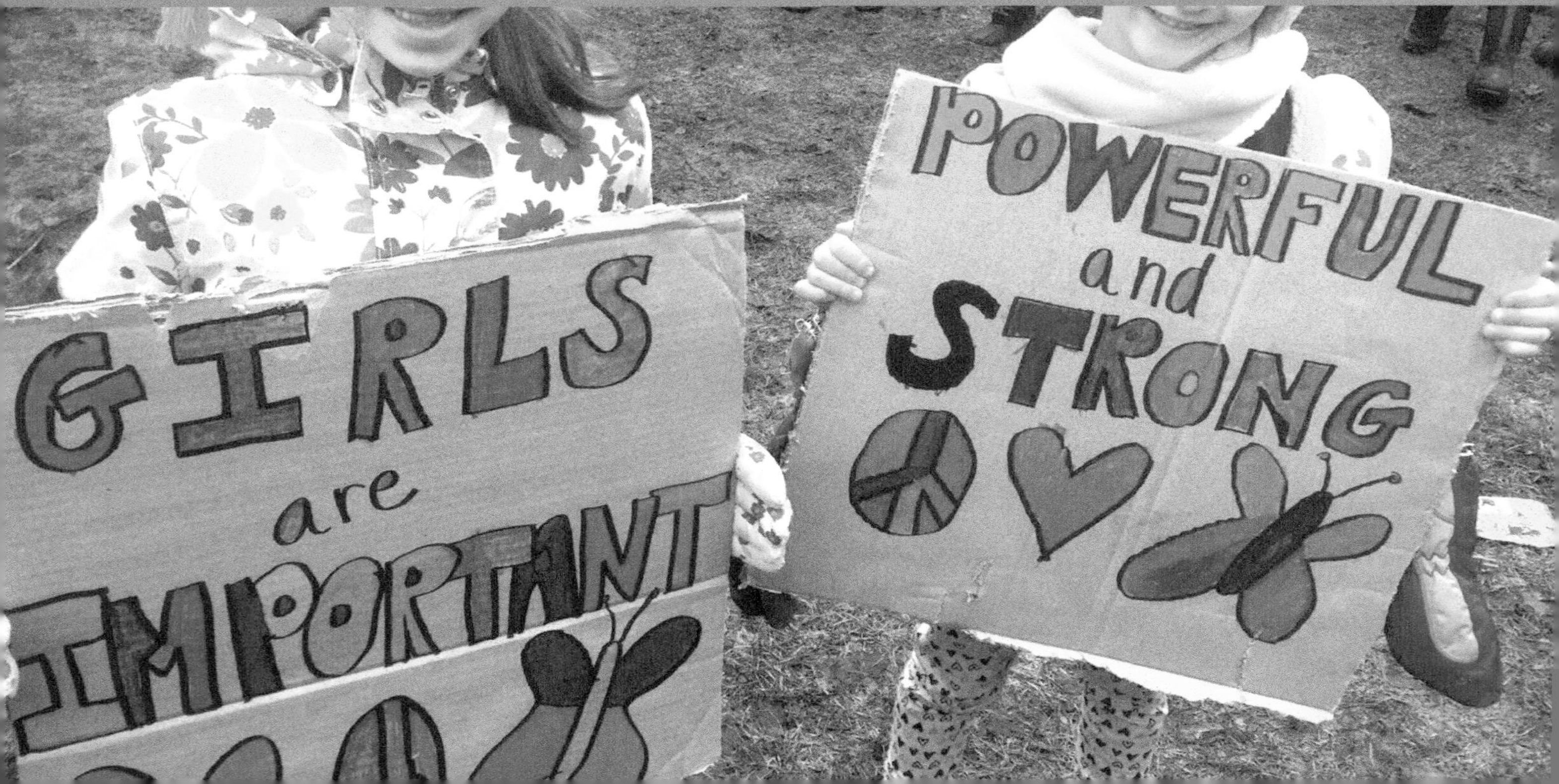
GIRLS
are
IMPORTANT
POWERFUL
and
STRONG

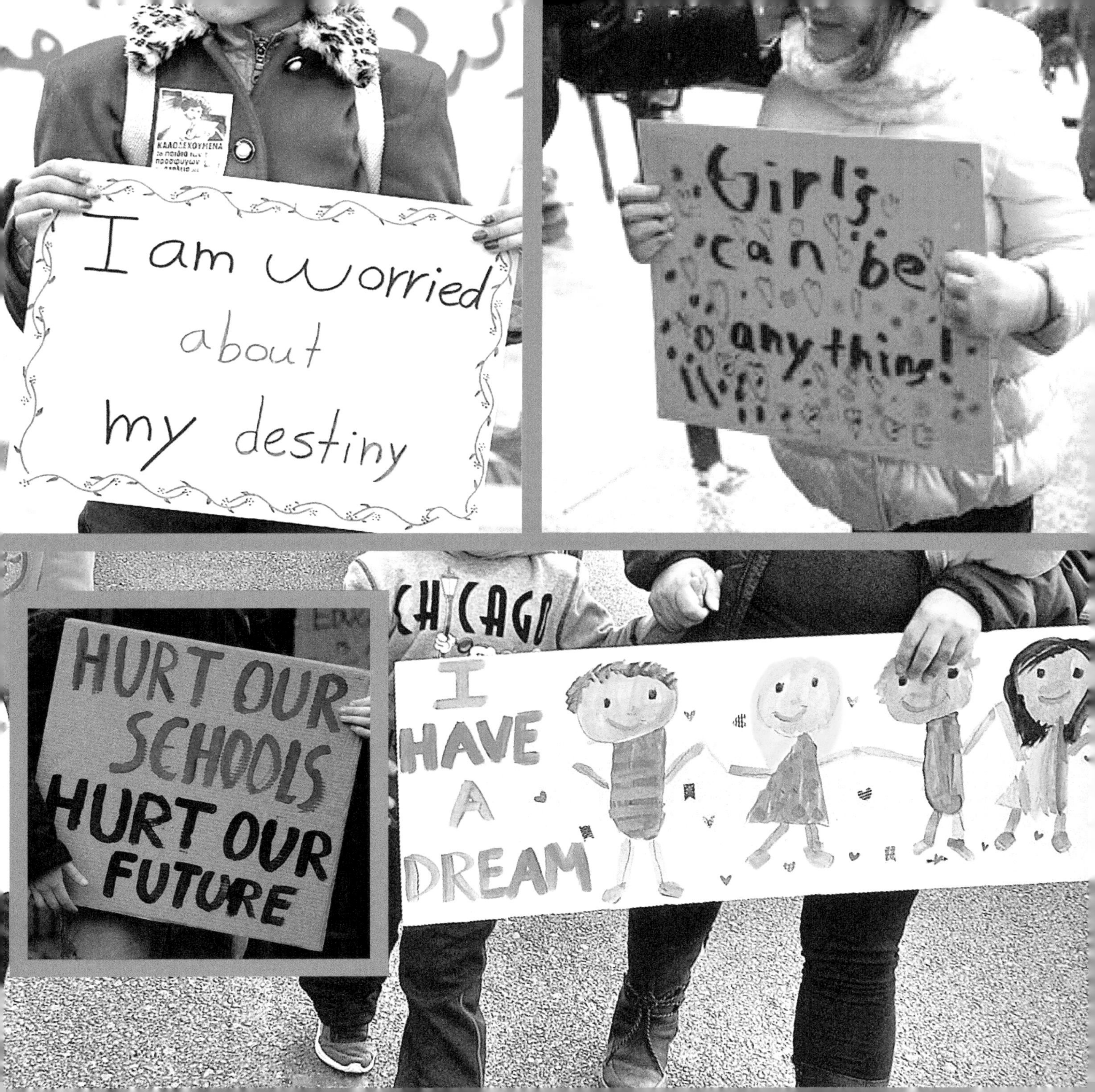
I am worried about my destiny
Girls can be anything!
HURT OUR SCHOOLS HURT OUR FUTURE
CHICAGO
I HAVE A DREAM

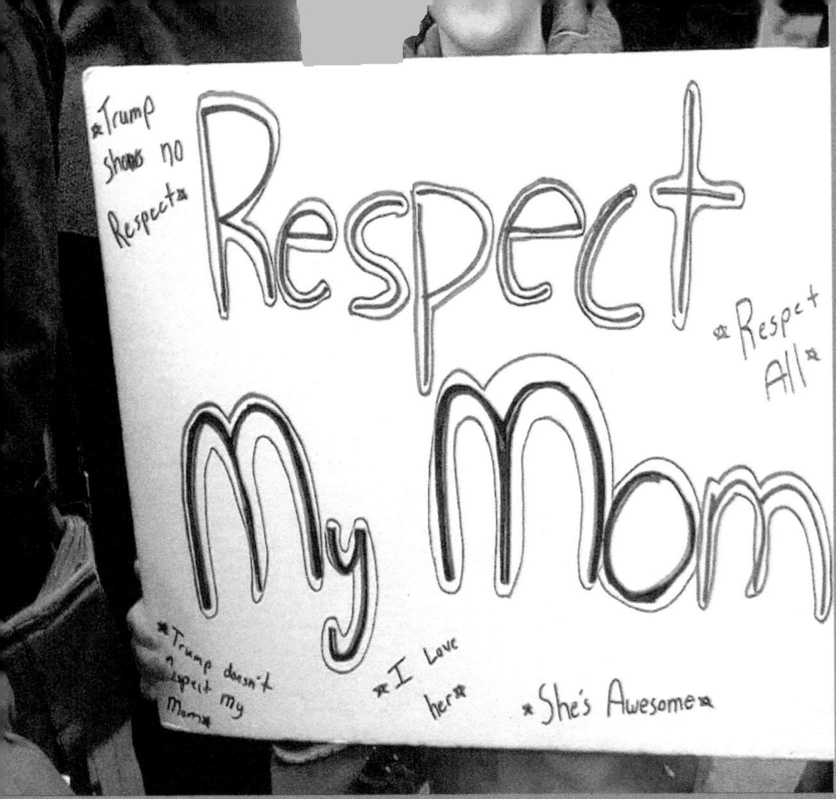
Trump shows no Respect
Respect My Mom
Respect All
I Love her
She's Awesome

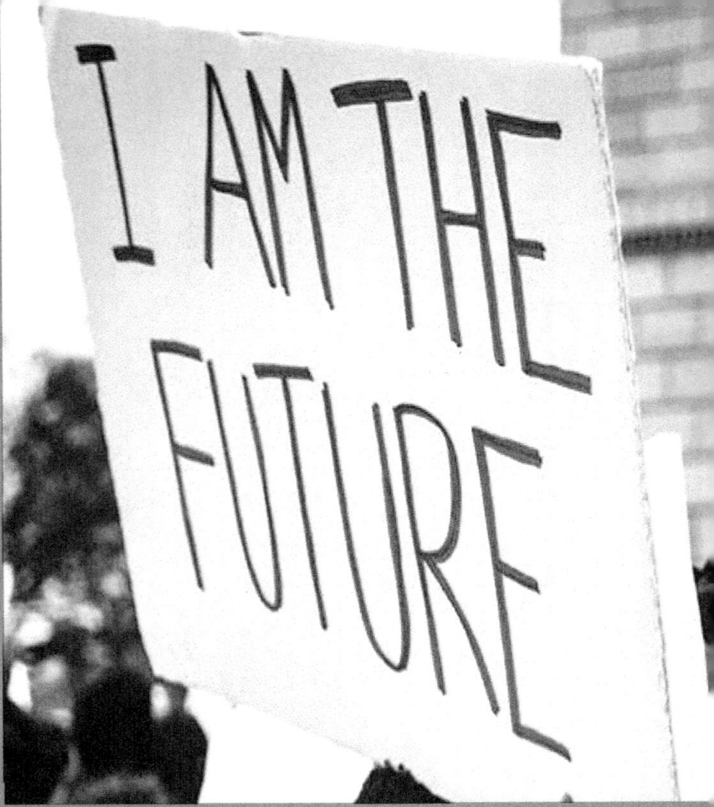
I AM THE FUTURE

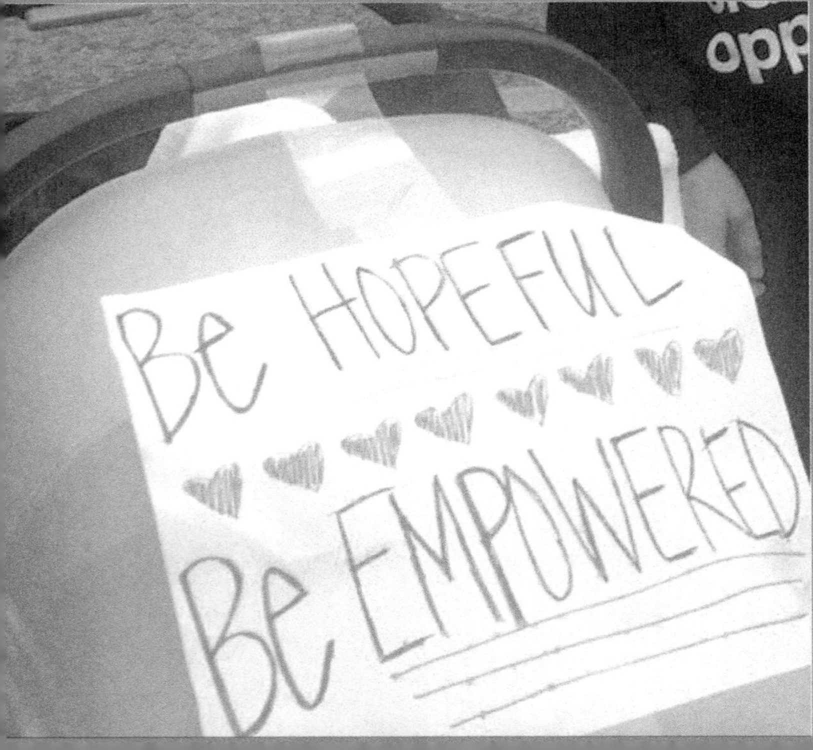
Be HOPEFUL
Be EMPOWERED

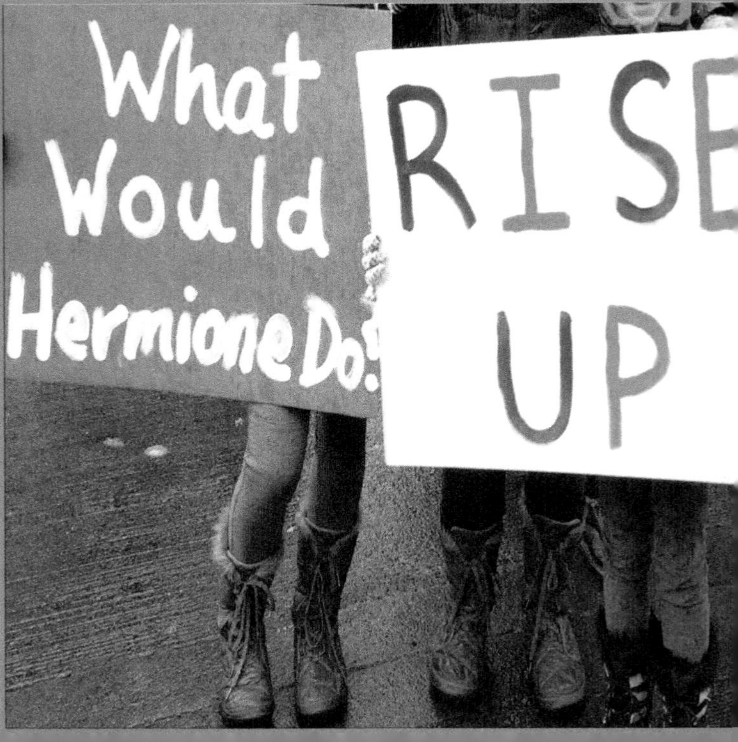
What Would Hermione Do
RISE UP

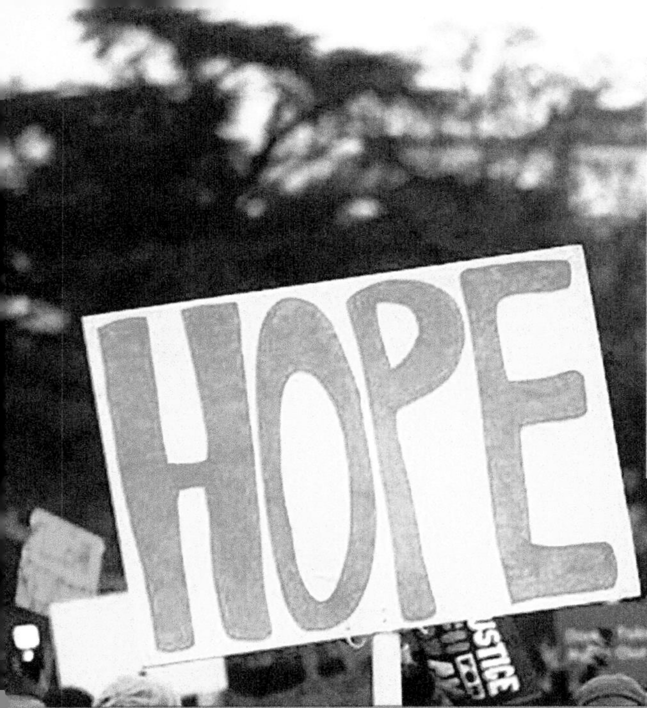
HOPE

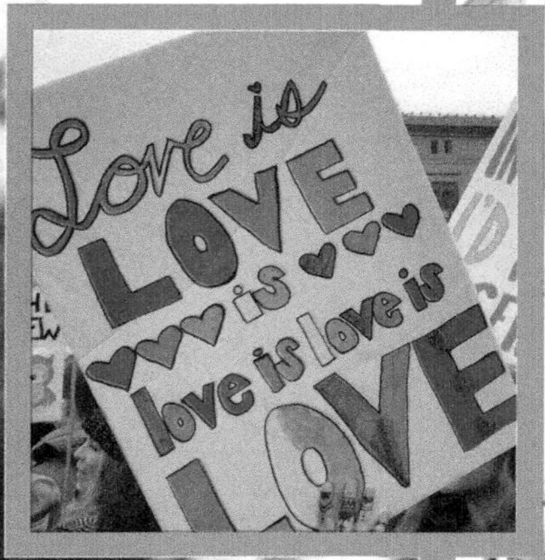
Love is
LOVE
is
love is love is
LOVE

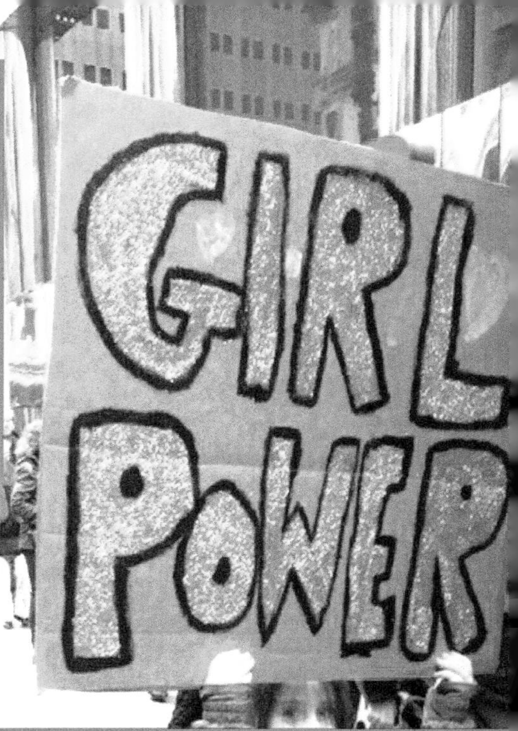
GIRL
POWER

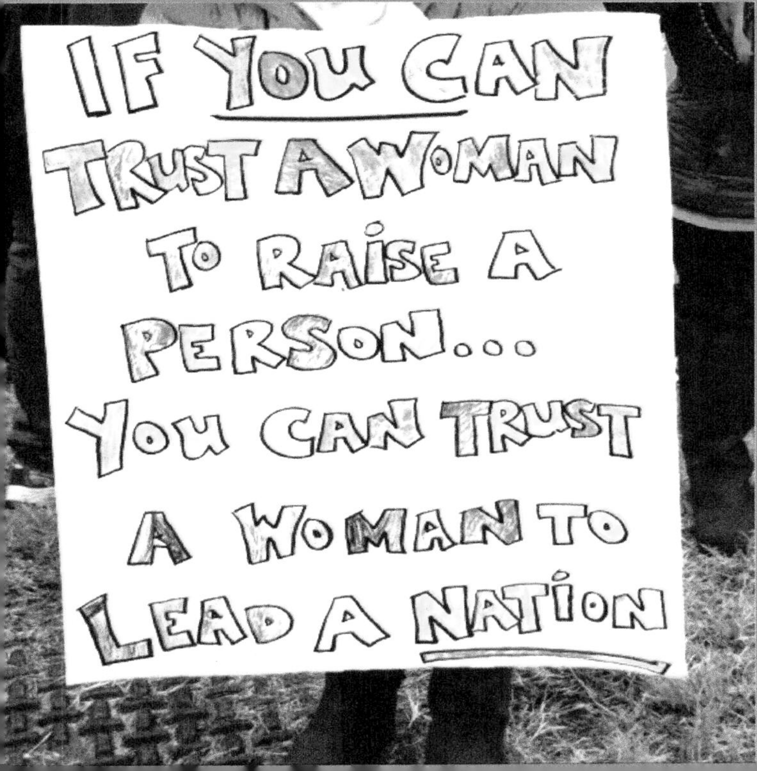
IF YOU CAN
TRUST A WOMAN
TO RAISE A
PERSON...
YOU CAN TRUST
A WOMAN TO
LEAD A NATION

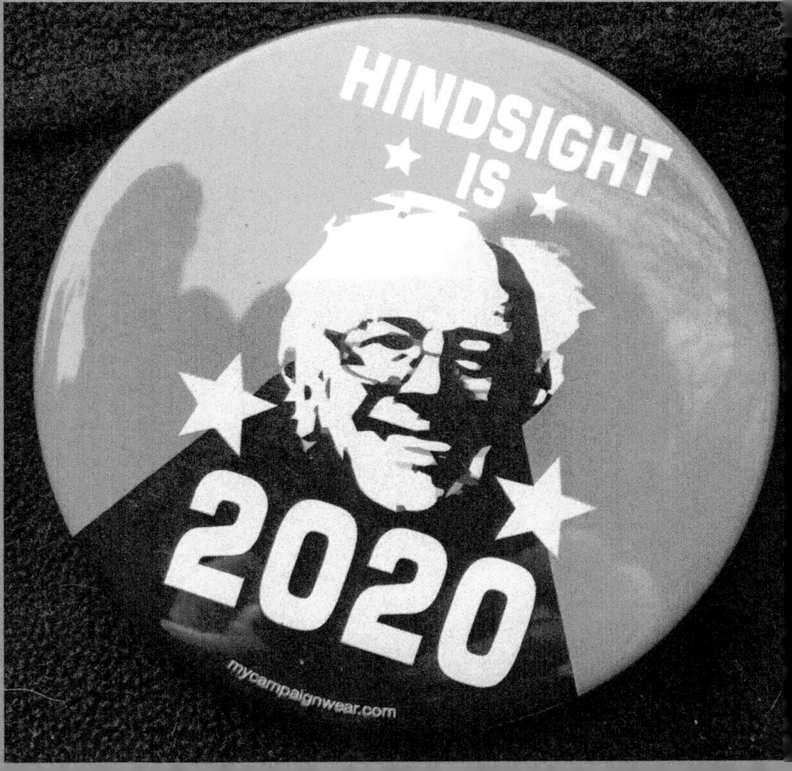
HINDSIGHT
IS
2020
mycampaignwear.com

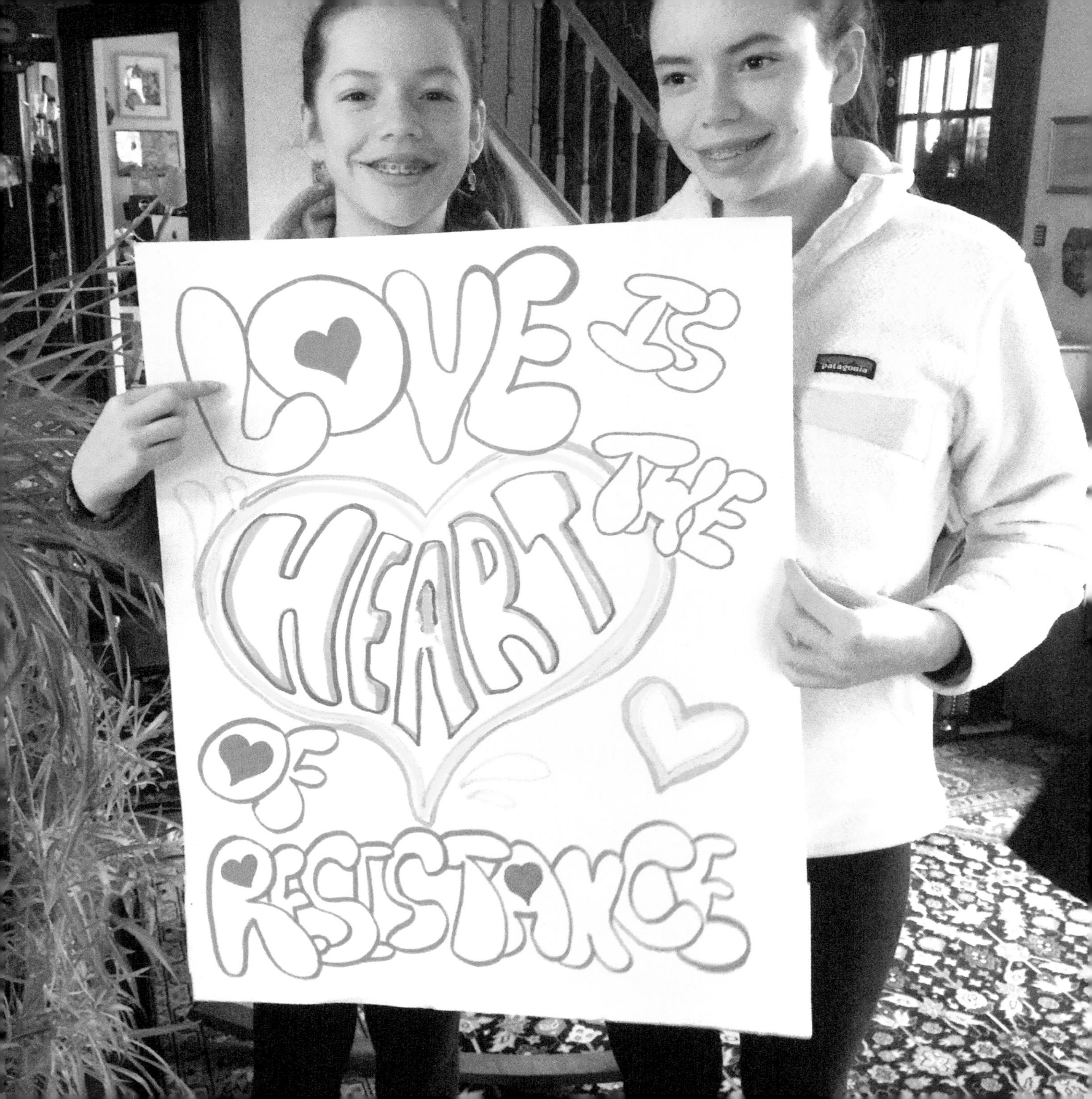
LOVE IS THE HEART OF RESISTANCE
patagonia

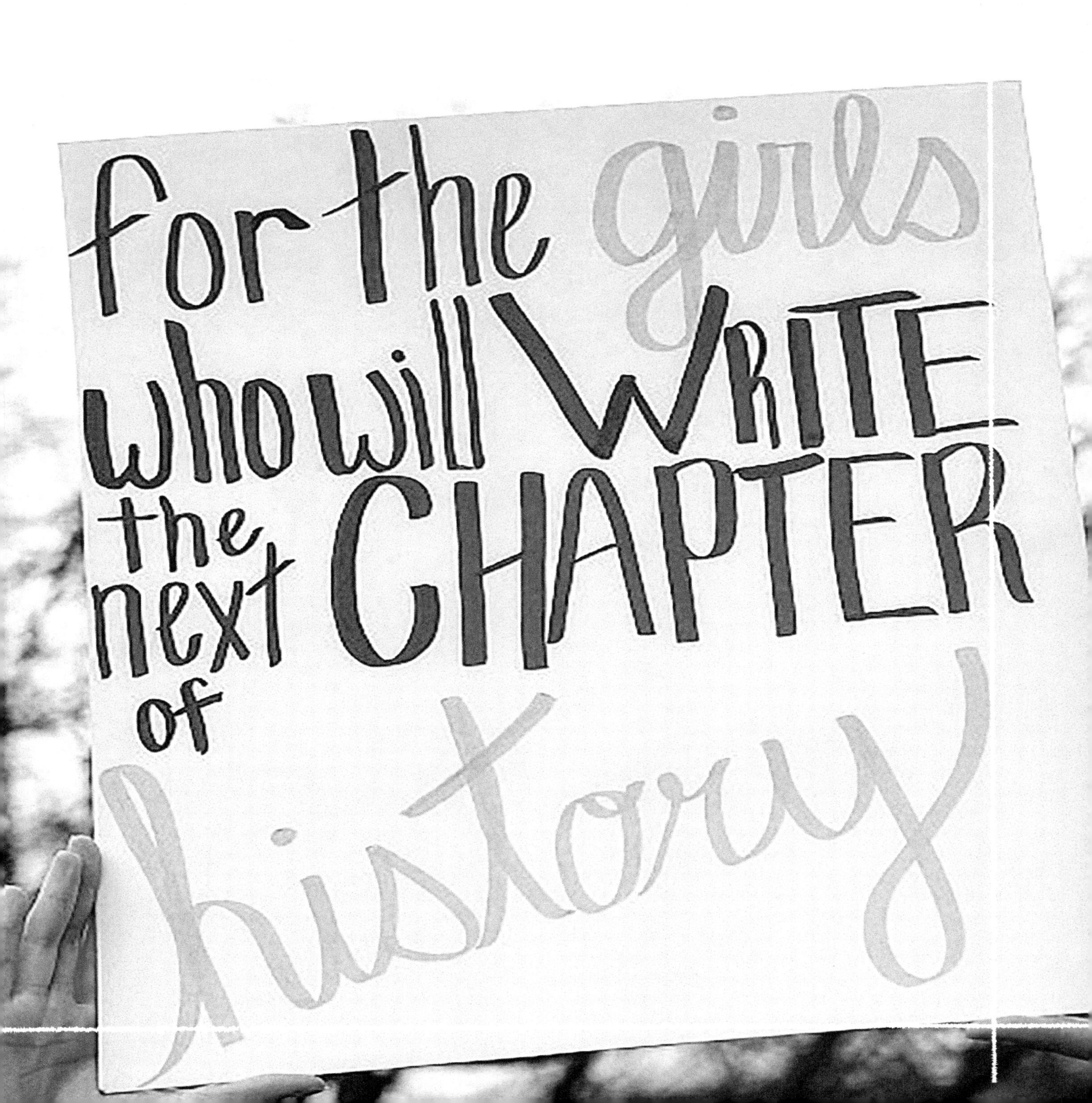
for the girls
who will WRITE
the next CHAPTER
of
history

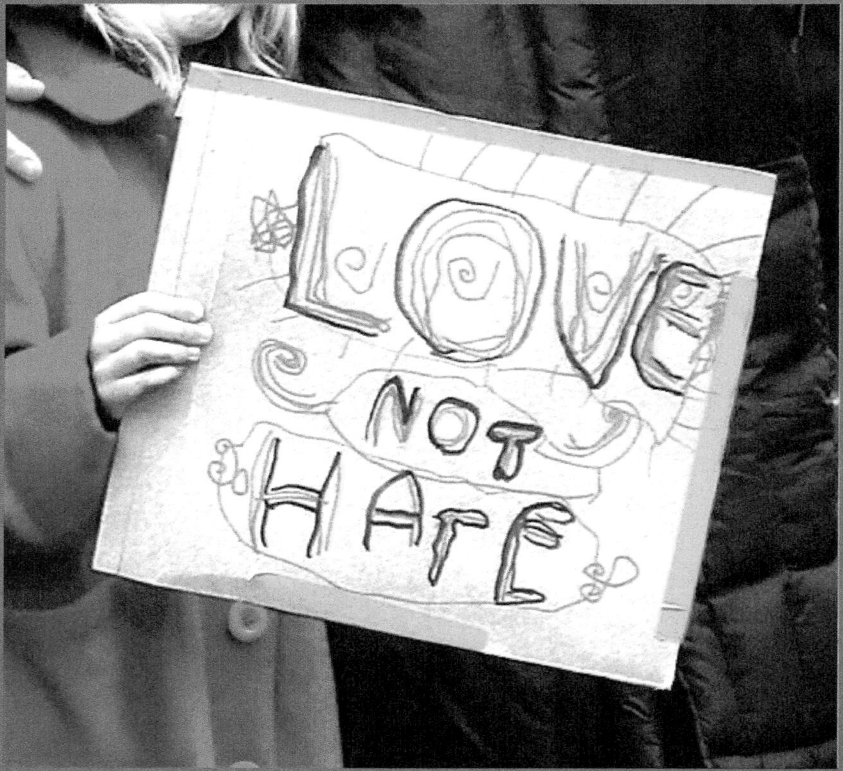
LOVE
NOT
HATE

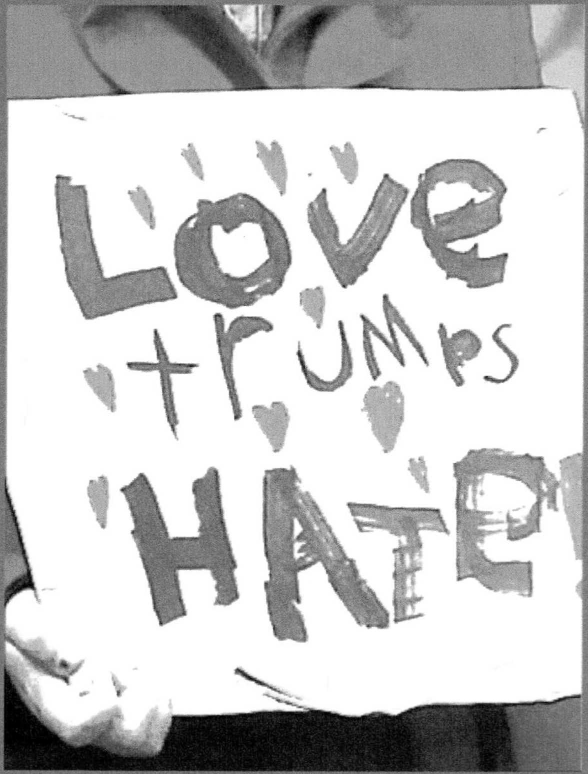
Love
trumps
HATE

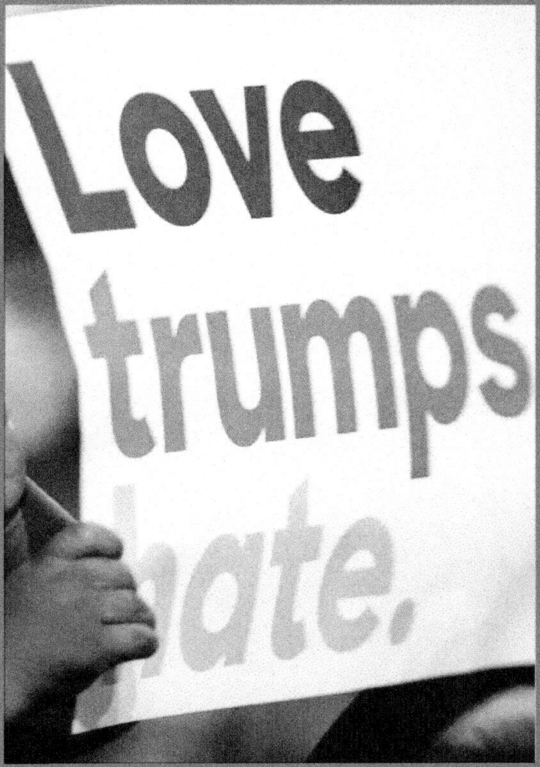
Love
trumps
hate.

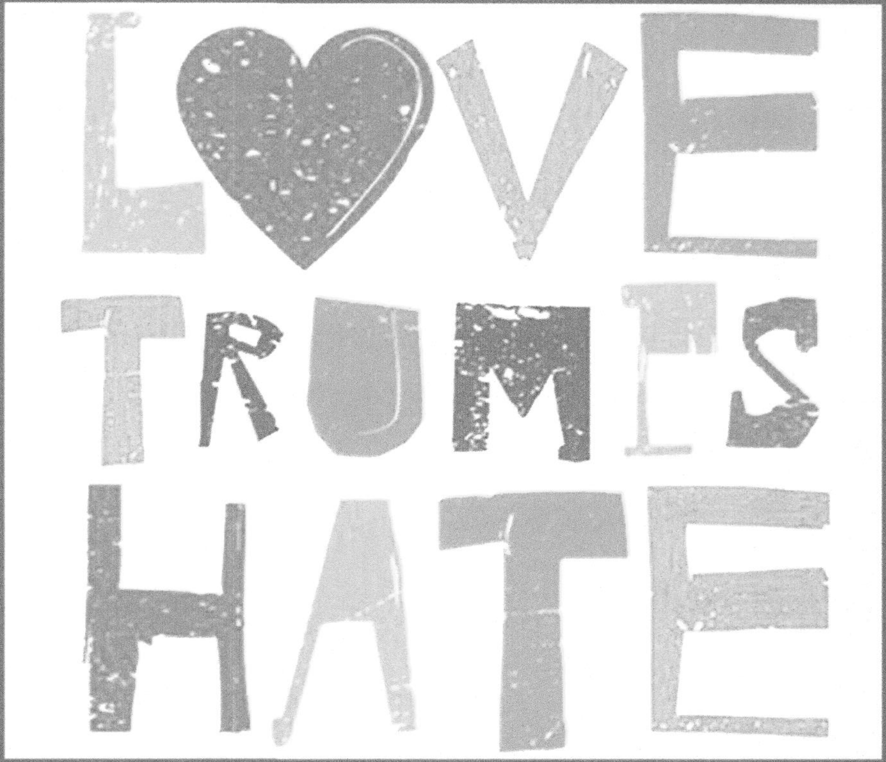
LOVE
TRUMPS
HATE

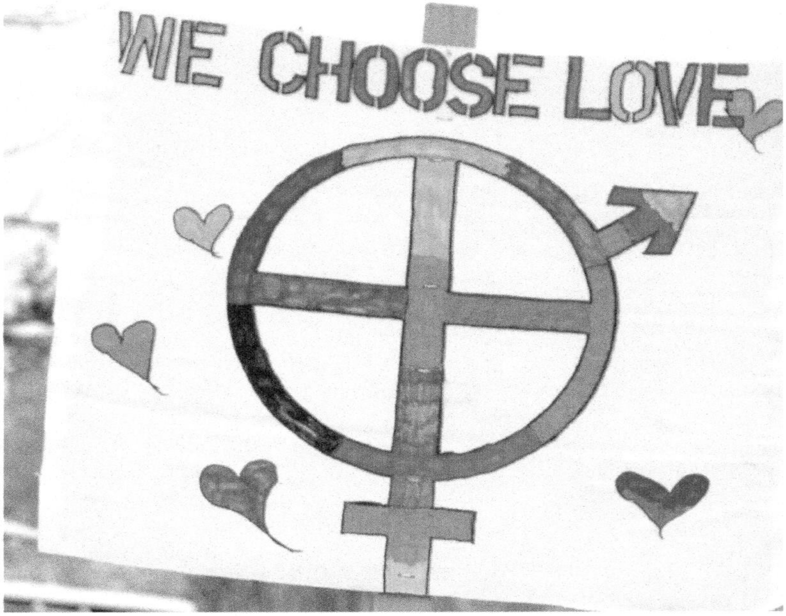
WE CHOOSE LOVE

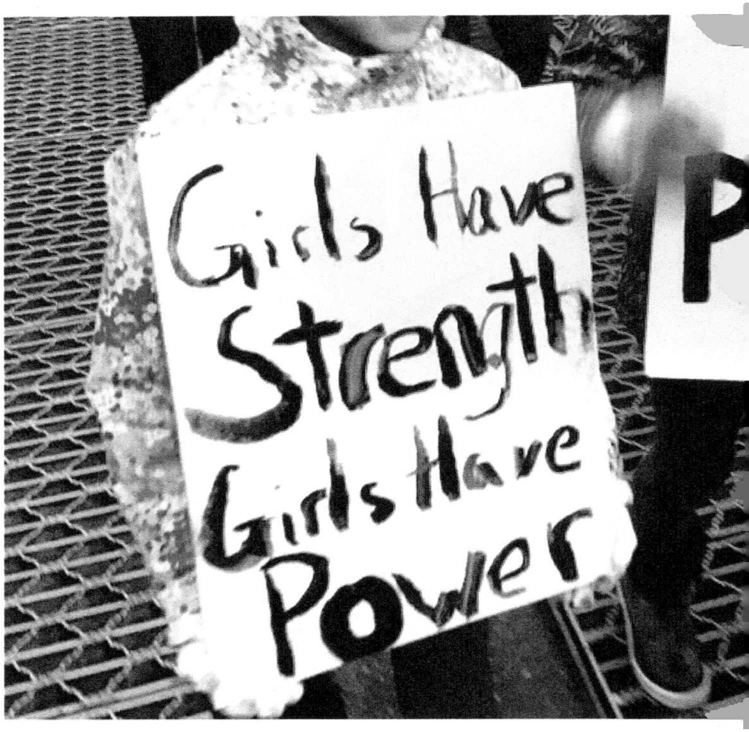
Girls Have
Strength
Girls Have
Power

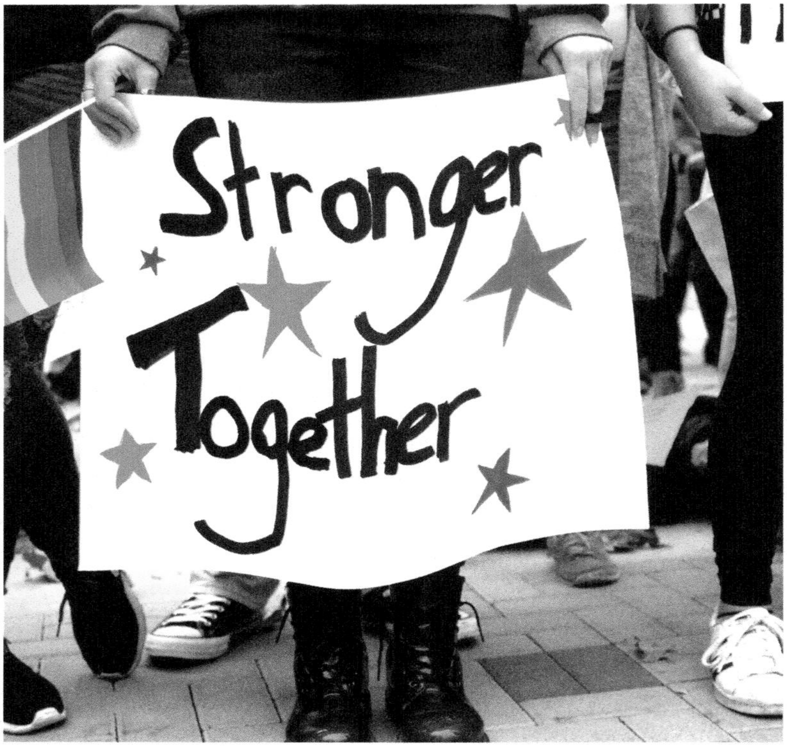
Stronger
Together

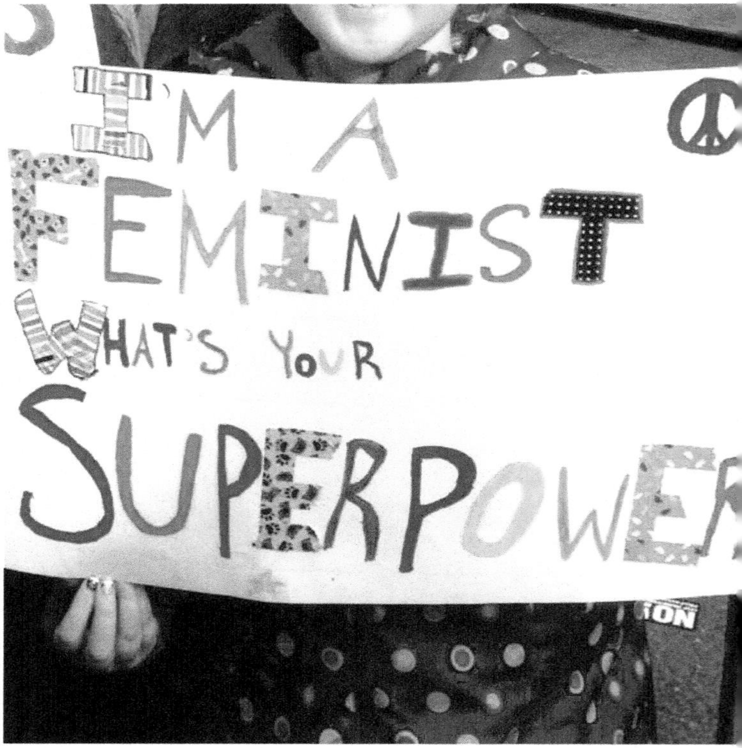
I'M A
FEMINIST
WHAT'S YOUR
SUPERPOWE

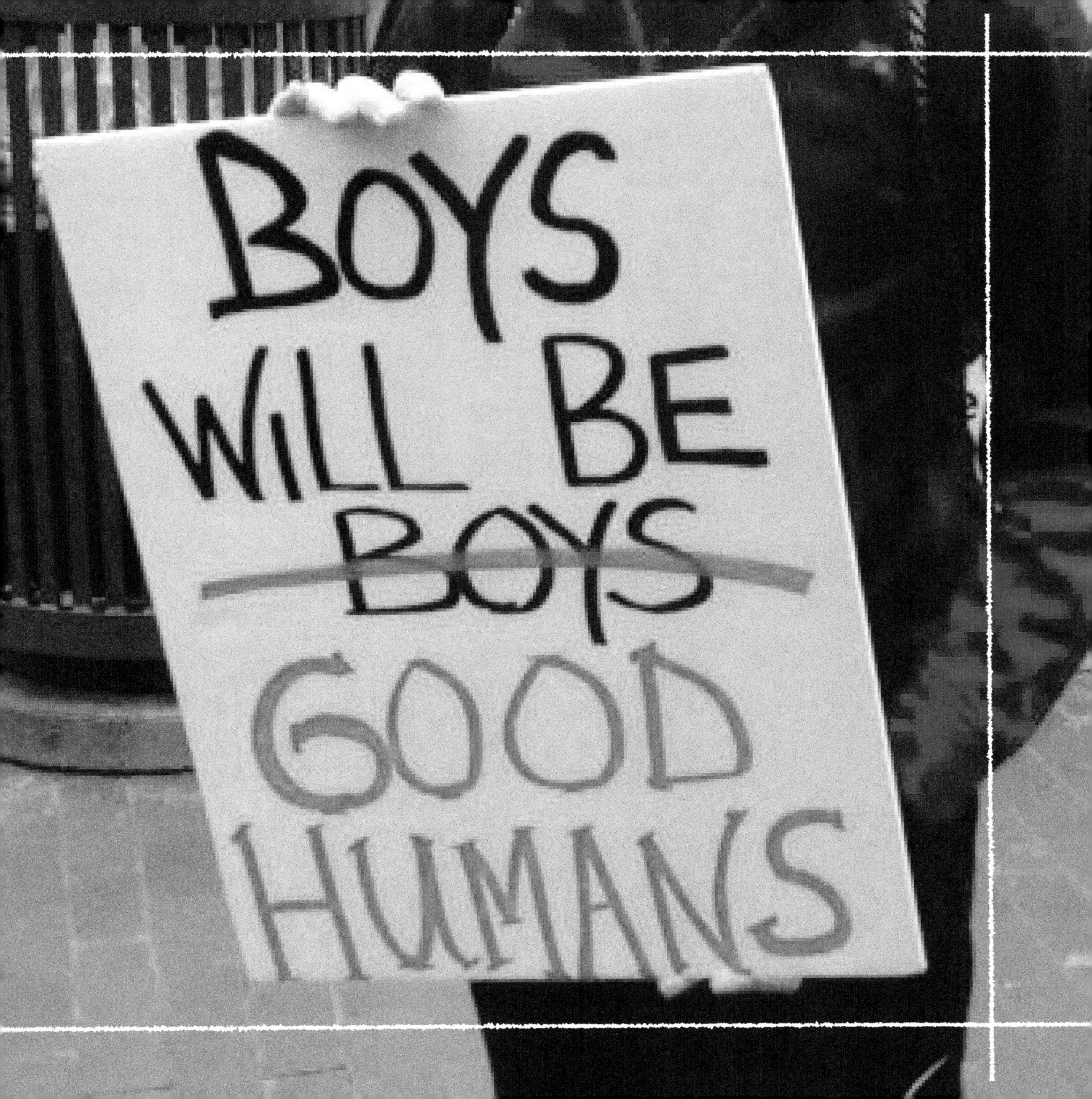
BOYS
WILL BE
BOYS
GOOD
HUMANS

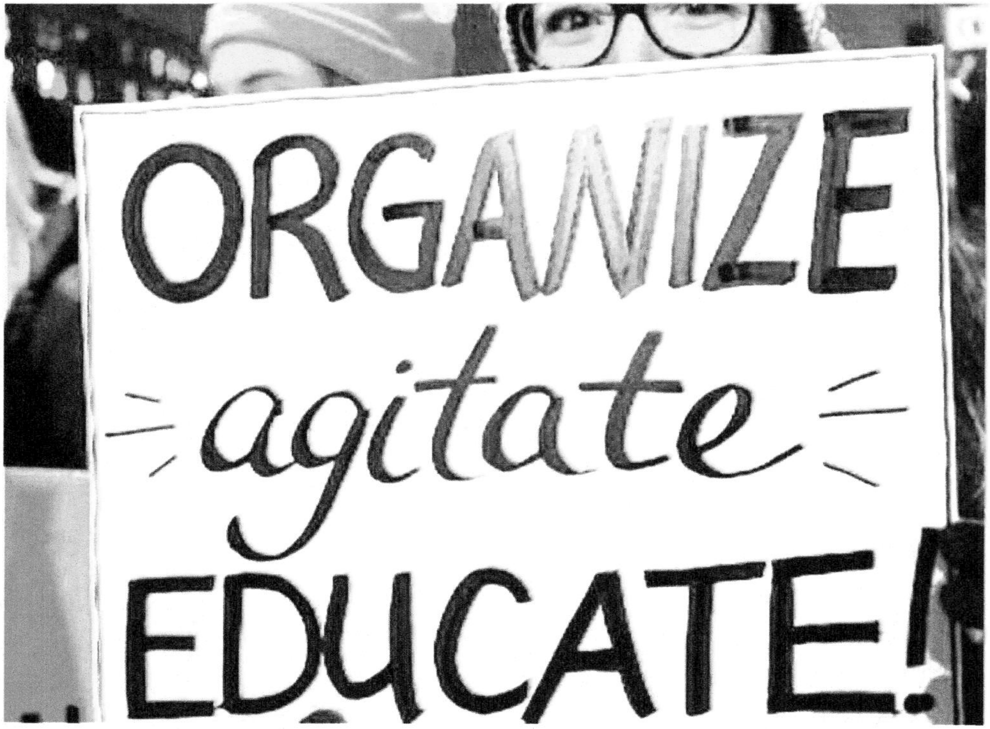
ORGANIZE
agitate
EDUCATE!

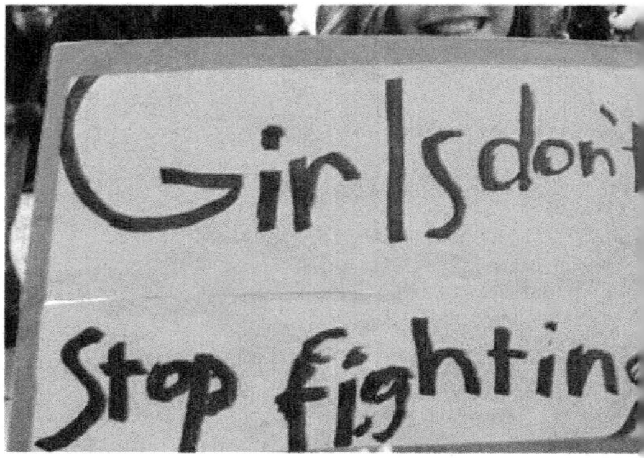
Girls don't
Stop fightin

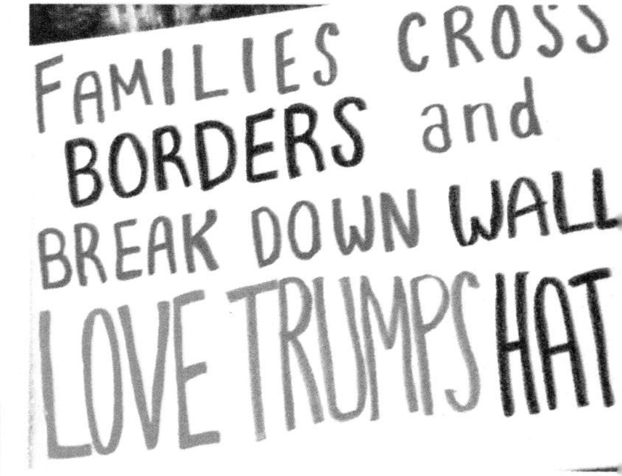
FAMILIES CROSS
BORDERS and
BREAK DOWN WALL
LOVE TRUMPS HAT

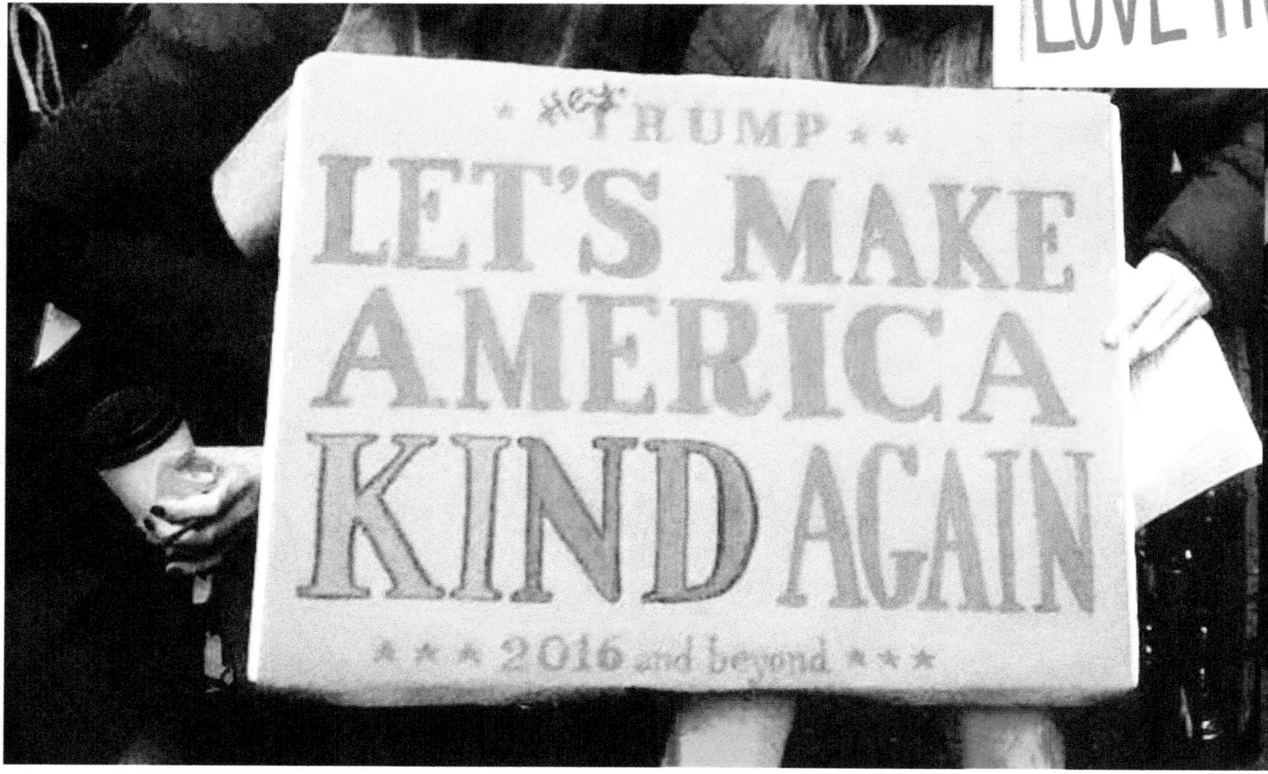
Hey TRUMP
LET'S MAKE
AMERICA
KIND AGAIN
2016 and beyond

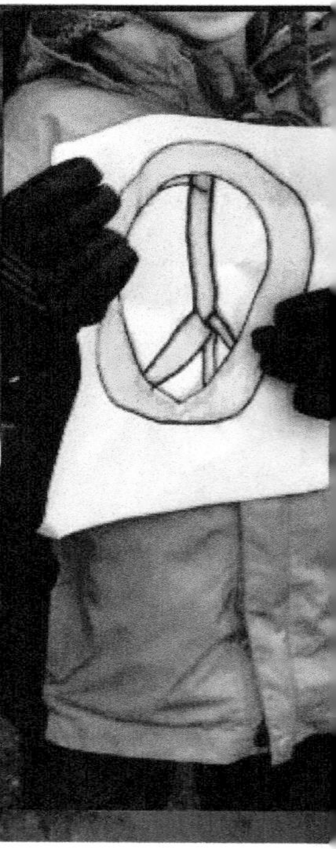

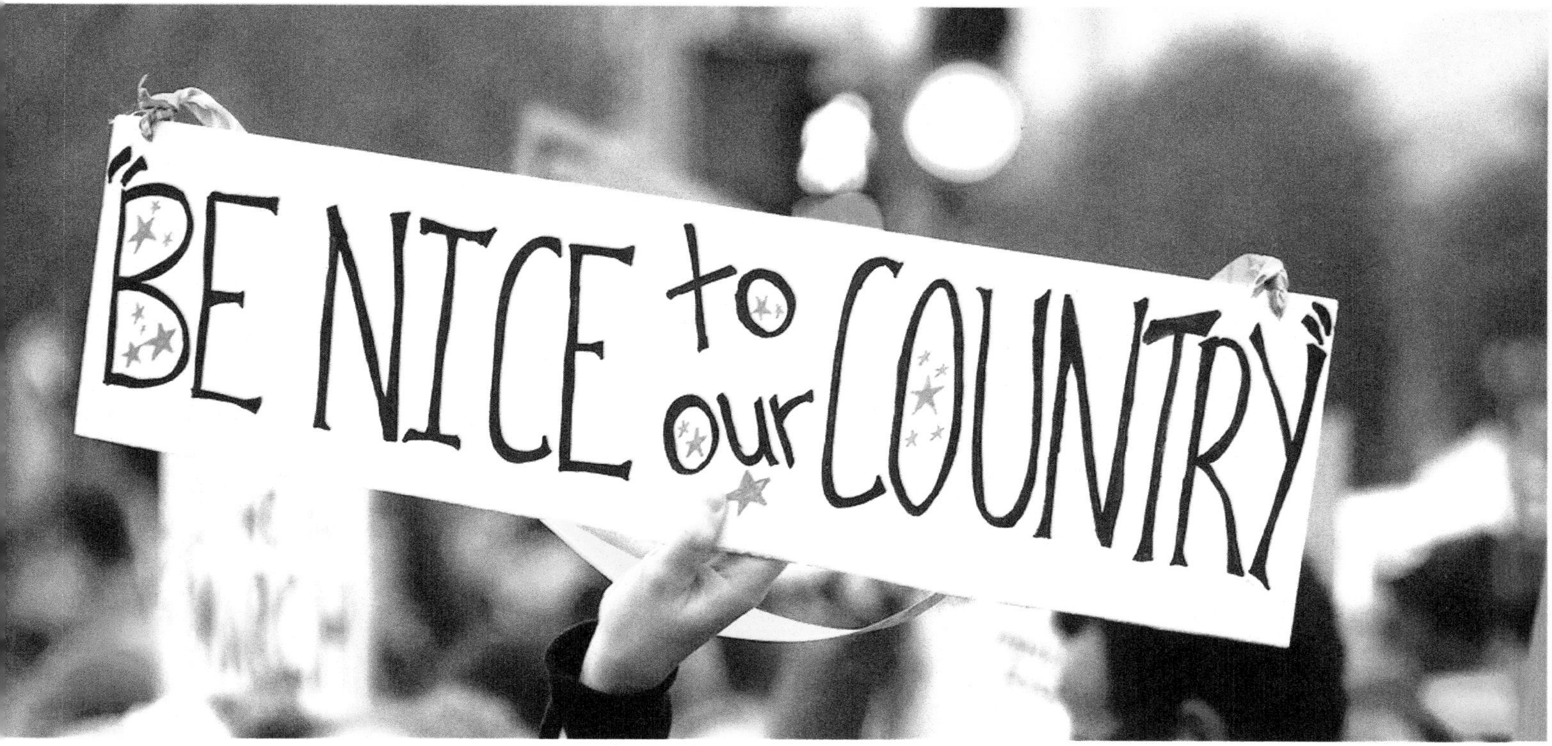
"BE NICE to our COUNTRY"

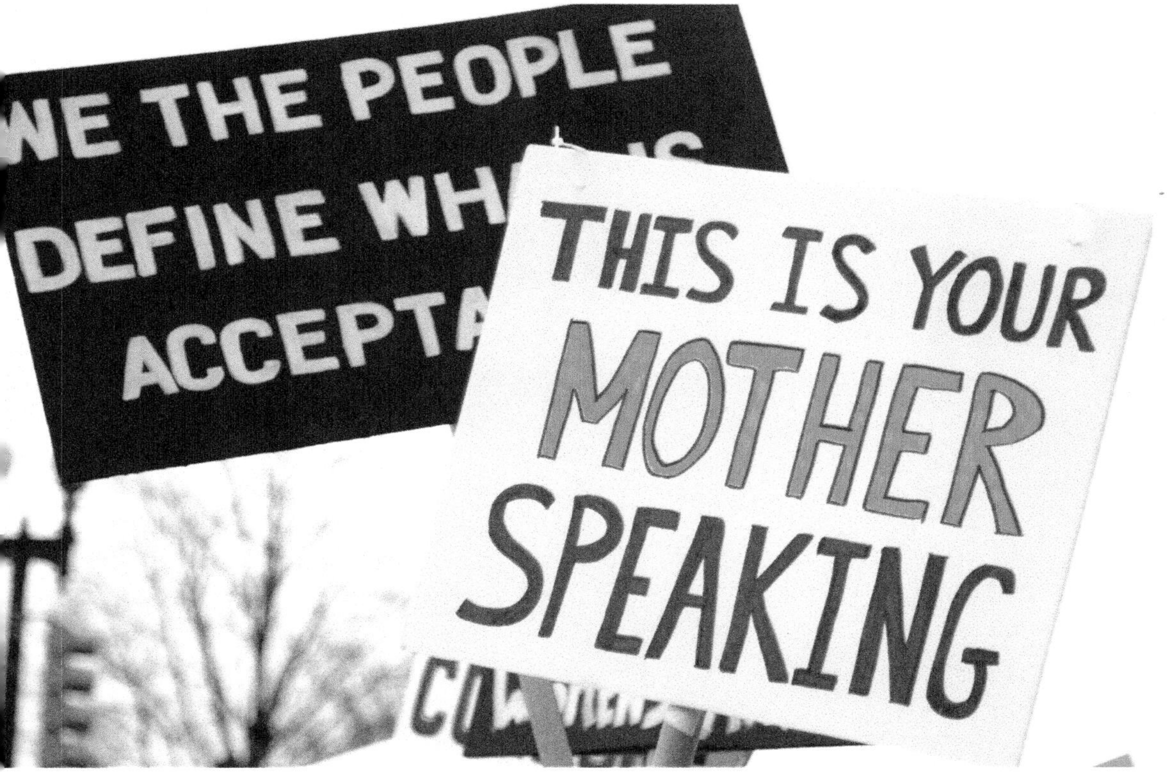
WE THE PEOPLE
DEFINE
THIS IS YOUR
MOTHER
SPEAKING

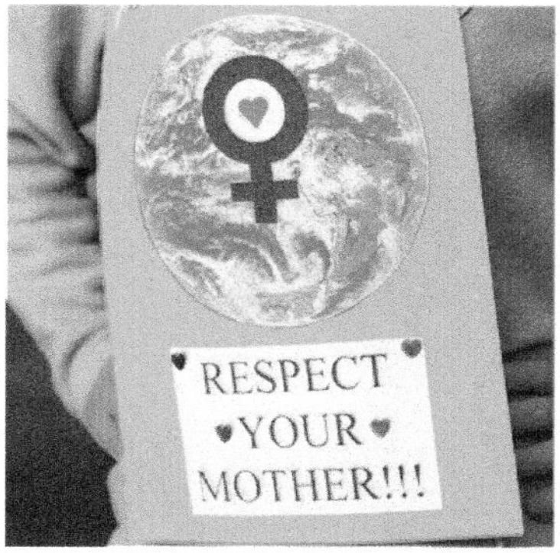
RESPECT
YOUR
MOTHER!!!

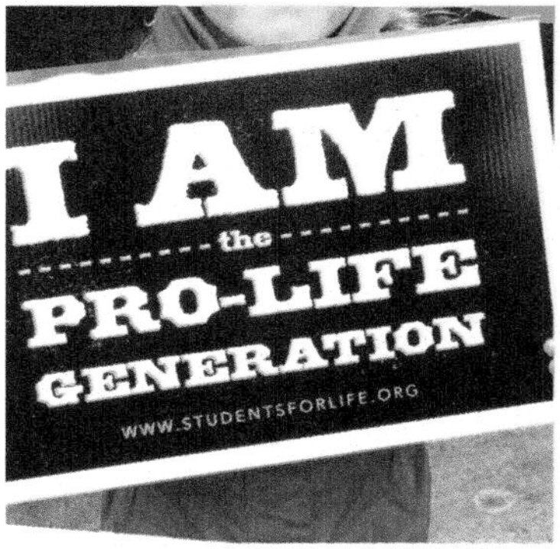
I AM
the
PRO-LIFE
GENERATION
WWW.STUDENTSFORLIFE.ORG

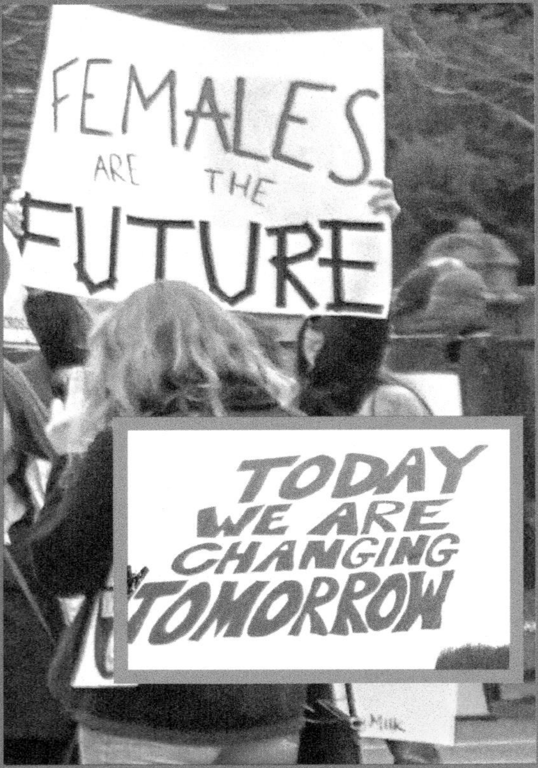
FEMALES ARE THE FUTURE
TODAY WE ARE CHANGING TOMORROW

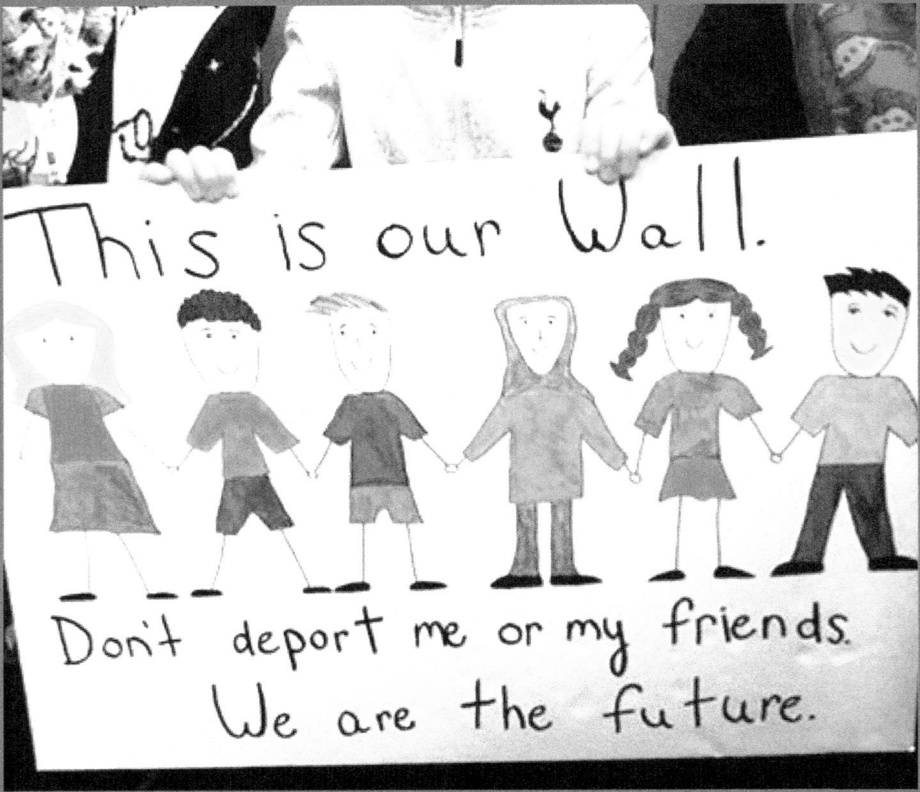
This is our Wall.
Don't deport me or my friends.
We are the future.

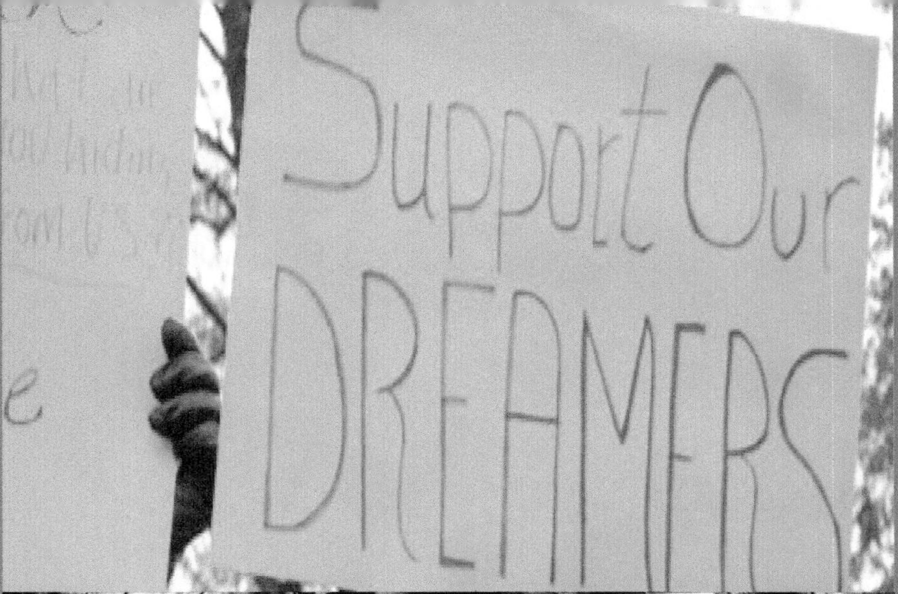
Support Our
DREAMERS

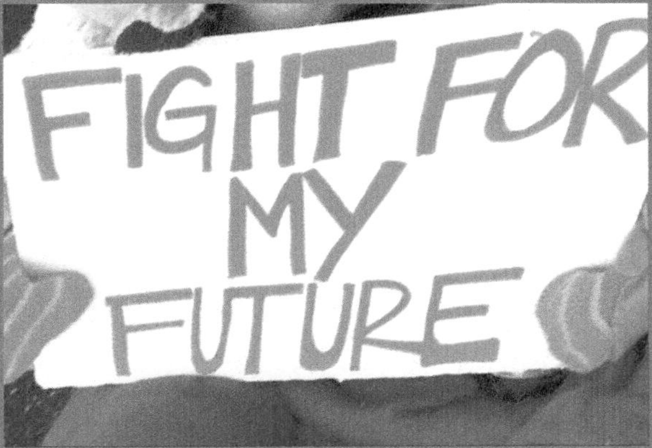
FIGHT FOR
MY
FUTURE

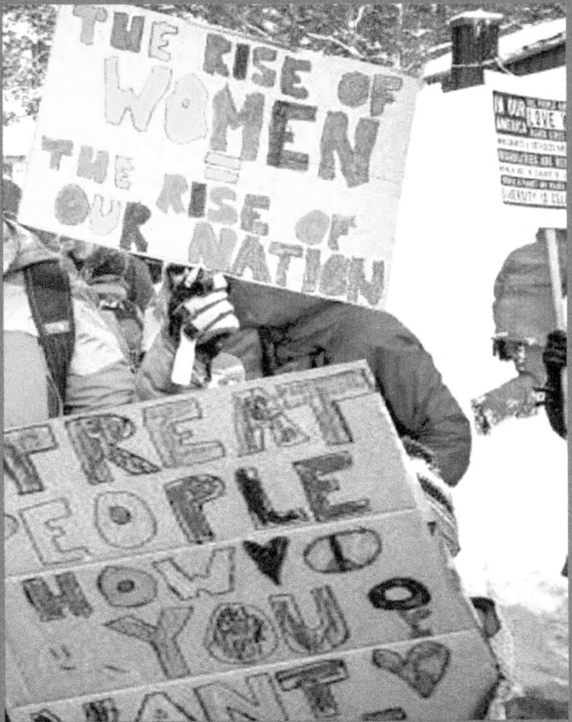
THE RISE OF
WOMEN
=
THE RISE OF
OUR NATION
TREAT
PEOPLE
HOW YOU

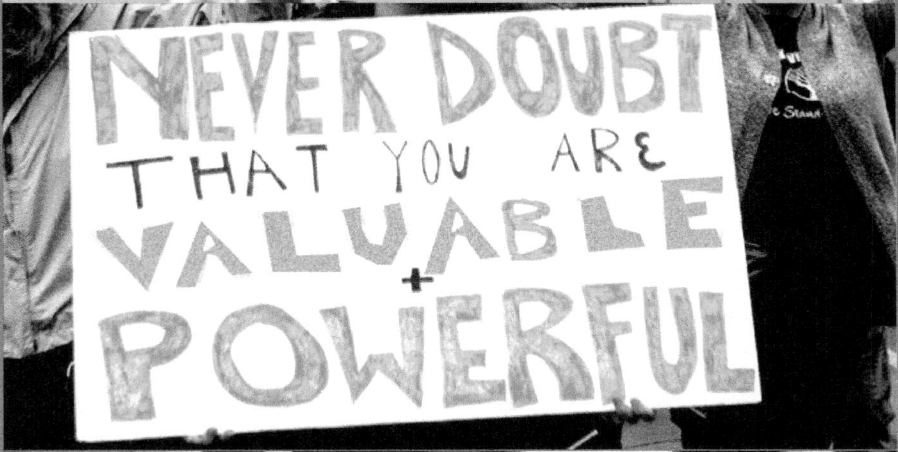
NEVER DOUBT
THAT YOU ARE
VALUABLE
+
POWERFUL

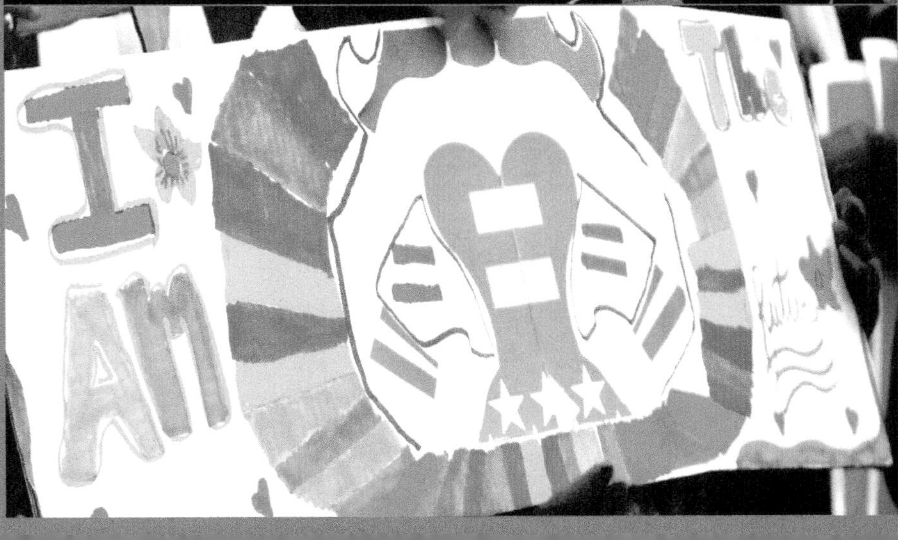
I
AM

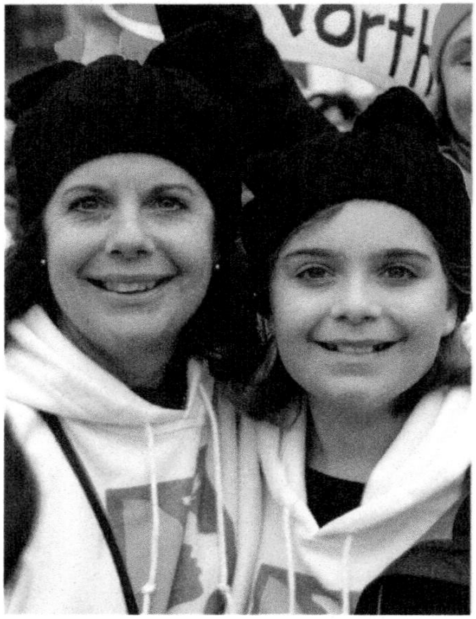

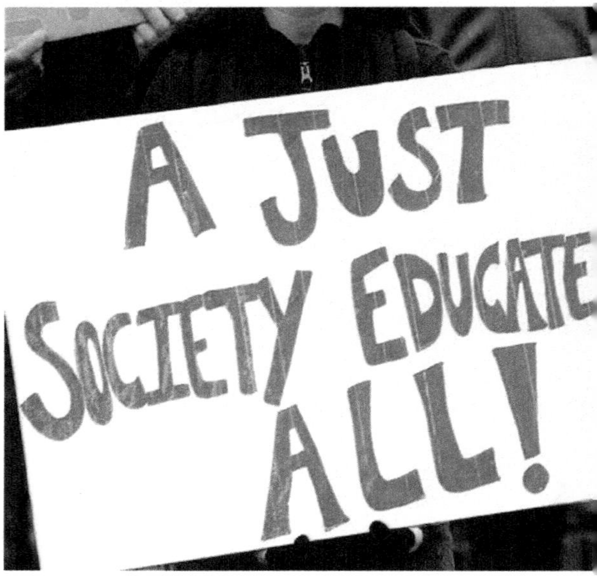
A JUST
SOCIETY EDUCATE
ALL!

Whatever pathways and hurdles we face, we are connected.

Karen Gross

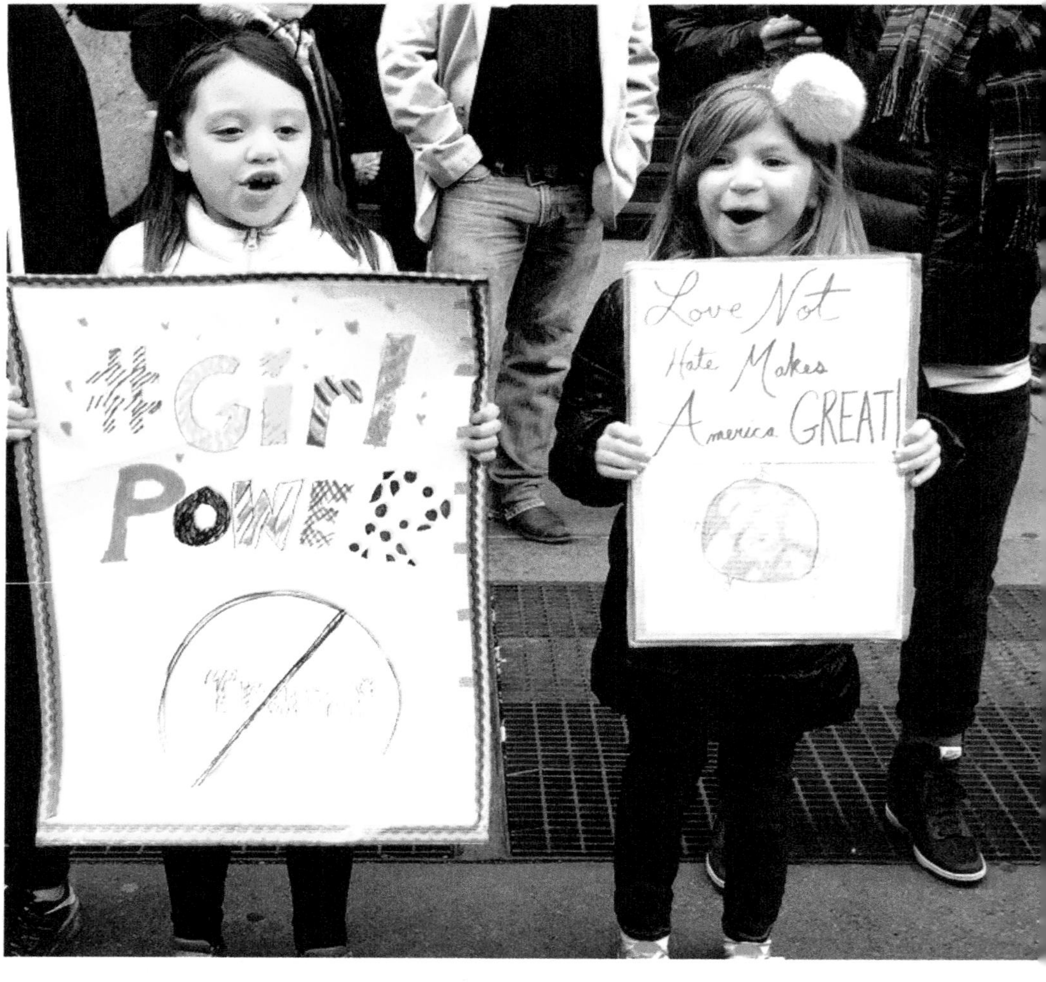
#Girl
POWER
Love Not
Hate Makes
America GREAT!

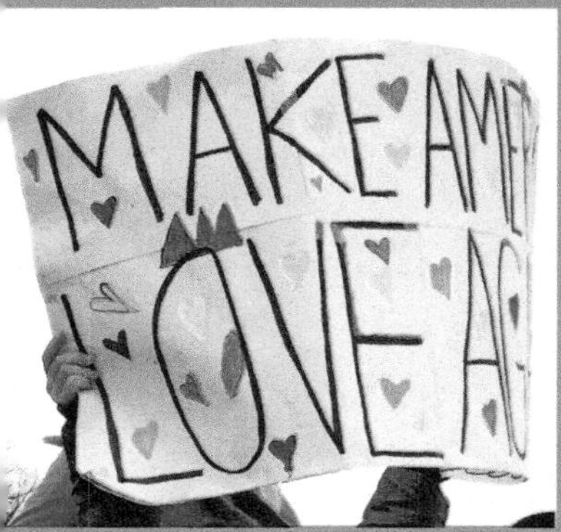
MAKE AMER
LOVE AG

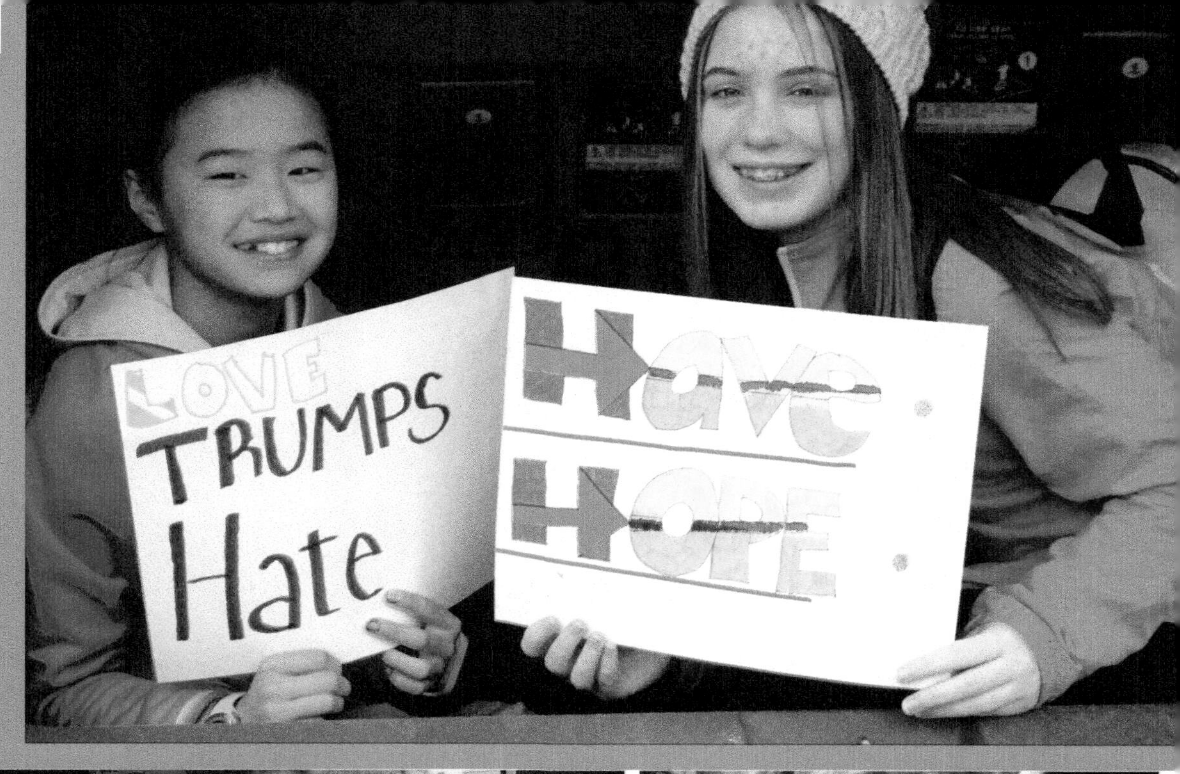
LOVE
TRUMPS
Hate
Have
HOPE

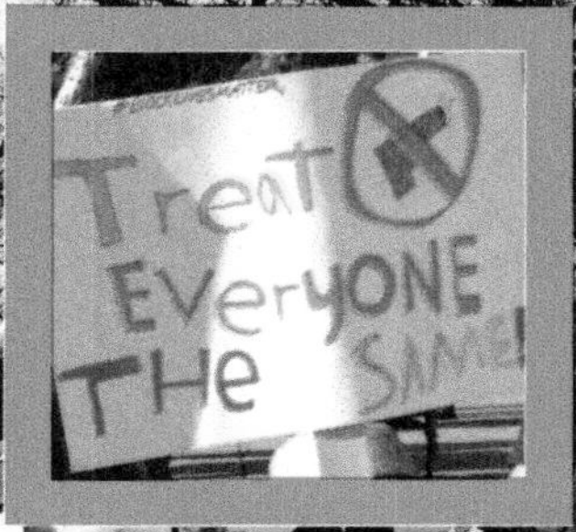
Treat
EveryONE
THe SAME!

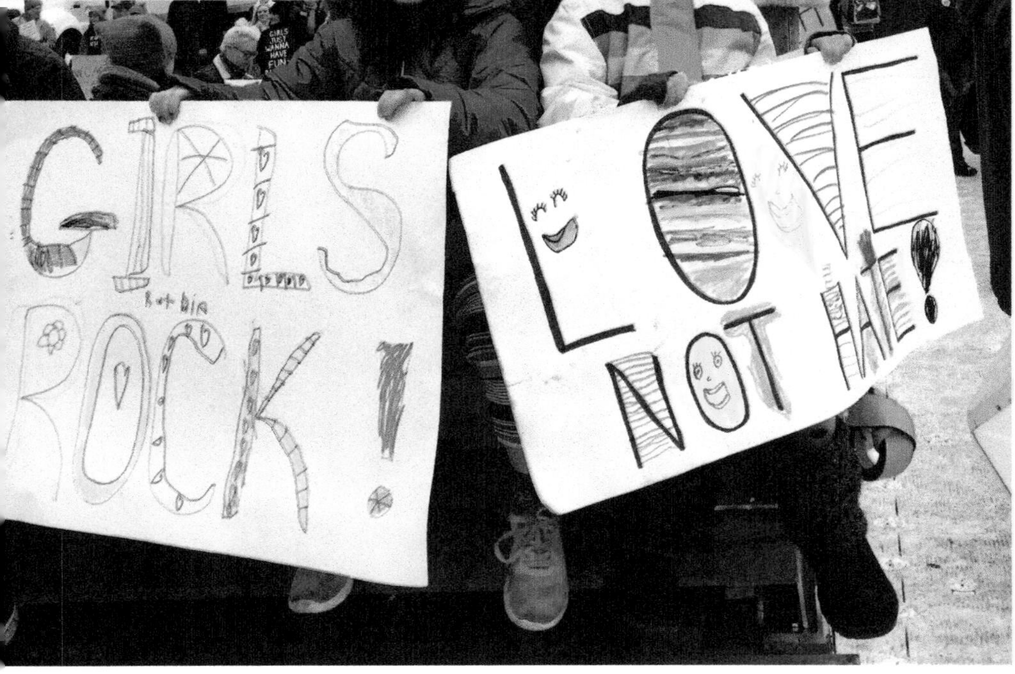
GIRLS
ROCK!
LOVE
NOT HATE!

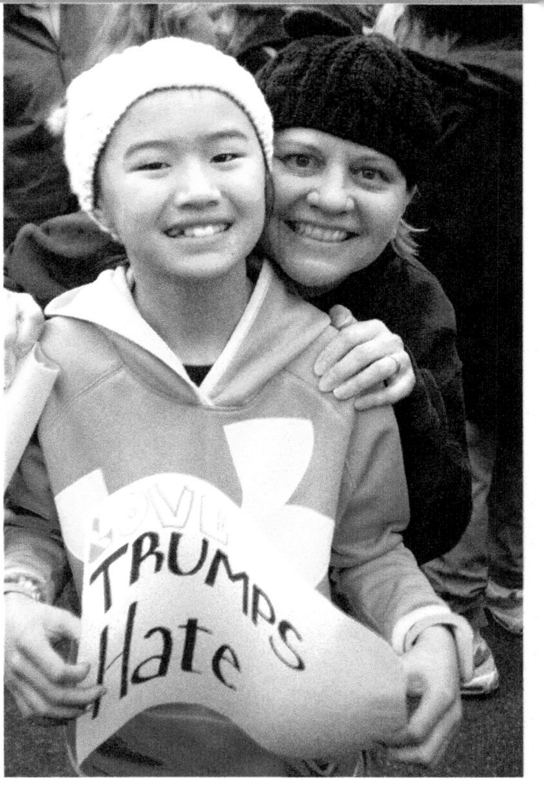
LOVE
TRUMPS
Hate

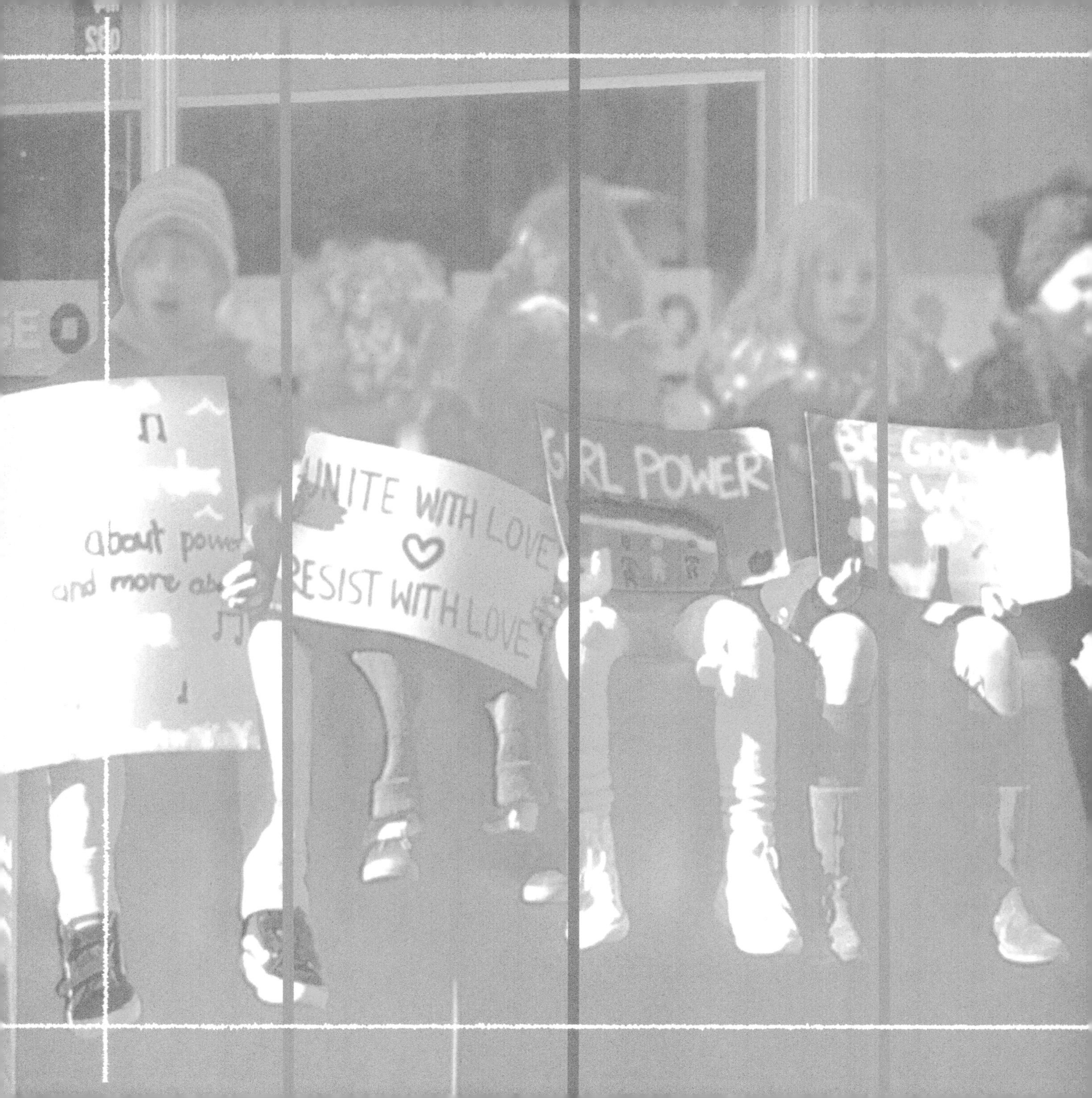
UNITE WITH LOVE
RESIST WITH LOVE
GIRL POWER

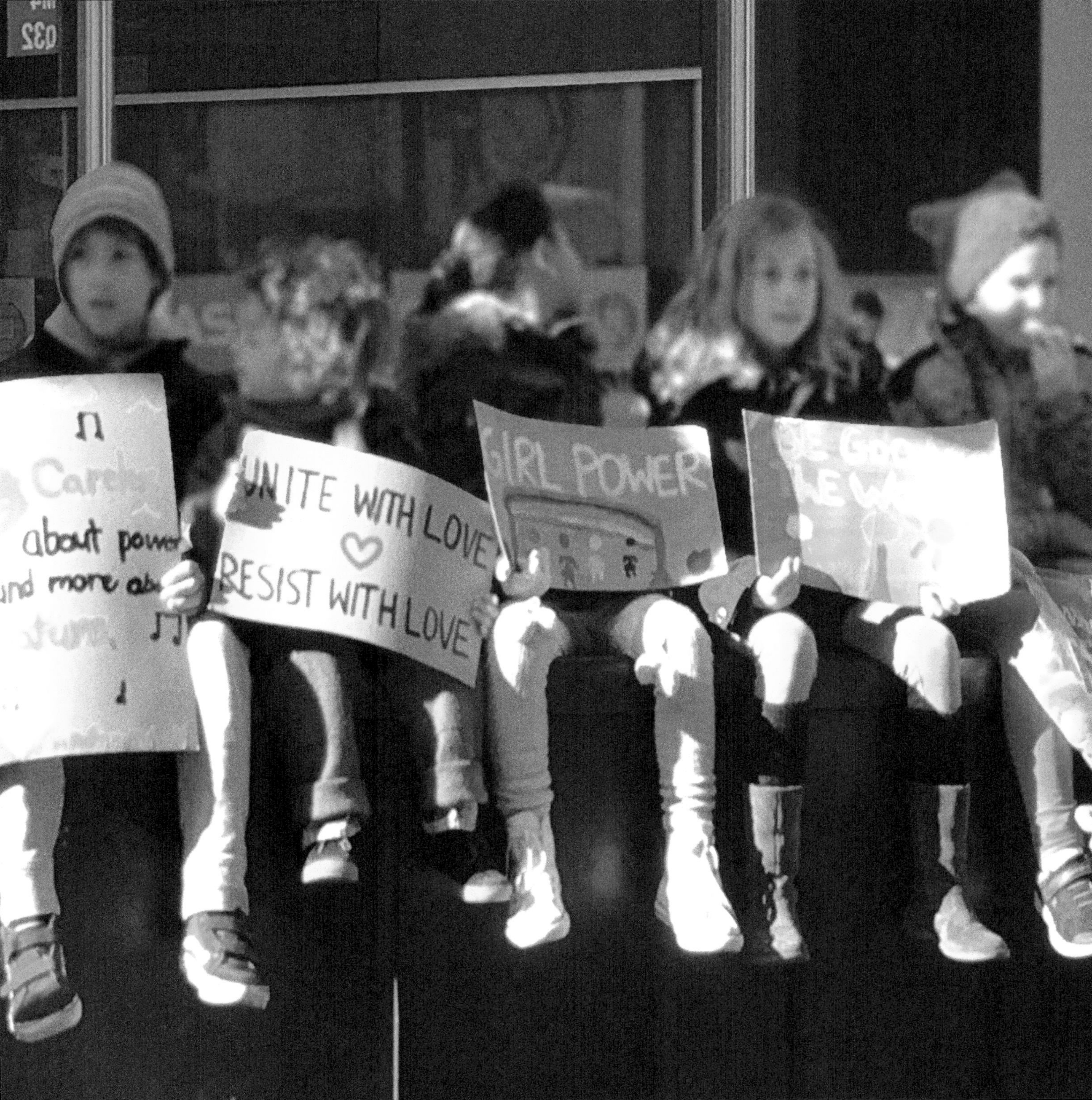
UNITE WITH LOVE
RESIST WITH LOVE
GIRL POWER

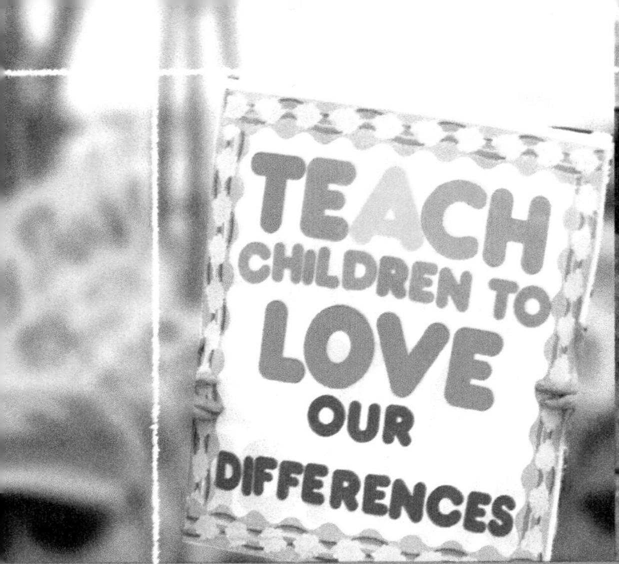
TEACH
CHILDREN TO
LOVE
OUR
DIFFERENCES

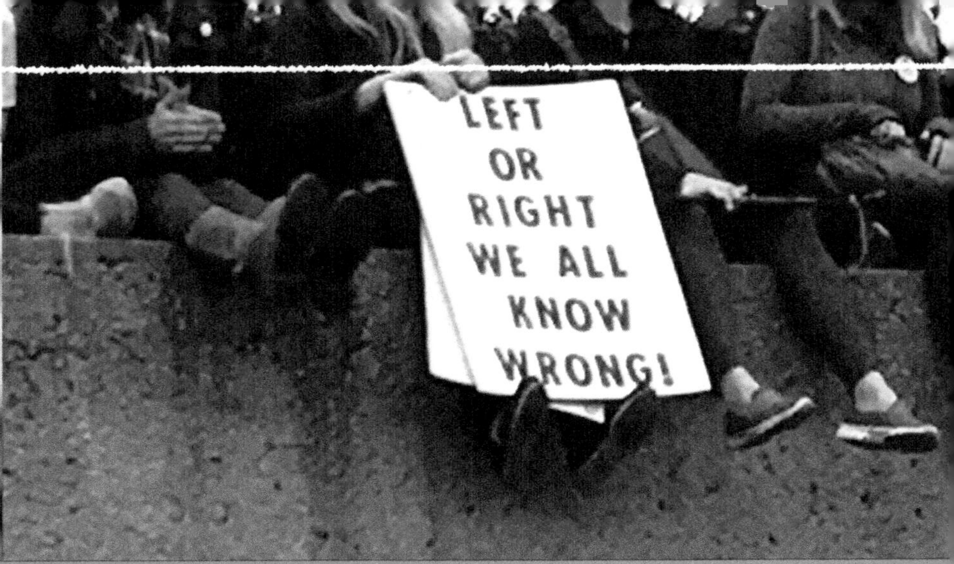
LEFT
OR
RIGHT
WE ALL
KNOW
WRONG!

For the children who will write the next chapter of history.

Karen Gross

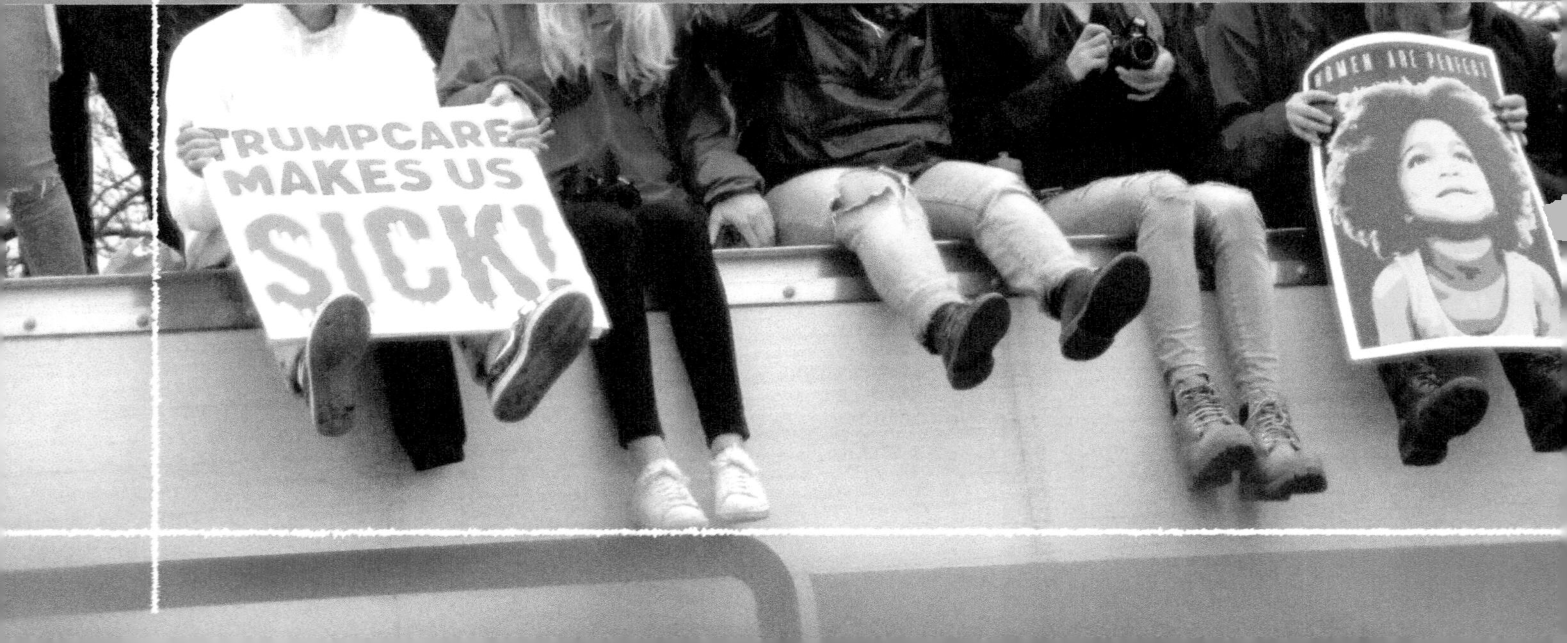
TRUMPCARE
MAKES US
SICK!

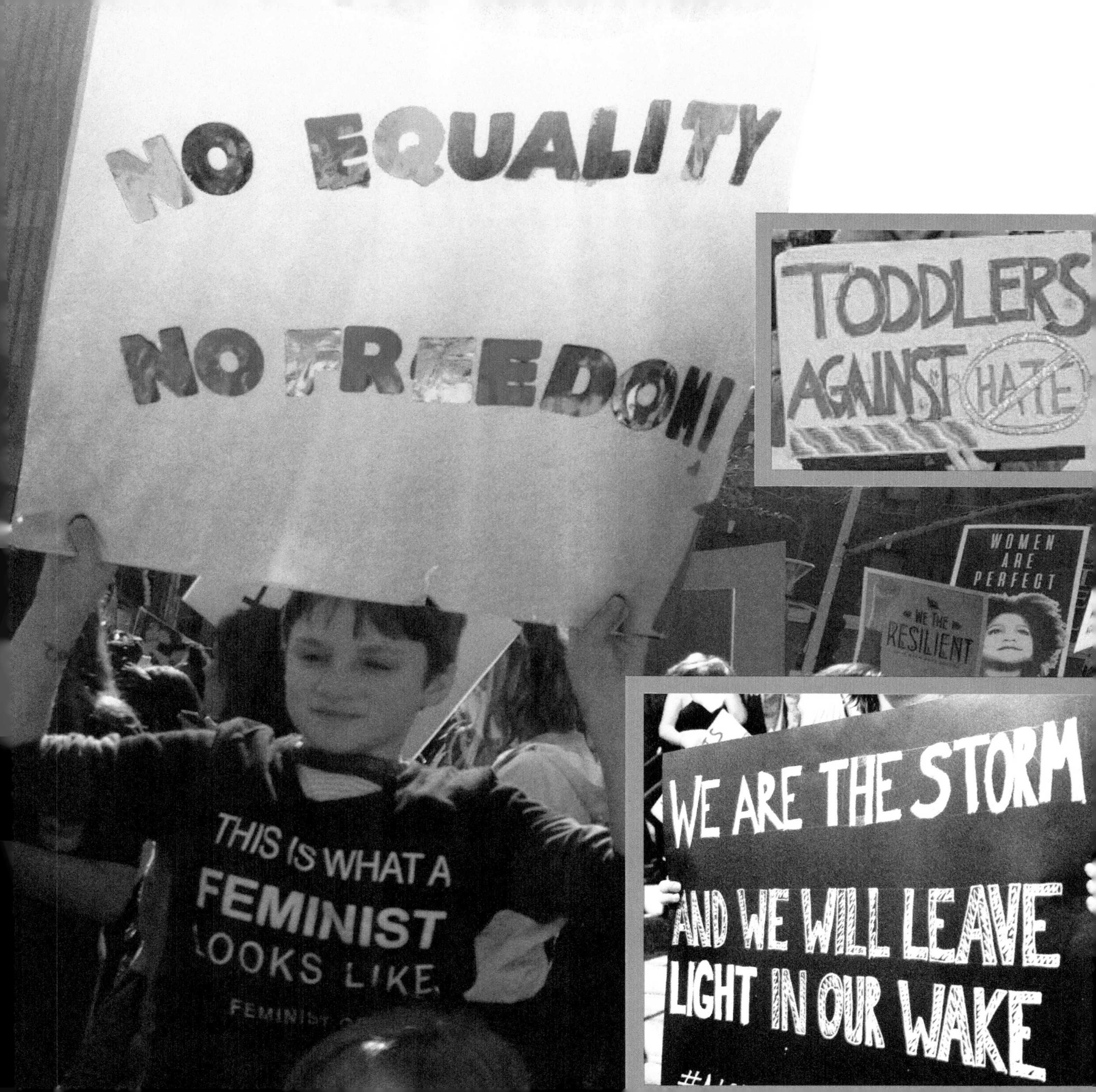
NO EQUALITY
NO FREEDOM!
TODDLERS AGAINST HATE
THIS IS WHAT A
FEMINIST
LOOKS LIKE.
WOMEN ARE PERFECT
WE THE
RESILIENT
WE ARE THE STORM
AND WE WILL LEAVE
LIGHT IN OUR WAKE

Gloria Steinem

at March

"Thank you for understanding that sometimes we must put our bodies where our beliefs are. Sometimes pressing send is not enough. And this also unifies us with the many in this world who do not have computers or electricity or literacy, but do have the same hopes and the same dreams."

> To paraphrase a famous quote, I just want to say: I have met the people, and you are not them," she continued. "We are the people."
>
> — Gloria Steinem

"Make sure you introduce yourselves to each other and decide what we're going to do tomorrow, and tomorrow and tomorrow," she said. "We're never turning back!"

— Gloria Steinem

in DC on January 21, 2017

We are here and around the world for a deep democracy that says we will not be quiet, we will not be controlled, we will work for a world in which all countries are connected. God may be in the details, but the goddess is in connections. We are at one with each other, we are looking at each other, not up. No more asking daddy. We are linked. We are not ranked. And this is a day that will change us forever because we are together. Each of us individually and collectively will never be the same again.

"And remember the Constitution does not begin with 'I, the President.' It begins with 'We, the People.'"

— Gloria Steinem

Janet Mock at March in DC on January 21, 2017

"But I cannot survive on righteous anger alone. Today, by being here, it is my commitment to getting us free that keeps me marching. Our approach to freedom may not be identical, but it must be intersectional and inclusive."

"It's been a heart-rending time to be both a woman and an immigrant in this country."

— America Ferrera
at March in DC on January 21, 2017

"This darkness we are experiencing today is not of the tomb, but of the womb- and it is female- and we are laboring and we need to push and to breathe for a true America to be born."

— Anonymous

Sophie Cruz at March in DC on January 21, 2017

"I also want to tell the children not to be afraid, because we are not alone. There are still many people that have their hearts filled with love and tenderness to snuggle in this path of life. Let's keep together and fight for the rights."

"We can whimper, we can whine or we can fight back."...
"Me, I'm here to fight back."

— Senator Elizabeth Warren
at March in Boston on January 21, 2017

Author Elie Wiesel

tells the story of the one righteous man of Sodom, who walked the streets protesting against the injustice of this city. People made fun of him, derided him. Finally, a young person asked: "Why do you continue your protest against evil; can't you see no one is paying attention to you?" He answered, "I'll tell you why I continue. In the beginning, I thought I would change people. Today, I know I cannot. Yet, if I continue my protest, at least I will prevent others from changing me."

"We must always take sides. Neutrality helps the oppressor, never the victim. Silence encourages the tormentor, never the tormented."

— Elie Wiesel

Tamika Mallory at March in DC on January 21, 2017

"Today is not a concert. It is not a parade, and it is not a party. Today is an act of resistance. Now, some of you came here to protest one man. I didn't come here for that. I came here to address those of you who say you are of good conscience. To those of you who experience a feeling of being powerless, disparaged, victimized, antagonized, threatened and abused, to those of you who for the first time felt the pain that my people have felt since they were brought here with chains shackled on our legs, today I say to you, welcome to my world. Welcome to our world. I stand here as a black woman, the descendent of slaves. My ancestors literally nursed our slave masters. Through the blood and tears of my people, we built this country. America cannot be great without me, you and all of us who are here today. Today you may be feeling aggrieved, but know that this country has been hostile to its people for a long time. For some of you, it is new. For some of us, it is not so new at all. Today I am marching for black and brown lives, for Sandra Bland, for Philando Castile, for Tamir Rice, for Aiyana Stanley-Jones, for Eric Garner, for Michael Brown, for Trayvon Martin and for those nine people who were shot at the Emanuel African Methodist Episcopal Church. We have a chance, brothers and sisters, to get this thing right. We can do it, if women rise up and take this nation back!"

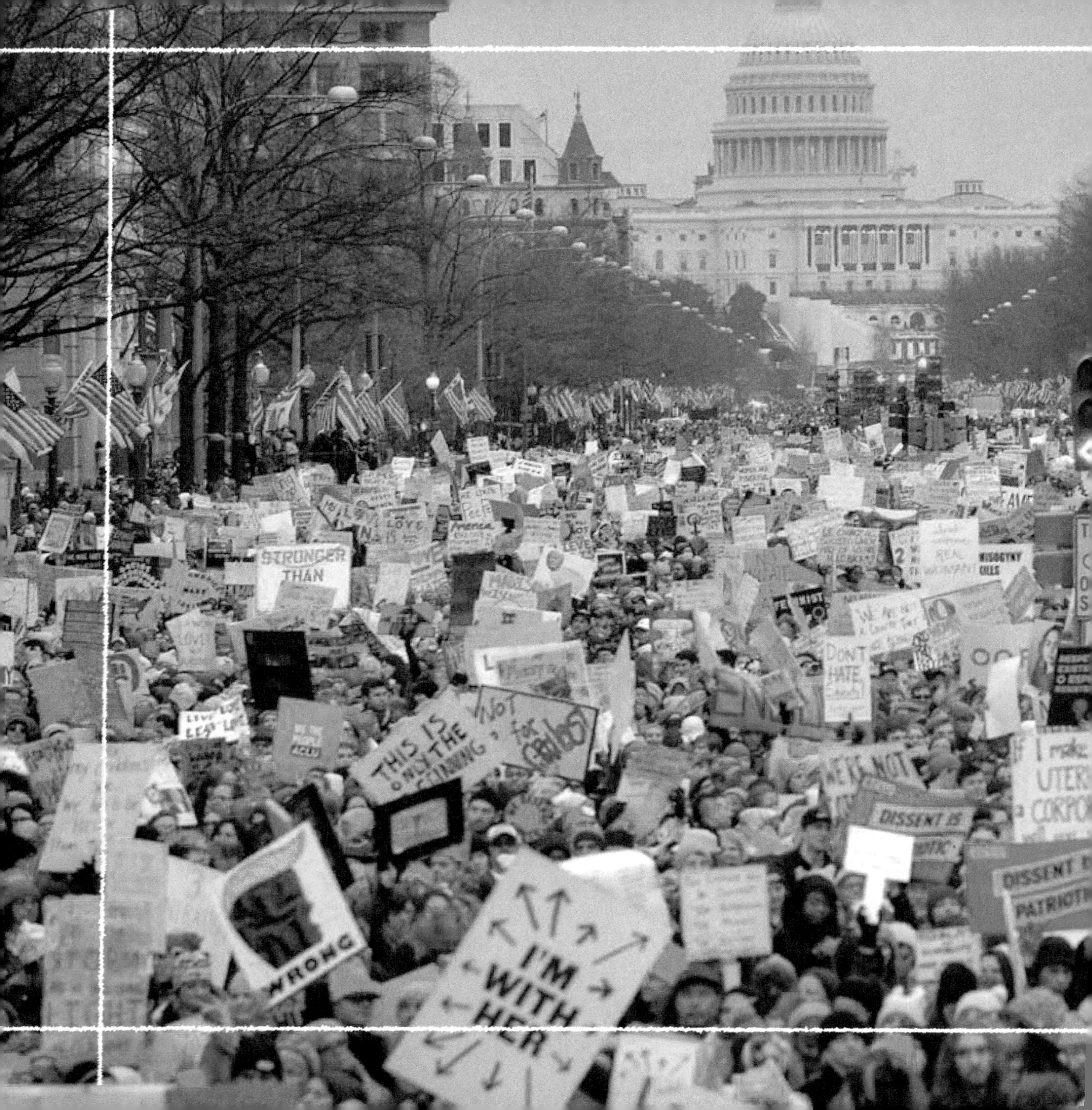
STRONGER THAN
THIS IS ONLY THE BEGINNING
DON'T HATE
DISSENT IS PATRIOTIC
I'M WITH HER
WRONG

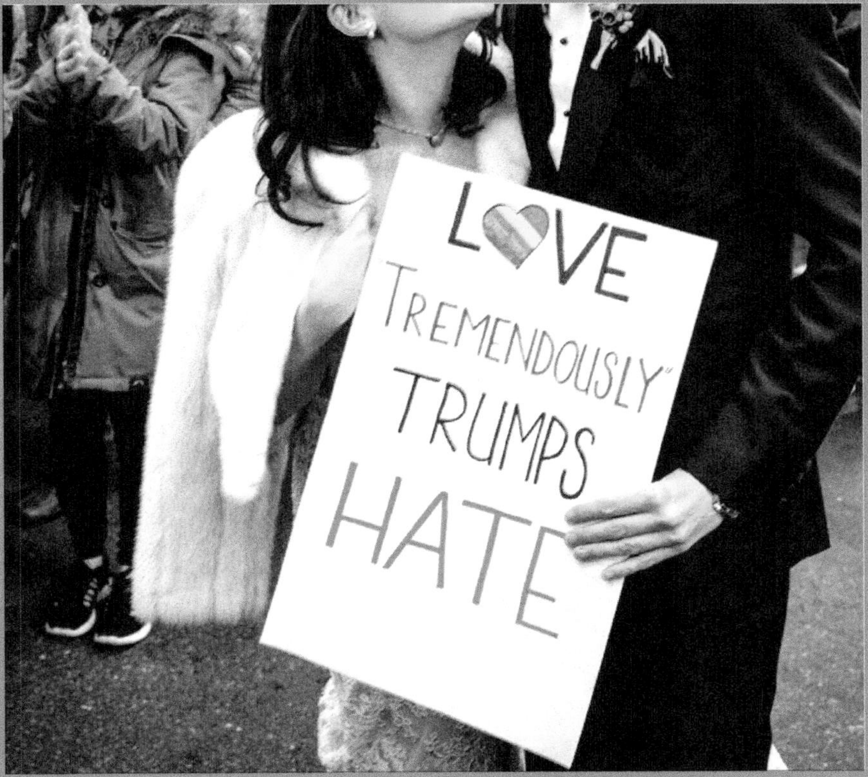
LOVE
"TREMENDOUSLY"
TRUMPS
HATE

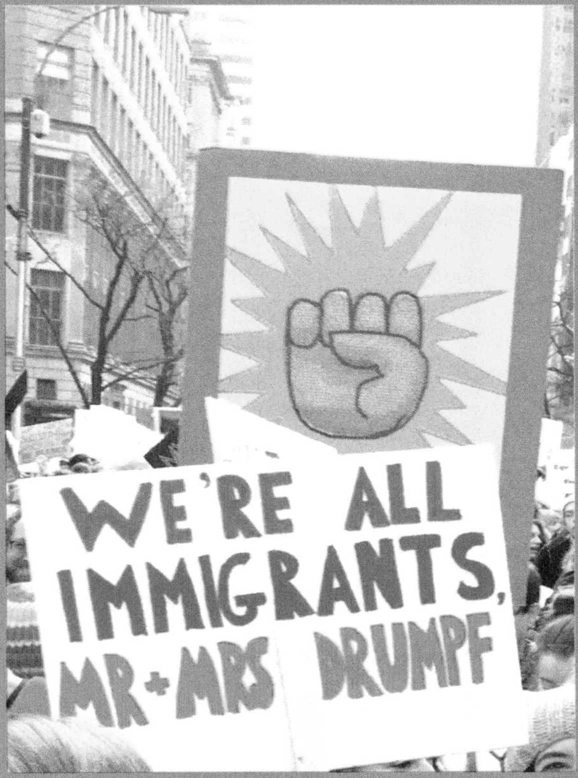
WE'RE ALL
IMMIGRANTS,
MR+MRS DRUMPF

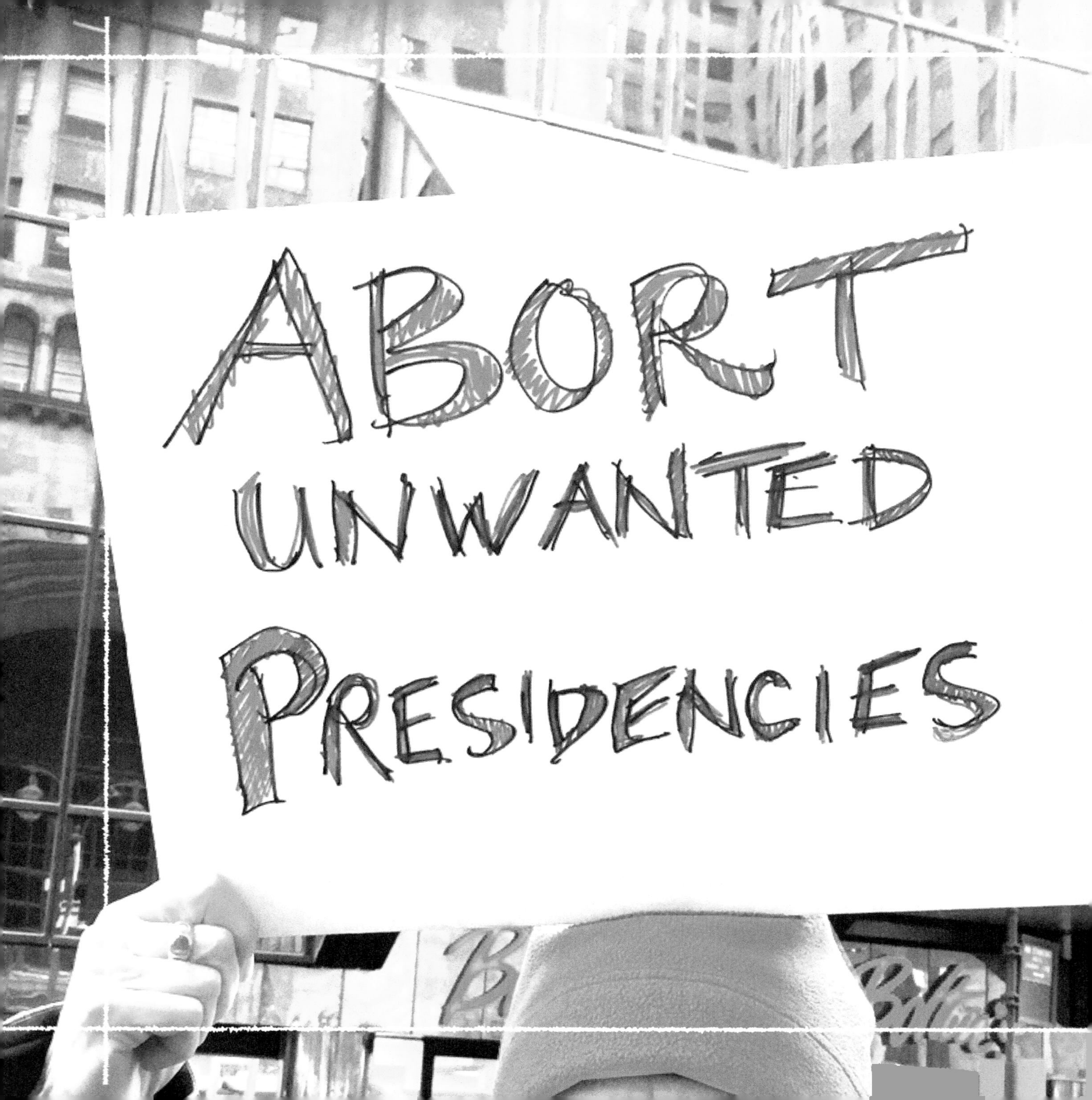
ABORT
UNWANTED
PRESIDENCIES

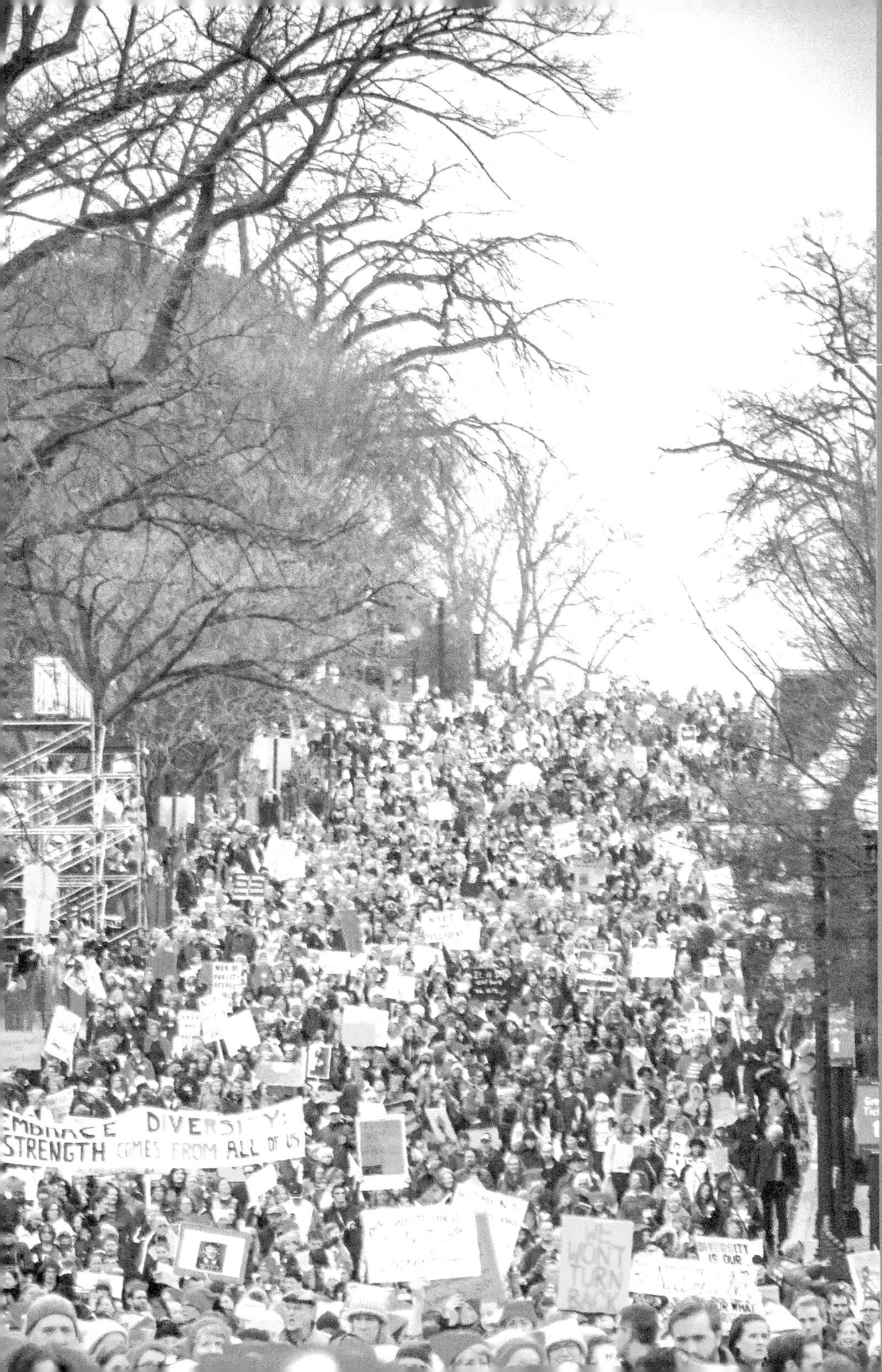
DIVERSITY:
STRENGTH COMES FROM ALL OF US
WE WONT TURN BACK
DIVERSITY IS OUR

We can do this.
We must do this.
We will do this.
Individually
and
together.

Karen Gross

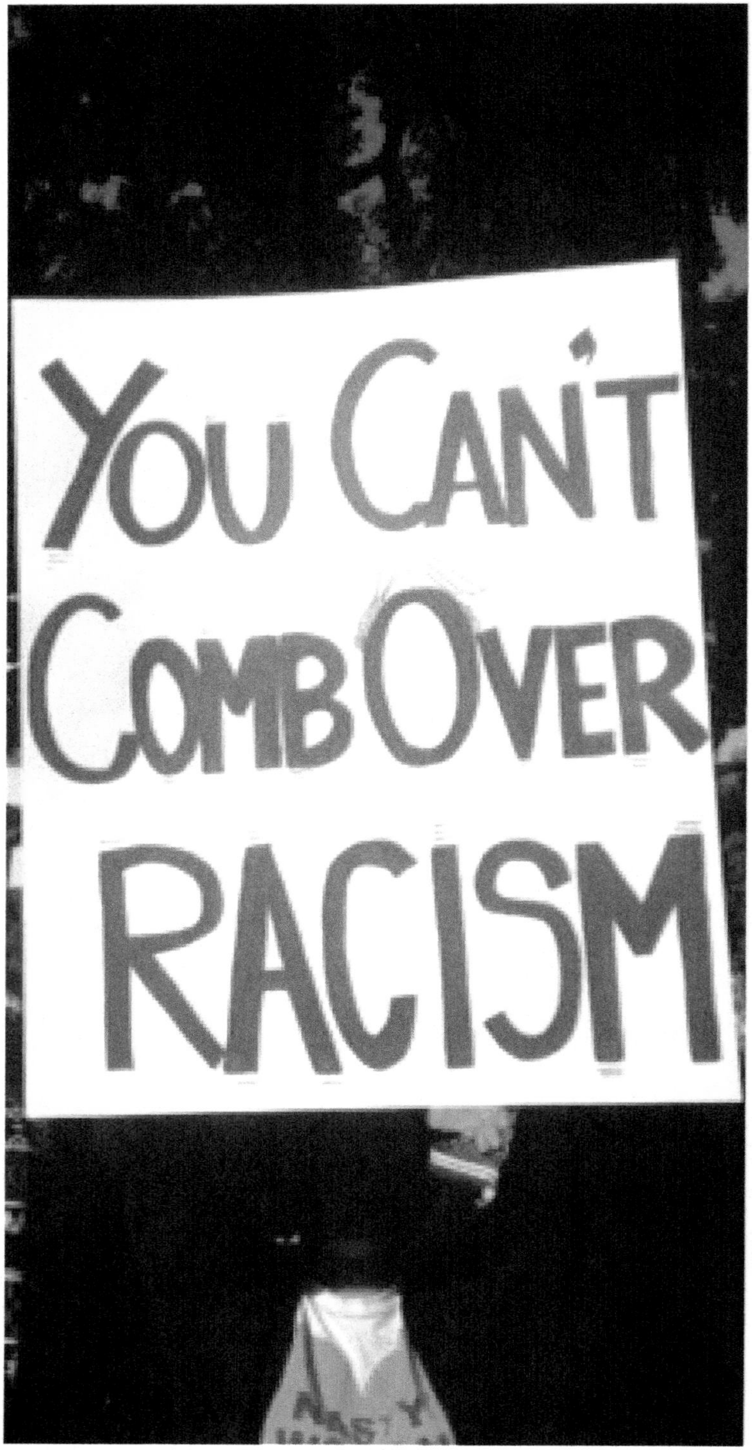
YOU CAN'T
COMB OVER
RACISM

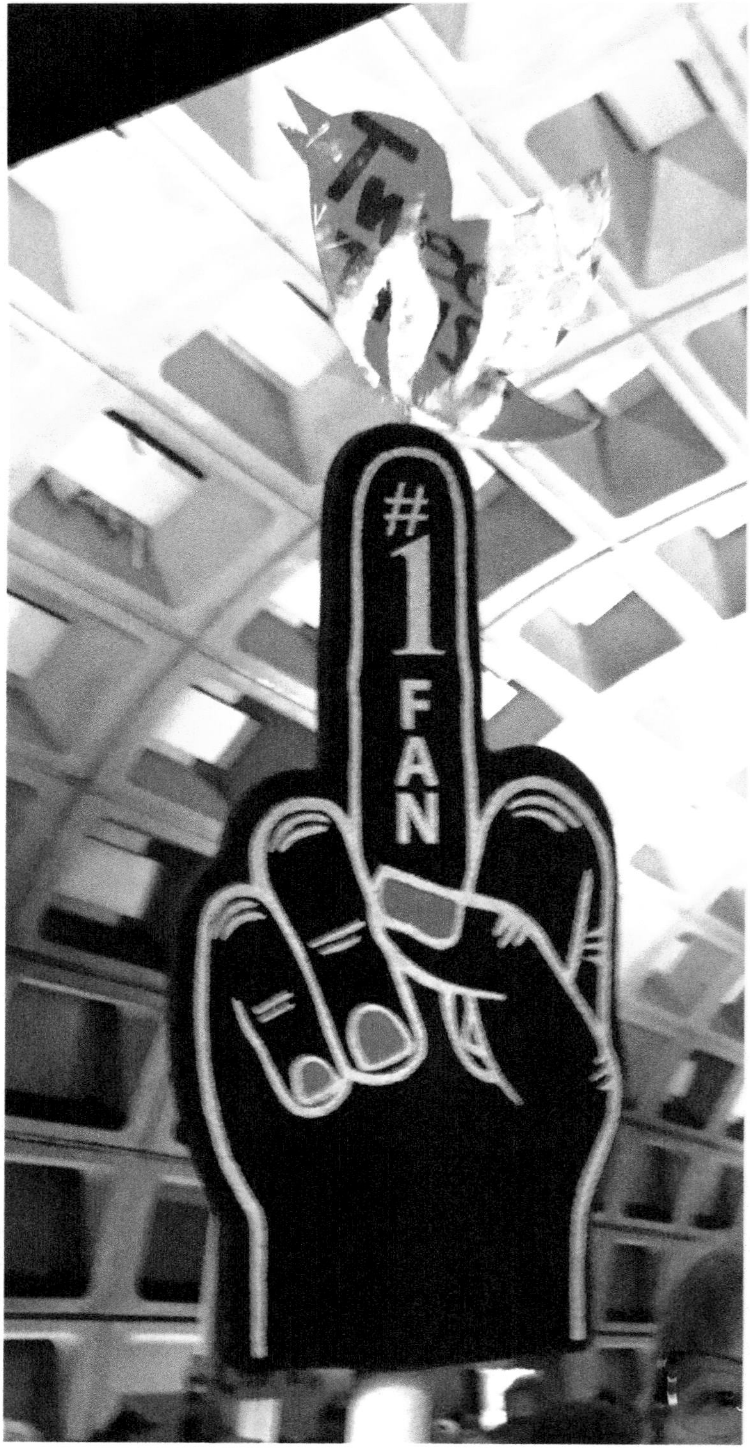
#1
FAN

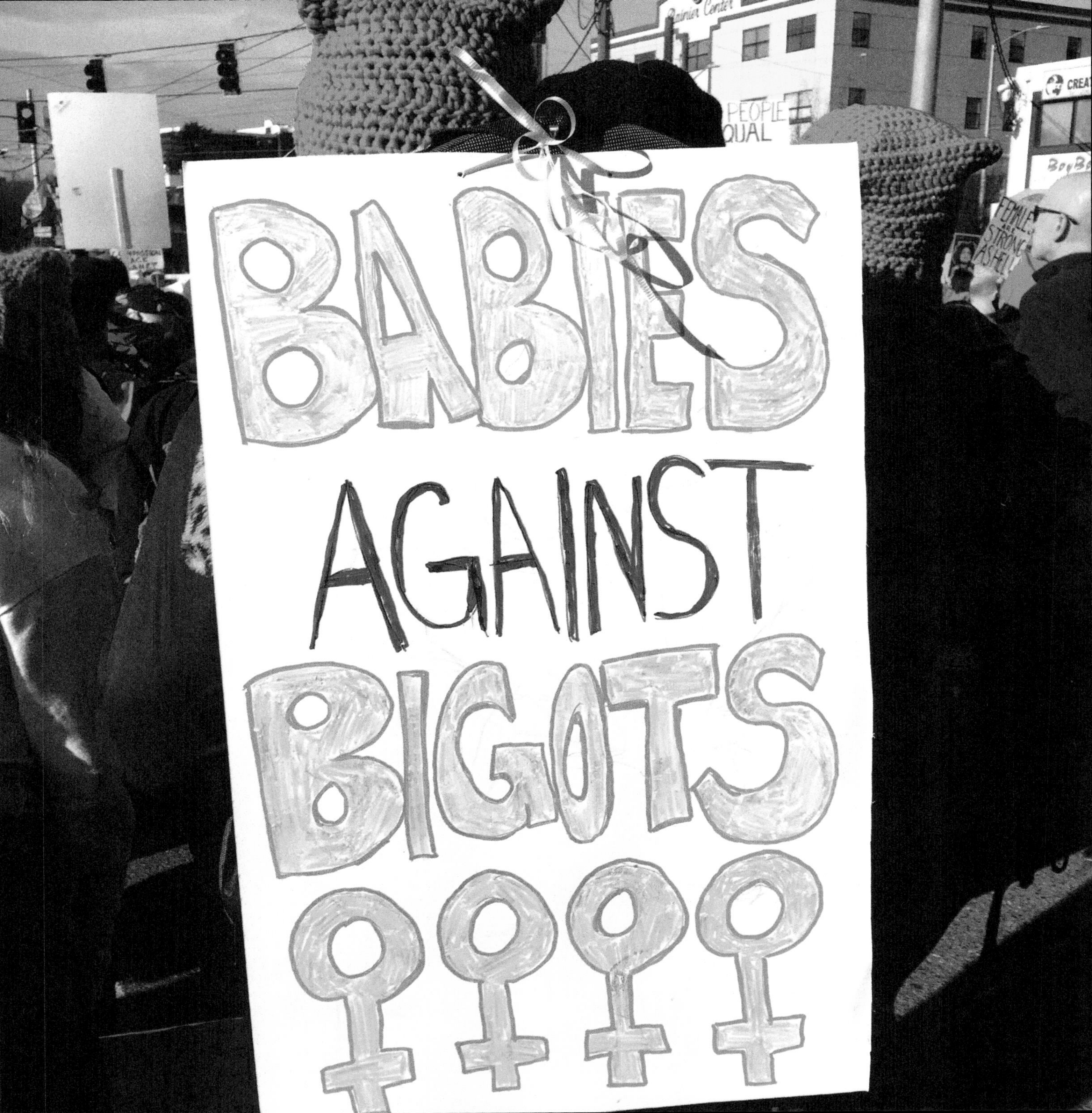
Rainier Center
PEOPLE
BABIES
AGAINST
BIGOTS

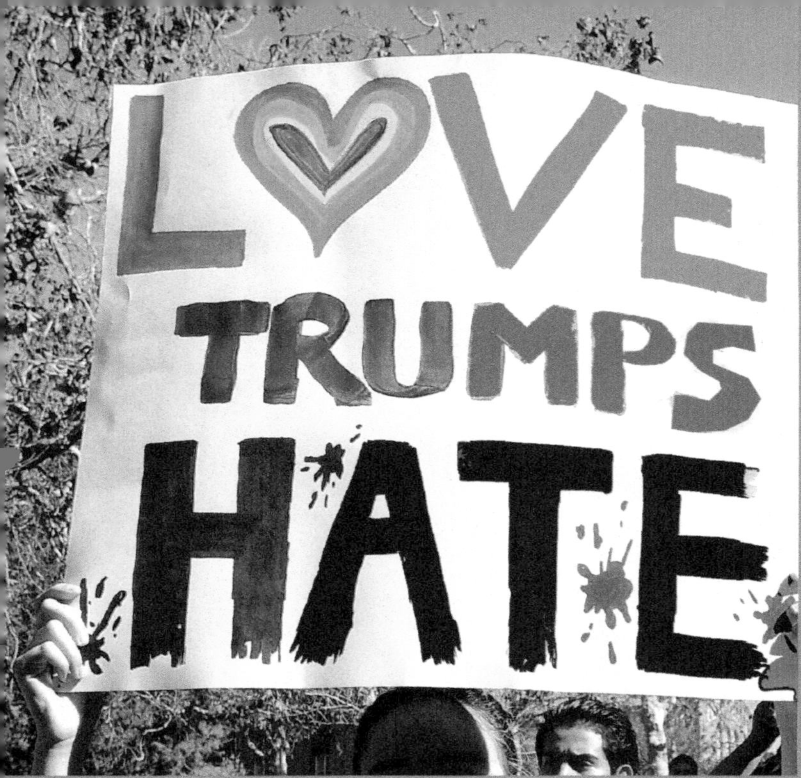
LOVE
TRUMPS
HATE

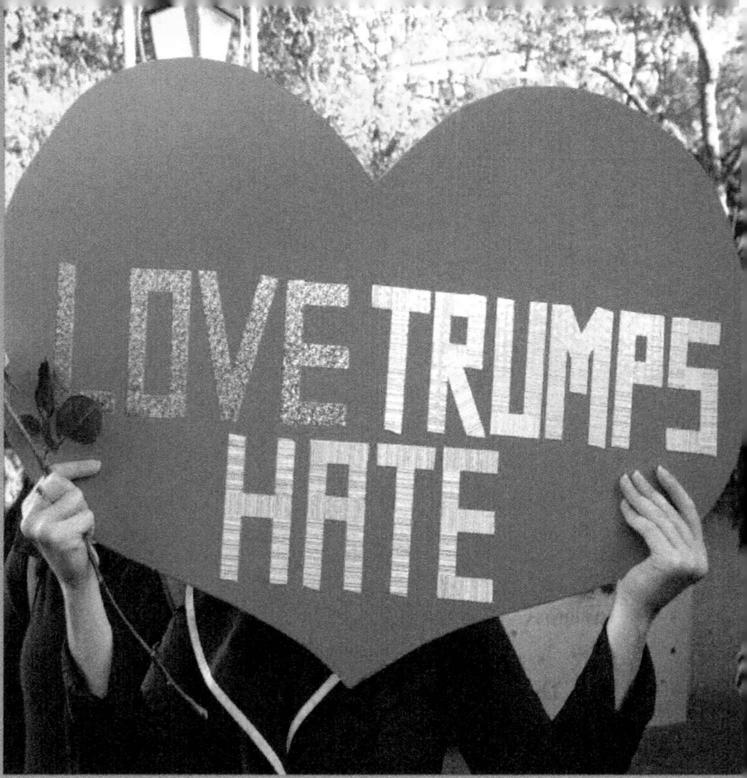
LOVE TRUMPS
HATE

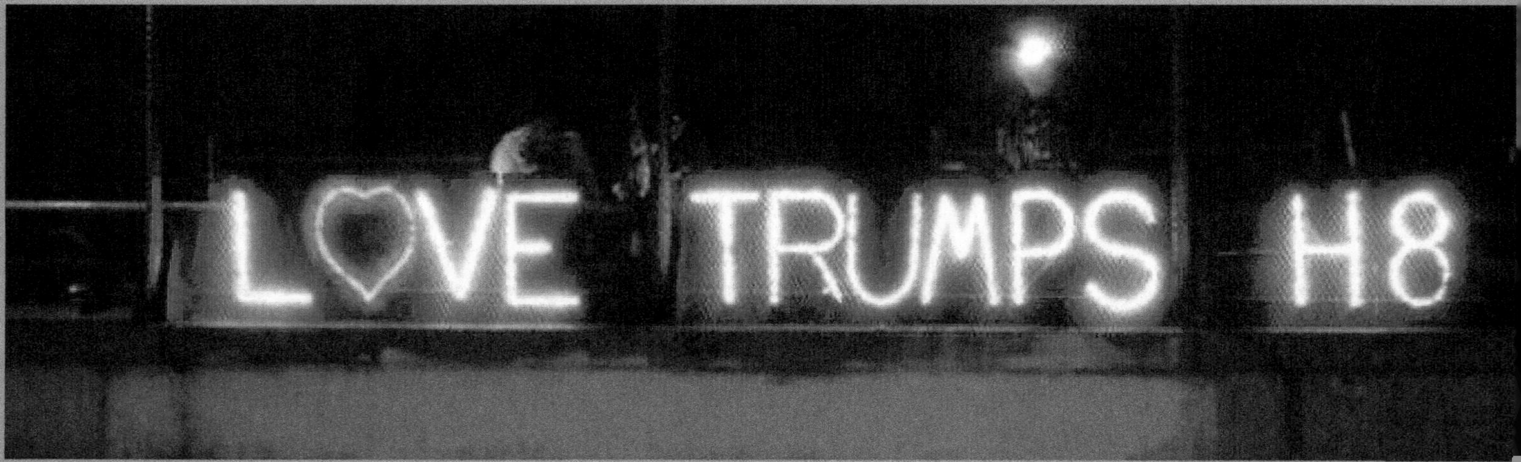
LOVE TRUMPS H8

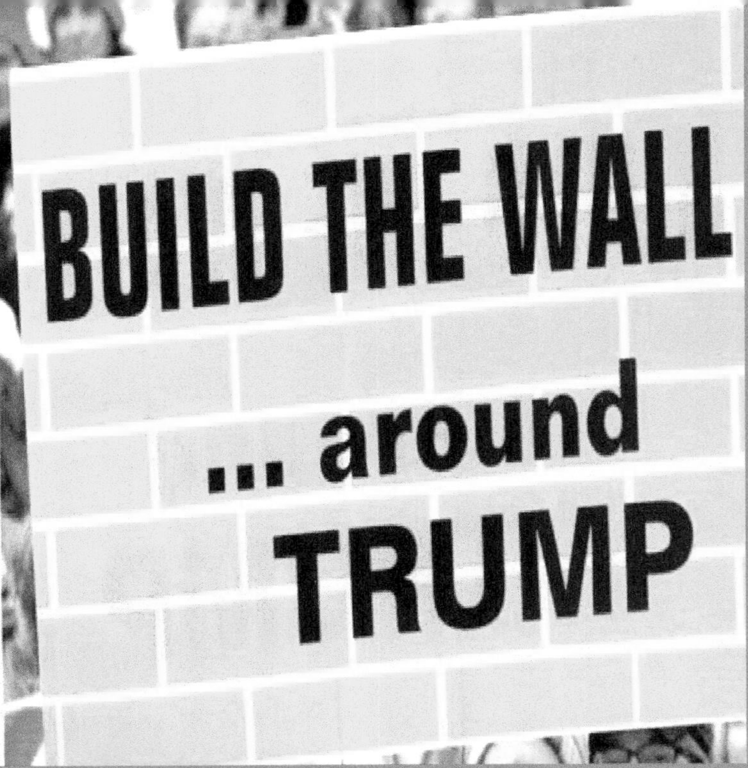
BUILD THE WALL
... around
TRUMP

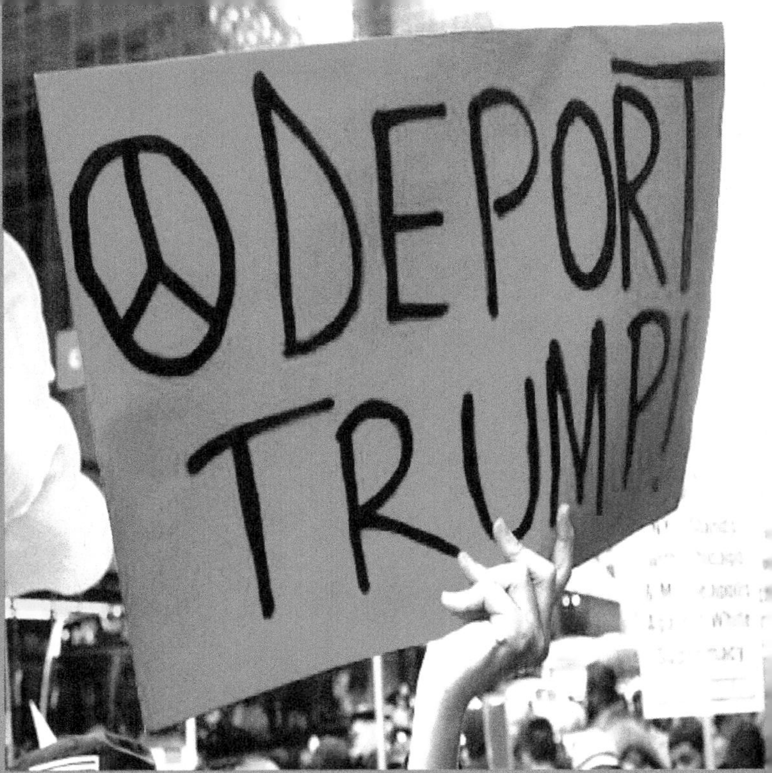
DEPORT
TRUMP!

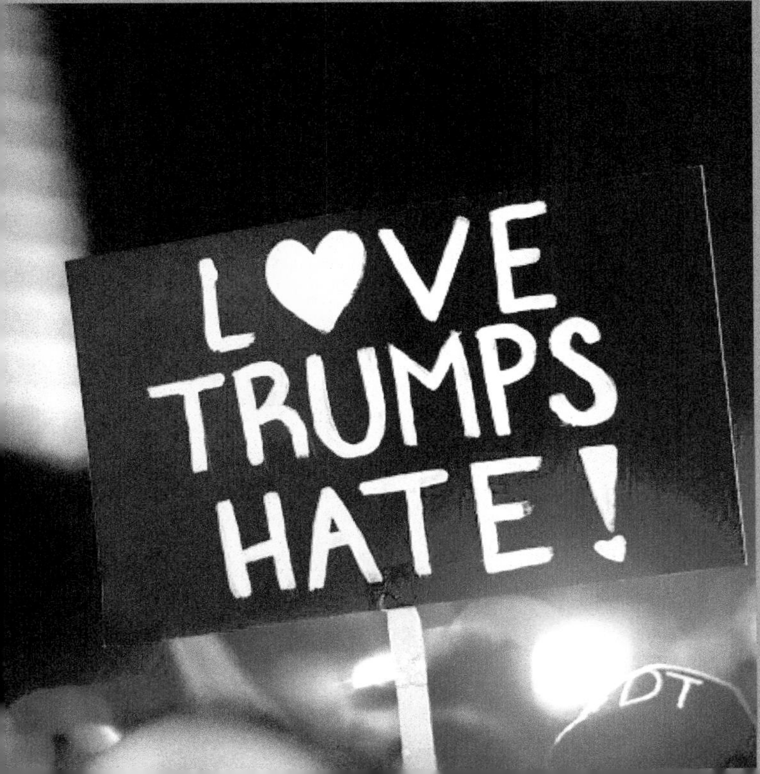
LOVE
TRUMPS
HATE!

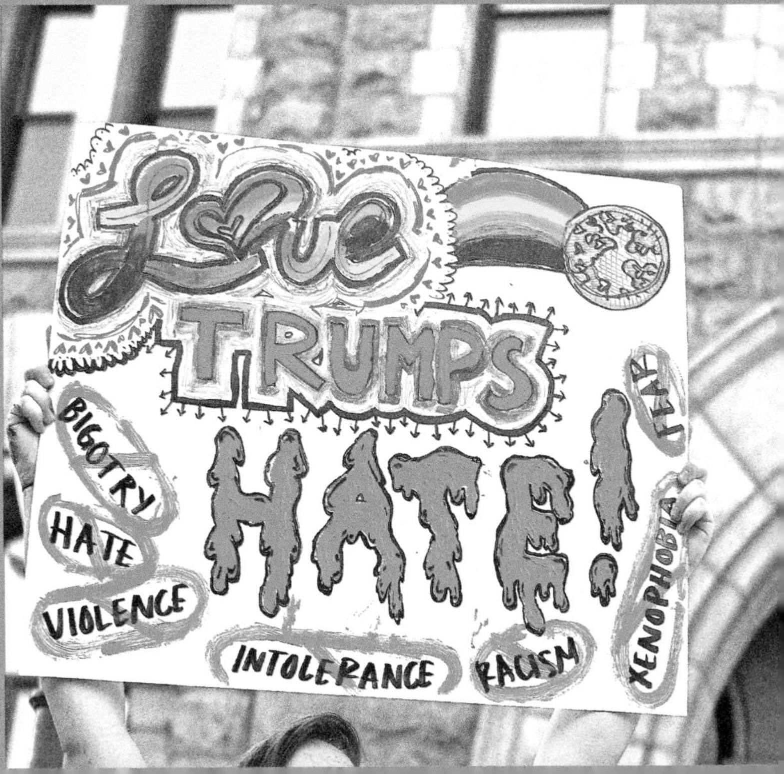
Love
TRUMPS
HATE!
BIGOTRY
HATE
VIOLENCE
INTOLERANCE
RACISM
XENOPHOBIA
FEAR

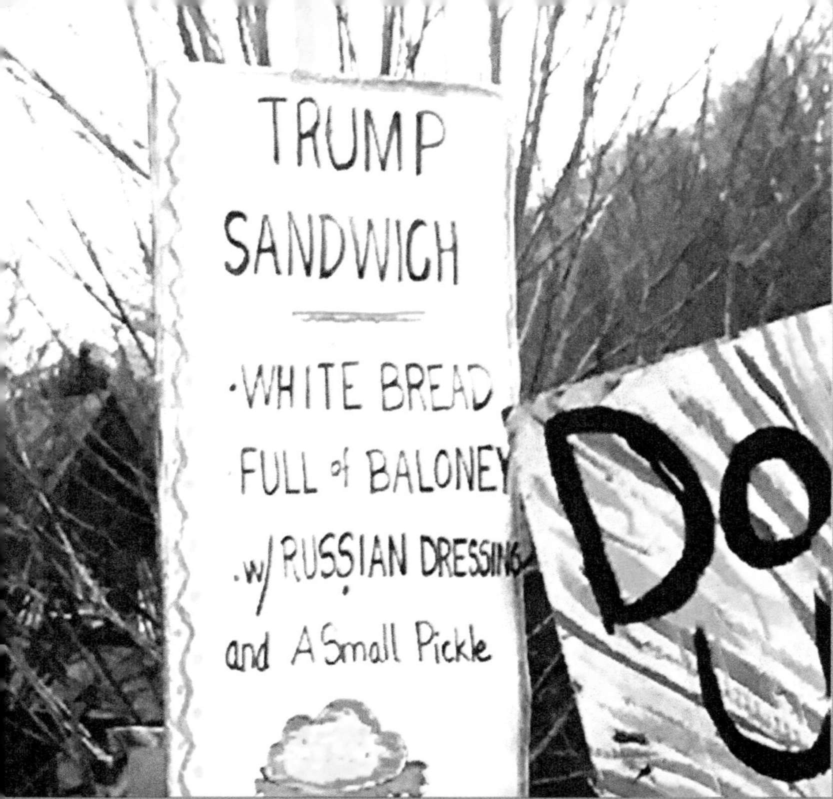
TRUMP
SANDWICH
·WHITE BREAD
FULL of BALONEY
·w/ RUSSIAN DRESSING
and A Small Pickle
Do

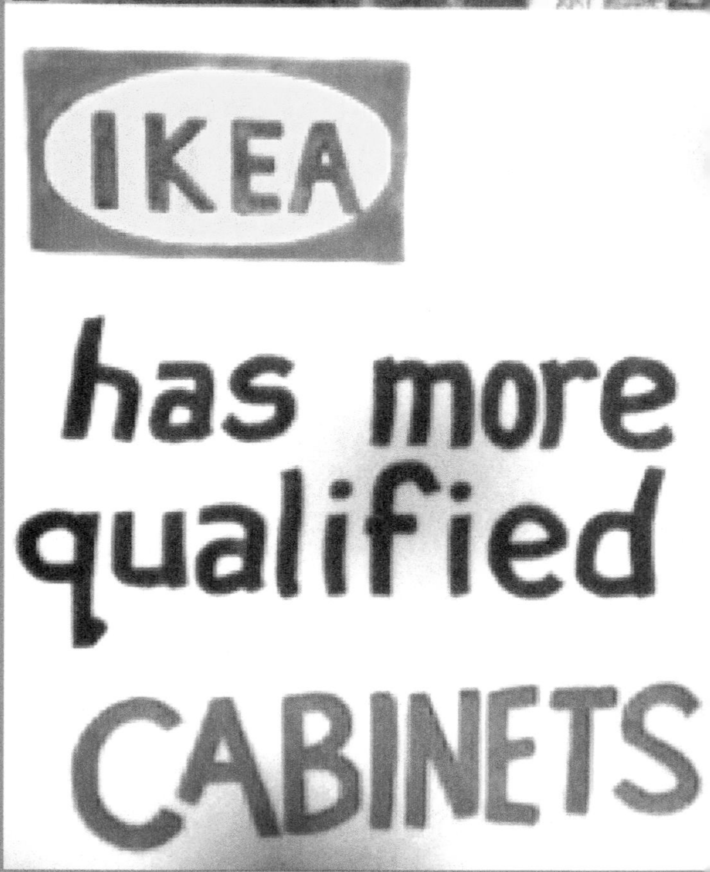
IKEA
has more
qualified
CABINETS

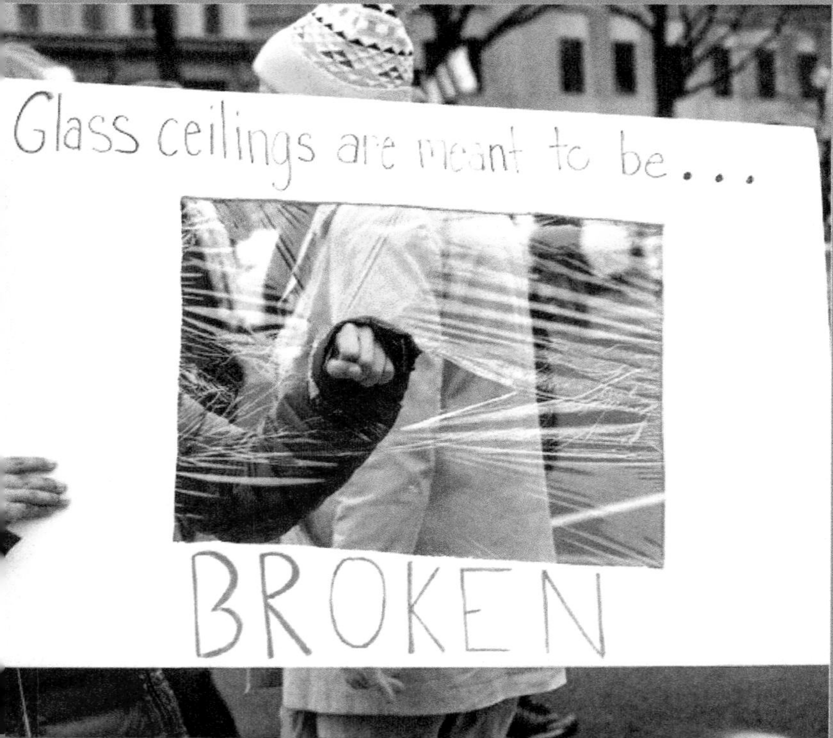
Glass ceilings are meant to be...
BROKEN

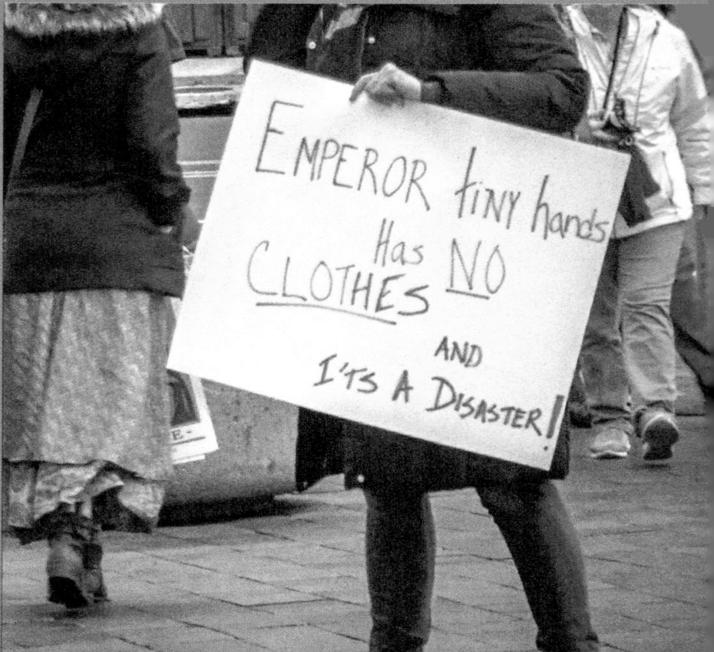
EMPEROR tiny hands
Has NO
CLOTHES
AND
IT'S A DISASTER!

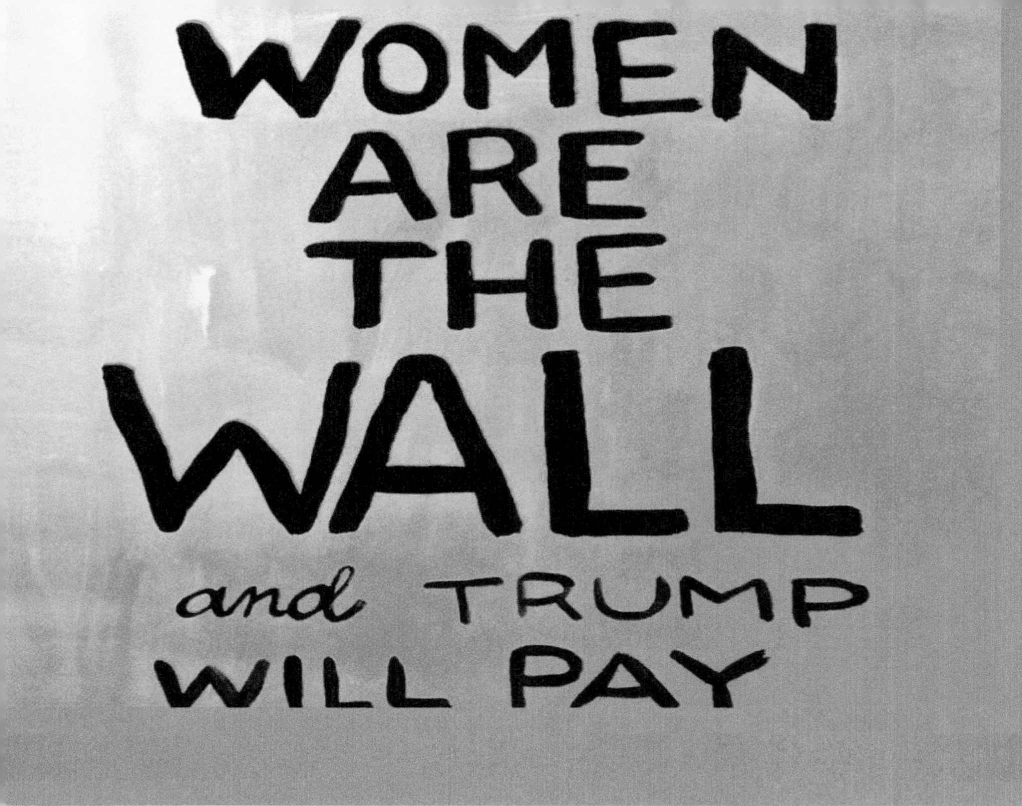
WOMEN
ARE
THE
WALL
and TRUMP
WILL PAY

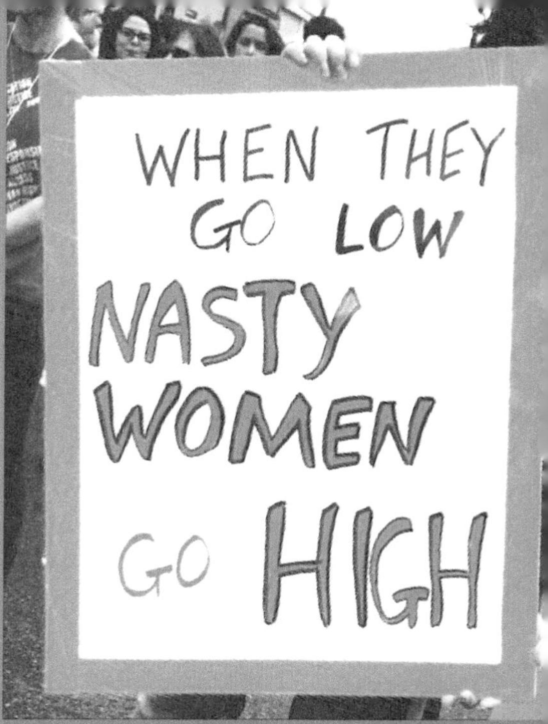
WHEN THEY
GO LOW
NASTY
WOMEN
GO HIGH

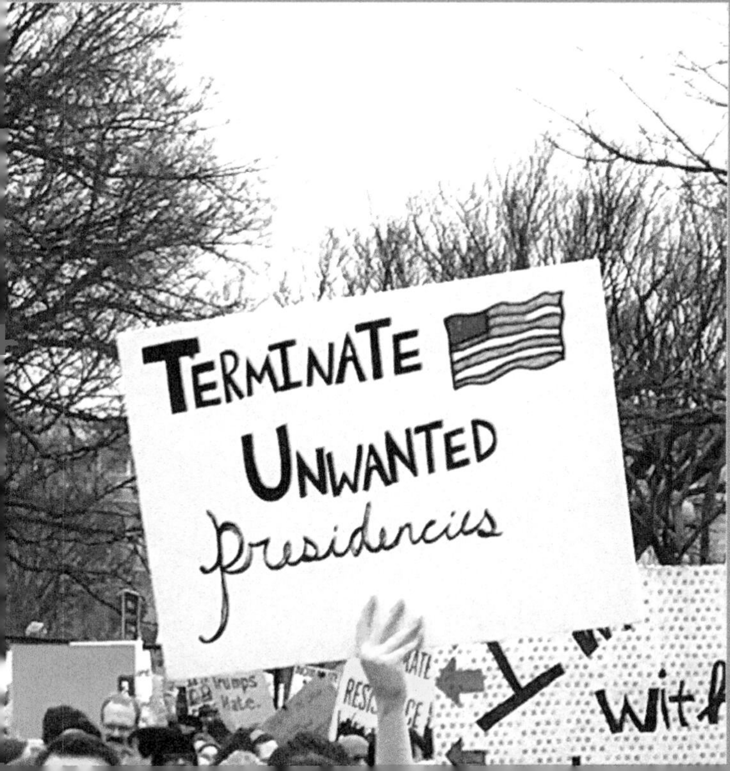
TERMINATE
UNWANTED
Presidencies

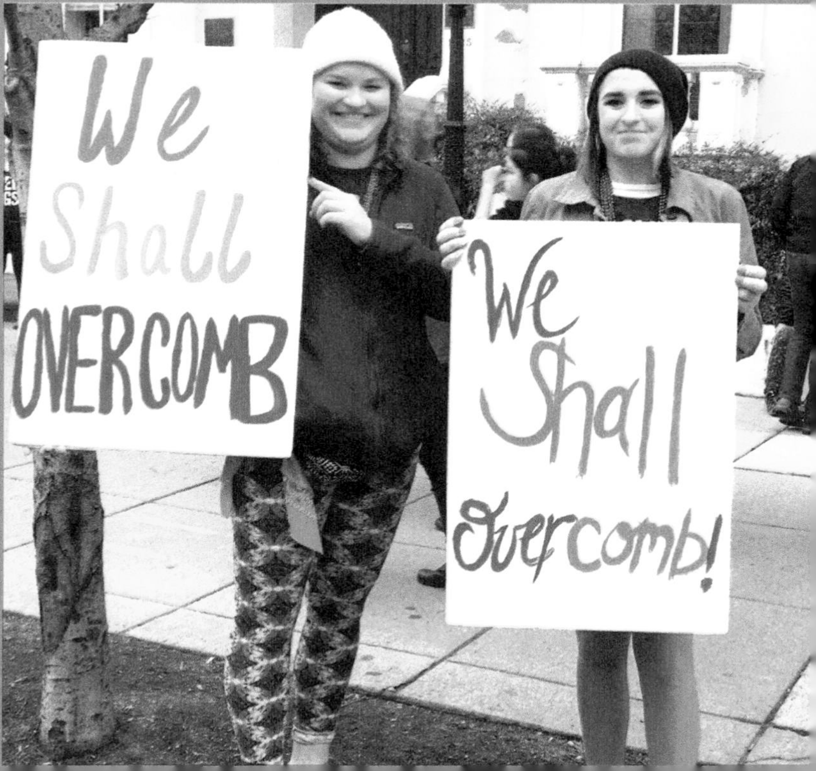
We
Shall
OVERCOMB
We
Shall
Overcomb!

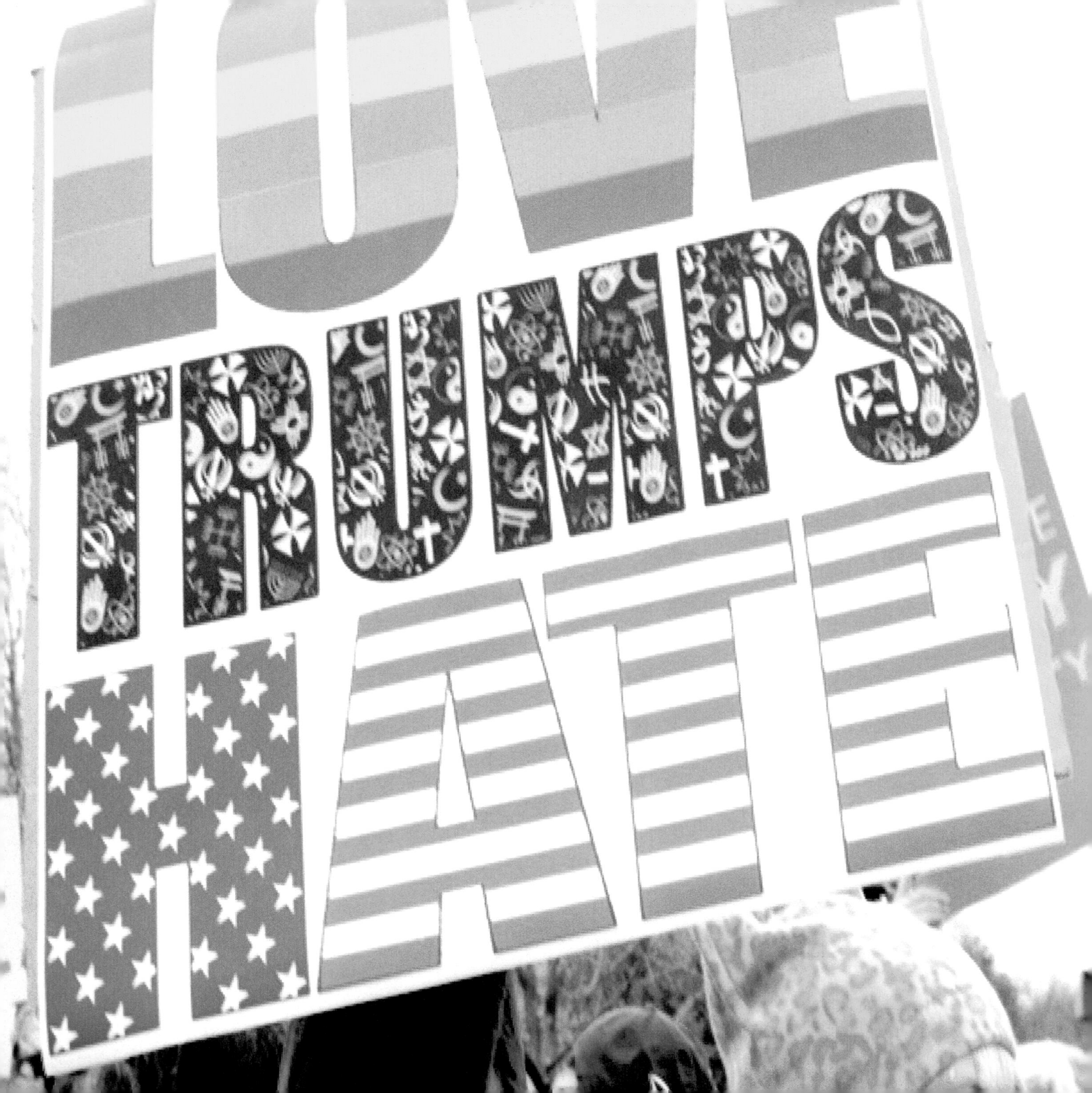
LOVE
TRUMPS
HATE

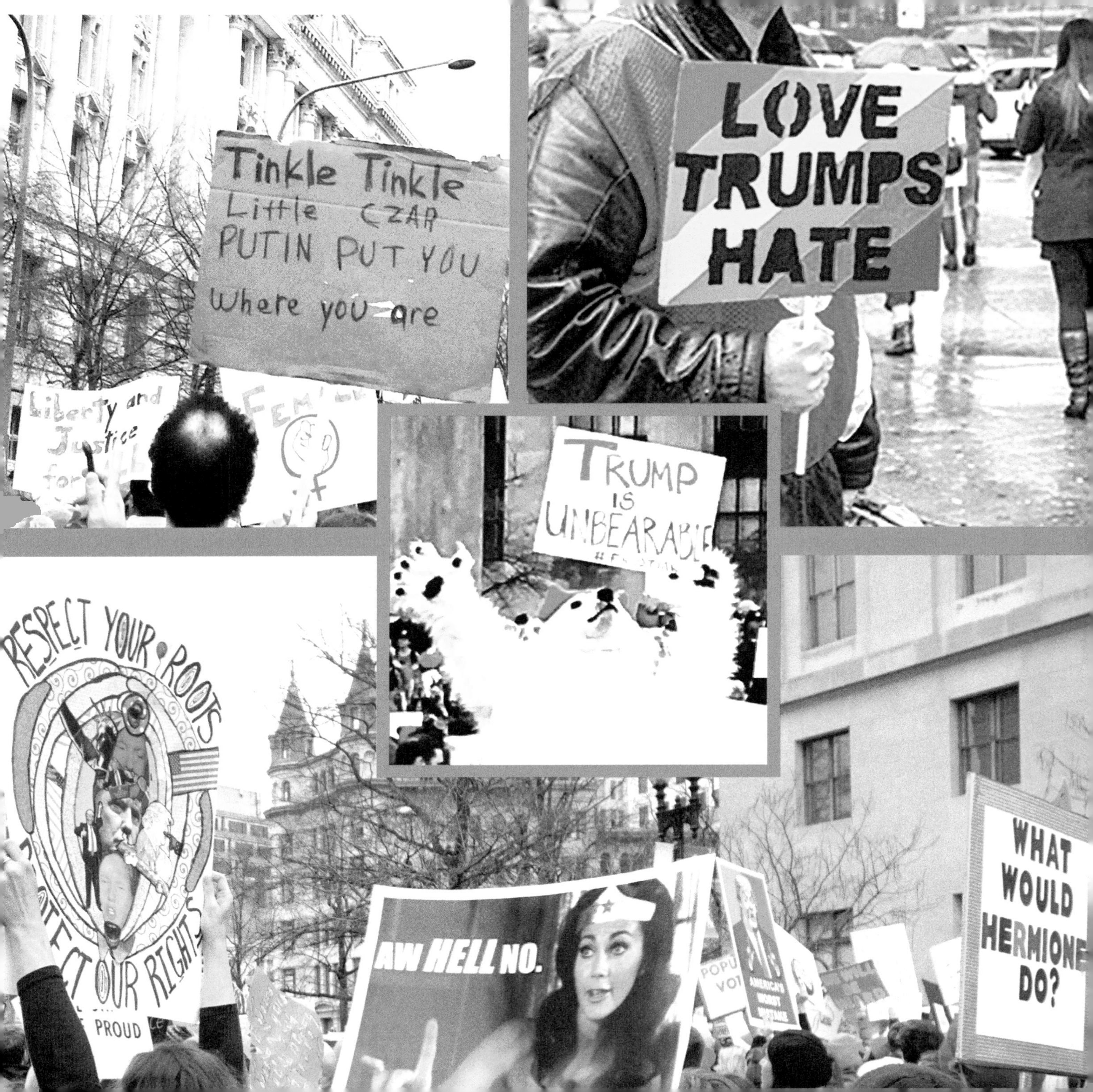

Tinkle Tinkle
Little CZAR
PUTIN PUT YOU
Where you are
LOVE
TRUMPS
HATE
Liberty and Justice for
TRUMP
IS
UNBEARABLE
RESPECT YOUR ROOTS
PROTECT OUR RIGHTS
PROUD
AW HELL NO.
WHAT
WOULD
HERMIONE
DO?

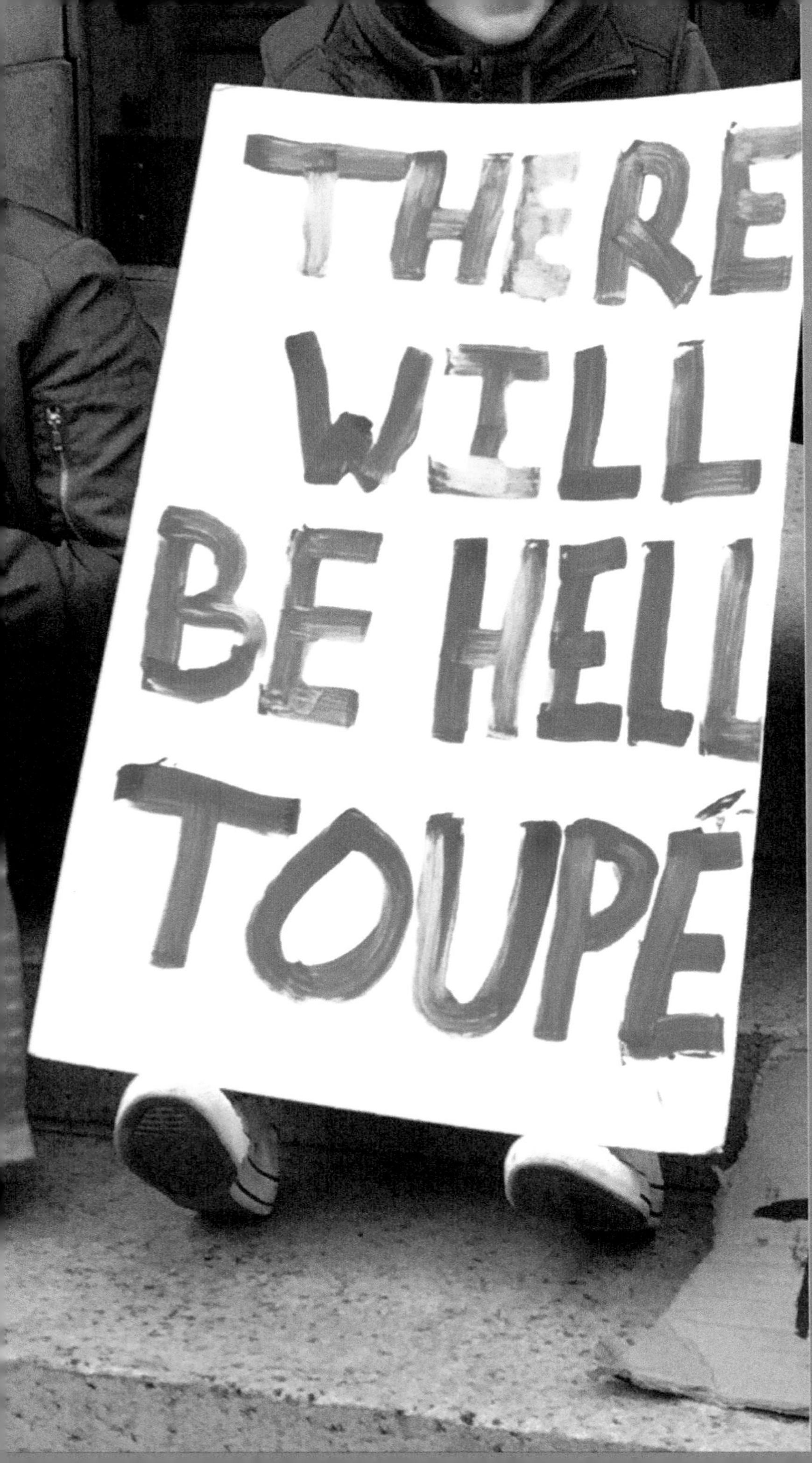
THERE WILL BE HELL TOUPÉ

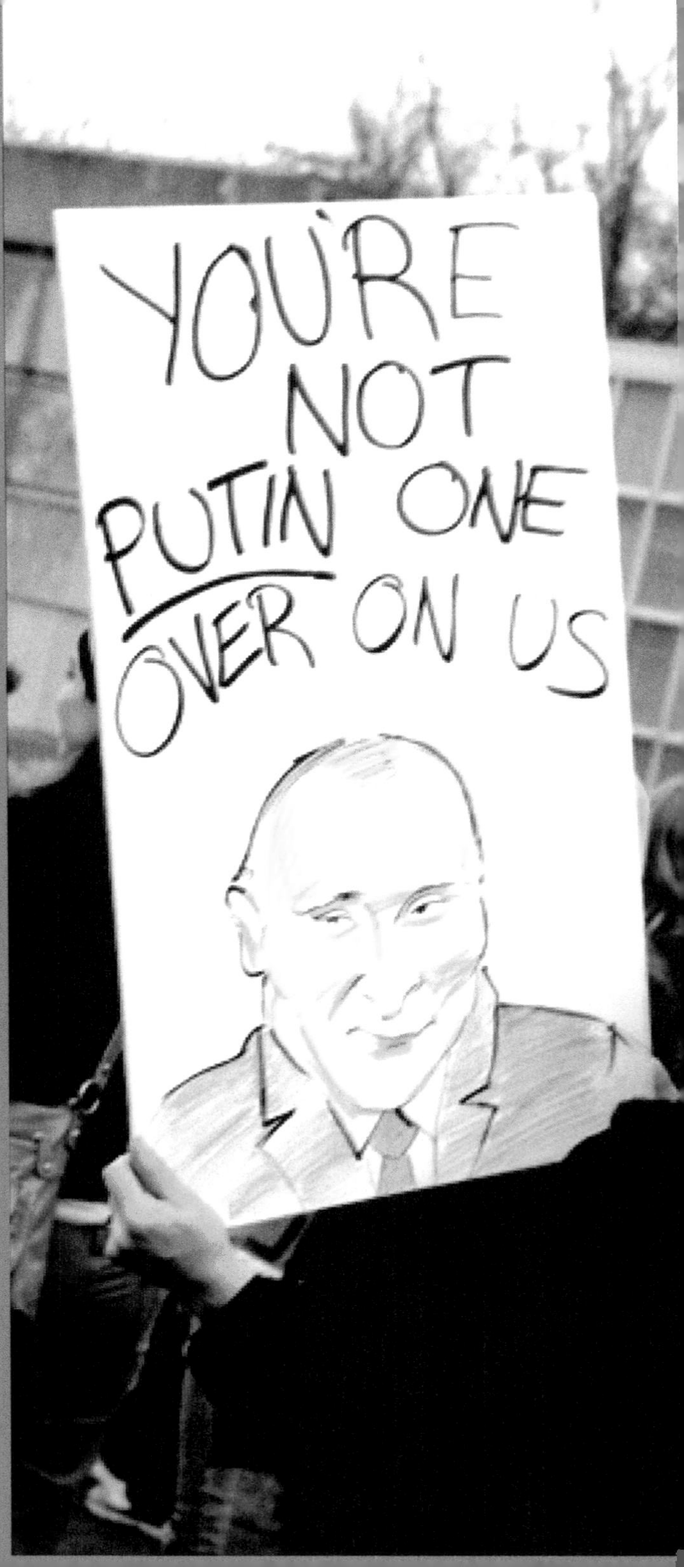
YOU'RE NOT PUTIN ONE OVER ON US

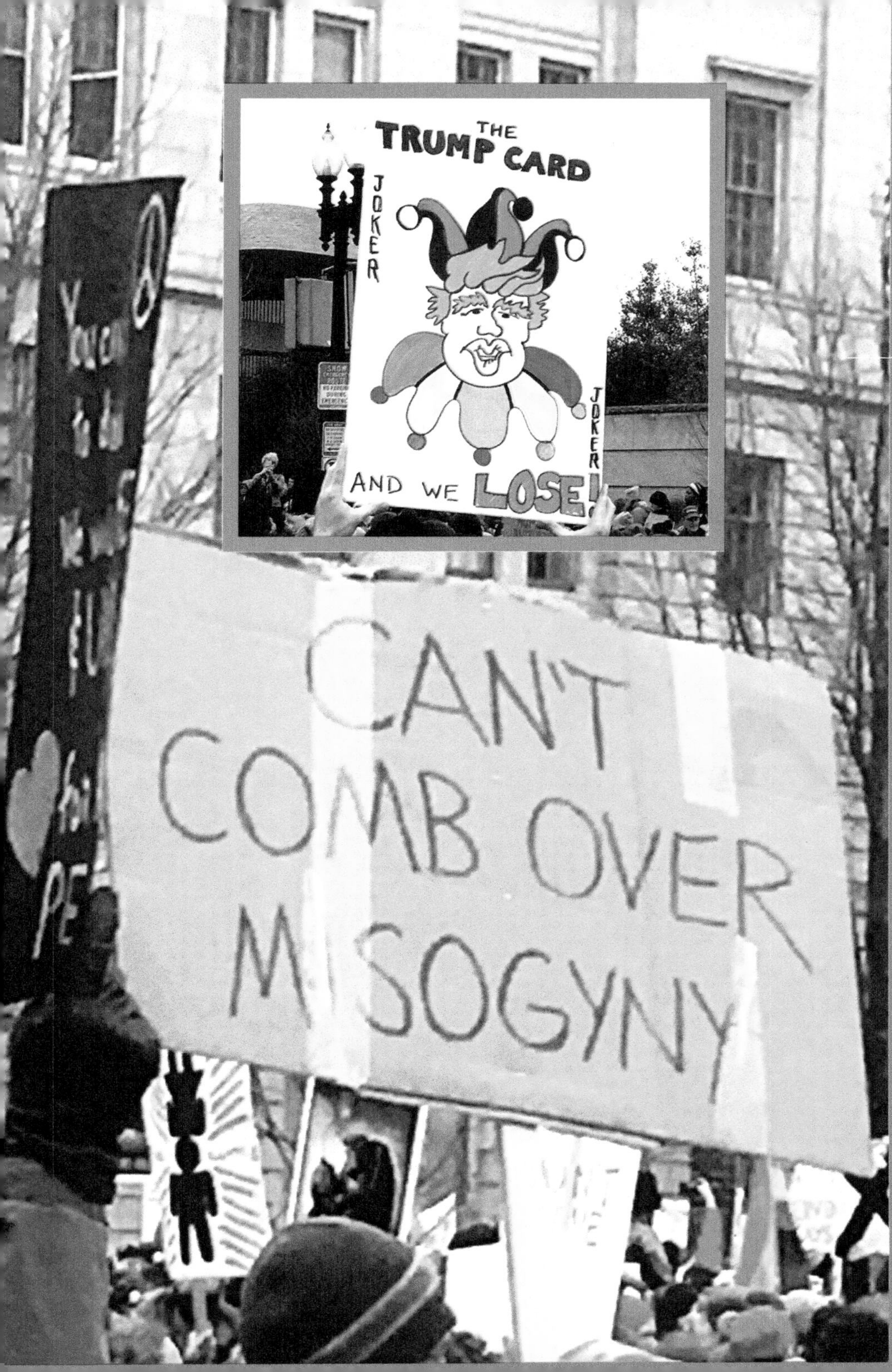
THE TRUMP CARD
JOKER
JOKER
AND WE LOSE!
CAN'T COMB OVER MISOGYNY

We can be Patriots by serving in the military but we can also be Patriots by writing protest songs and litigating issues in courts across the land to fight for rights in which we believe.

Karen Gross

WE WILL NOT BE SILENCED
Think
before
YOU

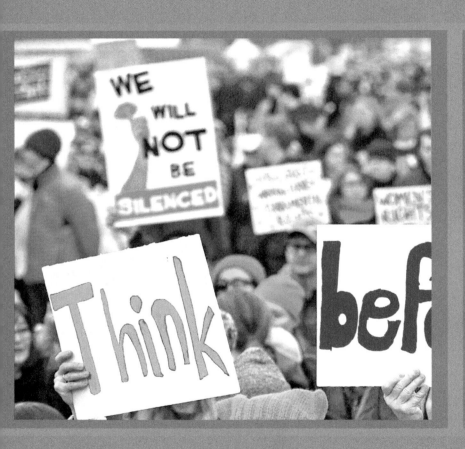

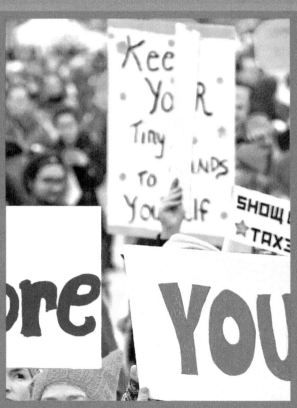

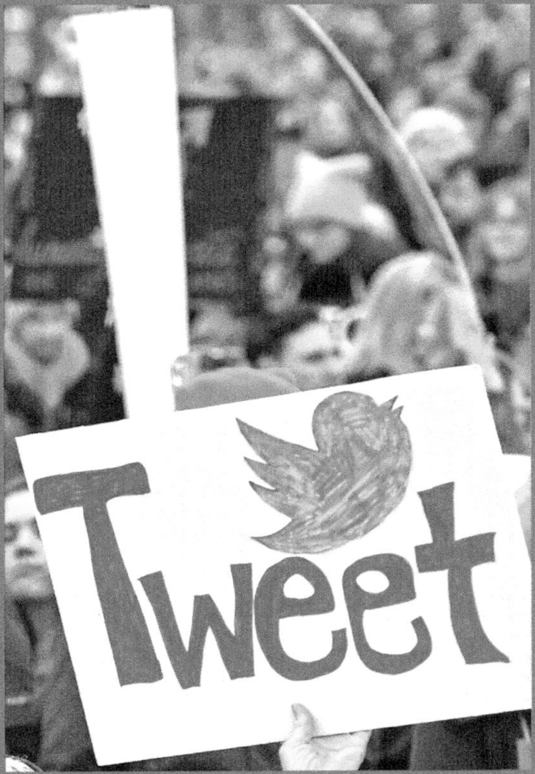
Tweet

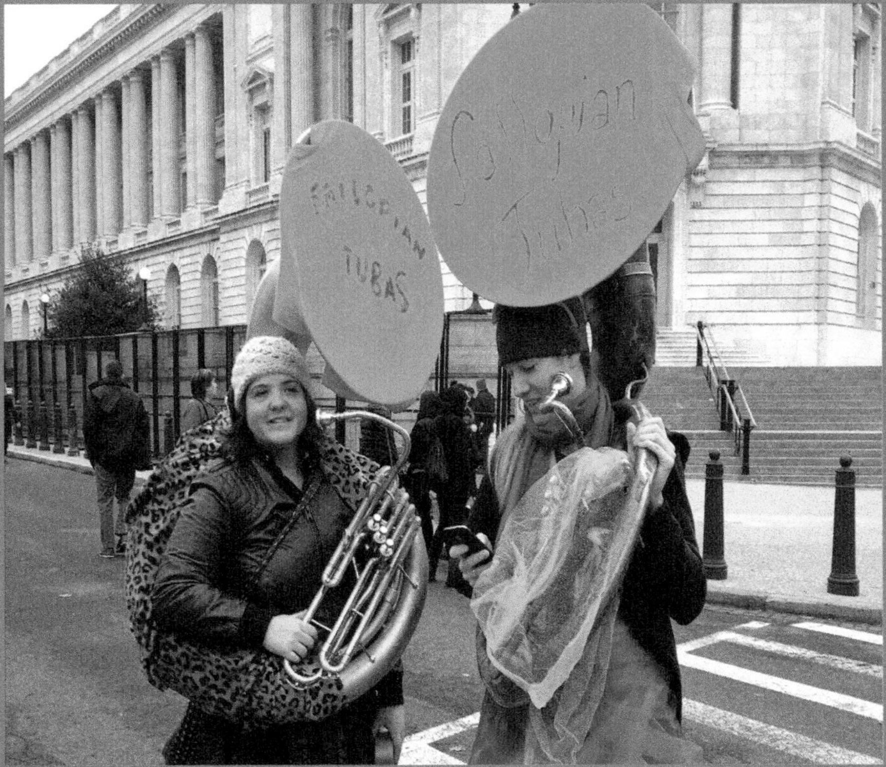
TUBAS

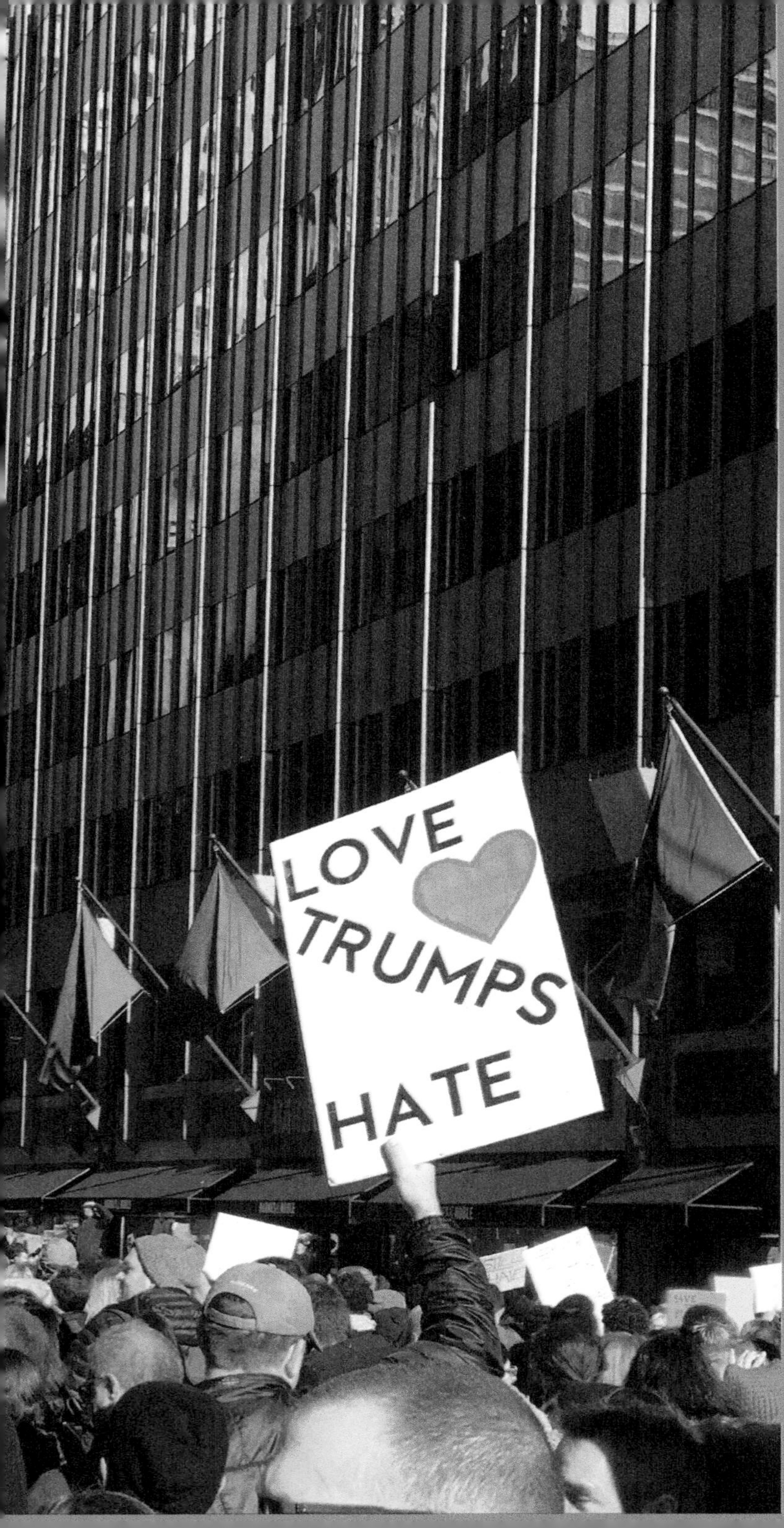
LOVE
TRUMPS
HATE

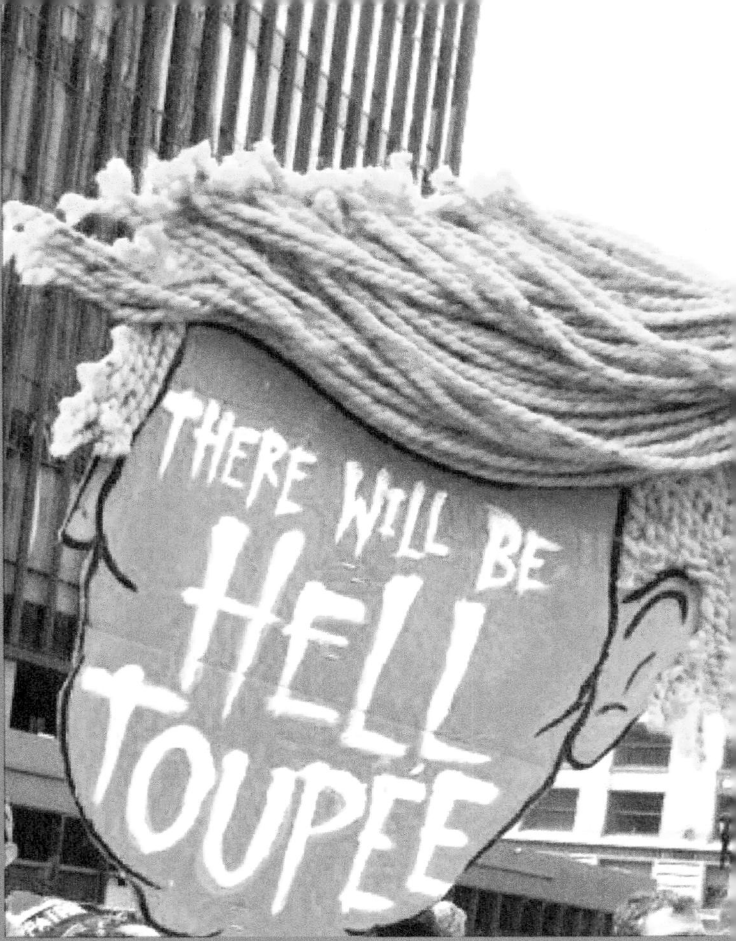
THERE WILL BE
HELL
TOUPÉE

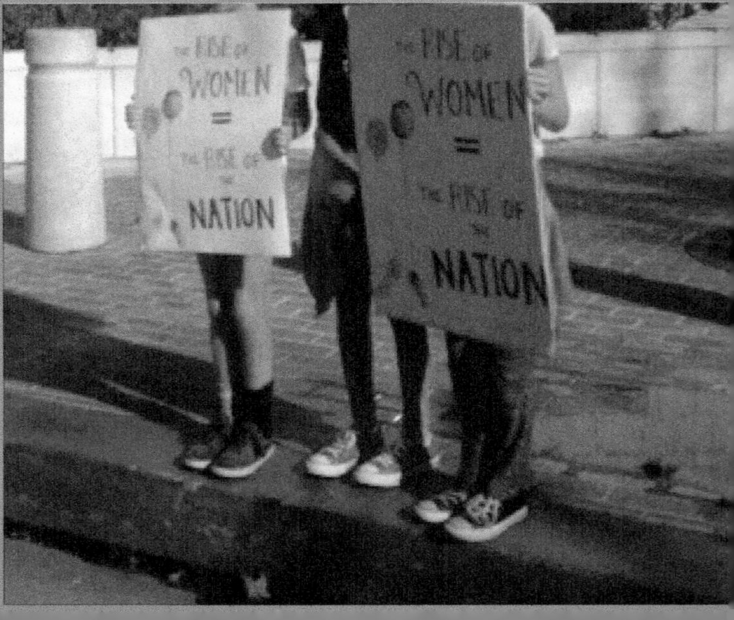
WOMEN
=
NATION
WOMEN
=
NATION

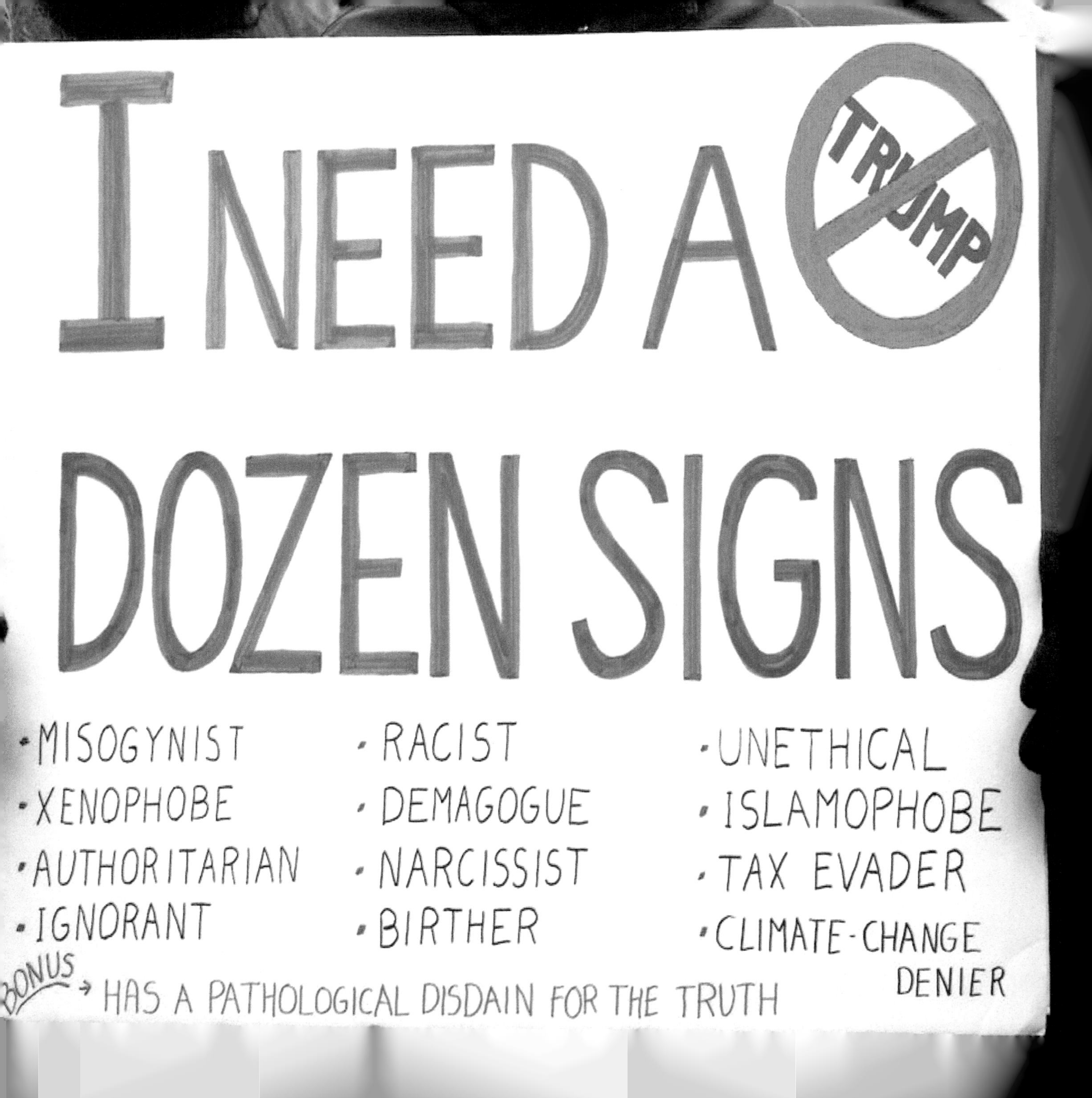
I NEED A
TRUMP
DOZEN SIGNS
• MISOGYNIST
• XENOPHOBE
• AUTHORITARIAN
• IGNORANT
• RACIST
• DEMAGOGUE
• NARCISSIST
• BIRTHER
• UNETHICAL
• ISLAMOPHOBE
• TAX EVADER
• CLIMATE-CHANGE DENIER
BONUS → HAS A PATHOLOGICAL DISDAIN FOR THE TRUTH

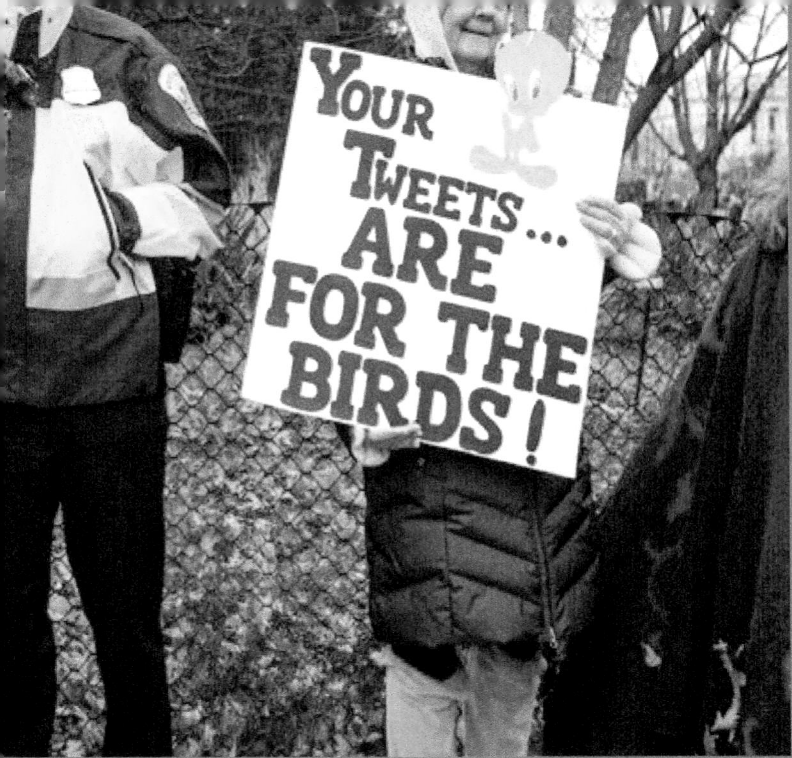
YOUR TWEETS... ARE FOR THE BIRDS!

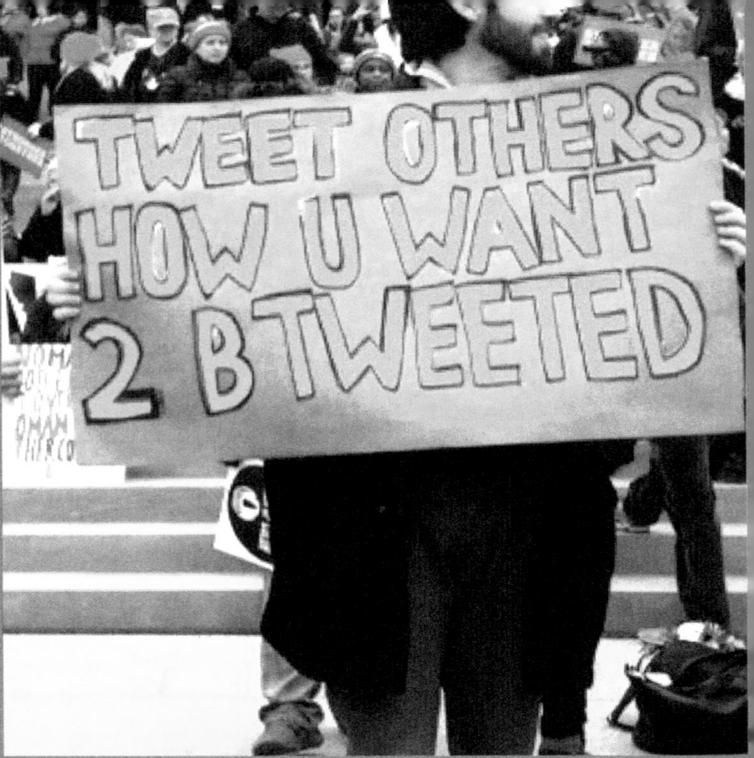
TWEET OTHERS HOW U WANT 2 B TWEETED

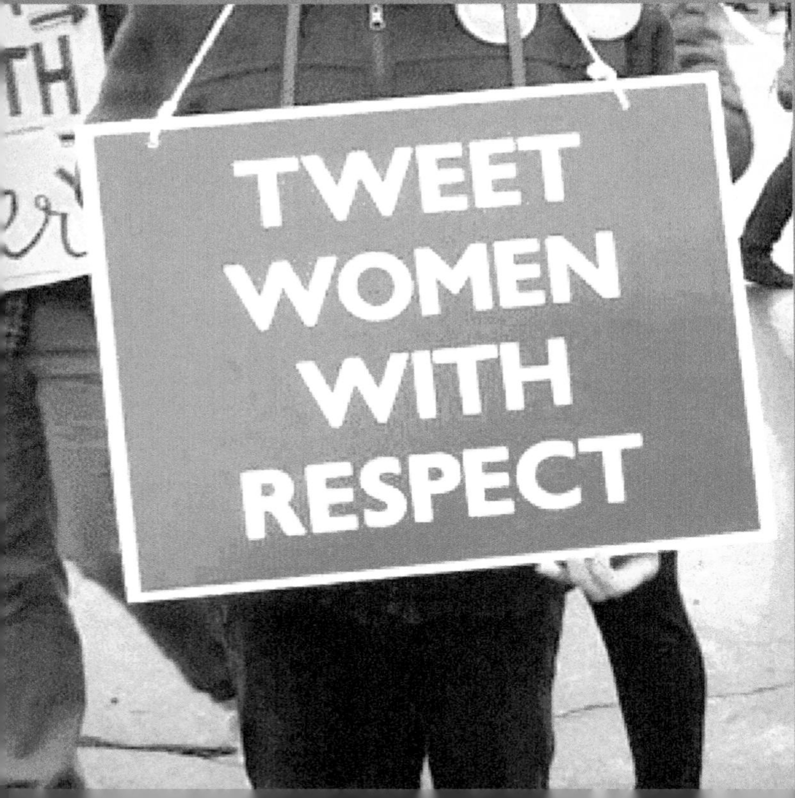
TWEET WOMEN WITH RESPECT

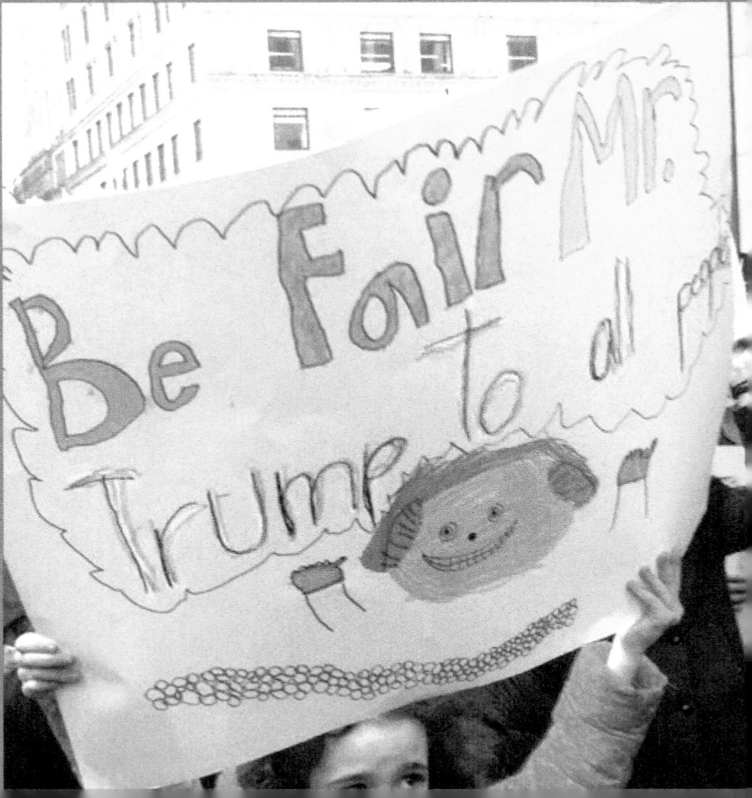
Be Fair Mr.
Trump to all

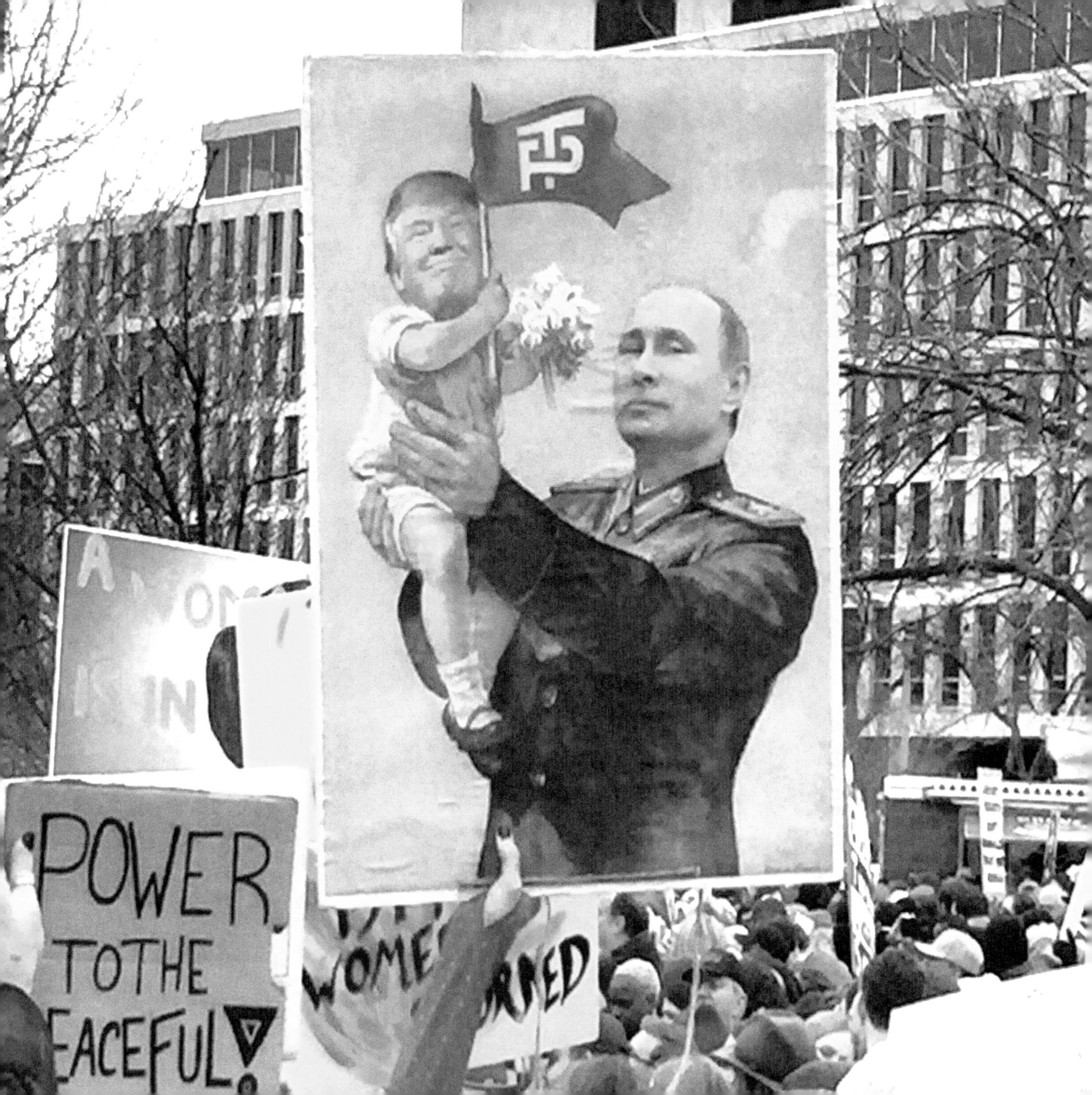
POWER
TO THE
EACEFUL!

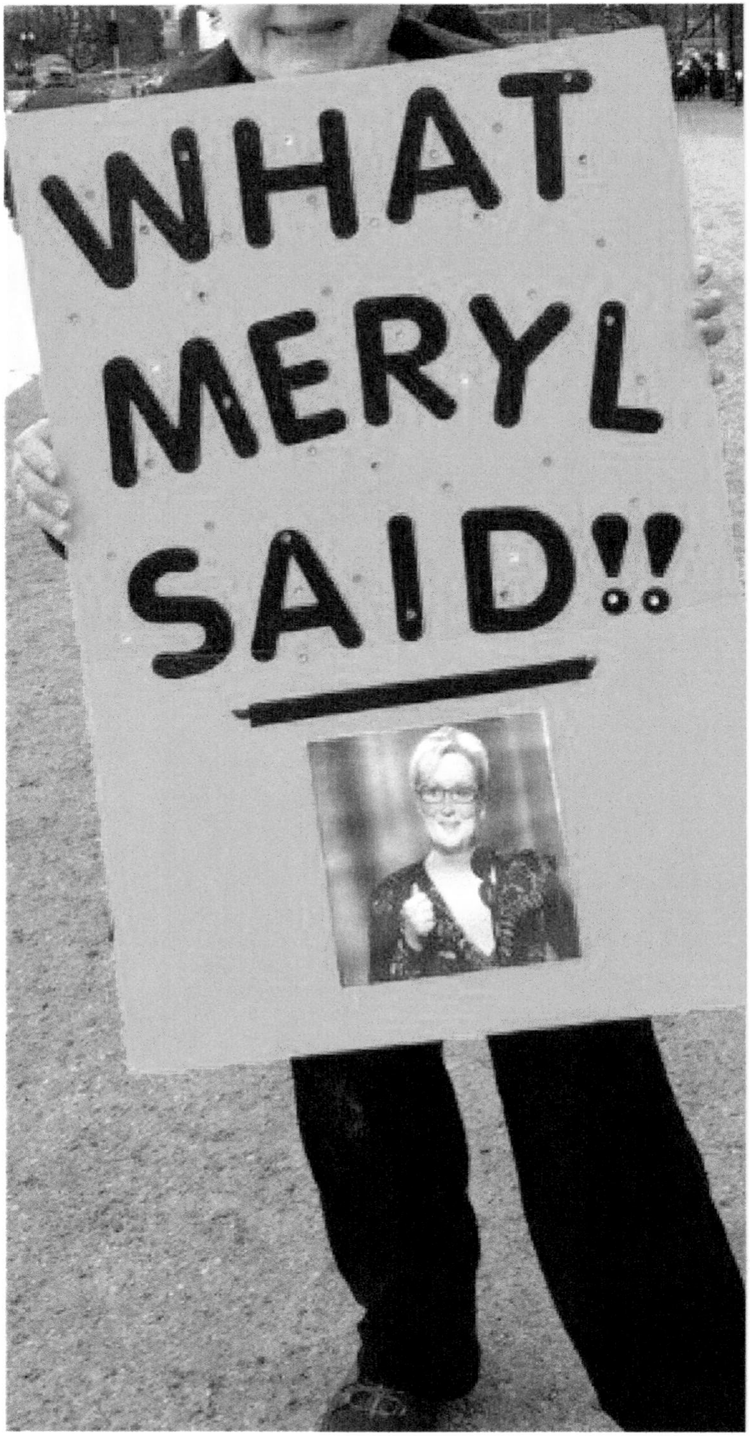
WHAT
MERYL
SAID!!

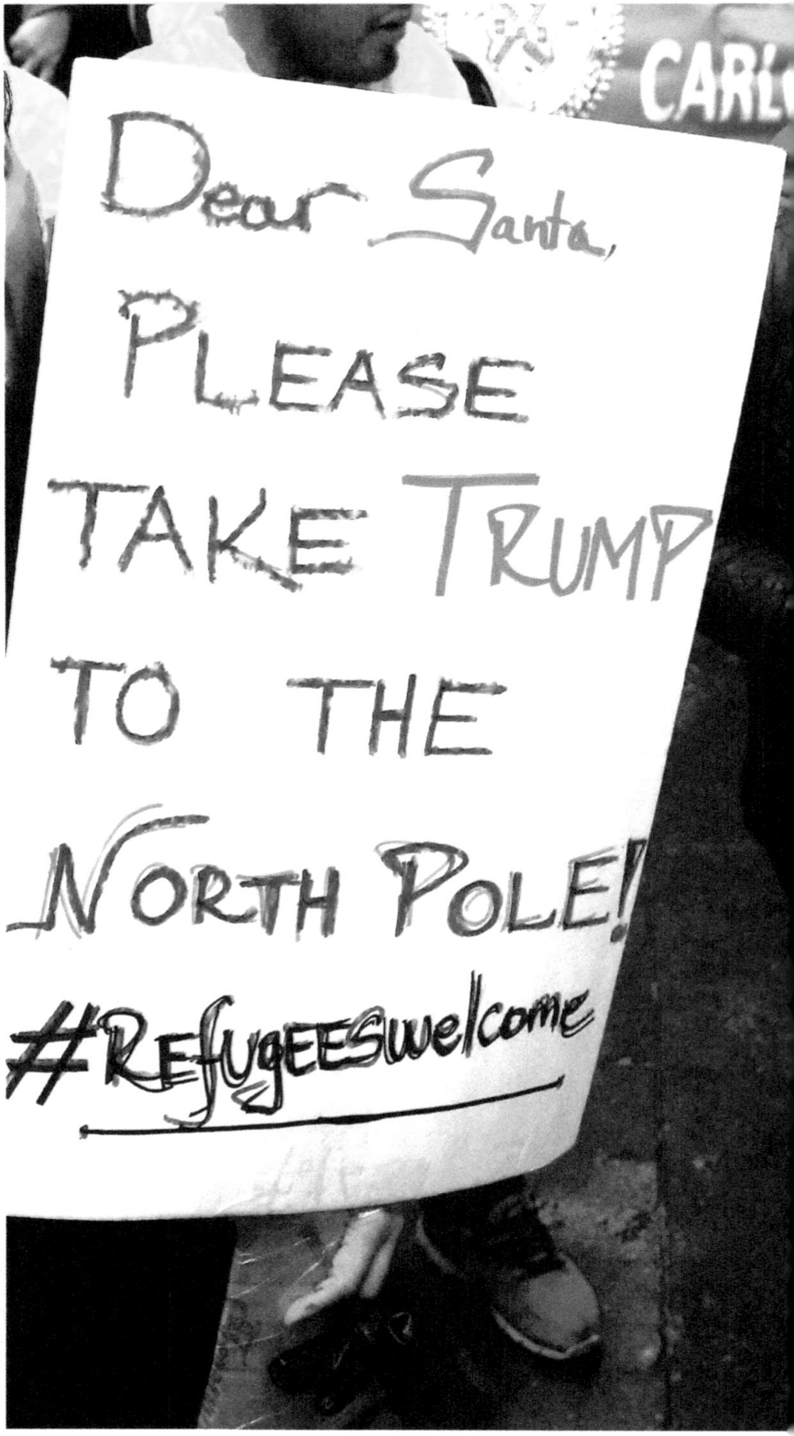
Dear Santa,
PLEASE
TAKE TRUMP
TO THE
NORTH POLE!
#Refugeeswelcome

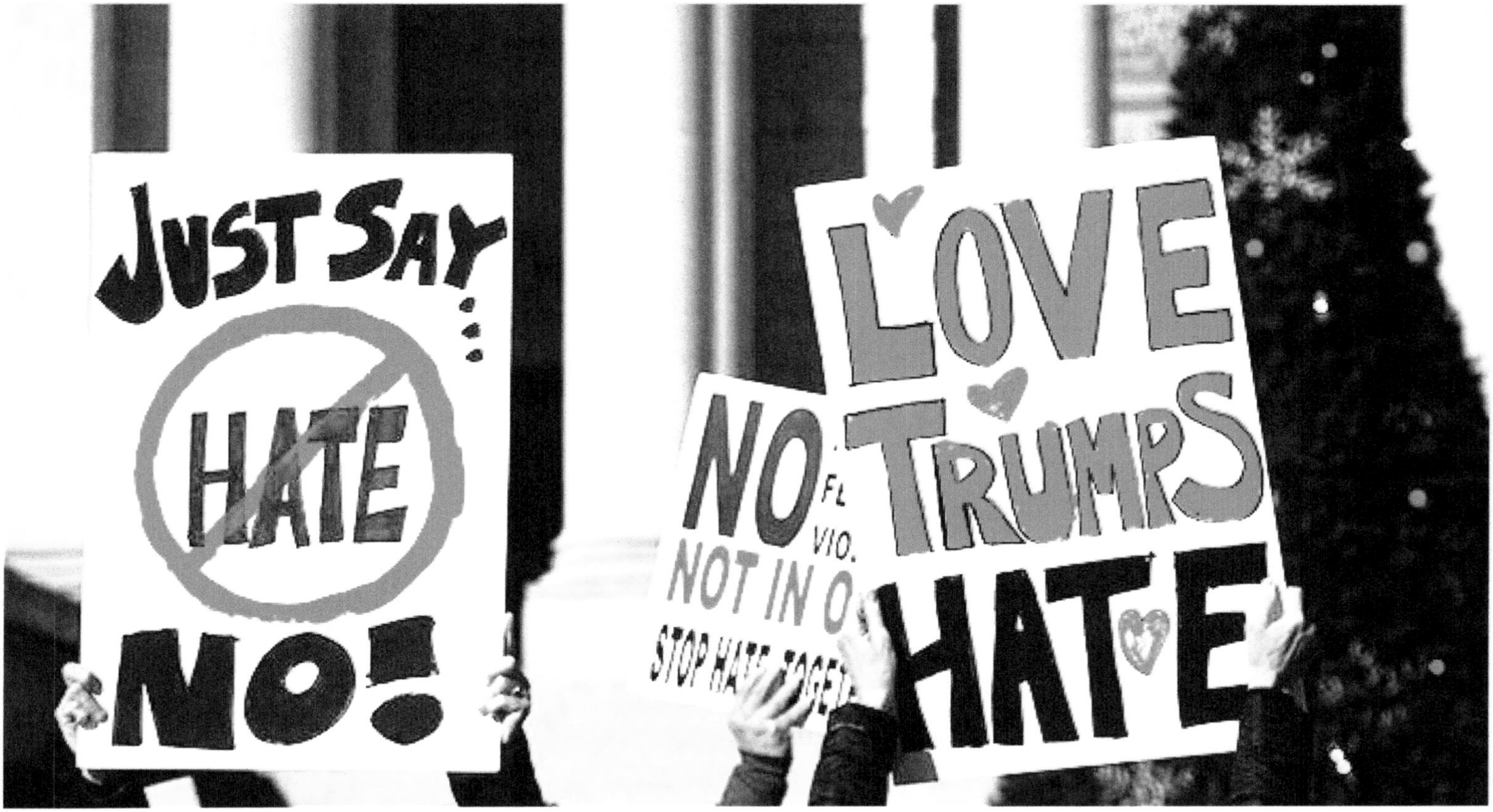
JUST SAY...
HATE
NO!
NO
LOVE TRUMPS HATE

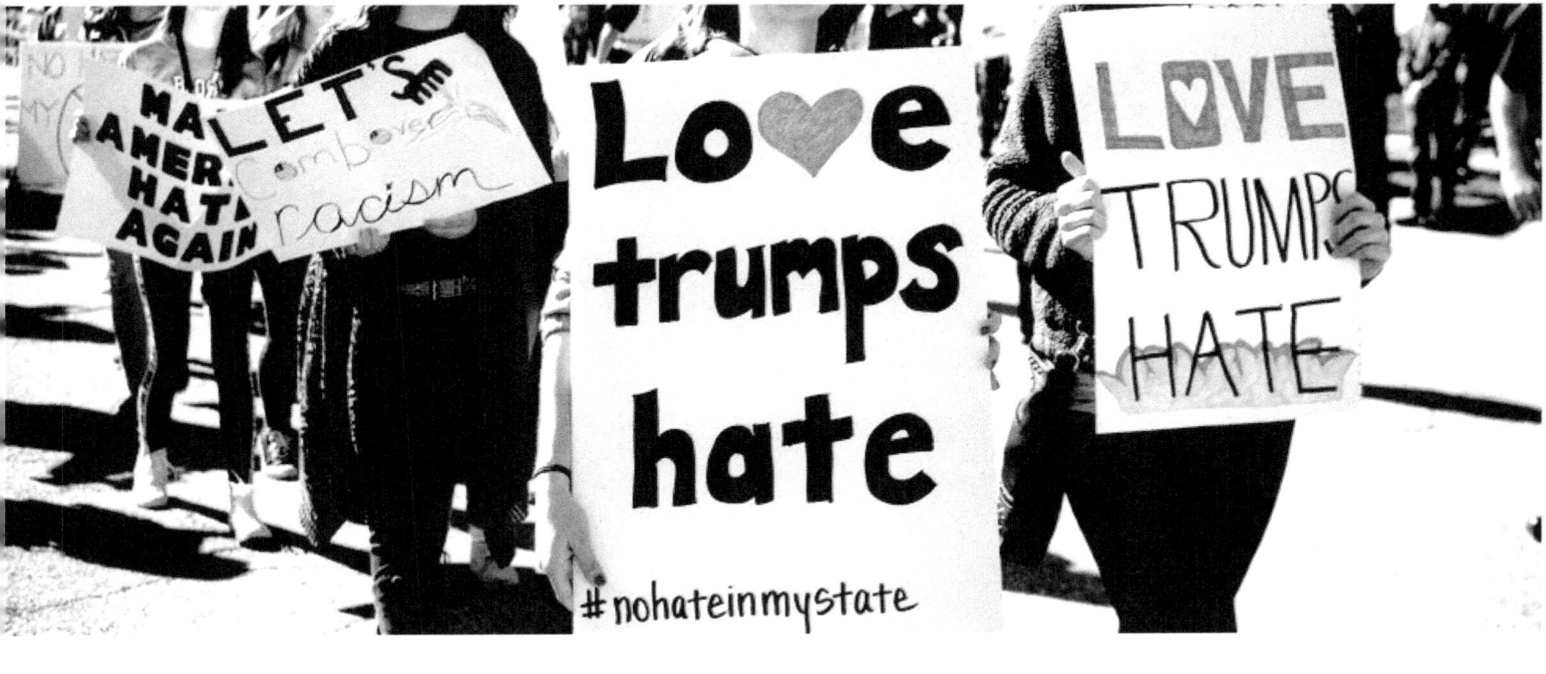
Love trumps hate
#nohateinmystate
LOVE TRUMPS HATE

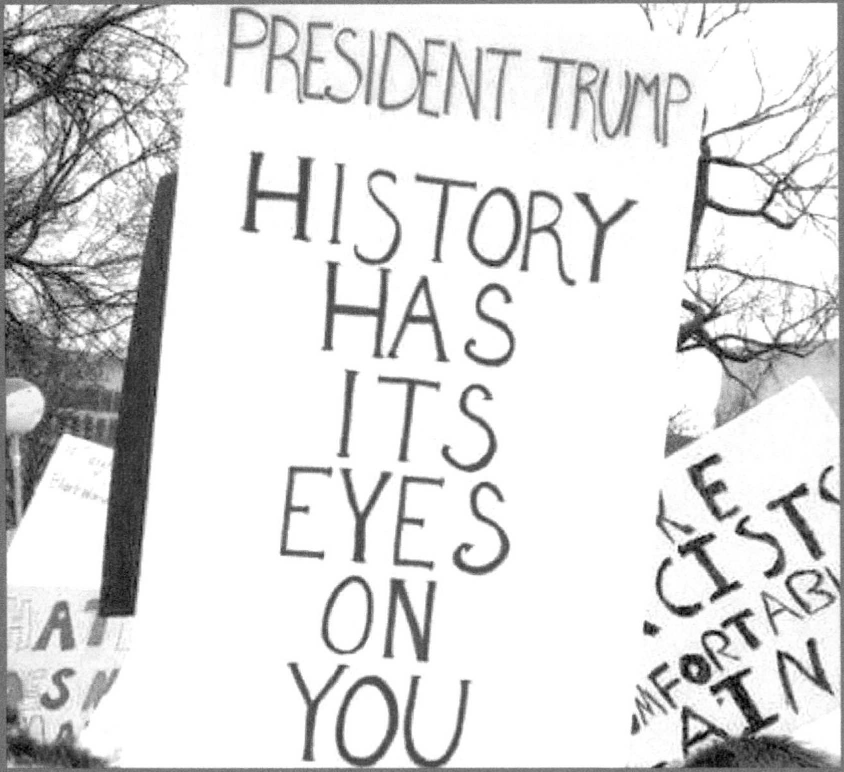
PRESIDENT TRUMP
HISTORY
HAS
ITS
EYES
ON
YOU

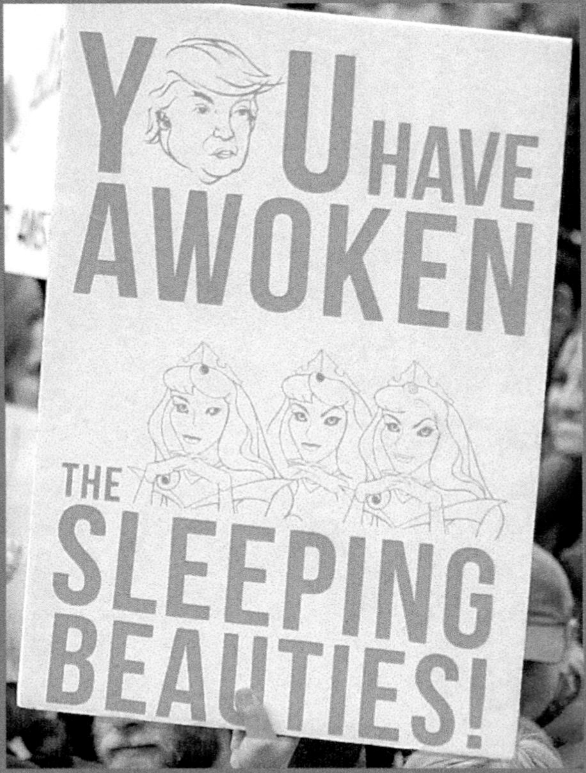
Y U HAVE
AWOKEN
THE
SLEEPING
BEAUTIES!

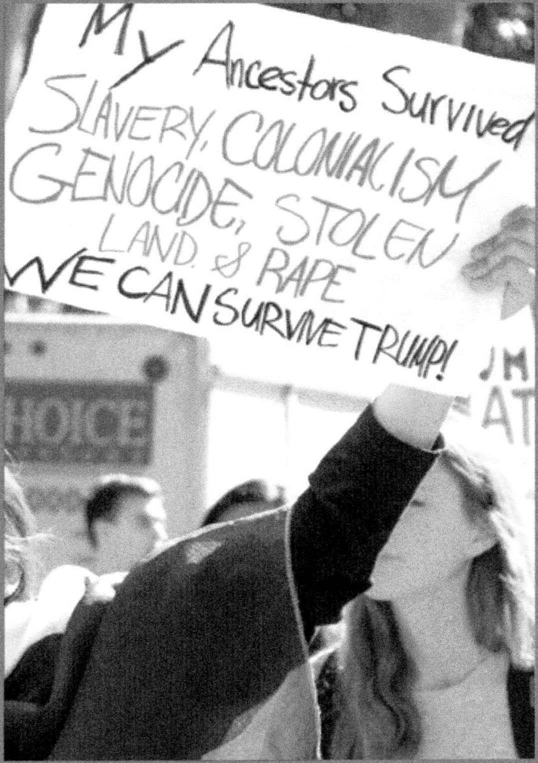
My Ancestors Survived
SLAVERY, COLONIALISM
GENOCIDE, STOLEN
LAND & RAPE
WE CAN SURVIVE TRUMP!

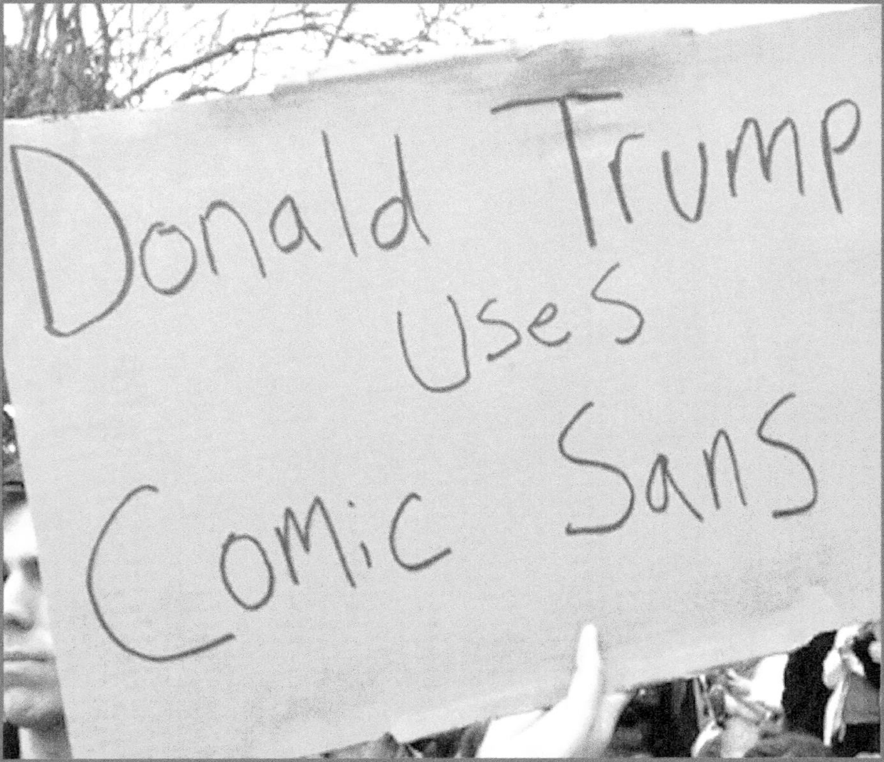
Donald Trump
Uses
Comic Sans

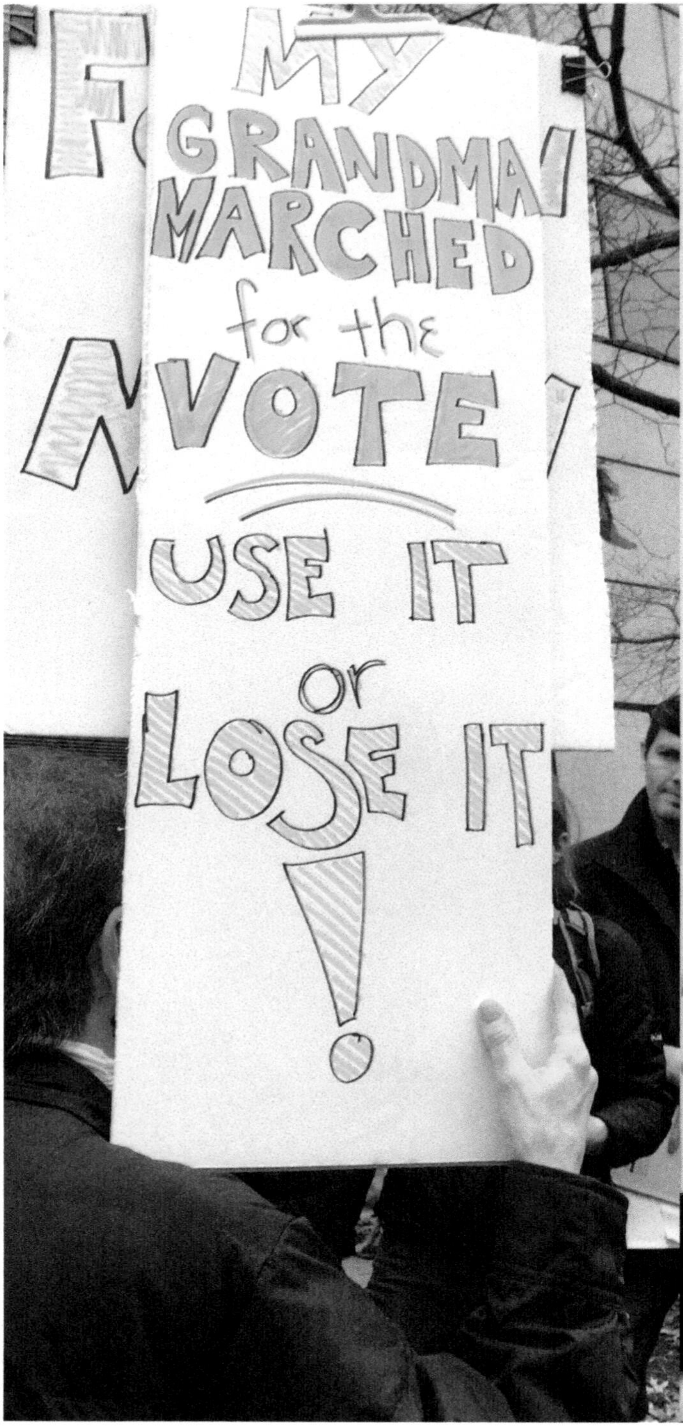
MY GRANDMA MARCHED for the VOTE
USE IT or LOSE IT !

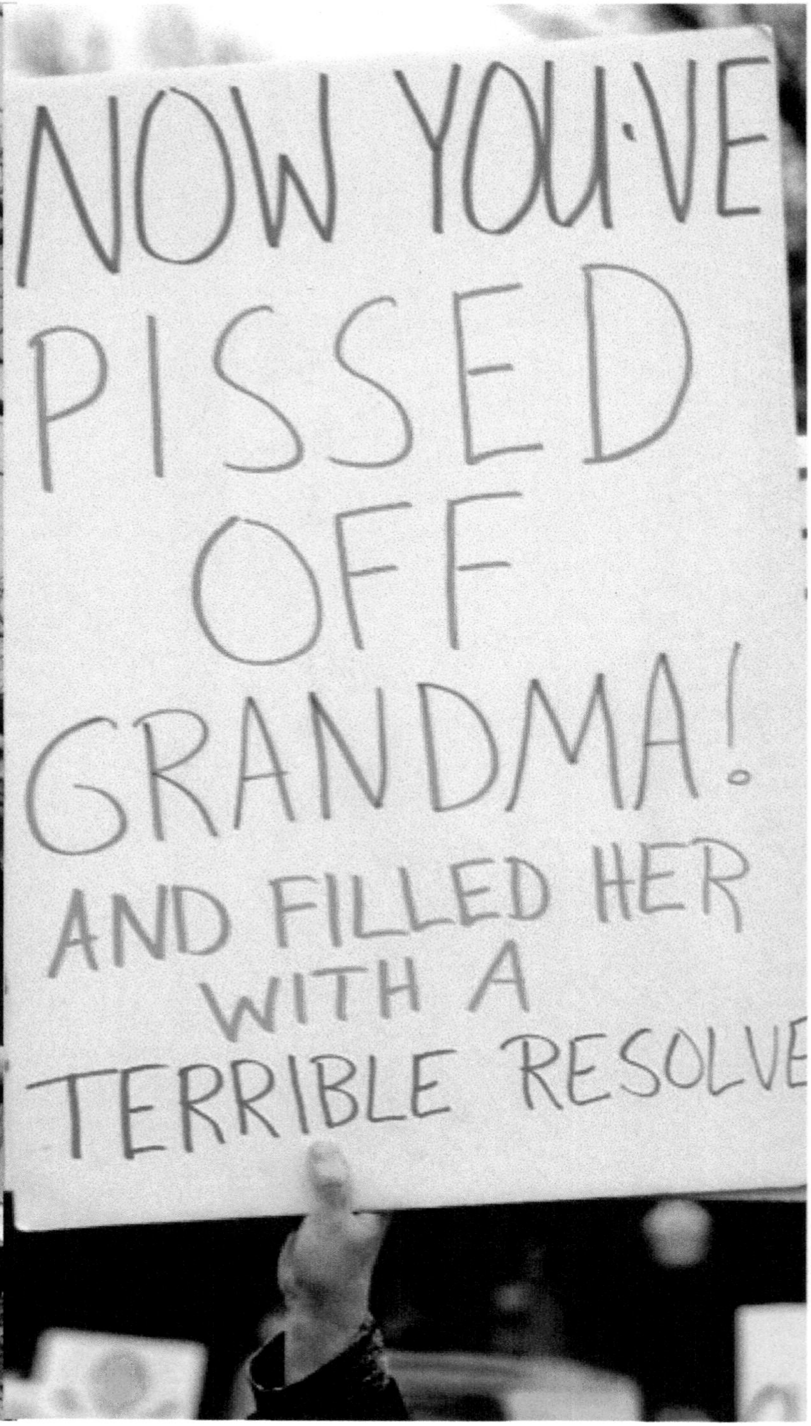
NOW YOU'VE PISSED OFF GRANDMA!
AND FILLED HER WITH A TERRIBLE RESOLVE

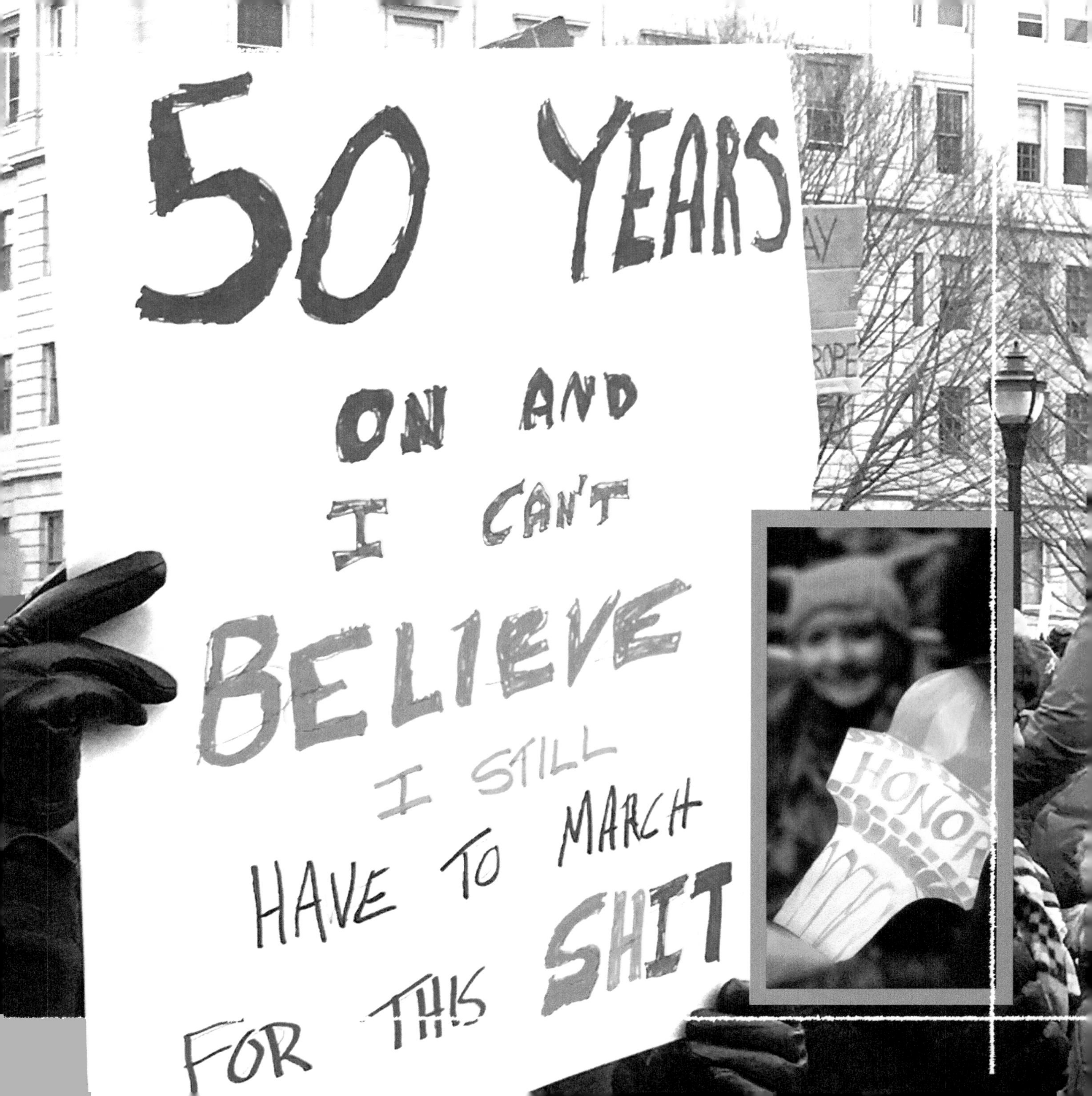
50 YEARS
ON AND
I CAN'T
BELIEVE
I STILL
HAVE TO MARCH
FOR THIS SHIT
HONOR

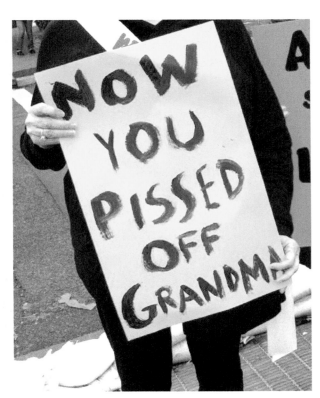

NOW YOU PISSED OFF GRANDMA

NEVER

AGAIN

EQUALITY

SAME SHIT. DIFFERENT CENTURY

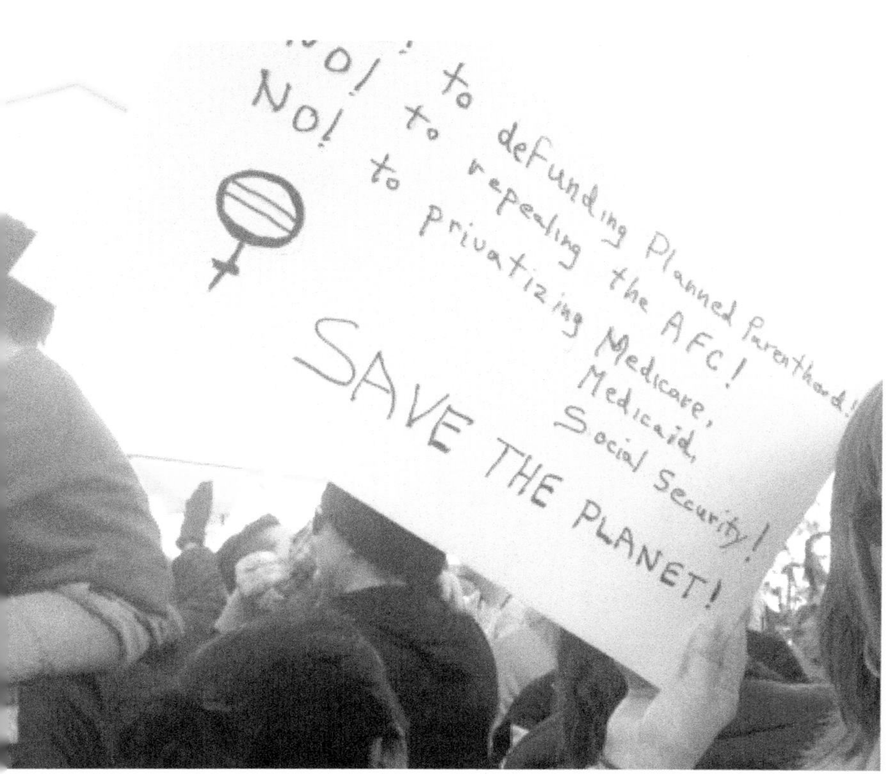
to defunding Planned Parenthood!
No! to repealing the AFC!
No! to privatizing Medicare,
Medicaid,
Social Security!
SAVE THE PLANET!

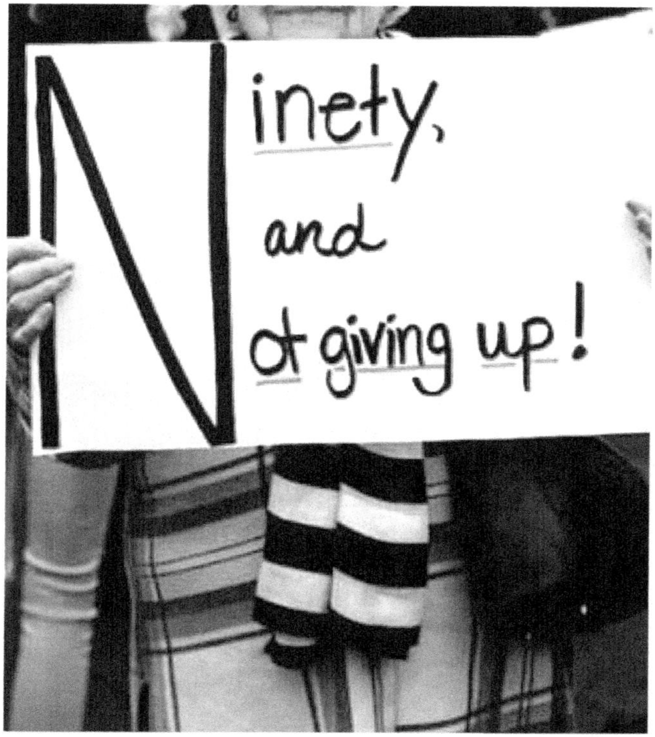
Ninety,
and
Not giving up!

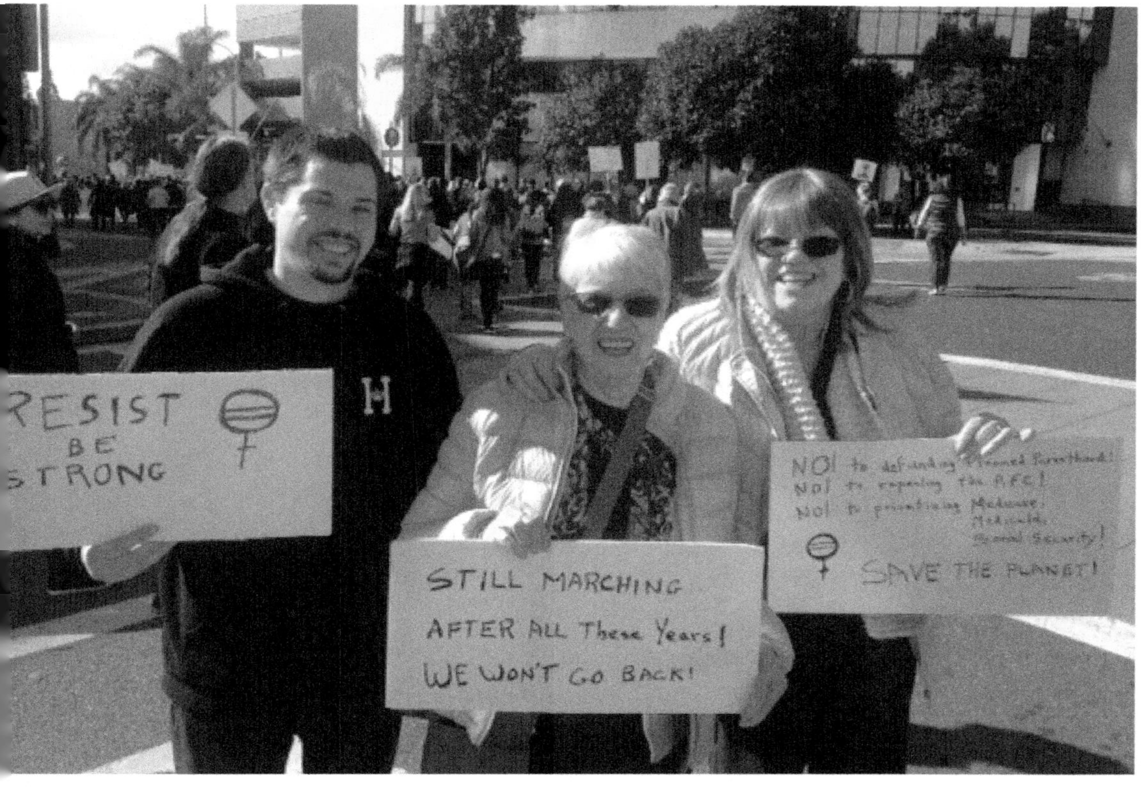
RESIST
BE
STRONG
STILL MARCHING
AFTER ALL These Years!
WE WON'T GO BACK!
NO! to defunding Planned Parenthood!
No! to repealing the AFC!
No! to privatizing Medicare,
Medicaid,
Social Security!
SAVE THE PLANET!

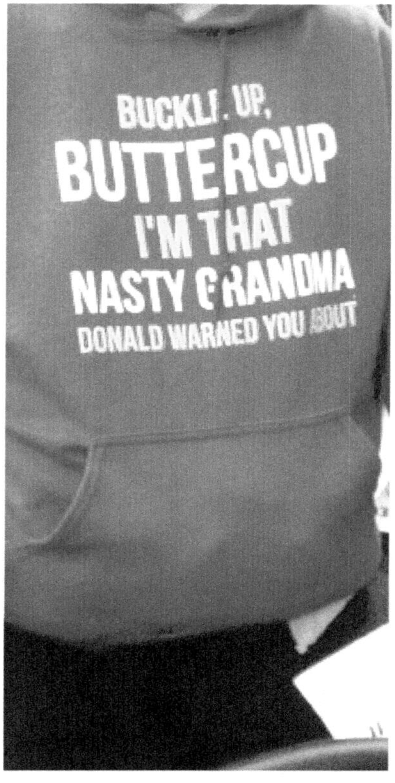
BUCKLE UP,
BUTTERCUP
I'M THAT
NASTY GRANDMA
DONALD WARNED YOU ABOUT

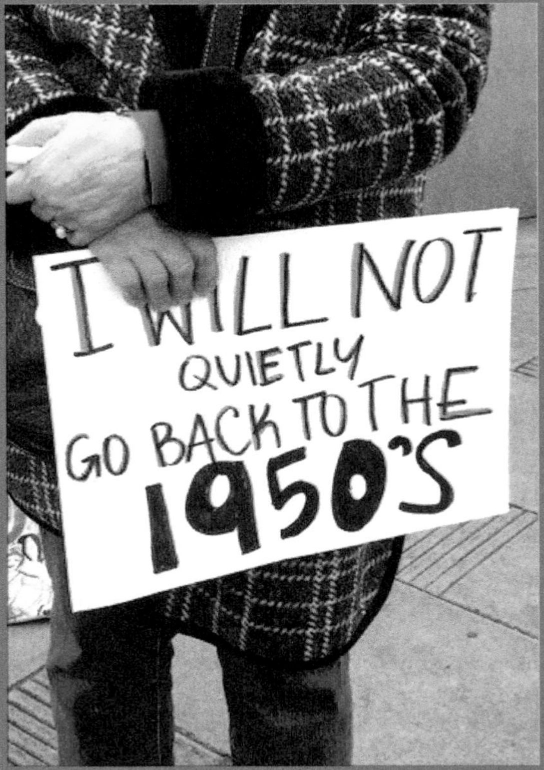
I WILL NOT
QUIETLY
GO BACK TO THE
1950'S

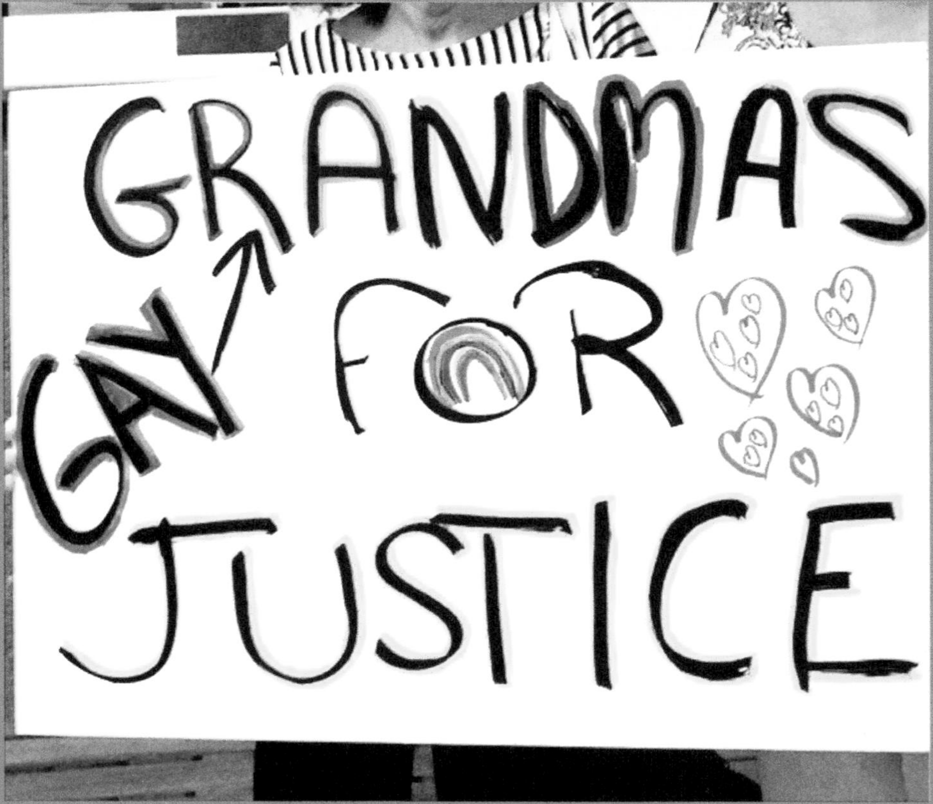
GRANDMAS
GAY
FOR
JUSTICE

"But the President is not America. His cabinet is not America.
Congress is not America. We are America! And we are here to stay."

Anonymous

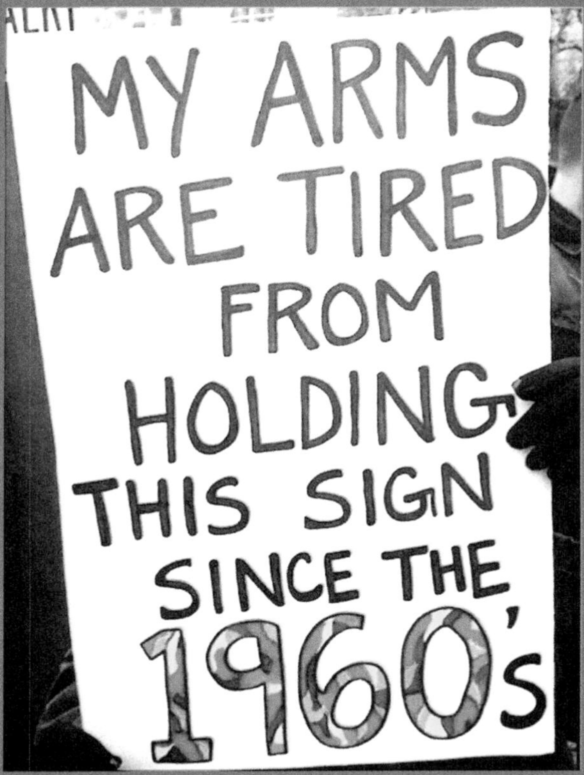
MY ARMS
ARE TIRED
FROM
HOLDING
THIS SIGN
SINCE THE
1960's

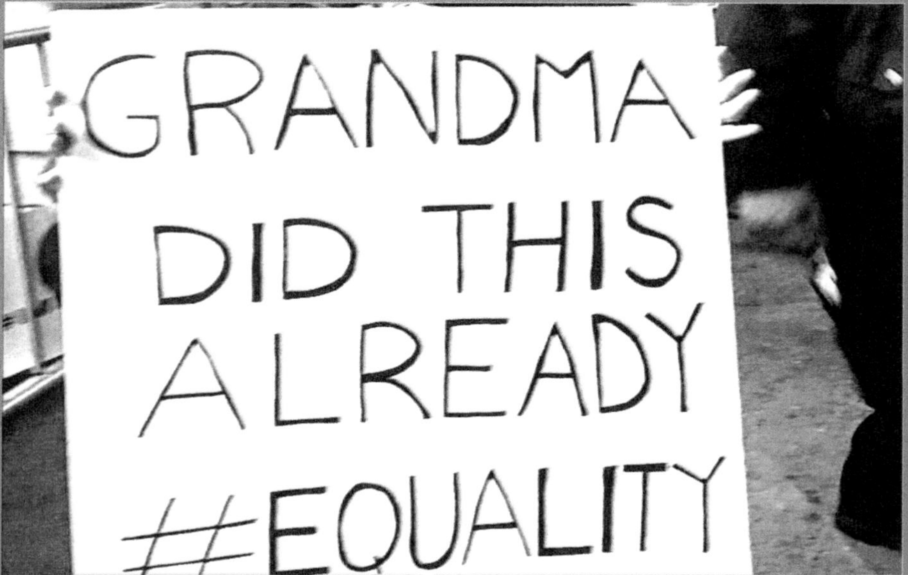
GRANDMA
DID THIS
ALREADY
#EQUALITY

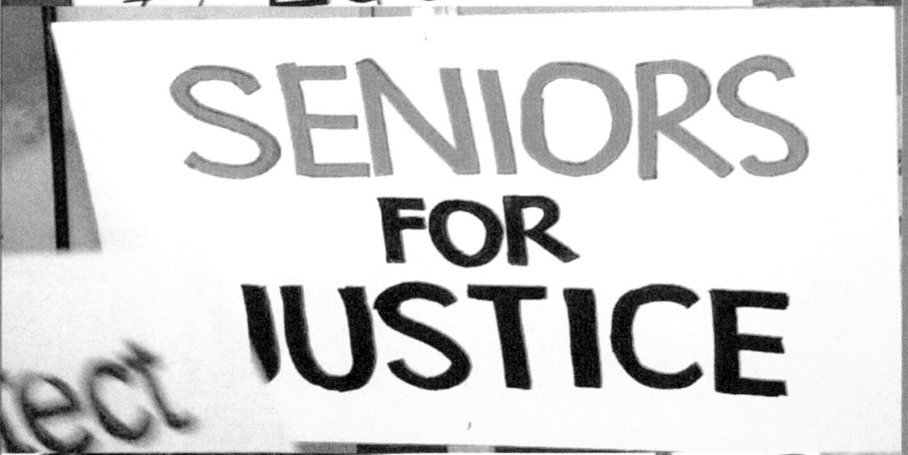
SENIORS
FOR
JUSTICE

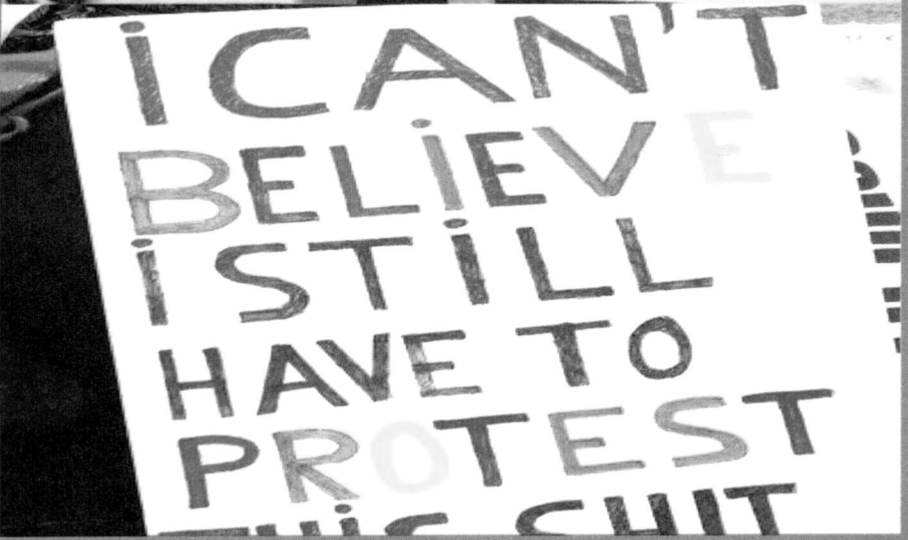
I CAN'T
BELIEVE
I STILL
HAVE TO
PROTEST

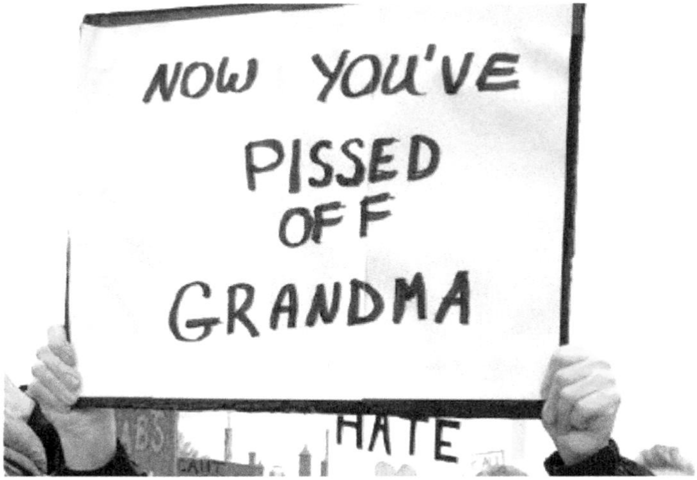
NOW YOU'VE PISSED OFF GRANDMA
HATE

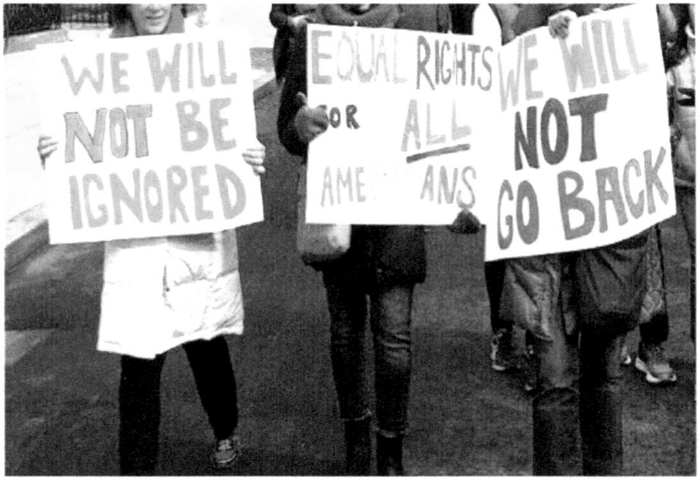
WE WILL NOT BE IGNORED
EQUAL RIGHTS
ALL
WE WILL NOT GO BACK

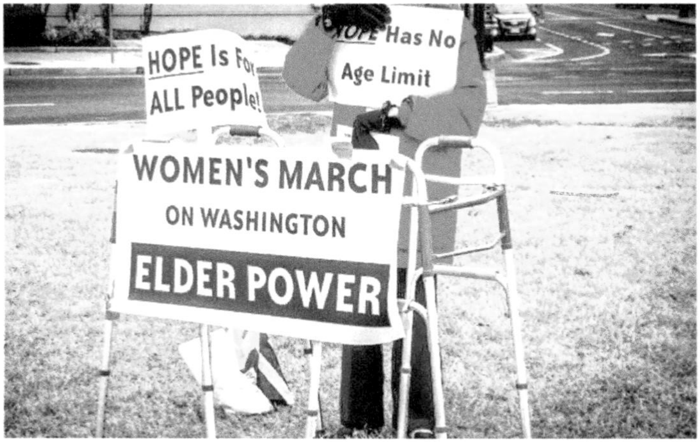
HOPE Is For ALL People!
HOPE Has No Age Limit
WOMEN'S MARCH
ON WASHINGTON
ELDER POWER

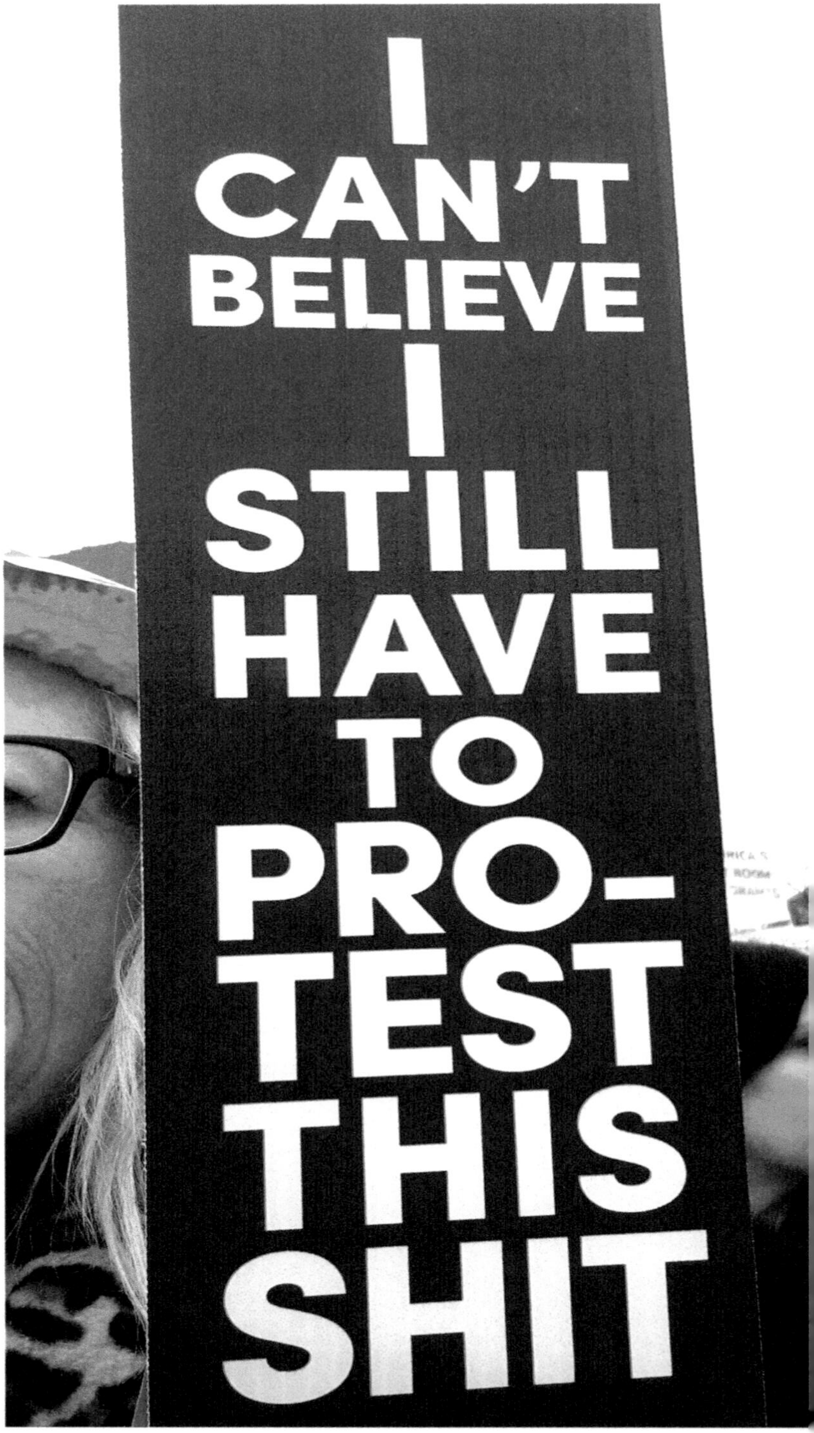
I CAN'T BELIEVE I STILL HAVE TO PRO-TEST THIS SHIT

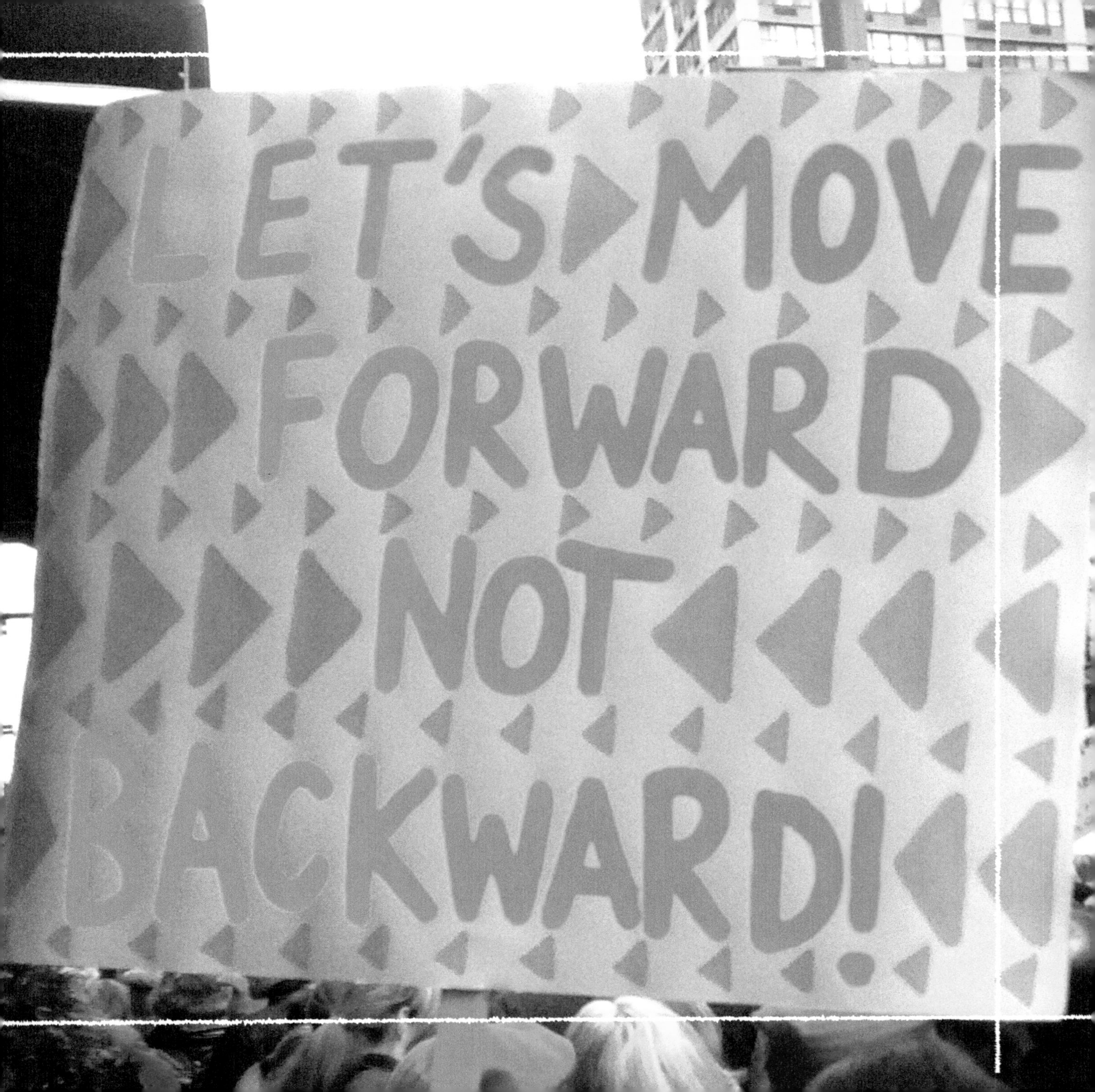
LET'S MOVE
FORWARD
NOT
BACKWARD!

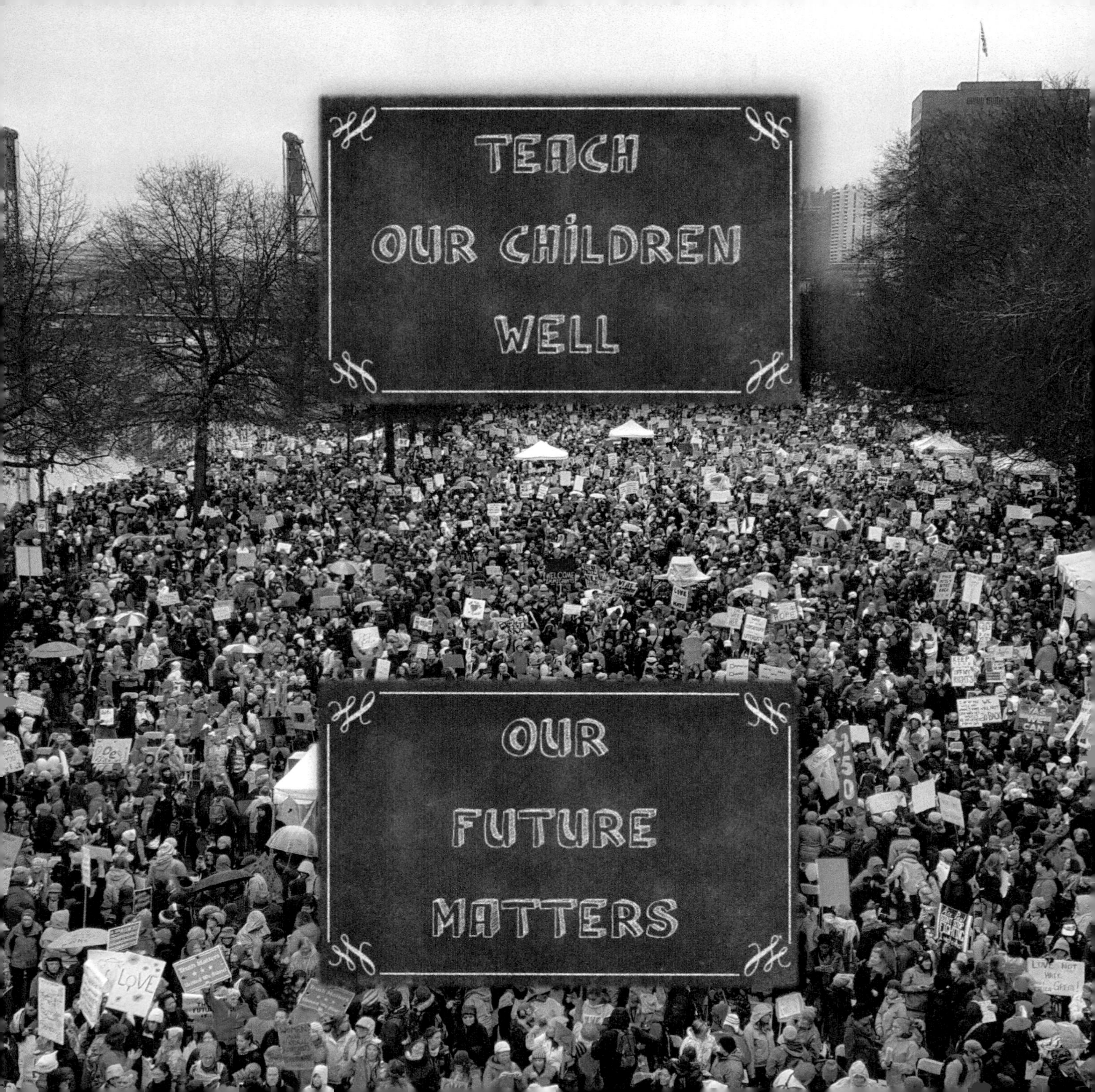
TEACH OUR CHILDREN WELL
OUR FUTURE MATTERS

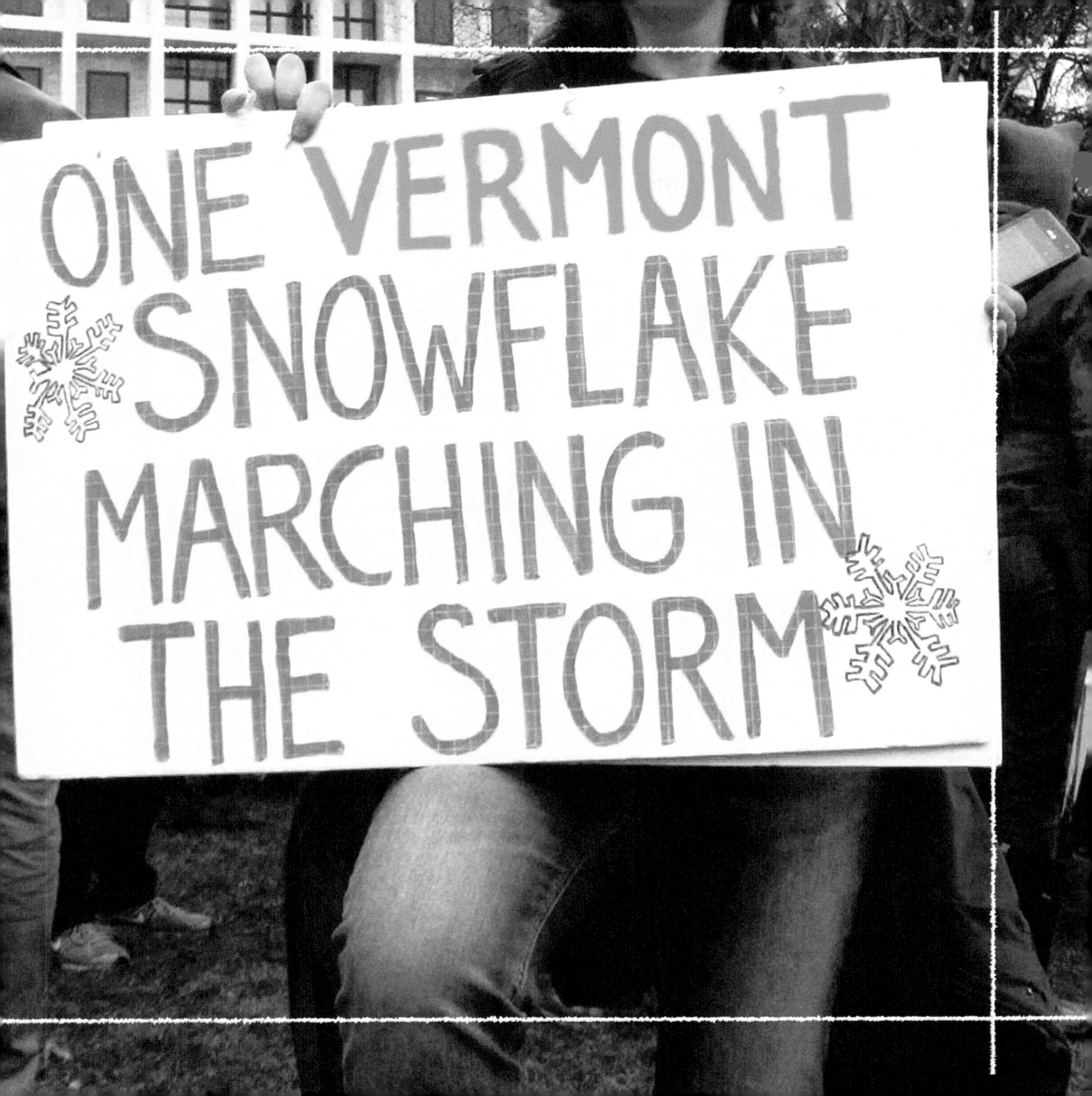
ONE VERMONT
SNOWFLAKE
MARCHING IN
THE STORM

Recently, the word "snowflake" has been used as a demeaning and derogatory term

to describe individuals who are weak, whiny or coddled or fragile, melting at the first sign of disagreement or dissent. It is commonly applied to students who protest (particularly students of apparent privilege without any actual or factual awareness of their true life experiences). And, in the current political climate, the descriptor "snowflake" refers to those who have not fully accepted Donald Trump as our President-elect. Instead of saying "buck up" or "grow up" and realize the election has happened and the results fully in force, there is a charge made that those who are unhappy with the state of the US (or the world perhaps) and its leaders are dreamers or romantics or non-pragmatists.

I beg to differ on what it really means to be a snowflake and how that term can and should be turned on its head into a positive. Start here: in the holiday season, people display snowflakes everywhere – on houses, in trees, in windows, on wrapping paper, cards and clothing. Skiers beg for snowflakes.

Those of us who live in a cold climate also have a rapport with snowflakes. We relish the flakes falling from the sky, particularly at night when they sparkle and twinkle in the light. And we watch with wonder as these flakes accumulate, creating a winter wonderland for folks of all ages and stages.

I have been particularly struck by the photographic images of snowflakes taken many decades ago by Vermonter Wilson A. Bentley. He captured the many shapes and styles of snowflakes, sending a loud and clear message that they are not all the same. Their variety is stunning actually and the level of detail, when seen through a microscope, is an affirmation of the power of nature and the complexity of its designs. Yes, with his 5000 images, he has created a legitimate snowflake generation.

For me, then, snowflakes are anything but weak, coddled or fragile. They are strong and individualized -- architectural and artistic marvels. We would be wise to recognize the power of and inherent in snowflakes and those of us on whom that name has been placed (as a stain of dishonor) should wear it proudly. We are symbolic of a different time, a more beautiful time, a time when marveling at the world and its potential was a plus.

And, if snowflakes are those of us who fight for (not melt away from) a fairer world, a better world, a more genuine world in which there is both respect and awe, you can call me snowflake anytime. I will wear that moniker proudly. So, go decorate your home – holiday or not – with snowflakes and help rebuild a nation and the world in which we fiercely fight for the right to be independent thinkers, caretakers of each of other and the environment and recorders of a history written and to be written about 2016.

And the next time someone calls you a snowflake, say thank-you.

Karen Gross
Reprinted from a piece on LinkedIn December 22, 2016

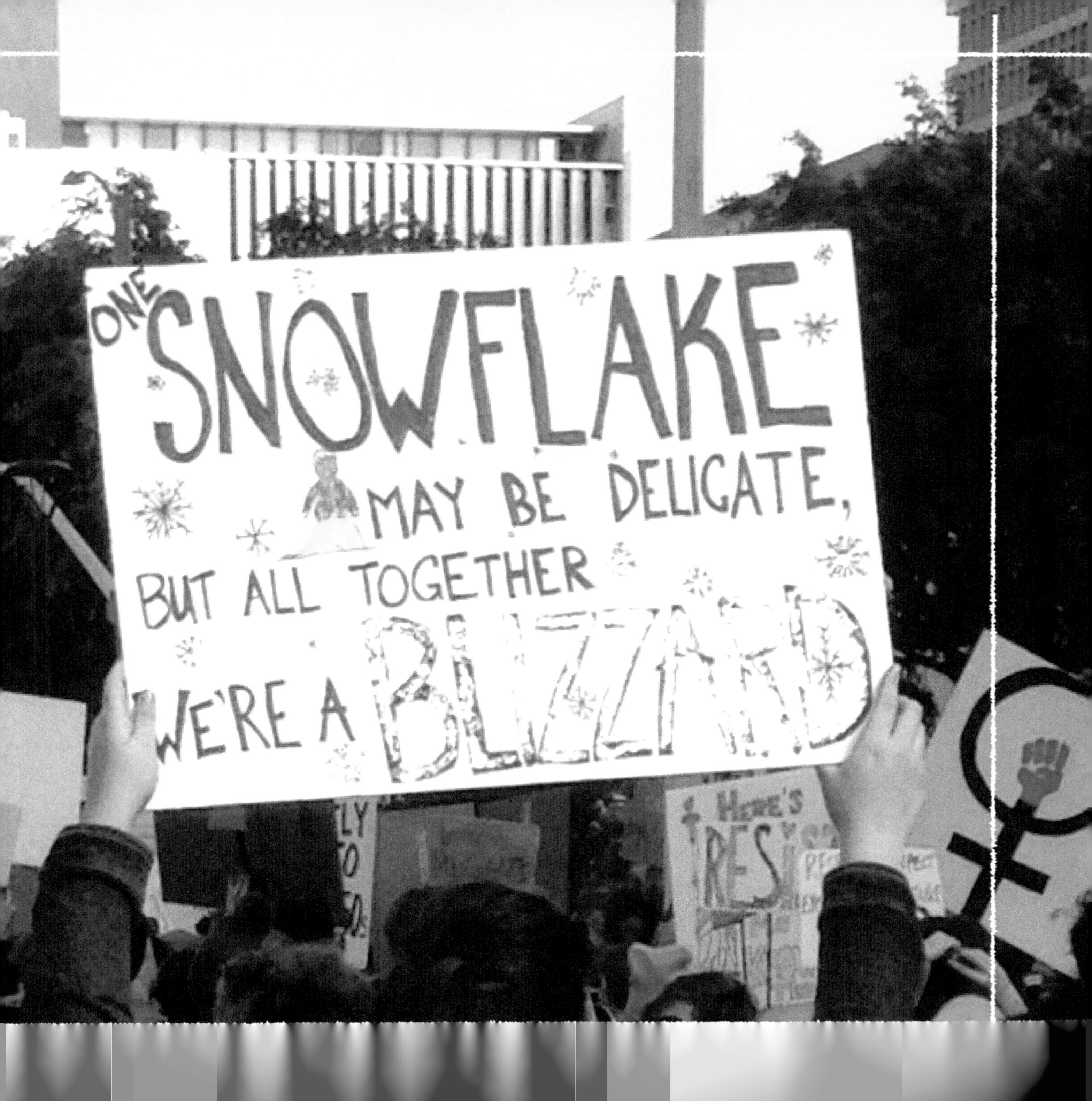
ONE SNOWFLAKE MAY BE DELICATE,
BUT ALL TOGETHER
WE'RE A BLIZZARD

Next Steps:
They Come in All Sizes and Shapes

The signs contained in this book can be seen and re-seen and with each viewing, we can garner new understandings, new feelings and added strength. The signs are, then, memorialized here but they are not static. The selections of the particular signs for this book (and their presentation) were chosen because they continue to make us think and feel and reflect. They were and are designed to give us a pathway forward. They are repeatedly signaling this message: we need to teach our children well.

The obvious question that confronts all of us concerned about our nation, our world and our children is: What can we do? What are our next steps? How do we convert feelings and thoughts into action? What approaches will work to make the world safer and better for our children and our children's children? What will restore and then reinforce values that we hold dear?

I wish there were a simple answer but there is no magic, single strategy for answering any of these questions. If there were, it would have been adopted already. So, I think we need to stop looking for an answer, an approach. Instead, as people are accustomed to doing, we need to see, experience and use our collective web-like power to utilize a myriad of strategies – simultaneously – to teach our children.

Here's why. Start with this reality. We lead complex lives and those lives are different at different ages and stages and in different locales and different contexts. Some people work outside the home, contributing in meaningful ways to society and the well-being of their families. Some people are caregivers, within and outside the home, whether or not they earn actual dollars. Some people are focused on raising their child or children and helping raise other children. Some women of a certain age are pushing to break glass ceilings and entering rooms previously occupied mostly by men. Some people are struggling with personal demons or illnesses and getting up each morning and putting one foot in front of another is challenging. Some people, those with gray hair in particular, are reflecting on how they can deploy the experience and talents they have garnered over generations. They may not be running marathons (although some are); they may not be entering the workplace daily (although some are). But, they have energy and wisdom that can help us make improvements in our world.

In other words, everyone will and can contribute to improving our world in different ways. Some can run for office; some can help candidates running for office; some can write and speak out to large groups; others can speak softly but firmly to smaller audiences; some can approach legislatures with ideas and sample legislation; others can make calls to key personnel; some can give money; some can raise money; some can push for change in their workplaces and communities;

others can push for change within their families; some can write books and essays that promote change; others can make art whether that is painting or music or dance.

Many years ago, Caroline Kennedy edited a book called *A Patriot's Handbook*. The book had and still has a powerful message: there are many ways to be a Patriot. Yes, one can be a President of a country (or a college or a company). But, one can also be a dissenter and a protester and fight hard against the tide to deliver a message. We can be Patriots by serving in the military but we can also be Patriots by writing protest songs and litigating issues in courts across the land to fight for rights in which we believe. The point of her book is particularly poignant because it signals that we all can contribute to being a Patriot but in our own way, using our own talents, recognizing the marked diversity among us as women, as workers, as thinkers, as mothers, as people.

So, for me and I hope for those who have this book, there will be many ways to work to improve our world. The point isn't that there is only one pathway forward. There are many – and they are not all straight. But, whatever pathways and hurdles we face, we are connected – as exemplified by these signs – to move forward, to use our individual and collective talents to teach our child and our children's children well.

We can do this. We must do this. We will do this. Individually and together.

Karen Gross

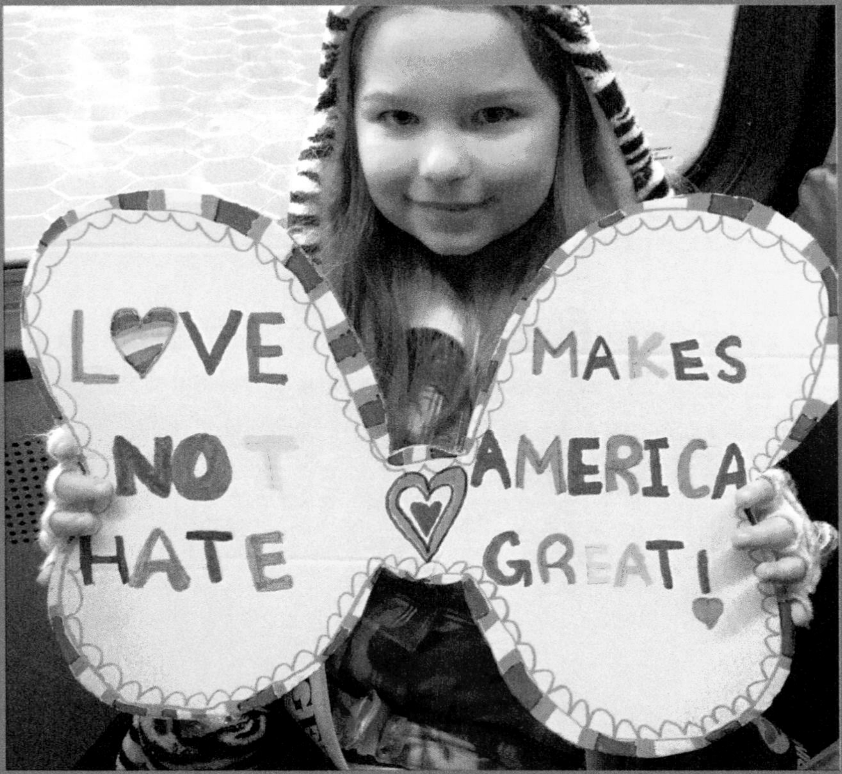
LOVE NOT HATE
MAKES AMERICA GREAT!

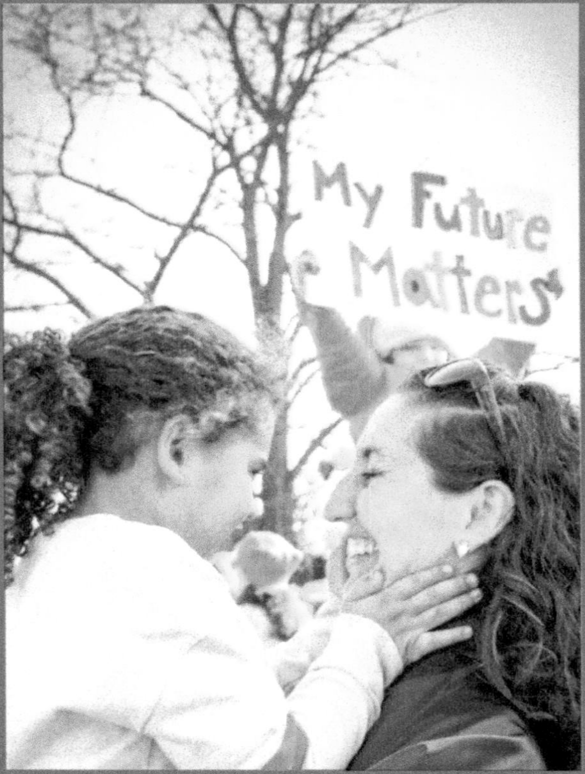
My Future Matters

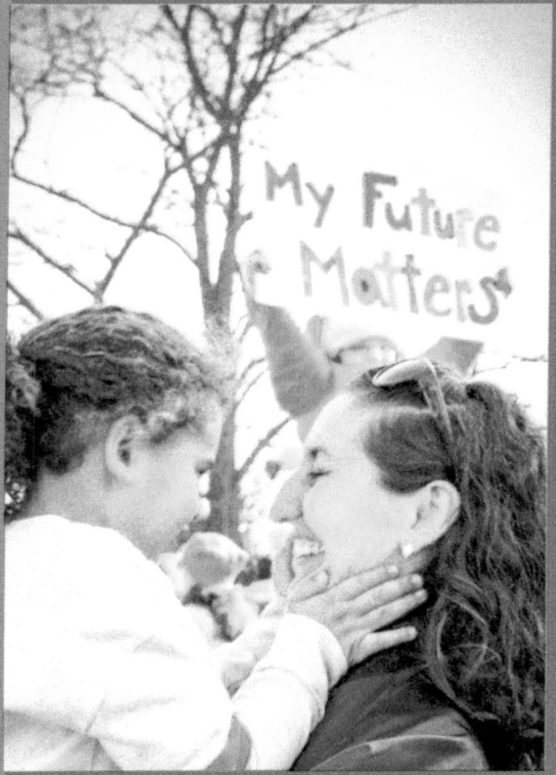
My Future Matters

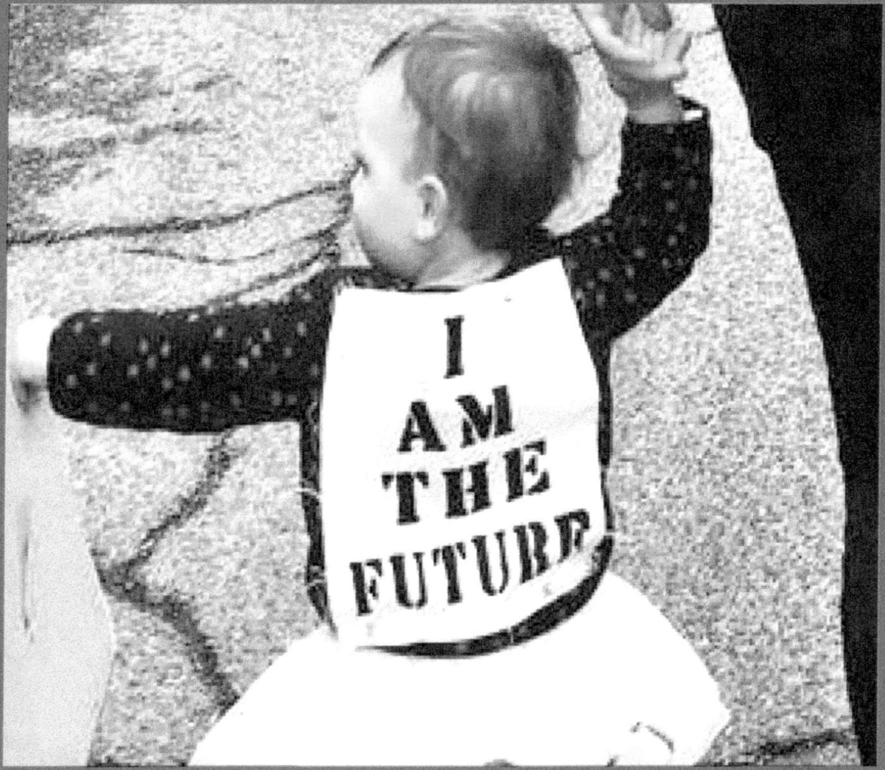
I AM THE FUTURE

Karen Gross

Karen Gross has taught and continues to teach across the educational pipeline. In Spring 2016, she taught at Bennington College in Vermont. She writes, consults and advises on how to improve student success and has a forthcoming book from Columbia University Teachers College Press titled *Breakaway Learners* (pub. date 2017—www.breakawaylearners.com) on this very topic. She is the author of a children's book series titled *Lady Lucy's Quest* (www.ladylucysquest.com). A former college President and Senior Advisor to the US Department of Education, she currently serves as Senior Counsel to Widmeyer Communications, a Finn Partners Company and as an Affiliate to the Penn Center for MSIs at the University of Pennsylvania Graduate School of Education. She blogs/writes for many education outlets including Huff Po, WPo, InsideHigherEd, MSI Unplugged, DiverseEducation, Evolllution, NAIS, and CollegeAD.

Debbi Wraga

Debbi Wraga joined the Northshire Bookstore in 2009 and continues to run the independent publishing program in Manchester Center, Vermont and Saratoga Springs, New York. She is thrilled by the incredible books and covers she has been able to design for authors. Collaborating with Karen on *Teach Your Children Well* and *Lady Lucy's Quest* has allowed Debbi to touch the hearts of children all over the world.

While enjoying the creative challenges presented to her, Debbi enjoys the fusion of an author's vision with the creative process and continues to freelance graphic design work.

Debbi lives with her husband in Vermont, and enjoys spending time with her two grown children and her fur babies.

CPSIA information can be obtained
at www.ICGtesting.com
Printed in the USA
FSOW03n1721120917
38448FS

9 781605 713472